The Invention of Creativity

The Invention of Creativity

Modern Society and the Culture of the New

Andreas Reckwitz

Translated by Steven Black

polity

First published in German as *Die Erfindung der Kreativität. Zum Prozess gesellschaftlicher Ästhetisierung* © Suhrkamp Verlag, Berlin, 2012

This English edition © Polity Press, 2017

The translation of this work was funded by Geisteswissenschaften International – Translation Funding for Humanities and Social Sciences from Germany, a joint initiative of the Fritz Thyssen Foundation, the German Federal Foreign Office, the collecting society VG WORT and the Börsenverein des Deutschen Buchhandels (German Publishers & Booksellers Association).

Polity Press
65 Bridge Street
Cambridge CB2 1UR, UK

Polity Press
350 Main Street
Malden, MA 02148, USA

ISBN-13: 978-0-7456-9703-1
ISBN-13: 978-0-7456-9704-8 (pb)

A catalogue record for this book is available from the British Library.

Library of Congress Cataloging-in-Publication Data

Names: Reckwitz, Andreas, author.
Title: The invention of creativity : modern society and the culture of the new / Andreas Reckwitz.
Description: Malden, MA : Polity, 2017. | Includes bibliographical references and index.
Identifiers: LCCN 2016043495 (print) | LCCN 2016057624 (ebook) | ISBN 9780745697031 (hardback) | ISBN 9780745697048 (paperback) | ISBN 9780745697062 (Mobi) | ISBN 9780745697079 (Epub)
Subjects: LCSH: Cultural industries. | Creative ability. | Social sciences–Philosophy. | BISAC: SOCIAL SCIENCE / Sociology / General.
Classification: LCC HD9999.C9472 R43 2017 (print) | LCC HD9999.C9472 (ebook) | DDC 338.4/77–dc23
LC record available at https://lccn.loc.gov/2016043495

Typeset in 10.5 on 12 pt Sabon by Toppan Best-set Premedia Limited
Printed and bound in the UK by CPI Group (UK) Ltd, Croydon

The publisher has used its best endeavours to ensure that the URLs for external websites referred to in this book are correct and active at the time of going to press. However, the publisher has no responsibility for the websites and can make no guarantee that a site will remain live or that the content is or will remain appropriate.

Every effort has been made to trace all copyright holders, but if any have been inadvertently overlooked the publisher will be pleased to include any necessary credits in any subsequent reprint or edition.

For further information on Polity, visit our website: politybooks.com

Contents

Preface to the English Edition

The first German edition of this book appeared in 2012. This English translation provides the occasion to re-evaluate the book within the context of the Anglophone discussion around creativity and society that has been emerging since the beginning of the new millennium. An aspect of this re-evaluation is the question as to what degree the book reflects a specifically German context.

The role of creativity as a cultural blueprint and an economic factor in the formation of late modern society first emerged as an object of inquiry around 2000, particularly in Great Britain, North America and Australia, where it has remained prominent in discussion in sociology as well as in broader intellectual and political discourse. Two of these contexts are of particular note here. First, a mainly academic but also popular discourse has been taken up on the relevance of 'creativity' to the economic prosperity of contemporary societies, regions and cities and the emergence of a 'creative class' of producers and consumers. This discussion has also carried over into political consulting and urban planning.[1] Second, research areas have developed in sociology and cultural studies dealing with the so-called creative industries, which have been spearheading this economic and social transformation. These industries encompass the audio-visual, print and digital media, as well as the arts and crafts, film, design, music, architecture and advertising. The abundant research in this field has been concerned mostly with the detailed analysis of creative labour and the cultural markets, the structural transformation of consumption and the global spread of the creative industries. It has also critically studied the increasingly global phenomenon of the state subsidising of the creative industries.[2]

The Invention of Creativity takes a step back from these sociological and economic analyses of the creative economy of the present and takes in a more historical and theoretical view of society as a whole. The book regards today's creative industries as the tip of a much bigger iceberg, which conceals below the surface a more fundamental and historically far-reaching transformation of modern Western society. The main claim of the book is the following: late modern society has been fundamentally transformed by the expectation and desire to be creative. What is meant here by creativity is the capacity to generate cultural and aesthetic novelty. Modern society has become geared to the constant production and reception of the culturally new. This applies to the economy, the arts, lifestyle, the self, the media, and urban development. We are witnessing the crystallization of what I have called a *creativity dispositif*, which is increasingly determining the shape of late modern society.

The term *dispositif* signals a certain influence coming from Michel Foucault. The book undertakes a genealogical analysis. I reach from the present back into the past, through the twentieth century as far back as the late eighteenth. Creativity is taken not as a given but, rather, as an enigma, as sexuality was for Foucault. How did creativity come to be accepted as a desirable norm? In which heterogeneous complexes of practices and discourses has the dispositif of creativity gradually been developing? The genealogical approach avoids economic reductionism. The economy is certainly one of the main places where the culture of the new develops – a complex I refer to in the book as *aesthetic capitalism*. Yet the scope of the creativity dispositif extends beyond that of the economy. It also takes in the internal dynamics of media technologies and the human sciences, above all psychology, with its techniques of the self. Since the 1980s, the dispositif has also been propped up by state control in the form of what I have called *cultural governmentality*, urban planning being among the most conspicuous examples of this. Yet political reductionism must also be avoided. As such, the study undertaken here is not orthodoxly Foucauldian. It is concerned less with revealing the creativity dispositif as a new system of domination than it is with working out the internal dynamics and the internal contradictions of what can be called *the society of creativity*. For my line of argument, the following point is crucial: in modern culture, the orientation towards creativity began in romanticism in the marginalized niche of the arts. Ever since, it has been spreading to more and more parts of society. Sociology therefore has to take the field of the arts more seriously than it did in the past. The arts do not merely watch from the sidelines; instead, they are a structural blueprint for late modern society as a whole.

In this process, the tension between an anti-institutional *desire* for creativity and the institutionalized *demand* for creativity has continued to mount to the present day and has now become acute. For this reason, it is important to take seriously the affective dimension of the creativity dispositif, the importance of aesthetic practices in contemporary society, the existence of what I have termed *aesthetic sociality*, and the way the dispositif directs audiences' sensuous, affective attention. These aspects have been left underexposed by the tradition following Foucault. Yet they need to be brought to light if we are to be able to take up a critical stance towards the society of creativity.

But we have still not answered the question 'Is the book informed by a specifically German perspective or not?' While it was being written, the question did not occur to me, but it comes up now as the book is presented to an Anglophone readership. I completed part of my studies in Great Britain in the 1990s, and my approach has since then been strongly influenced by the international, Anglophone and also Francophone discussion in social theory and cultural sociology. Moreover, the creativity dispositif embraces a diversity of phenomena that have assumed international dimensions, having become a major force shaping society, whether in London, New York, Copenhagen, Amsterdam, Melbourne or Berlin. This internationalism tends to mute the specifically German accent of the book altogether. Nevertheless, there remains a certain German timbre which likely has three main sources.

First, German sociology is strongly characterized by a fundamental interest in theorizing *modernity*. This stretches from Max Weber and Georg Simmel to Jürgen Habermas's *The Philosophical Discourse of Modernity* and Ulrich Beck's work on the society of risk. The theory of modernity is also a key concern of the present book. A characteristic of this tradition is that it equates modernity a priori not with capitalism but rather with what it calls 'formal rationalization' and 'social differentiation'. Underlying the book is a re-engagement with these two concepts: the late modern creativity dispositif pushes modernity's optimization imperative to the limit, while at the same time it is driven by a deeply anti-rational affectivity. Further, the sociality of creativity is manifest in a broad spectrum of heterogeneous, occasionally autonomous social spheres ranging from the arts to economics, human sciences and the mass media. In each case it manifests in different ways, yet always as part of the one overall structure.

Second, the discourse of the aesthetic in philosophy and the humanities, or *Geisteswissenschaften*, has also influenced the book. Since Kant and Schiller, German philosophy has been intensely concerned with the aesthetic as an autonomous sphere of social practice. More importantly, the interdisciplinary humanities in the German-speaking world since the 1980s have gone outside the narrow confines of these idealist aesthetics to bring to light the social importance of aesthetic practices and their mediality, as well as the way in which they structure perception and feeling, thus recognizing the power of aestheticization in late or postmodernity.[3] Noteworthy in this context is also the prominence of German media theory. These newer branches of interdisciplinary German humanities (as distinct from what is generally understood in English as Cultural Studies) have significantly influenced the book's account of the creativity dispositif as a specific manifestation of aestheticization. One effect of this influence has been the reframing of the question of the relation between social modernity and aesthetic modernity.

The third German-language context from which the book originated is more difficult to outline because it is strictly contemporary. Since the mid-2000s, the members of a new generation of German social and cultural theorists have been working independently of one another to produce a series of studies adopting a new approach to the critical examination of late modern society and culture. Just as there has emerged since 2000 a new 'Berlin school' in German film, undertaking a uniquely sociological, microscopic inspection of the complexity of contemporary life,[4] so too are emerging the contours of a 'new German critical analysis' in social and cultural theory, taking a macroscopic view of late modern culture. Ulrich Bröckling's *The Entrepreneurial Self*, Hartmut Rosa's *Social Acceleration* and Joseph Vogl's *The Specter of Capital* can be counted among this movement. I see *The Invention of Creativity* as also situated within it.[5] These books are certainly distinct from one another thematically and methodologically. Yet they share in common an interest in critically penetrating to the deep structure of late modern culture and society, a task requiring an historically and theoretically informed optics. In the wake of the global financial crisis of the late 2000s, Germany has been increasingly pushed into a political and economic leadership role at the centre of Europe, a role it assumes with reluctance and hesitation. It is perhaps no coincidence that at about the same time German intellectuals began embarking on a fundamental meditation of the crises and contradictions of Western late modernity as a whole.

I would like to take this opportunity to thank Steven Black for his precise and sensitive translation. I am also indebted to Daniel Felscher for his assistance in sourcing the biographical details and quotations. Finally, my thanks go to *Geisteswissenschaften International*, without the generous support of which this publication would not have been possible.

Berlin, summer 2016

We could paint a picture... No, it's been done before.... We could do a sculpture too. Oh! But a clay or a bronze one?... But I get the impression that's been done before... We could even kill ourselves, but even that's been done before... Well, I thought that we could create an action without getting involved in it. Nooo. That's been done.... How about saying something?... Been done. To sell something right away, before you do it... That's been done. Done? And could we sell it again? That's been done, too. Done already? Twice?...

Grupa Azorro, *Everything Has Been Done I*, 2003
(Courtesy of Raster Gallery, Warsaw)

Introduction

The Inevitability of Creativity

If there is a desire in contemporary society that defies comprehension, it is the desire *not* to be creative. It is a desire that guides individuals and institutions equally. To be *incapable* of creativity is a problematic failing, but one that can be overcome with patient training. But not to *want* to be creative, consciously to leave creative potential unused and to avoid creatively bringing about new things, that would seem an absurd disposition, just as it would have seemed absurd not to want to be moral or normal or autonomous in other times. Must not any individual, any institution, indeed the whole of society, strive towards the kind of creative self-transformation for which they would seem, by their very nature, to be predestined?

The extraordinary importance attributed to creativity as an individual and social phenomenon in our time is illustrated by Richard Florida's programmatic text *The Rise of the Creative Class* (2002).[1] According to Florida, the main transformation that occurred in Western societies between the end of the Second World War and the present day is more cultural than technological. This transformation has been ongoing since the 1970s and consists in the emergence and spread of a 'creative ethos'. The bearer of this creative ethos is a new, rapidly spreading and culturally dominant professional group, the 'creative class', busy involved in producing ideas and symbols, working in fields ranging from advertising to software development, from design to consulting and tourism. In Florida's account, creativity is not restricted to private self-expression. In the last three decades, it has become a ubiquitous economic demand in the worlds of labour and the professions.

Florida's study is far from being a neutral account. Instead, it endeavours to promote the very phenomenon it is discussing. Consequently, his view is selective. Nevertheless, there is much evidence to indicate that the normative model of creativity, accompanied by corresponding practices aimed at harnessing institutionally those apparently fleeting bursts of creative energy, has been entering the heart of Western culture since the 1980s at the latest and is now stubbornly occupying it.[2] In late modern times, creativity embraces a duality of the *wish* to be creative and the *imperative* to be creative, subjective desire and social expectations. We *want* to be creative and we *ought* to be creative.

What does creativity mean in this context? At first glance, creativity has two significations. First, it refers to the potential and the act of producing something dynamically new. Creativity privileges the new over the old, divergence over the standard, otherness over sameness. This production of novelty is thought of not as an act occurring once only but, rather, as something that happens again and again over a longer period of time. Second, the topos of creativity harks back to the modern figure of the artist, the artistic and the aesthetic in general.[3] In this sense, creativity is more than purely technical innovation. It is also the capacity to receive sensuous and affective stimulation from a new, human-made object. Aesthetic novelty is associated with vitality and the joy of experimentation, and its maker is pictured as a creative self along the lines of the artist. Creative novelty does not merely fulfil a function, like mere useful technological invention; it is instead perceived, experienced and enjoyed in its own right both by the observer and by the person who brought it about.

From a sociological viewpoint, creativity is not simply a superficial semantic phenomenon but, rather, a crucial organizing principle of Western societies over the last thirty years or so. This development was initially most noticeable at the economic and technical heart of capitalist societies in the sphere of labour and the professions. What will be referred to here as contemporary 'aesthetic capitalism' is based, in its most advanced form, on forms of work that have long since moved beyond the familiar model of the routine activities performed by labourers and office workers, with their standardized, matter-of-fact ways of engaging with objects and people. These older forms of labour have been replaced by work activities that demand the constant production of new things, in particular of signs and symbols – texts, images, communication, procedures, aesthetic objects, body modifications – for a consumer public in search of originality and surprise. This applies to the media and design, education and consultation, fashion and architecture. Consumer culture has generated a desire for these aesthetically attractive, innovative products, and the creative industries are at pains to supply them. The figure of the creative worker active in the creative economy has become highly attractive, extending beyond its original, narrower professional segment.[4] The focus on creativity is, however, not restricted to work practices but extends also to organizations and institutions which have submitted themselves to an imperative of permanent innovation. Business organizations in particular, but increasingly also public (political and scientific) institutions, have been reshaped in order to be able not only to generate new products on a constant basis but also ceaselessly to renew their internal structures and procedures, honing their responsiveness to a permanently changing outside environment.[5]

Since the 1970s, the two-pronged advance of the creative urge and the creativity imperative has been overstepping the confines of career, work and organization to seep deeper and deeper into the cultural logic underlying the private lives of the post-materialist middle classes – and it has not stopped there. The late modern incarnations of these classes strive above all towards individualization. However, this tendency has assumed the particular form of the creative shaping of the individual's subjectivity itself. This is what Richard Rorty has described as a culture of 'self-creation'.[6] The aspects of self-development and self-realization implied in the late modern striving for self-creation cannot be understood as universal human qualities. They originate rather in a historically unique vocabulary of the self emanating from the ambit of the psychology of 'self-growth'. This psychology is in turn the preserver of a romantic heritage. It is within the context of this psychology that the concern originally arose to develop, in an experimental, quasi-artistic way, all facets of the self in personal relations, in leisure activities, in consumer styles and in self-technologies of the body and the soul. This preoccupation with creativity is often construed as a striving for originality, for uniqueness.[7]

Finally, there is another area where the social orientation towards creativity is readily apparent: in the transformation of the urban, in the reshaping of built space in larger Western cities. Since the 1980s, many metropolitan cities, from Barcelona to Seattle, from Copenhagen to Boston, have been re-creating themselves aesthetically with the aid of spectacular building projects, renovating whole quarters, establishing new cultural institutions and striving to generate appealing atmospheres. It is no longer enough for cities to fulfil their basic functions of providing living and working space as in earlier industrial society. Cities are now expected to pursue permanent aesthetic self-renewal, constantly seizing the attention of inhabitants and visitors alike. Cities want to be, and are expected to be, 'creative cities'.[8] Creative work, innovative organization, self-developing individuals and creative cities are all participants in a comprehensive, concerted cultural effort to produce novelty on a permanent basis, feeding the desire for the creation and perception of novel and original objects, events and identities.

In principle, this is all extremely curious. We need only take a small step backwards to become conscious of the strangeness of all this creativity, of the commitment to the idea of creativity as an unavoidable and universally valid blueprint for society and the self. It is the current omnipresence of this very commitment that obscures what a strange development this is. The idea of creativity was certainly not first invented by our post- or late modernity. However, from a sociological point of view, creativity was present in modernity yet was essentially limited until around the 1970s to cultural and social niches.[9] It was the successive waves of artistic and aesthetic movements starting with *Sturm und Drang* and romanticism that engendered the conviction that both the world and the self were things that had to be creatively formed. Rearing up against the bourgeois and post-bourgeois establishment, opposed to its morals, its purposive rationality and its social control, these movements defined and celebrated non-alienated existence as a permanent state of creative reinvention. This is true in equal measure of the early nineteenth-century romantics, the aesthetic avant-garde, the vitalist, lifestyle reform movements around 1900 and, finally, the 1960s counter-culture proclaiming the Age of Aquarius as the age of creativity. In these artistic and counter-cultural niches, creativity was deployed as a promise of emancipation. It was seen as capable of overcoming a repressive Western rationalism based on paid labour, the family and education.[10] The dominant, everyday rationalism of the nineteenth and twentieth centuries, to which these minority movements opposed their desire for creativity, would never have been able to conceive of an imperative for everyone to be creative.

Developments in late modern culture since the 1970s represent a remarkable reversal of this state of affairs. Ideas and practices from former oppositional cultures and subcultures have now achieved hegemony. The creativity ideal of the once marginal, utopian, aesthetic-artistic opposition has percolated up into the dominant segments of contemporary culture to condition the way we work, consume and engage in relationships, and it has undergone a sea change in the process. From a functionalist perspective, the aesthetic and artistic subcultures can be seen as resembling those 'seedbed' cultures that Talcott Parsons saw in ancient Greece and Israel, in Greek philosophy and the Jewish religion[11] – hotbeds of alternative and at first marginal cultural codes exercising a delayed revolutionary effect on the mainstream. Daniel Bell's insightful study *The Cultural Contradictions of Capitalism* (1976) already brought to light the unintended repercussions of the artistic opposition movements on the present, especially in contemporary consumer hedonism. In the spheres of work and organizations, Luc Boltanski and Eve Chiapello's more recent analysis of management discourse *The New Spirit of Capitalism* (2007) has traced ideas from the artistic counter-culture that have tipped over into the current 'new spirit' of the network economy. The formerly anti-capitalist 'artistic critique' from 1800 to 1968, the critique of alienation in the name of self-realization, cooperation and authenticity, is already built into the current project-based way of working and to the organizations with their flattened hierarchies. The tradition of artistic critique thus seems to have been rendered superfluous by becoming an omnipresent reality in the economy.[12]

Yet the coupling of the *wish* to be creative with the *imperative* to be creative extends far beyond the fields of work and consumption. It encompasses the whole structure of the social and the self in contemporary society. We have not even begun rightly to understand the process by which previously marginal ideas of creativity have been elevated into an obligatory social order, gradually solidifying into a variety of social institutions. The yet unanswered question of how this has come about is the point of departure for the present book. The claim is that what we have been experiencing since the late twentieth century is in fact the emergence of a heterogeneous yet powerful *creativity dispositif*. This dispositif affects diverse areas of society, from education to consumption, sport, professional life and sexuality, and conditions their practices. All these fields are currently being restructured according to the creativity imperative. The current study is an attempt to contribute to our understanding of the origins of this creativity complex, to retrace its composite, non-linear prehistory. This is not a history of the idea of creativity. Instead, it will be a reconstruction of the contradictory process by which techniques and discourses emerged simultaneously in different social fields, causing social practices and the agents performing them increasingly to reshape themselves in terms of a seemingly natural and universal focus on creativity. This has taken place in the arts, in segments of the economy and the human sciences, in the mass media, and in the planning of urban space. The once elitist and oppositional programme of creativity has finally become desirable for all and at the same time obligatory for all.

This approach to what can be called the creative ethos of late modern culture does not frame the rise of creativity as the result of individuals and institutions being released from oppression and so finally being free to be creative. From within the viewpoint of post-structuralist ontology of the social, we are justified in assuming that social, psychological and organic structures in general consist in continuous processes of emergence and disappearance, ceaselessly reconstituting and dissolving.[13] Even when we begin with individuals and their everyday practices, we can presuppose as a general rule that their conduct, regardless of how routine it is, nevertheless contains unpredictable, improvised elements. Yet it would be rash to character-ize this becoming and disappearing of social forms and the incalcu-lability of individual behaviour as creativity, with all the specific cultural baggage the notion implies. This book is concerned not with the ontological level of becoming and passing away, the constant emergence of novelty as such in the world, but rather with a much more specific cultural phenomenon characteristic of our time. We are concerned with the social creativity complex as an historically unprec-edented manifestation belonging to the last third of the twentieth century, in preparation since the late eighteenth century and accelerat-ing markedly since the early twentieth century. This multipart complex has the effect of suggesting to us the necessity of reflecting on our own creativity with the aid of culturally charged concepts. It makes us desire creativity, gets us to use appropriate techniques to train it, to shape ourselves into creative people. As such, creativity as a social and cultural phenomenon is to a certain degree an invention.[14] The creativity complex does not merely *register* the fact that novelty comes about; it systematically propels forward the dynamic production and reception of novelty as an aesthetic event in diverse domains. It elicits creative practices and skills and suggests to the observer the impor-tance of keeping an eye out for aesthetic novelty and creative achieve-ment. Creativity assumes the guise of some natural potential that was there all along. Yet, at the same time, we find ourselves systematically admonished to develop it, and we fervently desire to possess it.

Sociological analysis has tended to relegate to the margins one particular social field which is of central significance to the genesis of the creativity dispositif. This is the field of art, the artistic and the artist. The emergence of the aesthetic creative complex is certainly not the result of a simple expansion of the artistic field. Further, creativity as an historical model appears at first glance not to be restricted to art; it has developed elsewhere as well, above all in the area of science and technology.[15] From the point of view of our current historical situation, however, it is precisely art that turns out to assume the role of an effective, long-term pacemaker, imposing its shape on the creativity dispositif in a way that surely runs counter to many of the intentions and hopes associated with art in modernity. In the end, the dominant model for creativity is less the inventor's technical innovations than the aesthetic creation of the artist. This role model function of the artist contributes to a process of social aestheticization.

The process by which the creativity dispositif crystallizes can be observed and dissected with cool equanimity. But, in the context of the culture of modernity, creativity and aesthetic are too laden with normative judgements and feelings actually to allow value-free judgement. In the last two hundred years, the access to untapped human resources of creativity has become one of the main criteria for cultural and social critique. Consequently, this book was written in a state of oscillation between fascination and distance. Fascination is elicited by the way the earlier counter-cultural hope for individual self-creation has assumed reality in new institutional forms, by how elements of former aesthetic utopias could be put into social practice against diverse forms of resistance. This fascination rapidly turns into unease. The mutation of these old, emancipatory hopes into a creativity imperative has been accompanied by new forms of coercion. We are thrown into frenetic activity geared to continual aesthetic innovation. Our attention is compulsively dissipated by an endless cycle of ultimately unsatisfying creative acts.

The principal methodological aim guiding the work on this book has been to interlock social theory with detailed genealogical analysis. The investigation seeks, on the one hand, to uncover the general structure of a society that has come to be centred on creativity. The systematic analysis of this dispositif of creativity as the specific form of a process of social aestheticization is concentrated in chapters 1 and 8, which thus make up a pair of theoretical flanks bracketing the book. At the same time, however, the book attempts to trace the genealogy of the creativity dispositif by studying in detail several particularly important complexes of practice and discourses. Consequently, chapters 2 to 7 are concerned with a series of very different specific contexts and their respective genesis: the development of artistic practices (chapters 2 and 3), techniques of economic management and the 'creative industries' (chapter 4), psychology (chapter 5), the development of the mass media and the star system (chapter 6) and, finally, the changes in the design of urban space and urban planning (chapter 7). In each of these chapters, the concern is to show how in each field, with its contradictory and conflicting configurations, a cultural focus on creativity and a corresponding process of aestheticization were gradually set in motion by illuminating the most important stations of these developments. The analyses cover the twentieth century, with the exception of chapter 2, which systematically investigates the field of art extending back into the eighteenth century. The different social fields are in no way harmoniously coordinated. Each has its own dynamic, yet they are all interconnected. Accordingly, these chapters constitute not so much a logical progression as a series of approaches to the growth of the culture of creativity from different angles. Together, these separate attacks form a mosaic, built up of individual elements, each with their own peculiar character, corresponding to the various main features of the dispositif of creativity and coalescing as a totality into its portrait.

1

Aestheticization and the Creativity Dispositif

The Social Regime of Aesthetic Novelty

The *creativity dispositif* is closely bound up with processes of social aestheticization but is not identical with them. Aesthetic practices and processes of aestheticization can be found in modernity and elsewhere, assuming diverse guises and following different tendencies. The creativity dispositif is one specific mode of aestheticization. The dispositif couples aestheticization with specific, non-aesthetic *formats*, or complexes of practices (such as in the context of economization, rationalization or mediatization), imposing on them a structure dominated by one narrowly specific aspect. The aesthetic is thus understood here as a broader context, of which the creativity dispositif is one specific form.[1] The social complex of creativity territorializes the floating processes of the aesthetic according to its own particular pattern. It moves in such processes already at work, transforming them in its own specific way, distinct from other trajectories and modes of aestheticization that have existed in the past and will presumably continue to exist in the future. The peculiarity of the creativity dispositif is that it intensifies an aestheticization process focused on the production and uptake of *new* aesthetic events. Now, modern society has from the start been organized to promote novelty, in politics and technology as well as in aesthetics. The difference is that the creativity dispositif reorients the aesthetic towards the new while at the same time orienting the regime of the new towards the aesthetic. It thus constitutes the intersection of aestheticization and the social regime of novelty.

1.1 Aesthetic Practices

What is the aesthetic and what is aestheticization? What do they have to do with modernity and with the creativity dispositif? The adjective 'aesthetic' entered philosophical discourse in the mid-eighteenth century in parallel to the development of art as a social field and has been undergoing career changes ever since. In some respects, the term is so ambiguous and so normatively charged that not a few authors have recommended doing without it. Paul de Man points to the existence of an 'aesthetic ideology',[2] particularly in Germany. From a sociological viewpoint there seems even more reason to avoid the notion of the aesthetic, with its apparent vagueness and remoteness from everything social. However, a socio-historical study of the creativity dispositif cannot afford to ignore it, since it has been responsible for bringing about a process of aestheticization. The society of late modernity is, in its own way, an *aestheticized* society. Analogous to the more customary, traditional sociological terms for historical movements of increase and intensification (rationalization, differentiation, individualization, etc.), the term *aestheticization* designates a force shaping society and postulates of this force that it is expanding and increasing in complexity. This force is the aesthetic. Talk of aestheticization therefore presupposes at least a basic notion of the aesthetic, a notion with sociological signification.

The concept of the aesthetic has been developing in philosophy since Alexander Baumgarten and Edmund Burke. It has had a decidedly anti-rationalist thrust, generating a variegated semantic field spanning sensibility, imagination, the incomprehensible, feeling, taste, corporality, creativity, the purposeless, the sublime and the beautiful.[3] We are dealing here with a discursive phenomenon all of its own, which will have to be inspected more closely in connection with the formation of the field of art in modernity. The aesthetic was reactivated towards the end of the twentieth century as a term in the humanities, often in distinction to idealist aesthetics. It would come to be expanded and accorded new functions – for example, in the aesthetics of the performative, aesthetics of presence or ecological aesthetics.[4] Despite this heterogeneity, the aesthetic always retained *aesthesis* as its common conceptual core, in the original meaning of sense perception in the broadest possible understanding. We should return to this original meaning as our starting point. The concept of the aesthetic shifts our attention to the complexity of the perceptual sensibility built into human conduct, the many-layered character of which undoubtedly makes it particularly relevant to sociology and cultural history. A sociological account of the senses could take a magnifying glass to the social modularization of sight, hearing, touch, taste and smell, bodily motion and the spatial localization of the self in different cultural settings and in their historical transformation.[5] Within the context of such an all-embracing concept, the aesthetic would be identified with sense perception in general – but in the end the concept would thereby become superfluous. Processes of *aestheticization* in particular are difficult to account for accurately using so broad a notion of the aesthetic, since aestheticization implies the expansion and intensification of the aesthetic at the expense of the non-aesthetic. However, equating the aesthetic entirely with sense perception robs it of an opposing term, since every human activity mobilizes the senses in one way or another. The result would be that entirely non-sensuous acts would be mere anomalies.

On the one hand, an analysis of the changing culture of the human senses – i.e., of *aesthesis* in the broadest meaning of the word – provides an indispensable background for any reconstruction of processes of aestheticization. But, on the other hand, a more specific concept of the aesthetic is required in order to understand these processes. Yet again, it must be a concept that seeks to avoid idealistic narrowness. This more sharply defined concept can fall back on another basic intuition from classical aesthetics that has remained relevant to the present day. In its narrower sense, which we will be reviving here, the aesthetic does not encompass all processes of sense perception; it embraces only those perceptual acts which are enjoyed for their own sakes – *auto-dynamic* perceptions, which have broken loose from their embeddedness in purposive rationality. *Aesthetic* perception in particular can then be distinguished from the broader realm of *aesthesis*, as the totality of sense perception.[6] The defining characteristic of aesthetic perception is that it is an end in itself and refers to itself; it is centred on its own performance in the present moment. When we speak here of the auto-dynamics of sense perception, what we mean is precisely this sensuousness for its own sake, perception for its own sake.[7] Relating the aesthetic to purpose-free sensuousness in this way follows an impulse from the classical discourse of modern aesthetics originating in Kant's notion of 'disinterested pleasure'. At the same time, a contemporary understanding of the aesthetic must free itself from the traditional attachments to good taste, reflexivity, contemplation and the notion of art as an autonomous sphere. Decisive for aesthetic perception is not whether the object being perceived appears beautiful or ugly, whether the experience is harmonious or dissonant, whether the attitude is introverted and reflexive or joyful and enraptured. The decisive feature of aesthetic perception distinguishing it from mere processing of information towards rational ends is that it is an end in itself.

The phenomenon of the aesthetic incorporates a further dimension. Aesthetic perceptions are not pure sense activities. They also contain a significant affectivity. They involve the emotions. They are therefore always made up of a coupling of 'percepts and affects'.[8] Aesthetic perceptions involve being affected in a specific way by an object or situation, a mood or stimulation, a feeling of enthusiasm, of calm or of shock. The domain of the aesthetic does not consist therefore of perceptions directed to objective and instrumental, affect-neutral knowledge of matters of fact; rather, it comprises sensuous acts distinct from end-oriented action, acts that affect us emotionally, touch us and alter our moods. Affects can here be understood as culturally moulded, corporeal intensities of stimulation or excitement, while aesthetic affects in particular can be understood as such intensities attaching to sense perceptions taken on their own terms.[9] Again, aesthetic affects should here be distinguished from non-aesthetic affects – i.e., from affects entirely subservient to pragmatic concerns of action. Life-world affects such as fear of danger or joy at success have a subjective and intersubjective signal and communication function. In contrast, aesthetic affects involve affects for their own sake (such as the fear felt watching a horror film or the enjoyment of nature) in which the individual probes her emotional possibilities. On the perceptual and emotional levels, the aesthetic presupposes the existence not only of human subjects perceiving and being affected, but also of objects being perceived and stimulating affects. Conglomerations of such objects can create whole environments replete with their own aesthetic atmospheres, presenting themselves to people and drawing them in. The aesthetic in this sense is therefore never merely an internal, psychological phenomenon. It operates in a social space made up of people and objects in which new percept–affect relations are continually coming into being.

Many of these relations are one-offs, disappearing immediately, but there exist also more durable socio-cultural practices, which at once promote and inhibit, stimulate and moderate the growth of different types of perception and feeling. A sociological understanding of sense perception and affectivity calls for a *practice-oriented concept of the aesthetic* – that it to say, a concept in the framework of a theory of social practices, within which two modes of the aesthetic – aesthetic episodes and aesthetic practices – can be distinguished. In *aesthetic episodes*, an aesthetic perception appears momentarily and unexpectedly. Someone is affected by an object and so breaks through the cycle of instrumental rationality; then the event subsides. Meanwhile, in *aesthetic practices*, aesthetic perceptions or objects for such perceptions are produced repeatedly, routinely or habitually. If practices can be understood in general as repeated, intersubjectively intelligible and embodied forms of behaviour, occasionally in interaction with artefacts, involving the processing of implicit knowledge and always organizing the senses in a specific way, then aesthetic practices are practices in which self-referential sense perceptions and affects are shaped on a routine basis. At the heart of such practices is the eliciting of aesthetic perceptions in oneself or in others.[10] Aesthetic practices therefore always entail aesthetic knowledge, cultural schemata, which guide the production and reception of aesthetic events. As practices, they are therefore, paradoxically, not at all free of purpose. They are as teleological as any other practice. Their telos, or purpose, is to generate purpose-free aesthetic events.

This understanding of the aesthetic accentuates an aspect of social practice that has long been marginalized by rationalist philosophy and sociology. The term opposed to that of the aesthetic as autodynamic sense perception and affectivity is that of rational, purposive and rule-guided activity. This binary allows us to set up an ideal distinction between, on the one hand, a mode of rationally *acting upon the world* that covers goal-directed and normative action and, on the other hand, an aesthetic mode of *experiencing the world* through sense perception. At one extreme, social practice can assume the form of an activity guided by interests or norms. This kind of practice is largely non-aesthetic, though naturally not entirely devoid of sense perceptions, and follows normative or technical rules. Here, perception is subordinated to cognitive processing of information, which assumes the function of a means to some end of action. Emotive, stunned or libidinous responses to objects, to other people or to environments are then subordinated to the technical or normative context, which on the ideal definition is emotionally neutral. This is the ideal type of activity traditionally presupposed by sociology.

This rational mode of acting on the world is opposed to the mode of self-referential experiencing and working *in* or *with* the world involved in aesthetic practices. In aesthetic practices, the proportion of end-directed or norm-oriented action is reduced to a minimum. These acts of sense perception – by the visual, aural, tactile and olfactory senses, whether alone or in combination – are self-steering processes that do not merely serve the effective regulation of action. The perceptions are joined to corresponding affects, meaning people are emotionally affected in specific ways by perceptions of objects, other people or environments. In general, these perceptions and affects are not acts of pure, immediate experience or feeling but, rather, entail the use of implicit schemata, patterns and criteria of selection, and culturally acquired skills. These kinds of practices of aesthetic perception and feeling include the cultural manifestations of Kantian 'disinterested pleasure' in the observation of an artwork but extend also far beyond it, ranging from the ecstasy of collective effervescence observed in archaic rituals by Émile Durkheim to the 'aesthetic of blandness' found by François Jullien in Chinese calligraphy; they embrace the aestheticization of politics in fascist mass rallies observed by Walter Benjamin and Charles Baudelaire's metropolitan *flâneur*.[11] Aesthetic practices are performed on a visit to Disneyland or in Jackson Pollock's drip-painting, when playing theatre or attending theatre; they are performed by the enthused onlookers in a football stadium and in courtly dance.

Two components of human action – the body and the sign – assume special functions in aesthetic practice. They are employed differently in rational, end-oriented and normative action than in aesthetic practice. In the rational context, the body serves the attainment of a goal, with the consequence that it ceases to appear, although it is the bearer of all the requisite skills. Language and other sign systems are here the means to attaining a maximally unequivocal conceptual grasp of the world, to gathering information and assuring communication. Meanwhile, in aesthetic practice, the body figures as the site of a performance sensually perceptible to others. The body is then no longer primarily the means to an end but rather an end in itself; its sensibility and perceptibility are self-referential and process-oriented. When aesthetic practices employ language or other sign systems, the main purpose is not to transmit information but to exploit the signs' polyvalence and their capacity for producing narrative, iconographic and other entities able to stimulate the senses and the emotions. The point is then not that the signs have 'real' referents; instead, the play of significations, the production of fictional meaning and alternative narrative worlds come to the fore.[12]

The ideal opposition of purposive, end-directed action and aesthetic perception is first and foremost a heuristic aid in acquiring a precise conception of the aesthetic. However, it is a dualism that should be handled with care. The strict opposition remains infused by a classical aesthetics dating from Winckelmann and Baumgarten that has often incited attempts to cut off the aesthetic completely from the rational in order to ensconce it in the safe, autonomous reserve of what is sensuous, emotional, beautiful, sublime, non-conceptual and purpose-free. By making this distinction, classical aesthetics *performs* what it appears merely to describe from a neutral vantage point: it exiles the aesthetic from rationality, factuality and morality in response to the inverse exiling of the rational from the aesthetic in the corresponding utilitarian, cognitivist or moralistic discourses. Bruno Latour has studied these modernist efforts at purification, the aim of which is to create clear distinctions between humans and things, culture and nature, culture and technology.[13] A comparable modern technique of separation can be found in the relation between aesthetics and rationality.

When this dualism is viewed historically in this way it becomes clear that, in fact, there has frequently been a *mixing together* of rational, teleological or normative moral practices with aesthetic practices. Purely rational, purposive and rule-guided forms of practice devoid of aesthetics and emotions, on the one hand, and purely aesthetic activity oriented exclusively on the senses and the emotions, on the other, represent the extreme poles of a continuum. If we accept the existence of impure combinations, then we can see the aesthetic occurring not only in exclusively aesthetic practices but also in mixed social fields and mixed practices in which instrumentality and normativity are combined with *relatively* autonomous acts of perception and feeling. Religious ceremonies, for example, can contain traces of the aesthetic without being aesthetic through and through. Craftsmanship and trading in shares also incorporate aesthetic elements, auto-dynamic percepts and affects associated with engaging materials or being stimulated by the game of financial speculation. Analogous cases include belligerent activities, friendly interactions, moving in public space or gardening. In all these cases, perception and emotion need *not* be entirely subordinate to the pursuit of rational ends but can operate in part auto-dynamically and self-referentially. In effect, the whole history of culture can be reconstructed as a history of different forms of aesthetic activities or products that go far beyond what modernity understands as purpose-free art and are incorporated in diverse practices, such as the making of artefacts, communication, politics, religion and spirituality. A distinction can therefore be made within the totality of aesthetic practices between *purely* aesthetic practices and *mixed*, aesthetically permeated practices, whereby here too the two types are part of the one continuum.

Against the background of this understanding of the aesthetic, the phenomenon of *aestheticization* becomes more sharply contoured.[14] Aestheticization is a precisely definable transformation of society. In processes of aestheticization the segment of aesthetic episodes and aesthetically oriented or permeated practices expands within society in general, at the expense of exclusively non-aesthetic practices. This aestheticization can assume extremely diverse cultural and historical forms and orientations. Such processes can be concentrated within certain classes, institutions or spaces or can cross over the thresholds between them. They can be distinguished in two ways: according to the degree to which they are quantitatively and/or qualitatively oriented and according to the degree to which they are intended and/or unintended. In quantitative aestheticization processes, the proportion of aesthetically oriented and permeated practices increases, whether because they are more frequently performed or because they are executed by a greater number of agents (such as readers of novels or the amount of novel reading in general) or, inversely, because the non-aesthetic practices decrease in scope and relevance (for example, as a result of the decline of machine labour). Aestheticization processes can involve a qualitative component, as when new aesthetic processes come into being and are supported by new aesthetic discourses or when current aesthetic practices are intensified. This sort of aestheticization can be intended, as when entities such as political leadership, intellectuals, subcultures, architects or managers, wielding aesthetic utopias and schemes, promote the aesthetic in definite directions and with complex justifications. Aestheticization can also happen by chance, as the side effect of other processes, such as an increase in the number of artefacts capable of assuming aesthetic qualities. The comprehensive process of aestheticization leading to the creativity dispositif has occurred on all four levels at once.

1.2 (De-)Aestheticization and Modernity

While we may be justified in assuming the existence in recent history of a broad zone of mixed aesthetic and rational practices that has been veiled by their strict conceptual opposition, this modernist dualism of the aesthetic and the rational governing classical aesthetic discourse is nevertheless more than a merely terminological phenomenon. It reflects a real bifurcation actively promoted by modern society, though never with absolute success. We can thus see a self-contradiction within the process of modernity. On the one hand, there is a broad rationalization of social practice, which indeed leads to a far-reaching de-aestheticization. Yet, at the same time, opposing forces are at work reinjecting the aesthetic into the social, while we also observe the mixed forms of aestheticization and rationalization described above.

If we look to classical social theory for aid, to Marx, Weber and Durkheim, we find that these theoreticians, despite fundamental differences, are in tacit agreement with one another that modern society essentially brings about de-aestheticization. The fact that their analyses of society contain so little reference to the aesthetic is in no small part a result of this assumption. There are good reasons for this theory of aesthetic atrophy. According to the classical theories, there are four basic structures responsible for the modern form of society that should be understood not necessarily as competing but rather as complementary phenomena: industrialization (Durkheim, Marx), the rise of capital (Marx), rational objectification (Weber) and functional differentiation (Durkheim, Weber, Luhmann). A fifth structure of relevance here is the strict separation between the human world and the world of things (Latour). All these modern social constellations order subjects and things, knowledge and practices in such a way as to reinforce the complexes of rational purposive action, thereby systematically cutting them off from sense perceptions and affects experienced for their own sakes. This causes the latter to be pushed to the margins of social practice. Precisely for this reason, processes of aestheticization and the subsequent creativity complex in modernity inevitably appear anomalous. Industrialization was made possible by the objectification of nature, technology and space and their subjection to impersonal treatment as work materials. The rise of capital caused labour to be regarded exclusively as the production of value circulating in society and objects as essentially goods with exchange value – a process that can also lead to an objectification of relations between people. Formal, objective rationalization transformed institutions into organizations regulated by charters. The functional differentiation effectuated a strict separation between spheres of activity, in which forms of behaviour were fixed according to specialized functions and forms of observation. Finally, the split between the human world and the world of things caused both natural entities and artefacts to be engaged with primarily as objects for scientific study and instrumental control.

Industrialization, the rise of capital, formal objectification and the separation between human and thing would at first seem parts of a downright *de-aestheticization machine*. They cause the atrophy and inhibition of auto-dynamic sensuous perceptions and affects, albeit incompletely. This applies especially to the economic, scientific, governmental and legal complex, which is, according to Max Weber, the core of rationalized modernity. This fact makes any remaining aesthetic practices and elements look like mere leftovers from a pre-modern past. From its inception, this process of de-aestheticization has been the object of a cultural critique stretching from Rousseau and the romantics through the English cultural critics of the mid-nineteenth century such as Matthew Arnold to Benjamin and Bataille in the 1920s and, finally, to the early Frankfurt School's critique of reification.[15] These authors' critique of alienation is essentially a critique of the repression of the aesthetic.

The functional differentiation of various spheres of action diagnosed by the sociologist Georg Simmel also has a broad, de-aestheticizing effect on social practice, though, interestingly enough, it produces the opposite effects. While it leads to a general de-aestheticization of the economy, politics, education, etc., it can at the same time promote the growth of its own special sphere concerned primarily with the intensified production of pure percepts and affects. This is precisely the proper place of modern, initially bourgeois, art. From the point of view of classical social theory, this provides the image of a main axis running through modernity towards a decisive de-aestheticization and objectification accompanied by a significantly weaker auxiliary axis containing the specialized sphere of the aesthetic in art. The separation of the aesthetic and the rational in bourgeois aesthetics can then be interpreted as a means to create legitimate art and secure the independence of the artistic.

In reality, the de-aestheticization of modernity was never complete. This fact was rightly pointed out within the context of postmodernist theory in the 1970s, albeit confined to late modernity.[16] Aestheticization has indeed come to assume a particular intensity and breadth since the last quarter of the twentieth century, and the creativity dispositif constitutes the structural core of this process. Yet, at the same time, modern society has never been a mere monolith of one-dimensional objectification. Aestheticization is not the exclusive property of postmodern culture, not a mark of the great rupture between modernity and postmodernity. On the contrary, the whole history of modernity contains at various places and times numerous concrete instances of aestheticization, of aesthetically dominated practices, as well as mixtures of the aesthetic and the non-aesthetic (aesthetically mixed or permeated practices). These processes are not restricted to a superficial 'aesthetic of beautiful appearances' (although they also contain it). Instead, they embrace the whole range of the cultivation of auto-dynamic percepts and affects. Whether we are referring to the middle-class practice of communing with nature, to the aesthetic image maintenance of the modern man since the 1920s, to pop culture, to the appropriation of Eastern meditation by Westerners, to proletarian pigeon-breeding, to late modern cycling as a leisure activity, or to the atmospheres arising from bourgeois or modernist architecture, in every case we find a great diversity of both aesthetically pure and aesthetically mixed practices.

Now, how does the powerful de-aestheticizing objectification go together with these heterogeneous forms of aestheticization, which seem bound together rhapsodically rather than according to any ordered principle? My claim is that there is good evidence to indicate that these complexes of the aesthetic do not occur at random but result systematically from structural features of modernity, albeit largely unintentionally. This systematic production of the aesthetic intensifies over time in successive waves. Modernity is not only a de-aestheticization machine but also an *aestheticization machine*. The aesthetic formats of modernity have roots going back to pre-modern times. Particularly robust or reactive relicts of pre-modern practice continued to reassert themselves into early modernity. This is especially true of those aesthetic practices which developed within religious contexts. It applies, however, also to aesthetic practices rooted in aristocratic and courtly society, as well as to practices from popular rural culture and craft culture preserved by the modern urban proletariat. In addition, throughout modernity there have existed specifically modern constellations providing basic conditions for processes of aestheticization that can be referred to as *agents of aestheticization*. Five such agents are characteristic for modernity.

1   *The expansionism of art*   The most prominent wave comes from art movements and from bourgeois art. In this respect, the artistic field that formed in the nineteenth century had a paradoxical effect. On the one hand, it strictly confined the aesthetic to the reception and production of what is regarded as art, thereby reinforcing the modernist dominance of objectification. But, on the other hand, bourgeois art, with its notions of the artist and of artistic training, in cooperation with the expanding discourse around art and aesthetic since 1800, was able to overstep its own boundaries in a variety of ways. Within the middle classes, the ways of engaging with art lost their niche character when the emotional, sensuous satisfaction they produced became a constant, unsatisfied promise threatening the other, objectified segments of middle-class life (an example being the bourgeois desire to be an artist) or when the freedom from necessity supposed to arise from contact with art turned into the hidden, aesthete centre of the totality of bourgeois life.[17] Nonetheless, modern art had from the beginning incorporated elements of aesthetic-political utopian visions of total aesthetic emancipation. The utopian infusion of the aesthetic, extending beyond artworks to encompass, among diverse objects, the wish to *transform life into art*, was part of a radically modern aesthetic way of life and way of thinking that was practised by romanticist subcultures, bohemians and the avant-garde.

2 *The media revolution* With the development of audio-visual
   recording and reproduction devices, modernity has seen an unprecedented revolution in media technology.[18] After the development
   of writing in early civilization and the printed book in the early
   modern period, a further transformation of the patterns of sense
   perception and feeling was brought about from the 1830s on by
   the invention and distribution of technologies of visual and aural
   reproduction and again in the late nineteenth century with photography, film and the telephone, then television and video, and
   finally the high-quality digital revolution of the computer and
   internet. These media technologies fundamentally altered the basic
   conditions of human *aesthesis*. Whereas the culture of writing
   required endowing the sense of sight with the cognitive capacity
   to decipher non-pictorial signs, audio-visual culture has brought
   about a major reorientation towards reproductions of image and
   sound sequences. The audio-visual and digital media thereby
   introduce a systematic aestheticization of their own. Technically
   reproduced images and sounds in cinema, television, radio or
   recordings can be experienced non-instrumentally and appropriated and enjoyed at any time as autonomous sequences of stimulation free from the need for urgent action or the fulfilling of social
   duties. Made images and sounds were already capable of lending
   impulses for affects in paintings, music and the voice, but the
   newer audio-visual media technologies provide a qualitative and
   quantitative leap to this generation of affects by freeing the production and appropriation of images and sounds from face-to-face
   interaction and thus rendering it omnipresent.

3 *The rise of capitalism* Capitalism can be understood as an expansionist economic system for producing and selling goods with the
   aim of reinvestment and capital accumulation. Modern capitalism
   suppresses traditional aesthetic practices on a significant scale,
   especially in rural and pre-industrial craft milieus. Moreover, it
   fosters anti-aesthetic objectification in relations between people
   and things as well as between people. At the same time, however,
   capitalism produces its own version of aestheticization centred on
   the world of commodities. This process started immediately and
   picked up speed in the course of capitalism's historical development.
   This commodity aestheticization was able systematically to promote
   aesthetic relations and practices on account of two factors. First,
   commodities belong to no fixed, antecedent social context but are,
   rather, purchased individually and then embedded in a lifestyle,
   which means they lend themselves to what Marx calls fetishism –
   i.e., to appropriation – where they are turned into autonomous
   objects for the user's sense perceptions and subjective feelings that

can extend to idolatry.[19] Second, the expansionist tendency, the constant search for new markets, led capitalism, in two large historic waves, systematically to promote the production of such aesthetic consumer goods, signs and feelings by 'immaterial labour'. This applies to Fordism, which began recalibrating the capitalist economy to mass consumption in the 1920s, and it applies more especially to post-Fordism, which since the 1970s has led both the diversification of consumer objects as determinants of lifestyles and the corresponding mode of labour centred on the production of sensuous, symbolic goods.[20] With this 'aesthetic capitalism' we thus encounter a special version of aestheticization.

4 *The expansion of the world of objects*   A general characteristic of modernity has been the unprecedented growth in the invention, production and distribution of new artefacts. Latour speaks of these artefacts as a hybrid type of *quasi-object*, at once material and cultural.[21] The expansion of the world of things in technological society is connected both to the development of capitalism and to the media revolution, but it also extends beyond them. The expanded set of objects includes consumer goods, technical appliances, architecture, human-influenced nature, art and design objects, body accessories, media images and sounds. The explosion of the world of things in modernity suggests at first sight the predominance of technology and objectification, but it actually turns out to provide a basic precondition for diverse forms of aestheticization. Naturally, relations between people can be aestheticized – examples being love relations or mass events – but aesthetic relations appear to come about just as effortlessly between subjects *and objects*.[22] The artwork is here just one prominent example among others. In contrast to the special control to which relations between people are generally subject, objects are obviously characterized by less social regulation and greater openness to diverse interpretations, sensuous appropriations and pleasurable sensations. The extraordinary expansion of the world of objects in industrial and post-industrial modernity thus creates the preconditions for new types of aesthetic relations, whether these are intended by the producers of the objects or not. A high-density centre for the provision of such aesthetic relations is the modern urban metropolis – an agglomeration of diverse artefacts in various combinations converging in a totality of architecture and urban structures.

5 *The rise of the subject*   The modern expansion of the world of objects is accompanied by an equally unprecedented concentration of social and cultural practices and discourses focused on the human subject. The late eighteenth century saw the subject come

under the influence of technologies of subjectivization and a new individualist semantics subtended by the discourses of the emerging human sciences such as psychology. These modes of subjectivization encouraged concerted self-observation, drawing out the 'self' as an independent entity. Some of these technologies doubtless had moralizing and disciplinary effects and promoted a loss of sensuality and a neutralizing of affects. At the same time, however, the focus on the self since sentimentalism and romanticism was frequently accompanied by a focus on sense perception, desires and emotions, which could then become a source of aesthetic experiences in relations to the self and to others. The concentration on subjectivity has generated the notion of an interiority of the self, which in turn has nourished receptivity for self-reflexive emotions, perceptions and imaginings influenced by psychological discourse as it began to infiltrate everyday language.[23]

1.3 Social Regimes of Novelty

The rationalization and de-aestheticization dominating modernity is thus both accompanied and counteracted by heterogeneous forms of aestheticization. Within this broader context, the creativity dispositif represents one specific version of aestheticization forming since the early twentieth century. The aesthetic-artistic movements, the revolution of communication media, the growth of capitalism and the rise of the subject are at once its preconditions and its constitutive elements. Previously dispersed and marginal fragments of aesthetic culture are consolidated in the creativity dispositif, thus endowing them with general validity and influence. Yet under modern and late modern conditions there also exist a global set of aesthetic practices that do not belong wholly to the dispositif. As Raymond Williams might put it, the creativity complex represents the dominant culture, yet this does not exclude the parallel existence of aesthetic residual cultures, historical relicts and emergent cultures, subcultures and counter-cultures providing alternative aesthetic criteria not based on creativity.[24] Further, other individual segments of late modern society evade aestheticization, preserving or rediscovering principles of morality, the struggle for power or purposive rationality. This applies, for example, to certain technical, administrative, belligerent and juridical practices and to morally oriented faith communities.

What is the special feature of the mode of aestheticization established by the creativity dispositif in the last third of the twentieth century? As we established in the introduction, the word 'creativity' refers to an activity aimed at the constant production of new things, understood on the model of artistic production. A closer inspection of aesthetic practices and processes of aestheticization in their entirety permits this understanding to be more precisely contoured. Against the background of the countless possible contents and forms of aesthetic episodes and practices, the creative complex has two different effects. On the one hand, it commits the aesthetic to dynamic novelty; on the other hand, it attributes aesthetic novelty exclusively to the creative author responsible for bringing a new entity into existence. The figures of the individual recipient and the audience are the complement of the creative author. Their function is to develop a perceptual and affective attentiveness and receptivity to aesthetic novelty. The creativity dispositif thus constitutes an intersection between a process of aestheticization *and* a social regime of novelty. It is founded on a *regime of aesthetic novelty* while, at the same time, casting this aesthetic novelty into a *producer–recipient* mould. In this mould there is a mutual dependency between a 'creator', a novelty-creating subject (or group or practice), and an aesthetically sensitive audience attentive to novelty.

Decisively, in the framework of the creativity dispositif, the new is understood not as progress or as quantitative increase but as aesthetic – i.e., as a perceived and felt *stimulus* or, more precisely, as a continuous sequence of stimuli, affecting recipients *as* stimuli, independently of rational purposes. This applies equally to art and to economics, to the media, to urban space and to the self. A social regime of attention is established, causing subjects to develop this receptiveness to stimuli.[25] This form of aestheticization is harnessed to an ethos of creative production whose source is the creative individual. The creativity dispositif therefore presupposes that aesthetic novelty is generated by a person or other entity, such as a collective or the practice itself. This implies an understanding of creativity as the ability to produce aesthetic novelty. The classical and still valid model of this capacity is the artist. Creativity is thus understood to entail an aesthetic mode of production.

The complement to the creative producers is the audience as the collection of recipients. Aesthetic stimulation by novelty depends on an audience to determine and appreciate what is genuinely new. Novelty does not exist as an objective fact. It depends on the requisite attentiveness and evaluation to distinguish it from the old and prefer it over the old. Three well-known types from sociology and cultural theory converge at the point of this complement to the creative producer: the *recipient*, the *consumer* and the *audience*. From a communications theory point of view, the recipient assumes the function of the receiver as the complement to the sender. For the sociology of economics, the complement of the producer is the consumer. Finally, in system theory terms, the complement to the output function of the producer is the audience taking up the output.[26] However, the recipient/consumer/audience as the complement to the creative producer should not be understood in the traditional sense of the terms: in the creativity dispositif, the recipients are not the receivers of information, nor are consumers the users of goods, nor is the audience primarily an integral participant in a functional system. The recipient and the consumer are instead the subject placed before an object in an attitude of aesthetic, perceptual and emotional excitability.[27] A modified version of the sociological concept of the audience or 'public' may be helpful in this context. Niklas Luhmann correctly points out that the social fields in modern society engender not only output functions but also audience functions – i.e., they involve participants whose role is to receive rather than to give.[28] In the case of the creativity dispositif, however, the audience assumes a special form. It orients itself towards what it observes, receives and uses, not by processing information but by its symbolic, sensuous and emotional excitability. The essential feature of the modern audience is that it is aesthetically interested.[29] In this capacity, the audience becomes the pacemaker of transformation in modern society.

In the past, the exact relation between the producer and the audience in the context of the creativity dispositif turned out to be as inconclusive as it was controversial. We know that in the bourgeois field of art an extreme asymmetry reigned initially between the artistic genius and the receptive audience. However, in the long run, the distinction between the two proves to be unstable. The continued intensification of the creativity dispositif in the course of the twentieth century led to a gradual assimilation of the producer and the recipient, a strengthening of the productive role of the recipient, and an inverse weakening of the importance in production of the creator, who increasingly assumes a receptive function in the creative process. However, this does not collapse the distinction between producer and recipient altogether. Rather, it renders it flexible, with the ideal of the creative subject broadening beyond the exclusive realm of the artist to become universal. The ideal subject of the creativity dispositif is consequently both the audience and the producer of new aesthetic stimuli, either in alternation or simultaneously.

If the producers and the audience are fundamentally focused on novelty in the creativity dispositif, then it still remains to be explained what the special characteristic of this social regime of novelty is. Modernity has seen different regimes of novelty that can be distinguished precisely from one another. One standard diagnosis of modern society states that its institutions and semantics are generally oriented not towards repetition and tradition but towards change; it is inclined towards revolution, implying an approach to time that favours the future over the past. In the political, scientific, technical and artistic spheres, modernity has apparently always strived to produce novelty, whether in the form of political revolutions, the circulation of goods, technical invention or artistic originality. Along these lines, Reinhart Koselleck's semantic investigations have revealed an understanding of society oriented towards progress and time as characteristic for modernity since the 'saddle period', the epochal threshold around 1800.[30] Postmodernist discourse has introduced the contrary thesis that such an orientation towards innovation and progress is admittedly a feature of classical modernity but is no longer as significant to current culture as was previously assumed.[31]

However, if we accept the existence of a creativity dispositif, we clearly cannot speak of the general dismissal of novelty as a structural feature of late modernity. It would be more plausible to suggest that the ideal of novelty has changed and no longer implies progress or historical discontinuity. The ideal of novelty entails most basically the development of a sense of temporality that distinguishes the past, the present and the future and favours the new over the old. If *old* is the opposite of *new*, then the alternative to the new/old distinction would be to think in terms of reproduction, repetition and cycles. A regime of novelty, however, connotes a specific conception not only of the temporal but also of the phenomenal and the social.[32] On the level of phenomena, the new signifies otherness as opposed to sameness. On the social level, the new is that which diverges from the normal and from normative expectations. Whether on the temporal, phenomenal or social level, the new is never objectively given. Rather, it always depends on often controversial patterns of observation and perception that allow things to appear as *not old*, as dissimilar, as divergent from the habitual. The regimes of novelty typical for modern society not only keep an eye out for the new, they prefer it and attempt to promote it. They actively advance dynamic social change. The new does not appear to them as worthless or aberrant, whereby their positive evaluation of novelty is dependent on social criteria that dictate *which* novelties are valuable and which are not. In ideal terms, three modern regimes, three modes of structuring the focus on novelty can be distinguished, the newer taking over from the older ones without the latter disappearing entirely: *the new as stage* (novelty I); *the new as heightening and supersession* (novelty II); and *the new as stimulation* (novelty III). These regimes of dynamism correspond roughly to three different models of modern society: modernity as perfection; modernity as progress; and aesthetic modernity.

The *first* regime of novelty strives to overcome older structures, replacing them once and for all with new, more progressive and rational ones. Here, novelty is total and revolutionary. After the revolution has been successful there will be no further need for anything fundamentally new. At the most, incremental improvements may be required. This is the model behind the ideal of political revolution. It is characteristic of the old juridical, moral dispositif of modernity with its orientation towards rules and rights. Exemplary here is the leap from tradition to the state of law, to formal bureaucracy, to socialism, to moral self-enlightenment – even to functionalist architecture. After all these changes no larger breach is to be expected. Once the desired stage has been reached, society and the individual will be forever reorganized around continually perfecting it. In 'novelty I' the new is thus subordinated to *finite* goals of political and moral progress.

The *second* regime of novelty, the new as heightening and supersession, has the different goal of the permanent production of novelty stretching into an infinite future. The characteristic trait here is the model of progress in the natural sciences and technology, but also in economic market innovation, the supersessions of the artistic avant-garde[33] and psychological self-optimization. At the same time, this model is characteristic of a politics of prosperity. The term *heightening* is meant here to include both quantitative increase and qualitative leaps.[34] For the constellation 'novelty II', the individual act of creating novelty typically entails a normative demand for improvement. The series of these improvements is *infinite*. Institutions and individuals organized on this model strive for continual progress, either gradually or in leaps.

The *third* regime of novelty, characteristic of the creativity dispositif, is organized differently again. It is also centred on the dynamic production of an infinite series of new acts, but it views particular novelties with equanimity, their value determined no longer by their place in a progressive sequence extending into the future but by the momentary aesthetic, sensuous, affective stimulus they provide in the present before it is replaced by the next. The object of concern is not progress or supersession but rather the movement itself, the series of stimuli.[35] The new is determined here purely by its difference to previous events, as otherness, as a welcome relief from the usual. It is as such the *relatively* new event. It does not mark a structural rupture. In the context of the regime of aesthetic novelty, it locates the new in the same semantic field as the interesting,[36] the surprising and the original.

None of the three terms implies progress or supersession; they are concepts of pure difference with affective connotations. The third regime is interested in novelty that affects the individual sensuously and symbolically. Here, the production of novelty does not follow the model of political revolution or technical invention; it is concerned with the creation of objects or atmospheres that stimulate the senses and the feelings in the same way art does.

The creativity dispositif brings about a paradoxical kind of aestheticization. It effectuates an *aesthetic normalization*. This concept may seem at first unusual. When Michel Foucault spoke of processes of normalization or Jürgen Link of 'normalism', they had very different phenomena of standardization in mind, such as the normalization of calculable body motions in disciplinary institutions, the behaviour of participants in market activities or the standardization of sexual desire.[37] In contrast, aesthetic normalization is a second-order phenomenon. The disparate practices and discourses of the creativity dispositif are aimed *not* at the creation of calculable, standardized behaviour – at least not on the first level – but rather at the production and reception of novelty for its own sake. Now, in order to arouse attention, novelty must always diverge from the past and the habitual, and it must involve an element of surprise and unpredictability. This can be put in terms of information theory: communication rests essentially on redundancy, whereas information presupposes a minimum of novelty. This applies even more to aesthetic information.[38] Now, the creativity dispositif 'functions' in a way which would appear counter-intuitive in a social context. It *requires divergence* from the standard in artistic, economic, medial, psychic and urban contexts. It demands surprise and unpredictability and encourages the flourishing of creative people, practices and collectives capable of fulfilling these requirements. Yet precisely for this reason the creativity dispositif leads to aesthetic normalization, to normalization on a second level, based on a paradoxical attitude of expecting the unexpected and awarding it. The creativity dispositif's opposite is therefore not social divergence as such, but rather, on the one hand, the undifferentiated and thus aesthetically uninteresting repetition of the eternally same and, on the other, those divergences that explode the limits of what is sensuously and affectively bearable.

Is aesthetic normalization a result of the colonization of aesthetic practices from the outside? We are adopting the view here that the explanation that capitalism or formal rationalization have appropriated the pure, autonomous aesthetic and shaped the creativity dispositif on their own terms is deficient.[39] Certainly, in contemporary culture, the creativity dispositif not only encompasses purely aesthetic practices but is also intertwined with normative and purposive practices. At this point we should make a distinction between aesthetic practices and 'aesthetic apparatuses'. Individual aesthetic practices (such as viewing a film, going for a walk, performing religious rites) can be purely aesthetical or at least aesthetically permeated. However, as soon as broader aestheticization processes are under way, these practices tend to abandon their isolation and gravitate to the centre of more capacious aesthetic apparatuses, larger institutional complexes aimed at the production and reception of aesthetic events, such as the film industry, football, museums and galleries, the fashion industry, tourism or experimental gastronomy. These apparatuses are generally not restricted to aesthetic practices; rather, as institutional complexes focused on results, they always involve non-aesthetic, purposive and normative practices (administration, advertising, craft, technology, service, etc.). These practices constitute a precondition for the permanent production of aesthetic events. This applies particularly to the creativity dispositif, which encompasses, among others, practices of attention management and instrumental training of creative processes that provide the general conditions for aesthetic processes.

Consequently, the creativity dispositif cannot be understood within the context of a strict opposition between the aesthetic and the rational, since it represents a necessarily impure combination of the two. We can here observe an auto-dynamical process of aestheticization that is *not* merely a product of rationalism or capitalism and yet is intertwined with both. The economization and rationalization of the social are not the principal cause and motor of aestheticization, but they do provide a general framework for the social diffusion of the creativity dispositif while, at the same time, helping to restrict aesthetic practices to the specific form of the dispositif. We will see that the economization of the social does not contradict the creativity dispositif's aesthetic logic. In fact, the two are structurally homologous. This homology makes it easier for the creativity dispositif to spread throughout society. Yet it also enables the creativity dispositif aesthetically to charge the economical and thereby 'colonize' it.[40]

1.4 Creativity as a Dispositif

Michel Foucault's concept of the dispositif is useful for understanding the creative complex.[41] A dispositif is not merely an institution, a closed functional system, a discourse or a set of values and norms. It encompasses a whole social network of scattered practices, discourses, systems of artefacts and types of subjectivity, recognizably coordinated with one another by orders of knowledge without being thereby entirely homogeneous. A dispositif comprises four different social elements: practices and everyday technologies informed by implicit knowledge; forms of discursive truth production, imaginary and collective problematization or thematization; artefacts (instruments, architecture, media technology, accessories, vehicles, etc.); and patterns of subjectivization – that is to say, ways in which people are shaped, and the way people adapt their abilities, identities, sensibilities and desires to the dispositif and so help to carry it. The dispositif is coordinated, despite its internal heterogeneity, by a specific order of knowledge. The cultural logic of the dispositif disposes people to a certain way of being; it strategically and actively produces specific social and individual conditions, though this need not be consciously intended by the agents. The dispositif has a transformative power directed against other dispositifs and discourses, forms of life and systems, all of which it endeavours to suppress.

The dispositif runs obliquely to the different specialized fields within modern society as conceived by the theory of social differentiation. It connects segments of various fields, arranging them into a new order. To name just one example, a dispositif can simultaneously extend to specific economic practices and discourses as well as to practices and discourses of upbringing and education. Dispositifs thus flatten differences by throwing down the boundaries between social fields and institutions. They take networks of heterogeneous practices and discourses and homogenize them. Instead of coming into existence instantaneously, they are formed by the gradual diffusion of social *formats*[42] between disparate fields and institutions, such as when psychological techniques are appropriated by the arts or subcultural discourse is deployed in urban development.

Following Foucault, a dispositif is a 'formation which has as its major function at a given historical moment that of responding to an *urgency*'.[43] A dispositif therefore responds to a specific historical and local situation. Resistant to attempts to grasp it as historically linear, it can be understood only from within a social context whose end results are undecided, and its analysis calls for a long-term genealogical approach with an eye to what Foucault refers to as 'emergence', as 'the entry of forces; it is their eruption, the leap from the wings to center stage, each in its youthful strength'.[44] The genealogy does not presuppose specific structures of the social but, rather, traces the historical paths along which the corresponding elements have assembled and concentrated. From the point of view of the genealogical approach, the traditional attempt to 'explain' a phenomenon by discovering an anterior and logically independent causal origin is unprofitable. The genealogy replaces *why* questions with *how* questions: How can we trace the emergence and spread of a cultural pattern in social and historical contexts?

However, emphasis must be placed on one main feature of social dispositifs that Foucault omitted: their *social affectivity*. By eliding the affective and emotional character of the seemingly coercive demand made on people, Foucault necessarily overlooks how people are motivated to pour themselves into social moulds in the first place. The reason they do so is because they are 'passionately attached', because the social forms somehow manage to appear attractive and satisfying.[45] A dispositif too has its own kind of affective structure. In order to be taken up by a group and to establish its power, a dispositif needs, in addition to pure effects of domination, a cultural imaginary promising fascination and satisfaction – i.e., durable affective stimulation.

The thesis of the emergence of a dispositif of creativity as a specific mode of social aestheticization satisfies all these criteria. In the form it has been assuming since the 1980s, the creativity dispositif encompasses processes and complexes of practices developed independently of one another in different social fields before gradually forming networks and mutually interpenetrating. It draws on such diverse phenomena as aesthetic subcultures and the artistic field, post-industrial labour, fashion and experience-oriented consumption, psychological discourses of human creativity, philosophical vitalism, developments in media technology, 'cultural regeneration' in urban planning, and political measures for fostering creative potential. Creativity is therefore the culminating point of a broadly diffused movement of cultural problematization within diverse social formats. It encompasses manifold everyday techniques, from creative work processes to private fashion decisions and discourses on creativity, as well as truth discourse from psychology and narrative and imaginary notions of the ideal creative person. The creativity dispositif incorporates typical sets of artefacts, ranging from digital data streams to gentrified suburbs and corresponding forms of subjectivation for creative workers and global city tourists. Importantly, the dispositif develops its own affective structure, cultivating the sense of novelty, the fascination for the creative subject's perfect body, enthusiasm for creative teamwork and constant creative activity.

For the purpose of understanding the genealogy of the creativity dispositif, four historical phases can be distinguished: *preparation*, *formation*, *crisis and concentration* and *domination*. The first phase, preparation, extending from the late eighteenth to the late nineteenth century, sees a gathering of discourses, practices, artefacts and forms of subjectivity, all of which turn out to be long-term preparatory factors for creativity as a social model. This preparation takes place in the specialized artistic field. The formation of the 'originality' of the artist goes hand in hand with the growth of a bourgeois art audience, a counter-cultural bohemia, an articulation of aesthetic utopias and a discourse of pathological artistic decadence. The model of creation assumes its characteristic form in the creation of the *artistically* new.

The second phase in the crystallization of the creativity dispositif covers the period from around 1900 to the 1960s. This period can be described as the formational phase, a time of incubation. Bits and pieces of different social and cultural practices emerge here and there in various social fields, promoting (aesthetic) novelty and its creative production. An analysis of this second phase must remain incomplete, but four disparate fields, already interwoven in 1900, can be identified as belonging to it. The first field encompasses diverse economic practices and discourses such as the arts and crafts movement, the late bourgeois discourse of entrepreneurship, the beginnings of the 'creative industries' of fashion, design and advertising, the organizational discourse around the motivation of employees, and innovation economics. Second, a positive psychology gradually grows up on the margins of psychoanalysis, gestalt psychology, intelligence research and 'self-growth' psychology, defending artistic genius against its stigmatization as pathological. Third, the field of audio-visual mass media sees the rise of interest in creative stars from film, music and the art scene. Finally, the further development of the artistic field in the twentieth century also contributes to the constitution of the creativity dispositif as the avant-garde brings about a far-reaching dissolution of the boundaries within and around artistic practices and aesthetic objects while breaking down the myth of artistic individuality. These changes cause the aesthetic and creativity to break out of their containment within the classical, bourgeois conception of art.

The third and fourth phases of the creativity dispositif can be traced back to all these fields. The third phase precipitates a crisis by concentrating the various elements of the dispositif. This occurred in the 1960s and 1970s with the emergence of the counter-culture, youth cultures and the critical protest movements. Individual elements of the creative complex previously existing in isolated social pockets now attracted wider attention, occasionally becoming radical and giving rise in their turn to varyingly radical alternatives to the dominant forms of the economy, art, self-technologies and urbanity. This critical concentration can be found equally in postmodern art, in the critical psychology of self-realization, in design, fashion and advertising made for a progressive audience, in the rise of pop and rock culture, and in critical urbanism. In the fourth phase, in force since the 1980s, the creativity dispositif has assumed a new predominance with the growing power and influence of the creative industries, creative psychology, the expanded star system and the political planning of 'creative cities'. The transformation of urban space and urban politics thus constitutes more fertile ground for the creative complex. This field first becomes relevant in the phase of critical concentration. Since the 1980s, the political planning of urban creativity has been an especially conspicuous manifestation of the societal influence of the creativity dispositif. The dispositif now appears complete and well on its way to successful cultural dominance – a development that is already provoking resistance. The dispositif is becoming a system, working concertedly to mobilize its own resources and casting aside in the process what it can make no use of.

2

Artistic Creation, the Genius and the Audience

The Formation of the Modern Artistic Field

2.1 Art as a Social Form

The gradual spread of the creativity dispositif in social practices and discourses since the early twentieth century was made possible by developments in the artistic field.[1] In its genuinely modern, middle-class or 'bourgeois' (*bürgerlich*) form, the artistic field grew up in the sphere of the visual arts, literature, music and theatre in the last third of the eighteenth century and established itself firmly in the course of the nineteenth century.* The artistic field is of fundamental importance to the later creativity dispositif, but their relation is also ambivalent. Art developed a social blueprint that was unusual for the time, an *aesthetic sociality*, which later influenced the social form of the creativity dispositif as it extended beyond the confines of art. This aesthetic sociality originating in art is based on a regime of aesthetic novelty and consists of four elements: the subjectivization of the artist as the creator of novelty, initially in the form of the 'original genius'; the aesthetic quasi-object, initially in the form of the artwork;[2] the

---

* The term 'bourgeois' is used here for want of a better translation of the German *bürgerlich*. *Bürgerlich* and its cognate *Bürgertum* (roughly equivalent to the middle classes, citizenry or civil society) do a good deal of work in German discussions of modernity and politics, both academically and in ordinary speech. The terms denote more than merely an economic class, connoting importantly a whole form of life with an emphasis on personal education and political participation. As such, *bürgerlich* has a positively connoted discursive tradition and breadth of meaning that none of the usual translations – 'bourgeois', 'middle class' and 'citizen' or 'civil society' – can do justice to.

audience, the community of recipients interested in aesthetic novelty; and an institutional complex – markets or state academies – for regulating audience interest. A social regime of aesthetic novelty emerging from the interplay of these four elements existed at first only in the arts, before spreading, together with the creativity dispositif, into diverse social fields.

In its early version, the modern artistic field set its own outer limit, preserving internally the autonomy of artistic practices. Initially, this prevented the broader social dissemination of art practices. Art maintained its exclusivity for a bourgeois audience with bourgeois taste, preserving the aesthetic of the work and, importantly, the cult of artistic genius. At the same time, however, countervailing forces in the artistic field – the focus on lifestyle among artistic bohemians and the growth of discourses around aesthetic utopias – also began dissolving the field's outer borders. In order for art to unfold its aesthetic intensity, it had first to render the aesthetic rare and concentrated. In order for art to pave the way for the creativity dispositif, it had then to loosen its ties to bourgeois aesthetics and intensify the dissolution of its own borders. This was brought about in the twentieth century by the avant-garde and postmodernism.

An account of the origins of modern art must be developed from this sociological perspective, avoiding the temptation to explain art as the product of a specific underlying social structure while also rejecting the notion of the autonomy of art as a functional system. The alternative view being offered here is that art acted as a *blueprint* for the creativity dispositif, as the model on which society as a whole was to develop in the twentieth century. In principle, a sociological analysis of art can concern itself only secondarily with the contents or forms of works of art. It must concentrate primarily on the social processes of the production, circulation and reception of artworks. As Howard Becker demonstrates in *Art Worlds*, art is from this viewpoint neither a sequence of works or styles nor just a place for aesthetic engagement with social questions. It is, rather, a collection of social practices and conventions in which artists as well as markets, media, critics and the public participate.[3]

There is, however, a tradition in the sociology of art of treating art as deriving from more general social structures. In their attempt to demythologize the bourgeois cult of art, sociologists have often explained how social structures that have their origins outside art find expression in works of art and reshape them. Since Marx and Weber, we have often been reminded of the impact of capital, the market and rationalism on the institutions of art, on the system of art forms (literature, music, visual arts, etc.), and on the meaning of art as an object of struggles for social distinction. Art's dependency on developments in media technologies has also been a fixture of the discussion since Walter Benjamin. The sociological theory of the origins of art has in this way created an awareness of the external framing conditions for art. But by the same token it has remained blind to the dynamics of aestheticization radiating out from art itself.[4]

In the sociological context there has always existed a point of view opposed to the theory that art has external origins and which accords the artistic field in modernity a degree of autonomy. This approach has been adopted above all in the theories of social differentiation following Georg Simmel. It is then interpreted in a way conforming broadly to the established notions of bourgeois art as a product of processes of functional differentiation, as an emerging sphere of values or a social system with its own peculiar norms and codes of communication, readily distinguishable from those of other systems.[5] Modern art is understood on this model as having emerged by proclaiming the purity of art, freeing it from the imperatives of other social spheres, especially religion, morality and politics. This theory of autonomy has the advantage of drawing attention to what is specific and novel about the artistic field as it emerged in the late eighteenth century. Art in modernity is a specialized, self-perpetuating microcosm of social practices, forms of subjectivization, discourses, and systems of artefacts with clear aesthetic functions. Nevertheless, the particular nature of art cannot be understood, as the differentiation theory traditionally frames it, as a mere alternative system of norms and values (see Parsons's system of expressive symbolism) or an alternative communication code (see Luhmann's binaries beautiful/ugly and success/failure).[6] Instead, the artistic field constitutes a holistic social constellation, a unique type of actor network of *aesthetic sociality*. Art provides a unique kind of blueprint, a structural model of the social with its own actors and relations. This aesthetic sociality is characterized by three structural features.

1   Modern art constitutes a social field focused on engendering aesthetically oriented practices – i.e., practices involving the production and reception of aesthetic events in maximally *absolute* form, practices of self-dynamic sensuousness and affectivity freed of all rational purpose. This concentration of 'pure' aesthetic practices in art both opposes and complements the processes of massive de-aestheticization in other social fields.

2   The aesthetic practices of modern art are embedded in a social regime of aesthetic novelty geared towards the continual produc-

tion of new aesthetic events, new artworks, presenting themselves as sensuous and affective offerings with the value of surprise.

3   The actor network of art is made up of the four components of aesthetic sociality mentioned above. First, the artistic field shapes the figure of the artist as a 'creative producer' endowed with the special ability to introduce novelty, in this case aesthetic novelty, into the world. Second, it nurtures an aesthetically sensitized audience as the opposite and complement to this producer of originality. Third, producer and audience are connected by aesthetic objects, artworks and art events that are produced and received. Fourth, the triad producer–work–audience is embedded in an institutional framework, the primary function of which is to direct audience attention towards certain artworks and artists. Collectively, these four components set in motion the endless cycle of sensuous, affective novelty. The core of the sociality of art is therefore neither rational purposive production, nor social interaction, nor exchange. Instead, it is focused on a *social process by which sensuous, symbolic and emotional stimuli are produced for an audience*.

As the nucleus of aestheticization, the modern artistic field thus develops its own form of sociality, yet this sociality is not as autonomous as the differentiation theory of art suggests. The view we are adopting here is that the artistic field is in reality characterized on the one hand by a demarcation of the aesthetic, which sets limits on it, erecting borders to keep the outside out, and on the other hand by the dissolution or breaching of these same borders. The practices in the artistic field involve a variety of strategies for attaining autonomy for art, marking off the purely aesthetic from morality and normativity, from purposive rationality, and also from the impure aesthetics of popular art and kitsch. The intensification of the aesthetic in the development of 'pure', concentrated aesthetic practices – the production of artworks and the enjoyment of literature, music, theatre and museums – necessitates a regime of exclusion on its outer borders to keep out the kind of 'illegitimate' aesthetic activities that early bourgeois art liked to attribute to both courtly society and popular culture. This regime operates by limiting the elements of artistic sociality recognized as legitimate in the following ways: addressees of art must develop an inwardly turned attitude of reception and orient themselves towards bourgeois tastes and ideals of beauty; further, the artworks are fixed in conventional formats (literary genres, pieces of music, etc.); art critique and canonizations organize attention and legislate taste; finally, the artist is defined as a figure of genius dedicated to absolute creativity.

At the same time, it cannot be overemphasized that the border lines in the history of the artistic field were always contentious and always accompanied by movements of aesthetic transgression passing from the domain of art to that of non-art. These movements imply a loss of distinction and of autonomy for art which counteracts its functional differentiation. The breaching of the border is not imposed on art from outside – for example, by order of the state or the church – but mobilized by art itself. Art does not constitute a closed social system but, instead, systematically breaks down its own borders as it begins to strive to be radically modern. The bohemian culture that attributes creativity to a collective lifestyle rather than to artworks can be understood as one such artistic force of border dissolution emerging after 1800. Further examples are the aesthetic utopias and cultural revolutions, such as romanticism, which elevate the figure of the artist to a social role model.

The set of practices collected under the name of *art*, in this, its first modern, bourgeois form, thus includes simultaneous tendencies towards systematic closure and tentative opening, exclusion and expansion. In what follows, we will explore in more detail the individual elements of this historically potent aesthetic sociality of art with its dialectic of limitation and dissolution. The question guiding this investigation will be: How did art as a social field come to be systemically oriented towards aesthetic novelty?

2.2 The Regime of Novelty in Art

Artist-creators

Disparate 'artistic' elements have converged in the artistic field since the last third of the eighteenth century. Art obtained its identity as a social field by virtue of its ability to develop aesthetically oriented practices that distanced themselves from other practices and ways of thinking from the religious, social (e.g., courtly society) and moral fields with which they formerly intermingled. The artistic field unified different arts under Charles Batteux's influential collective single definition as 'art',[7] though it did not develop synchronically in the various European societies. The field comprises artefacts, above all artworks – singular and definable objects such as paintings, sculptures, musical compositions and literary texts – as well as buildings in which to display these objects, such as museums, theatres, concert halls, etc. It includes the practices by which artworks are produced, their distribution via the art and literature markets and exhibitions, as well as their uptake by recipients. It encompasses the socialization of artists and recipients alike. It includes the collectivization of artists into milieus and urban quarters and also the social knowledge of the aesthetic circulating in philosophy, criticism and literature.

This heterogeneous field was shaped most forcefully by the restructuring of artistic production practices and the transformation of the artists themselves as the bearers of this practice.[8] The field positioned the artist as the producer of *novel* aesthetic objects that break with society's usual aesthetic expectations. This cultural development presupposed the discourse of the aesthetic of genius, which became established in Germany, Great Britain and France in the mid-eighteenth century. The aesthetic of genius stylized the artist as the creative progenitor of works whose novelty consisted in violating existing rules and generating surprise,[9] and its identity was secured by being marked off from humanistic and classicistic aesthetics of imitation. It was prepared semantically in the late seventeenth century by the context of the 'Querelle des Anciens et des Modernes', in which art was to function as an anti-classicist activity directed towards novelty. For the aesthetic of imitation, the task of the artist was to implement and perfect the rules of an ideal art in the masterly reproduction of time-honoured universal forms. In contrast, the new aesthetic reinvented the artist as the opposite of the copyist, as the creator of original works no longer derivable from generally valid rules.[10] This made it both possible and necessary to draw a clear distinction between art and craft.[11]

At the heart of the aesthetic of genius is the model of the subjective origins of novelty. The individual artwork is sourced to an individual, non-interchangeable 'creator' in possession of an out-of-the-ordinary soul. 'Genius' is the general title for these qualities of the psyche. Alexander Gerard provided the following definition in his 1774 essay: 'Genius is properly the faculty of *invention*; by means of which a man is qualified for making new discoveries in science, or for producing original works of art.'[12] The concept therefore clearly implied a disposition, faculty or power to invent, as opposed to the imitation of canonical rules. Of primary importance here is the assumption that both the work and its author shared a common freedom from rules known as 'originality'. In order for the artwork to be distinguished by its originality, the artist must also be an original. Work and artist are connected by a relation of expression; the uniqueness of the artist is expressed in that of the work. In antiquity, the artist's singularity had been founded on innate *ingenium*, while in the early modern era it had been associated with inspiration, both of which notions bore religious connotations. The modern notion of the genius was largely secular, even where metaphorical references to the divine nourished the fascination for the artist as an exceptional being.[13]

Within the geography of a modernity increasingly centred on economics, law and politics, the figure of the artist thus assumed a special place. He was an *exclusive type*, thus implying a strange duality. On the one hand he was a socially identifiable figure providing the special service of producing artworks. But at the same time he was a socially exclusive figure, since not everyone can be an artist. Being an artist demands the exceptional qualities denoted by the words 'genius' and 'ingenium', and these qualities tend to prohibit social inclusiveness. If the notion of social inclusion entails that every person is permitted to participate in society as long as she fulfils requirements attainable by all, then exclusivity entails that such universal participation is fundamentally impossible.[14] This is precisely the situation of the artist, though in a very special way. Artists fitted neither into the old exclusive class nor into the new class where inclusion was by merit. Their exclusivity was not based on parentage, as in the aristocracy of the *Ancien Régime*, nor were their status and their achievements potentially open to all, as the official version claims of all other modern professions.[15] Like their work, artists came to be surrounded by a cultural aura, in which they appeared capable of producing out-of-the-ordinary percepts and affects and were therefore exempt from having their achievements assessed and graded. The artist can evidently be classed as the generator of aesthetic novelty only when this class is restricted to geniuses. Artists are indeed as specialized as other professionals, but they are distinct from the latter to the extent that their activity is bound up with the aim and expectation of an undifferentiated and non-rational relation to a natural, psychic and social totality.[16]

The modern artistic field assigned the artist's capacity for creating novelty to an aesthetic faculty of imagination. Moreover, the subjectivization programme for generating the artist as an original genius was also closely bound up with the valorization of the imagination.[17] The imagination had been regarded from antiquity to the Renaissance as a primitive and perilous sensuous faculty, either performing the simplest kind of registration or at worst producing irrational fantasies. The modern artistic field reversed this evaluation. Now the imagination appeared in its capacity to produce the unexpected by combining different sense perceptions. This was exactly the precondition for original genius. Accordingly, genius was defined in the *Encyclopédie* published by Denis Diderot as 'expansiveness of the intellect, the force of imagination and the activity of the soul'. The man of artistic genius is someone 'whose soul is more expansive and struck by the feelings of all others; interested by all that is in nature never to receive an idea unless it evokes a feeling; everything excites him and on which nothing is lost'.[18] Consistent with this assessment, artistic activity began to veer away from materiality in the context of the aesthetics of genius. The strict separation of *artes liberales* and *artes mechanicae*, which now opposed art in the singular as the totality of the known individual arts since antiquity to mere functional manual craft, framed artistic activity as most essentially about the spiritual, affective shaping of objects rather than the mere working of their material constitution. Artistic practice was then, as Schelling claimed, 'the activity of an idea'.

What the artist-creator produced in the context of the modern artistic field was therefore the individual work as a quasi-object, a cultural, material duality.[19] This object consisted of various materials ordered by the maker and sensuously perceived and assigned a cultural meaning by the recipient. As such, artworks had both a 'form' and a 'spiritual content'. The individual works were as heterogeneous as the socially legitimated genres of art themselves, as sculpture, painting, poetry and prose, musical composition and drama fixed for performance on paper.[20] As artworks in the modern sense, as first systematically conceived by Karl Philipp Moritz, these disparate objects shared a set of common properties.[21] They were understood as purely aesthetic objects for two sorts of subjects: the artist and the recipient. At the same time, artworks were presumed to be auto-dynamic and internally complex; they were *'living, highly organized natures'*.[22] Although the bourgeois artistic field framed the artwork as internally unified and complete, it was also supposed to embody aesthetic novelty and originality. It should do this in two ways, both as an 'historical singularity' not subject to conventional rules and as the source of potentially infinite new forms of appropriation compliant with its nature.

The audience

The aesthetic form of social interaction developed by the modern artistic field needs an audience. It needs readers of literature, viewers of artworks, listeners to music or visitors to the theatre just as much as it needs the figure of the artist as their creator.[23] Art is not the only social field in eighteenth-century modernity to develop an audience to fulfil the functions of observation and evaluation. The audience or public also emerges in this period in science and politics.[24] These various publics are dependent on networks of communication media and are particularly interested in *new* events, new scientific insights, new political developments, new decisions and problems and, of course, new artworks. In the case of the artistic field, the audience is interested in *aesthetic* novelty; their attention is directed towards artistic originality rather than towards new ways of thinking and the progress of the sciences or towards new political decisions and social reform.

The emergence of the modern artist and the development of a general, anonymous audience in the late eighteenth century are two structurally interdependent events. The court artist could only be replaced by the modern original artist because of the rise of this bourgeois audience. It is well known that artists in the early modern era were usually dependent on aristocratic or church patronage. As such, they could lay little claim to original genius, their function being primarily to increase the fame of the patron.[25] The modern artist could advance to the status of original genius by addressing a circle of anonymous recipients capable of being surprised by unpredictable works made by artists of their own volition. This art audience comprised combinations of three different subject positions: first, consumers and users; second, private recipients and their internalized aesthetic appropriation; and, third, a collective audience in the narrower sense – i.e., a social form of observation, evaluation and affection. In bourgeois art, all three subject positions are regarded as receptive, in opposition to that of the productive artist.

The audience consisted at first of the aggregate of buyers and users. The artistic field developed through markets (the book market, the visual arts market) and public educational and cultural institutions (museums, theatres, concert houses). On this first level, the subject position of the audience was that of consumer, whose aesthetic intentions could be replaced by other aims, such as symbolic distinction or the fulfilment of the duties of the educated classes.[26] The formation of the aesthetic audience was thus crucially dependent on the second subject position, that of the recipient. Art in modernity presupposed reading, listening to or observing subjects training themselves in specialized aesthetic engagement with artworks. The investigations of the cultural history of reading, listening and viewing have shown how bourgeois individuals since the eighteenth century acquired these skills of aesthetic concentration. This applies to inner, silent reading aimed at following the strands of a narrative as well as to the concert-goer focusing her entire attention on the music while abstaining from interaction with fellow listeners, and, finally, to the viewer of a painting in a bourgeois museum spatially organized to favour the focus on single images one at a time. All these instances involve the utmost concentration of the senses on the object and away from the observer's own body; the act of reception is retracted into the inner psyche despite the presence of other people.[27]

The third subject position of the art audience is that of a collective engaged in the observation and evaluation of works and artists. The audience in this capacity can be physically present, can react spontaneously and be affected directly by a performance or an exhibition. However, in the eighteenth century, it developed mainly in the context of print media, which generated a communicative space for the observation and evaluation of art, paradigmatically in criticism and art history, both popular and academic.[28] This function of this type of audience is to direct collective attention for varying lengths of time at some works rather than at others. The direction of attention is influenced mainly by the expert critics who systematize and judge the body of new and old artworks. After the replacement of the imitative aesthetic by the aesthetic of genius, originality became the decisive criterion of judgement. With the spread of this expert discourse, the aesthetic experience of the works came to be accompanied by a reflexive, intellectual engagement with art involved in the recognition and comparison of artistic forms (genres, styles). A reflective discourse about art was therefore an integral part of the emergence of the artistic field. This reflection could intensify aesthetic experience but could also lead to a kind of anaesthesia and an intellectualizing of the field. Meditating on artistic forms can help to heighten recipients' aesthetic pleasure, but it can also end up *replacing* it. This audience is interested not only in the artworks but also in the artists. The public image of the artist and his biography became a privileged object of collective attention. The literary genre of the artist's biography, the artist's portrait and the public celebration of artists were indicative of this development.[29]

In the late eighteenth century, several forces contributed to raising interest in aesthetic novelty among the art audience, the community of users, recipients and participants in expert discourse. First, the aesthetic of genius since the 1770s was not only a programme for the subjectivization of artists; it also caused the recipient to *expect* the artist to produce original, surprising works that exhibited newness in some interesting or gripping way. Second, the audience was further attuned to novelty by the structuring of the artistic field by the market (for literature and visual art) and by cultural institutions (theatres, concert halls) working with gradually changing repertoires. The art market was already dependent by virtue of the uniqueness of its commodities on constant innovation, whereas the literature market tended to be repetitive – for example, printing classical authors and the Bible – but could expand only by introducing novel products. The same applied to public cultural institutions presenting a repertoire of works and promoting new productions. This is most evident in the development of theatre in Germany in the last third of the eighteenth century.[30] Both the art markets and some of the state cultural institutions thus pursued a type of attention management, systematically offering novel works and engaging audience interest in them. Third, the art criticism generated by the mass media, initially taking the form of journals and newspapers, was also oriented towards novel, current books, exhibitions and performances.[31]

Finally, the artistic field's reflection of art as divided into styles, which had been an influence on criticism and audiences alike since Johann Winckelmann's *Geschichte der Kunst des Alterthums* (History of the Art of Antiquity), also promoted the orientation towards artistic novelty.[32] The semantics of style can be applied to individual and collective styles, interpreting art as a play of differences across historical time. Every work from a new artist is then encountered as incomparable and interesting in terms of its individual style.[33] The individual artworks can in turn be ordered into collective historical styles. This stylistic observation schema sensitizes the comparative gaze for the ruptures between artistic modes of representation without passing judgement on the merits of one style over another. The new style is not regarded as better, just as interesting in its own way. The concept of style thus already shaped observation in relation to historical time before the advent of the avant-garde, though without avant-garde claims to supersede previous art.

However, the interest of the bourgeois art audience was not directed exclusively towards the cycle of artistic novelty. Traditional notions of timelessness and the classical, the culture of the museum, and the belief in 'good taste' ran counter to the interest in novelty. The bourgeois version of the modern artistic field was shaped by the tension between originality and classicism until the latter was gradually weakened in the course of the twentieth century. The modern artistic field entirely abandoned the classicist criterion of the perfect repetition of a universally recognized set of rules, yet the structural principle of the classical was revived in altered form.[34] Winckelmann's identification of the classical with the art of antiquity was influential here,[35] before the notion of the classical became so general that the term also came to be applied to more recent epochs and works, such as Weimar classicism (*Weimarer Klassik*) and Viennese classicism (*Wiener Klassik*). The notion of the classical only appeared to imply timelessness. In fact, it presupposes a temporal understanding of art by taking art formerly regarded as revolutionary and new and reinterpreting it retrospectively as the foundation of a paradigm. The classical is thus the 'idealized historical',[36] that which is regarded as deserving long-term cultural recognition. At the same time, a classical artwork is supposed to be so complex as to be 'infinitely interpretable' (Schlegel), interminably revealing ever new aspects of itself.

The way of seeing based on the notion of the classical thus proves to have ambivalent effects. It motivates a canonizing of earlier art and a concomitant devaluation of current art, the latter necessarily appearing inferior against the lofty heights of the past. This canonization is closely tied to the cultivation of bourgeois aesthetic 'taste' with claims to general validity and accompanied by a schematized sense of beauty, both to be trained as early as possible by familiarity with classical artworks in school and at home.[37] At the same time, the classical is clearly a temporal notion, since for a work to be classical it must once have been new and marked a rupture. In this context, the emergence of art museums also entailed an ambivalent institutional establishment of canons.[38] The spread of art museums in Europe after 1800 was founded on an historical and temporal approach which presented art as ordered into historical styles. The establishment of museums thus trained the aesthetic gaze by contact with what was held to be classical, while at the same time propagating an understanding of art as a sequence of ruptures.[39]

The paradoxical certification of novelty

The late eighteenth-century artistic field, structured by the genius aesthetic and the bourgeois audience, forced the regime of novelty in art into paradox. The audience certifies what is original art and which artist is a genius, and yet this competency can be denied by the artists themselves. This paradox became manifest in the nineteenth century in a permanent conflict between the makers of art and the audience over the attribution of originality to works of art and over the relevance of individual artists. The cult of genius presupposed an admiring audience at the same time as it cast doubt on that audience's ability to recognize 'true art'. In his analysis of the cult of genius, Edgar Zilsel pointed out that respect for the original work often took second place to the audience's affective relation to the authors themselves, which provided the observer with a 'personality experience'.[40] Further, the enthusiasm for the original personality was fuelled by a cumulative 'enthusiasm for enthusiasm'.[41] The original artistic genius is the one who sets the tone by virtue of his distinction from the masses, whereas it is the audience rather than the artist who judges the value of the work. The basic problem of judgement that then emerges is the danger that the audience falls into aesthetic conservatism, blinded to aesthetic novelty or disregarding it as worthless. This is the origin of the figure of the 'unrecognized genius'.[42] This judgement problem can be resolved only with the passage of time: the contemporaries have failed to recognize the new, but later generations will be able to give the creative achievement its due.

The permanent controversy within the bourgeois artistic field over who is the legitimate judge of an artwork's novelty value thus opposed the *logic of the producer* to the *logic of the audience*. The logic of the producer assumes that only the artists possess the appropriate criteria to judge the originality of their product. If the disparity in ability between the original genius and the mass is absolute, then only the authors can be capable critics. On this view, the audience inevitably misconstrues the originality of works frequently enough to result in conservative or popular misjudgement, which thus leads to the phenomenon of the 'unrecognized genius'. The audience devalues the work on account of its own insufficiencies, subjecting it to the conventions of good taste. In the extreme case, the original work is incommunicable beyond a small group of champions. This logic of the producers manifested in the 'anti-philistine critique' widespread after 1800, which consistently opposed art criticism and the art market, culminating in Johann Gottlieb Fichte's demand that the work of genius 'must first educate its audience'.[43]

This logic of the producer is opposed to the logic of the audience, according to which only the audience is able to judge artistic originality. In the bourgeois artistic field, the potential unpredictability of the audience was restrained by the social regulation of taste in the form of criticism and educational institutions. On the most extreme interpretation, the audience logic denies outright the producers of art the capacity to judge their own creativity. The discursive figure in which this self-empowerment of the (academic) public began to manifest around 1800 is the critique of the *genius inflation*,[44] the excessive self-definition as artist following in the wake of the aesthetic of genius. This mass self-attribution of a marker of exclusivity can be viewed by the audience as illegitimate. Friedrich Schlegel's critique of genius inflation is typical: 'The greater the body of original works that already exists, the more infrequent will be every new work of genuine originality. For this reason there are countless legions of derivative imitators [*Echokünstler*].'[45] The public can counter the self-empowerment of the artists with their ability to draw comparisons, which criticism deploys in its historical consideration of artistic forms. The comparison secured from the observer perspective through the study of history is required before the originality of so many artists and artworks can be judged. Moreover, only the audience possesses the relevant affective faculty. An artist is first made into a genius by the enthusiasm of an audience sensible to the total artistic connectedness to the world exhibited in his person and his works. This affection, this seizure by art, cannot be forced on the audience by the artist. Aesthetic novelty is therefore a question not only of evaluating but also of being affected.

In the mid-nineteenth century, the antagonism between production logic and audience logic, between the advocates of the 'unrecognized genius' and the critics of genius inflation, began to be supplemented by a third logic of the certification of novelty that combined the two and would finally be perfected by the avant-gardes: the *logic of scandal*. Here, the producer has the originality of her work certified by audience *rejection*.[46] The aggressive affects that accompany the rejection of a work as aesthetically or artistically worthless generate interest in the work. Its ability to provoke a reaction is a sign of originality, of misunderstood novelty upsetting traditional taste. The rivalry between the producer logic of genius, the audience logic and the logic of scandal established a permanent tripartite struggle over the valid determination of aesthetic novelty.

2.3 Dissolving Borders and Delegitimizing Art

The elements of aesthetic sociality – creative artists, artworks, the bourgeois audience, and the attention filtering of the market and institutions – are the four pillars of the bourgeois artistic field. However, in the course of the nineteenth century this structure was complicated by two tendencies extending the range of the aesthetic: first, the emergence of the bohemians as an artistic counter-culture; and, second, the establishment of discourses universalizing creativity and the aesthetic. Both employed strategies of breaching the outer limits of aesthetic practices and of assuming aesthetic forms of subjectivity which provided important foundations for the later advent of the creativity dispositif. At the same time, these tendencies of border dissolution were countered by attempts in early psychology and cultural critique to defame the aesthetic and stigmatize the artist as pathological.

La vie de bohème

The emergence of the bohemians must be understood as the translation of the aesthetic of genius into a subculture. As soon as the aesthetic of genius was no longer a discourse describing other people but had turned into a way artists moulded their own subjectivity, the bohemian became its collective product, an artistic, subcultural scene in urban centres at a remove from the bourgeois establishment. The Paris of the 1830s passes muster as prototypical for the bohemian scene that became established in the further course of the nineteenth century in such cities as Berlin, Munich and New York. Bohemian culture was made up of both young people who had fled to the city to become artists as well as more senior long-term members. In addition to artistic activity, the scene was a microcosm, mixing economic precariousness with opulence (such as in the *bright young things*) of a hedonistic way of life.[47]

Bohemian aesthetic practices undermined the wall put around the aesthetic by the cult of artistic genius, extending the domain of original artistic activity beyond the artworks to take in not only the totality of lifestyle but also, importantly, the persons of the artists themselves.[48] The elements of this lifestyle included leisure-time activities and intimate relations as well as artistic practices in the narrower sense. The artworks themselves were accorded no special privilege over these other everyday activities, if not treated as secondary to them. The bohemian form of life was invented aggressively as a *style* of living, as a totality of practices, the symbolic character of which was consciously moulded. This bohemian lifestyle operates in the mode of *subversion* deploying the above-mentioned strategy of scandal from modern art. The aim is constantly to mark a symbolic distinction to established lifestyles – in this case the bourgeois *juste milieu* – in dress, in the conduct of intimate relationships or in speech. The specific orientation of this non-conformist stylization can assume contrary forms – too much or too little, deliberate extravagance or conscious neglect – the main thing is to express divergence from the norm.[49] In a departure from the artist as framed by the aesthetic of genius, the bohemian lifestyle begins to hollow out the idea of originality of content, leaving only its outer husk. This is achieved in part by abandoning the experience of total connectedness with which the work of artistic genius promised to overcome the specialization and rationalization of modernity. In the bohemian, the new is a fantasy no longer of deliverance and reconciliation but rather of pure difference, the distinction from the established ways of life. The subversive bohemian lifestyle nevertheless does retain normative elements, albeit in a vastly more quotidian way than the cult of art. The bohemian life came to be seen as a place of opportunities for forms of individual expression otherwise held to the margins by a moralistic and materialistic society.

This involved collectivization, a transition from the individual existence of the artist to a common counter-culture. Bohemian culture performed its own sociological quasi-theory of itself, inwardly framing itself as a subculture while outwardly emphasizing its difference to the mainstream.[50] The antagonism between the art scene and society at large thus supplanted the polarity between the original genius and the bourgeois audience. In contrast to the individuality of the genius, the bohemian artist became a *social* type in the narrow sense, conceiving himself and conceived by others as bohemian. This had the effect of complicating the role of the audience. The art scene itself acted as an audience, albeit a minority one, subjecting the bourgeoisie as a class to critical observation while maintaining the greatest possible independence and distance from the bourgeois purchasing public. Conversely, the bourgeois audience was focused no longer on the individual artist alone but rather on the whole bohemian scene as a collective form of existence.

La bohème was indeed not a hidden subculture but, from the start, more a public media performance, reliant on a bourgeois dramaturgy, a prominent early expression of which was Henry Murger's *Scènes de la vie de bohème* of 1851.[51] Murger's portrayal oscillates between a domestic version of the bohemians as an idyll of hedonistic young adults, on the one hand, and a scandal and source of political and moral danger, on the other. Bohemian culture thus untethered aesthetic practices from the restraints of art while at the same time introducing a new restriction. The restraints were removed by transferring aesthetic work from the artwork to lifestyle and turning subversion into a general mechanism. The renewed restriction was social rather than psychological or character-based. The artists framed their own sociology of themselves as members of a counter-culture, a small, radical minority swimming to evade the mainstream.

The programme for universalizing creativity

It is well known that the formation of the artistic field from the late eighteenth century was accompanied by a discursive explosion encompassing not only aesthetics as a philosophical discipline but also adjoining areas of popular philosophy and programmatic theories of education. The aesthetic of genius constituted only a small section of a broader discursive field of the aesthetic and the arts. Large segments of this complex of discourses were concerned with securing the border between art and non-art or popular aesthetic practices. However, this border control was countermanded by the emphatic programmes to universalize the aesthetic, which start breaking though the border around 1800. Once razed, the borders stay down, allowing the aesthetic experience and the creative subject to overstep the confines of art. These universalist tendencies can already be observed in the mid-eighteenth century in philosophical and popular debate. In his *Conjectures on Original Composition* (1759), Edward Young introduced the concept of the creative genius and proclaimed that everyone possesses their own kind of originality and is therefore capable of creative achievement, though this originality is in most cases impeded by circumstances. 'She [nature] brings us into the world all *Originals*...Born *Originals*, how comes it to pass that we die *Copies*? That meddling ape *Imitation*...snatches the pen, and blots out nature's mark of separation....'[52] Young was not submitting a universal educational programme for creativity but rather quickly turned to concentrate instead on the singular artistic genius. Yet it is noteworthy that his basic presupposition about human nature is not its conformist character but its creative individuality, even if this is denied fruition in most cases on account of social obstacles.

These sporadic universalist tendencies in aesthetic discourse crystallized into systematic programmes around 1800 and began subsequently to seep into the bourgeois educational institutions. They can be interpreted as *cultural aestheticization projects*, opposing and at the same time presupposing the claims to autonomy for art and the aesthetic of genius. It emerged as necessary, first, to presuppose the autonomy of the aesthetic over against non-aesthetic practice and the independence of the creator of aesthetic works over against instrumental and moral conduct in order then to extend the aesthetic to all practice. If aesthetic creation and self-creation are not only legitimate ways of being but even superior to rationalist modernity, then the question arises as to why this aesthetic creation and self-creation shouldn't become the aim of a general programme for generating new human beings. After all, this would democratize the original genius.

The programmes for universalizing the aesthetic usually began with the *makers* of aesthetic works. The *audience*, the group of aesthetic recipients, was already universalized (albeit *de facto* restricted to the middle classes) but was merely passive and receptive towards the makers. It would now appear necessary to generalize the function of the active, creative subject. This can happen in two ways: by extending creative *personal skills* from the artist to the non-artist and by opening up the *scope of action* that counts as creative practice, extending it from the production of art to the whole of life. Within this framework, the artist and the artwork continue to appear as models, yet no longer as out of the ordinary, unattainable ideals but, rather, as available for imitation by everyone in the society.

Four programmes to universalize creativity in the writings respectively of Schiller, Emerson, Marx and Nietzsche had especially significant discursive impact, each pointing in different directions. Schiller and Emerson smoothed the way for a 'holistic' aesthetic education, influencing the humanistic secondary schools in Germany and the liberal arts colleges in the United States. Meanwhile, Marx and Nietzsche contributed anti-bourgeois programmes for cultural revolution, attempting to push aestheticization from the 'left' and the 'right' respectively.

Friedrich Schiller's aesthetic idealism in his *On the Aesthetic Education of Man* begins with a diagnosis of the social division of labour in modernity as constituting for individuals a 'splitting up of their being'.[53] The mobilization of an innate human 'ludic drive', drawing together both the sensuous and the formal drives, emerges as a strategy to regain the wholeness of the individual and at the same time enable the moral and political perfection of the 'aesthetic state'. Ralph Waldo Emerson's post-romantic transcendentalism may be understood as a reaction against a state of widespread social conformity that suppresses the true, expressive nature of human beings: 'For all men live by truth, and stand in need of expression.'[54] The artist, especially the poet, is therefore the model of creative self-reliance. For Emerson, the poet's spontaneity combines individuality with participation in an all-encompassing, religiously rooted current of nature. Schiller's model of aesthetic education still retains a link to the receptive experience of artworks, whereas Emerson's active creative subject frees itself more or less fully from any connection to art.

The essence of Marx's critique of alienation is the attack on the de-aestheticization of society as a denial of basic human needs. Marx identifies the division of labour inherent in bourgeois society and the capitalist manipulation of needs as the basic problems. Aestheticism and forced asceticism turn out to be two sides of the same coin. His normative model of human practice is essentially aesthetic, envisaging the fulfilment of the sensuous in its totality. The realization of this norm is contingent on a post-bourgeois society. As Marx writes, 'Only through the objectively unfolded richness of man's essential being is the richness of subjective *human* sensibility (a musical ear, an eye for beauty of form – in short, *senses* capable of human gratifications, senses confirming themselves as essential powers of *man*) either cultivated or brought into being.'[55] In this account, too, the artist functions as the model of the kind of creative existence that non-alienated labour would represent.

Finally, Nietzsche's aestheticization programme was also striving towards an autopoietic subject generating its own heightened self in autonomy from the bourgeois context of labour.[56] The moral subject, subtended by the dominant, essentially Christian ethic of duty, served here as contrast. Nietzsche opposes this ascetic morality with the figure of the *Übermensch*. An ideal aesthetic condition at the intersection of the classical traditions of the Apollonian and the Dionysian, the *Übermensch* is a subject of unlimited creation and enjoyment, her senses and affects freed from moral control. In distinction to Kant's restriction of the aesthetic to the disinterested recipient, Nietzsche's aesthetic subject is understood at the same time as both aesthetically productive and aesthetically affected. However, while Nietzsche frees the aesthetic from the narrow experiential scope of bourgeois art, he restores exclusivity to the creative subject by determining it as the *Übermensch*.

The pathological artist

As suggested above, the programmes to universalize the aesthetic, creativity and the artist met with the same kind of challenges as did the aesthetics of genius. After 1800, attempts were made to establish a discourse on the artist as a pathological figure, as a danger to himself and to society, countering the structural opening of aesthetic practices with endeavours to deprive it of social legitimacy.[57] It may at first seem surprising that the mystification of art and the artist effectuated by the aesthetic of genius and the pathology theory were simultaneous. In fact, both were based on the same distinction, differing only in preferring one aspect over the other. Both sides are predicated on the distinction between the *exceptional* character of the artist and the conformist majority. The aesthetic of genius saw in this exceptionalism the superiority of the original genius over the average person, while the pathology discourse opposed the dangerously abnormal artist to the alleged psychic health of normal people. For the aesthetic of genius, the creative capacity that would become universal in an aesthetic utopia was conditional on loosening up mental, spiritual routines. In contrast, the pathology discourse radically reduced the artist to his psyche. Deprived of his productive achievement, his psychic state is revealed as a menace to the public.

How does this strategy of rendering creativity as pathological work? Going back to Galen's theory of the humours, the history of ideas can draw on a rich semantic store of unusual artistic and intellectual character traits identified with 'melancholy'. Melancholy encompasses properties ranging from introversion and depression, not all of which carry negative connotations. Indeed, melancholy can be understood as a supplement to creativity.[58] Two factors made it possible to convert elements from this lexis of melancholy for the purpose of diagnosing the artist as pathological: first, the spirit of antagonism within the artistic field, arising from the confrontation between the genius and the audience as well as between the bohemians and the bourgeoisie; and, second, the transformation of the theory of character into a psychological and medical discipline. It was within this context that the notion of psychic 'abnormality' arose. Ironic stabs and aggressive diagnoses of the artist were deployed in a culture war between originality and subversion fought not only over artworks but also over ways of life. The discrediting of bourgeois morals by bohemians and artists was thus discredited in its turn. The artist was now not the maker of admirable works but, rather, psychologically unreliable. His unreliability could no longer be tolerated as merely the unavoidable downside of the originality of the artwork because that work itself had been denied its worth. Consequently, all that remained was the diagnosis of a failure of psychological adaptability on the part of the artist, now exposed as a fake, not a genius.

These pathologies of the artist begin with Louis Francisque Lélut's *Du démon de Socrate*, which undertakes the first pathographic descriptions, and *La psychologie morbid* by Moreau de Tours, which launches dubious theories of abnormal alterations in the nervous system of alleged artistic geniuses.[59] While the aesthetic of genius and the other idealistic programmes equated the peculiarity of the artist with his capacity for autonomous perceptual and mental acts, the pathologies employed a diametrically opposed materialism. The genius was for them no more than brain and psyche. His psychic unpredictability is opposed to healthy human common sense, placing the artist now no longer above it in the cultural hierarchy but rather down below it. In the worst case, this meant relegating the artist to the ranks of the abnormal, amoral and sick, such as in Max Nordau's attack of 'degenerate art'.[60] The artist fell from the hallowed heights to a debased *outside* – outside of the morality and health of the mainstream. The enthusiasm for the exceptional genius was turned into an aggressive act of exclusion that went as far as fantasies of extermination.[61]

However, it must be remembered that, despite their opposing tendencies, the pathology discourse, the aesthetic of genius and the bohemian subculture agreed on one basic assumption. Both sides regarded the figure of the artist as the *other* operating outside of the dominant cultural order. This determination of the artist as the other is typical of the bourgeois artistic field, despite the latter's various universalizing programmes.[62] The signification of the artist's otherness oscillates between three registers: charismatic-aesthetic, quasi-sociological and psycho-pathological. In the charismatic-aesthetic register the artist is an exclusive, auratic figure and the creator of original works with a relation of connectedness to the totality of human existence. This is the mystified other, the outside playing to the inside of the public – not a maker, not the provider of impulses, but their recipient. The inside depends on the outside for the intensities of aesthetic stimulation it receives from it. In the quasi-sociological register, the artist faces the mainstream as a member of the anti-authoritarian, marginalized bohemian collective: the consciously self-created other. The outside operates here as an aggressive force of disturbance, offering a serious challenge to the legitimacy of the inside. Finally, in the psycho-pathological register, the artistic genius is reduced to the status of psychological unpredictability and moral degeneration: the outcast other. He plays the outside to the inside of majority psychic normality, where he is the object of an aggressive rejection.

2.4 The Bourgeois Artistic Field and the Cartography of Its Affects

The most insightful sociological analyses of the origins of the modern artistic field can be found in Niklas Luhmann's *Art as a Social System* and in Pierre Bourdieu's *The Rules of Art: Genesis and Structure of the Literary Field*. However, both approaches evince failings. Luhmann rightly points out that the artistic field is clearly distinguished from other fields because it 'communicates by *using perceptions contrary to their primary purpose*'.[63] He also draws attention to the way the public and aesthetic novelty structure artistic communication. Yet Luhmann tends to intellectualize the artistic field, substituting the communicative reflection on art for the sensuous perception of artworks. Further, the conflicts between processes of demarcation and the dissolution of borders in art and the aesthetic are overlooked by the functionalist presupposition of systemic autonomy.

Bourdieu, on the other hand, uses the example of French literature to emphasize the antagonistic origins of the field, the competition between popular artistic practices and pure aesthetics, whereby the latter stood in an ambiguous relation to bohemian culture. The producer logic and the audience logic are here also in competition with each other. In his *Distinction*, Bourdieu also points to how the artistic field produces subjectivization effects in its bourgeois users as they teach themselves to acquire 'legitimate taste'. However, Bourdieu encounters the same difficulties as Luhmann in explaining the historical process of border dissolution in the artistic field, how it assumed an enduring paradigmatic character for other fields leading to the emergence of the creativity dispositif. For Bourdieu, border dissolution consisted primarily in the reception of art becoming popular. At the same time, he tends to reduce the social character of art to the struggle for distinction between the participating groups, neglecting the subject–object sociality between artworks and recipients as well as between artworks and producers.[64]

Therefore, certain elements from Luhmann's and Bourdieu's interpretations can be retained in order to arrive finally at a differently accented reading of the social relevance of the artistic field. To reiterate the basic statement of this alternative reading: by orienting the social on the production and reception of aesthetic objects and events, the artistic field constitutes a blueprint of the development of culture in modernity in general. Accordingly, the border regime of the autonomous artistic field is continually caused to overstep its own border by a politics of the aesthetic. As a model for society as a whole, all of the artistic field's constituent parts have been able to exercise enduring effects: art forces upon all involved an unusually strict obligation to recalibrate themselves towards aesthetic novelty, towards surprising, original divergence from the norm. The artistic field trains its participants' sensibility for auto-dynamic, sensuous, affective impulses at a remove from normative and purposive rational action. At the same time, it trains the artist to develop an ethos of aesthetic productivity. Art thereby reshapes sociality in general on the model of a specific audience situation in which aesthetic excitement is produced for recipients freed of the need to act.

Luhmann and Bourdieu leave underexposed another aspect of fundamental importance to this interpretation of the artistic field. On the model we are adopting here, art is characterized by a specific affective and political logic. The affect logic relates both to the field's internal structure and to its relation to other social fields. Gilles Deleuze is right to encourage the drafting of 'affect lists' of social entities to analyse the affective relations, nodes and diffusions inherent to social constellations.[65] This kind of affective cartography is indeed indispensable to an understanding of the modern artistic field. In comparison to the other modern social fields that emerged around the end of the eighteenth century, art can be observed to be unusually and systematically productive of affects. In the sea of modern cooling systems, art is a hot archipelago. This affective intensity derives from art's basic activity of generating aesthetic practices, practices of producing and receiving artworks. Artworks are by definition intended to intensify sensuous, affective relations: the feeling of aesthetic freedom, emotion freed from action, meditation, shock, perplexity, enjoyment or pleasure in engaging with the artwork and the sense of enthusiasm in the act of creating it. The aesthetic regime of novelty endows this affection with the specific form of a desire for constantly new, surprising objects.

It has become evident that the bourgeois artistic field was the place of convergence not only of these positive affective vectors – recipient-artwork and artist-artwork – but also of other vectors, positive and negative. The first set of affective relations between subjects and objects came to undergird a corresponding third set of affect relations between subjects. The audience admires the artist as a unique creative being, while the artist enthuses over himself, perceiving his work as the expression of his own individuality. The subject-oriented affects in the bourgeois artistic field appear in some respects to superimpose themselves over the object-oriented affects, until the act of reception revolves entirely around the enthusiasm for the ideal self of the artist as the creative unity of individuality and total connectedness – an enthusiasm that eclipses the works themselves. It is then possible to observe *affects of the second order*: being affected by being affected, enthusiasm for enthusiasm. Such affect-affects also ensue from the programmes for universalizing the aesthetic, within which the creative unfolding of the human being becomes an attractive general cultural aim independent of individual artworks and artists. Bohemian sub-culture further complicated the affective politics of the artistic, producing several new affective vectors: the emotional satisfaction the bohemian derived from the extension of creativity from the artwork to lifestyle; an emotional self-assurance within the artistic community as a collective avant-garde; the distinction this collective contemptuously makes between itself and the narrow-minded bourgeois audience; inversely, the aggressive polemic and even fear among parts of the bourgeoisie on account of the destabilization of the cultural order through the bohemians, and at the same time the bourgeoisie's secret attraction to precisely this libertarian lifestyle. The labelling of the artist as pathological inserted a final axis into the artistic field's affective cartography: the variably ironic and vitriolic defamation of the artist as a dangerous and immoral figure.

The modern artistic field in its early, bourgeois version was characterized not only by a high degree of affective intensity. Nor was this affectivity without inner contradiction and tension, since both positive and negative affects were at work simultaneously. Indeed, bourgeois art represented an *affective field of combat*, where the mystification of artworks, artists, the aesthetic and creativity is set off against the heated dispute between artists and the audience over the proper standards for measuring originality and the legitimate scope of the aesthetic, and where finally the artist is degraded to a despised symbol of the disintegration of the rational social order. These affective conflicts were fuelled by the tension between the granting of autonomy to the artistic and the attempts at border dissolution by aesthetic utopians and bohemians.

In the society of modernity beginning to form in the late eighteenth century, the artistic field was therefore more than just one more specialized and differentiated sphere striving for autonomy. Its aestheticization of the social and its orientation towards aesthetic surprise and divergence made it fundamentally distinct from the rationalizing effects of the other, dominant fields of modernity,[66] although the latter were never entirely devoid of aesthetic character. Since Schopenhauer, this special status of the artistic field has lent support to the functionalist argument that art in bourgeois society is a form of sensuous-affective compensation for that society's rationalist systems.[67] However, the notion of compensation does not quite do justice to the emotionally charged, belligerent political attitude the artistic field adopted in bourgeois society. In that society, the artist was an object of melancholic identification, a figure who could turn violent under unfavourable conditions.[68] The bourgeoisie identified itself with an ideal self, whom it must at first appear socially unthinkable to want to imitate. The artist was the fascinating other of the bourgeois self who could not be appropriated by it because he contradicted its rationalism and its morals of work and the family. The public admired the artist not only for producing artworks but also for his licence to follow his imagination, shaping his works and his person in deviation from social norms and historical precedent. The artist received social approbation for being other, for his non-conformity, often enough posthumously.

The emergence of the creativity dispositif would ultimately revolutionize the relation of the artistic field to other areas of society. In the course of the twentieth century and beyond, the inimitable ideal self of the auratic artist will have metamorphosed into the imitable ideal of the creative self. For the artist to become a universally acknowledged creative role model, both art and the other fields had to undergo change, beginning structurally to assimilate to each other. As we will see, processes of aestheticization at work, particularly in capitalist economy, the mass media, popular psychology and urban design, become increasingly oriented towards the creative subject and the whole social regime of aesthetic novelty as their blueprint. Conversely, artistic practices also change, as the artistic field extends the domain of artistic creativity and artistic procedures into the far reaches of everyday life. Finally, economy, mass media and psychological discourse become aesthetic, while the artistic field and the artist lose their aura. They all become equal, interconnected segments of the creativity dispositif. The artistic field will have both won and lost. It will have to surrender its exceptional status as a space of exclusive practices and identifications, while its disenchanted incarnation rises to become the paradigm of late modernity's focus on creativity.

3

Centrifugal Art

Dissolving the Boundaries of Art Practices

3.1 Namuth's *Pollock*

Hans Namuth's short film *Jackson Pollock* appeared in 1951. Namuth had already published a set of black and white photographs showing Pollock at work in his studio. The series was at first largely ignored. Edward Steichen, serving as director of photography at New York's Museum of Modern Art, dismissed them as inadequate. 'You know, Namuth, this is not the way to photograph an artist.'[1] To Steichen, 'the nature and personality of such a complex human being are only partially revealed when you show him at work.' However, the film that followed the photo series quickly aroused interest. In 1951, it was shown at MOMA and at the film festival in Woodstock. The medium of film had been used for the first time to show a visual artist in action. The attempt had been made to render something of the mystery of artistic creativity publicly accessible.

In some regards, Namuth's portrait belongs to the long tradition of writer's and artist's portraits going back to the Renaissance and smoothing the way for the cult of artistic genius. What is most noteworthy about the work is the way it makes manifest a reconfiguration in artistic practice, in the artist and his relation to his audience. This shift can be observed in its initial phases in the early twentieth century before beginning to erupt in the 1960s. At its core, the individual components of the artistic field can be observed to breach their own boundaries, driven by changes in the forms of creative practice and the creative practitioner. The artist is now no longer an exclusive figure, modelled on the auratic other of the cultural order of modernity, but has become a practitioner of 'aesthetic labour', employing learnable and partly shared skills and procedures as well as chance events. Namuth's images can be read as documenting this shift while at the same time promoting it by their contribution to the visual discourse around the figure of the artist. They reiterate the nineteenth-century trope of the artist as genius while representing the transformation of artistic creativity into what I will refer to later on as 'centrifugal artistic practice'.

The more than 500 photographs taken by Namuth can be divided into two groups.[2] One group shows portraits of Pollock and views of his studio house. The other shows him working in his studio. In the first group we see a simple country house in a natural setting, with Pollock as a kind of 'lonesome man' – leaning on a window sill, out on the meadow or sitting in his car, always with a cigarette, wearing jeans and a light-coloured open shirt or jeans jacket, or a black T-shirt, casual seeming and yet pensive, casting a pained expression into the camera. In the second group we see him in action. The canvas is rolled out on the ground and he is bent over, executing drip-paintings with swinging motions, the speed of which often blurs the image. The photographic interest is focused on the leg moves, evoking dance choreography.

Namuth's brief, ten-minute colour film takes up motifs from both of these groups, adding a soundtrack with Pollock's voice and atonal music by Morton Feldman.[3] We first see Pollock slipping into a pair of rough, paint-covered work boots. Perhaps meant to invoke Heidegger's discussion of a pair of farmer's boots in a Van Gogh painting,[4] they are repeatedly picked out throughout the film. Pollock is seen pouring and stirring paint before a longer sequence documents his dance-like motions of drip-painting. This first part of the film is followed by a change of scene and a shorter sequence showing Pollock in a gallery hanging his pictures. A visitor, actually Pollock's wife, is seen from behind, attentively studying one of the paintings. The short time allotted to the sequence in the gallery clearly subordinates it to the frenetic act of painting itself. This preference is made more obvious still in the third part of the film, which constitutes its dramatic climax. Here, we see Pollock painting in drip technique on a sheet of glass laid on the ground, over which he spreads pebbles, buttons and other small objects, the whole filmed spectacularly from below.

Namuth's portrait cites obvious elements of the model of the artist from the nineteenth-century aesthetic of genius. The impression of Pollock as a solitary, soliloquizing and palpably masculine figure is underscored by the isolated wooden house in its bucolic setting. In contrast, Alexander Liberman, in his 1960 photo book

The Artist in His Studio, shows all the painters included in his volume wearing suits in the style of urban industrial designers.[5] Namuth frames Pollock as an anti-bourgeois beatnik, an embodiment of the artist as an expressive subject hauling his interior depths up to the surface. Pollock's activity seems less premeditated than trance-like, the irrepressible expression of an inner world. The assumption seems to be that artistic practice consists of the creation of an enduring work in the studio away from the eyes of the public. This entails a symbiosis of introversion and extroversion. The manically self-absorbed artist is coupled with the seemingly obsessive activity of the painting process. Pollock's commentary underlines this notion of expressivity as a relation of fit between interior and exterior. With the words 'I lost contact with my first painting on glass',[6] he wipes off a jettisoned attempt.

But this is just one side of the story. Namuth's portrait also shows how the cultural meaning of art production is being fundamentally reconfigured. The film prefigures the normalization of artistic creation as artistic *labour*, which will assert itself in the 1960s and 1970s. Pollock's drip-painting makes the process of producing art so quotidian that it already seemed banal to some contemporary viewers. In drip-painting, the picture-making is reduced to the movement of the artist's body in space, randomly and automatically distributing paint over the canvas. The act of painting is not the deliberate action of a reflexive self but, rather, unfolds without his conscious intervention. When he distributes objects over the glass surface, Pollock shows up less as the creator of something completely new than as an arranger of found objects. By pointing the gaze at the drip-painting and the arrangement of objects, the film directs the viewer's attention away from the artist as an original genius in a state of rapture and towards the creative techniques and the material used. The artist is a worker of this material, becoming in a certain sense the mere medium by which it is organized.

From the observer's point of view, the production process thus turns into a performance for an audience, breaking open the privacy of the studio. Obviously with Namuth's film in mind, Harold Rosenberg referred to the style Pollock represents as *action painting* rather than abstract expressionism.[7] The aesthetic object is here no longer the finished, material work of art – not the painting in the museum – but, rather, the artist's performance in front of his audience, with the double meaning of performance as completion or execution and presentation or exhibition. The hermetically sealed artwork is replaced by the art event, such that performance art can be seen as paradigmatic for postmodern art in general since the 1960s.

In Namuth's film it becomes clear that not only is the performance an artistic event but the postmodern artist himself as individual rises to become an acknowledged and admired artist through the public performance, and especially through the media performance, of his own person. Namuth's film played a decisive part in elevating Pollock to stardom in the American art scene and among the general public, which his works, regarded as unwieldy and inaccessible, would have had trouble managing on their own. He could attain celebrity only by unveiling the intimate details of his practice before a wide audience, visually surrendering his body and addressing the viewer directly, thereby seeming to render his personality entirely visible. The features of the original genius – eccentricity, bohemian attitude, expressivity – resurface here in fragmented form in the artist's staging of himself and can be recognized without acquaintance with the artist's works. The film illuminates an aspect of performance in artistic practice that belongs to the repertoire of the artistic self. The artistic self does not simply create art in the solitude of the studio but strives above all to have his status as an artist certified by the fascinated gaze of the audience. The figure of the artist thus becomes an aesthetic object in its own right.

3.2 Breaching the Inner and Outer Borders of the Artistic Field

The transformation undergone by artistic practice, by the artist-subject and by the whole artistic field in the course of the twentieth century could be seen reflected in Namuth's work on Pollock. It remains to explicate the general features of this transformation.

As we saw in the preceding chapter, the earlier, bourgeois artistic field supplied the background for the following series of dramatic, emotional conflicts over artistic creativity: the inner conflict of the original genius; the conflict between the genius and the audience over the ultimate right to judge the artist's originality; the conflict between the auratic notion of the artist as creator and reconciler and the stigmatization of the artist as pathological; and, finally, the conflict between bohemians and the bourgeoisie. Then, in the post-bourgeois artistic field, the emotional drama gradually calmed down, most palpably in the so-called postmodern artistic field emergent since the 1980s. Superficially, the widespread deconstruction of the myth of the artist, undertaken in self-commentaries by artists such as Max Ernst, Martin Kippenberger and Bruce Naumann, contributed to this de-escalation.[8] The real transformation, however, was the dissolution of the borders between the four components of modern aesthetic sociality elaborated in the preceding chapter: the artist as the creator of novelty; the aesthetic objects; the audience; and the institutional framework for directing attention. This breakdown of borders occurred *internally*, within art itself.

This development can therefore be distinguished from the attempts at *external* border dissolution already beginning to occur in the bourgeois artistic field in the nineteenth century. The two most important border-breaching strategies we have already investigated were the universalizing programmes of aesthetic creativity and bohemian subculture. Strictly speaking, these programmes were no longer related to art as an independent field but aimed rather at transforming art into lifestyle. They were breaching an external border to the extent that they sought to shape non-artistic practice based on an artistic ground plan. The opening up of aesthetic borders, the extension of art beyond its own limits, has increased in the course of the twentieth century and beyond. The following chapters will be concerned with tracing this process in the social fields it affected. For example, the mainly philosophical and culture critical discourse of the universality of aesthetic creativity began to be absorbed into psychological and pedagogical models of the 'creative self' where they exerted influence on the educated middle class.[9] Inversely, the bohemian lifestyle was quoted, continued and finally anchored by youth and counter-culture as one of the preconditions for 'aesthetic capitalism'.[10]

While the external breaches of the aesthetic field exerted influence outside of art, an *internal* structural border dissolution within the artistic field began taking place around 1900. This time, components of the ground plan of aesthetic sociality extended over a broader area, causing the exclusivity that characterized the bourgeois artistic field to diminish. These internal border breaches are thus more than merely a quantitative expansion of people and objects, more than an increase in the amount of artists, artworks and audience members, although these were also factors. Above all, the shift involves a widening of what counts as a valid artwork, a valid artistic activity and a valid audience response.

Most significantly, the border has been breached that narrowed the determination of what is recognized as artistic practice and what is expected of the artist.[11] Artistic practice now encompasses a broad range of activities involving objects and signs, many of which are regarded as learnable and imitable, and draw on techniques from other social fields such as science, artisanship, media, advertising or design. Artistic method becomes more codified, turning the making of art into a profane, normalized work procedure that is no longer hidden but, rather, made explicitly public for further open-source development. The artists have lost their status as exclusive figures and become preoccupied with their professional skills profile. Theirs has ceased to be an out-of-the-ordinary activity and is now aesthetic labour, which can also be undertaken in groups.

Closely bound up with this development is the breakdown of the aesthetic object. Since the beginning of the century the definition of artworks as physically discrete, unique and unified entities has been eroded in a variety of ways. What counts as art has been broadening out to include performance and installation and the border zones between art and design. The art audience has also been gaining ground as the restrictions imposed by bourgeois taste loosen their grip,[12] allowing the viewer to emerge increasingly as an active participant in the artistic process rather than as a mere recipient. Finally, a further set of borders has been breached by the way the artistic field is regulated by the market and the state. The public's attention to aesthetic novelty is now no longer directed by the bourgeois canons and art critics. An indicator for this disappearance of the canon is the shift in the art museums' orientation from the classical to the contemporary and changing.[13] These internal breaches in the artistic field made it a structural model for the creativity dispositif as a whole in late twentieth-century society.

In what follows, the main stations of this gradual process of the dissolution of borders within and around the artistic field will be traced in greater detail. Two continuous historical contexts of dissolution can be identified: the avant-garde after 1900 and postmodern art after the 1960s.[14] Neither the avant-garde nor postmodern art are reducible to artistic styles but, rather, must be understood as shifting sets of relations between artistic production practices, the criteria for legitimate art, the form of the artistic subject, and the position of the public. In these complexes the form of creativity undergoes the following series of separate transformations: the codification of artistic practice since surrealism; the different tendencies of 'materialization' of art, from Bauhaus to minimalism; the readdressing of the audience as an equal partner since Marcel Duchamp; the redefinition of artistic creativity as the appropriation of found material; the shift from the work to the art event; and the dual role of the artist as arranger and as celebrity.

3.3 Avant-Garde Creativity

Procedures and automatisms

The first incisive transformation of the form of creativity was connected with the codification of its procedures. In the context of the avant-garde, this was undertaken most systematically by surrealism. Surrealism practised 'art as technique', to quote the title of an essay from 1917 by the Russian literature theorist Viktor Shklovsky,[15] evolving practical methods for solving the problem of producing aesthetic novelty. This came to have an effect on the status of novelty itself. The old model of the creative artist was here emphatically discarded, denigrated for example by Max Ernst, who wrote: 'the fairy-tale of the artist's creativity is Western culture's last superstition, the sad remains of the myth of creation.'[16] This thinking introduced a distinction between the subject and the procedure. The personal agent of creation was supplanted by the internal dynamics of creative processes proceeding by their own mechanisms and pulling the artist along after them. The artist was no longer the guiding force but was relegated to a passive or transmitting position from which to observe the emergence of the work. The demand placed on the original genius to bring works into being was replaced by the demand to clear the way to let the works brings themselves about.

In this way, surrealism broke down the opposition between novelty and normality. The creation of original, new, surprising works was no longer the exception but the rule, an event occurring without the interference of the author. The latter could figure only as a systematic hindrance to the natural flow of things. One of the main ways the surrealists promoted the codification of artistic procedures was by the use of random generators,[17] by which unpredictable events happen on their own, facilitated and recorded rather than created by the human subject. The production of novelty by letting random things happen provided an alternative to the model of an expressive vector between artist and work. This latter presumes that only a particular artist can generate a particular artwork, whereas random products cannot be unequivocally ascribed to a single author. These techniques of creativity, however, involve a paradox of programmed spontaneity, whereby it is supposed possible to access randomness with the help of learnable techniques, thereby rendering the unpredictable programmable.

Poets and artists such as André Breton, Max Ernst and André Masson developed a number of these creative techniques within the context of surrealism. Three different types of technique can be distinguished: inner-psychic; inter-objective; and intersubjective. Breton's well-known techniques of automatic writing and drawing[18] were creative methods drawing on inner psychic processes. Their two essential components were the unconscious and speed. They train the practitioner to enter a state of dreamlike consciousness (*état de rêve*), the floating concentration of the interval between the self-control of consciousness and the state of sleep in which images and words can arise in the mind spontaneously and unsorted. In the artistic production process, such as when applying paint to a canvas, speed was the elemental trick for making the process automatic and overriding conscious control. Masson recognized that the main problem arising from this production process was knowing when to stop. When creative production does not follow a pre-set plan, it is difficult to determine when the artwork is finished.[19]

A second version of the surrealist codification of method was supplied by Max Ernst. This time it was an automatism in the interaction with objects and materials. Making use of a children's game, Ernst developed the method of frottage.[20] Everyday objects with interesting surface structures are rubbed onto the paper with charcoal and the forms from various objects are superimposed. The rubbings automatically produce a negative of the object and the act of superimposition adds randomness of combination. Automatic writing and frottage were conceived as methods of producing art, but they exhibit structural commonalities with methods from the wholly different discourse of psychology, from which they were partly influenced and which they influenced in their turn. Automatic writing uses elements from Freud's 'free association', and frottage has similarities with methods of experimental creative psychology.

The third type of creative technique, the surrealist games known as *recherches experimentales*, consists basically of association techniques.[21] They are employed by a group and resemble the brainstorming of organizational psychology that has become familiar since the 1950s.[22] The *recherches experimentales* generate associations by intersubjective rather than by inner-psychic or subject-object processes, thereby removing the inventive genius from the creative process. The aim was not to produce art but, rather, mentally to limber up in preparation for producing improbable ideas. This liquefied the border between art and play. Howsoever they may have varied in their particulars, the games always ran on the same pattern, connecting two disparate phenomena in an intelligible way.[23] The group constellation can function in various ways as a motor of creativity, artificially placing the participants under pressure to solve a problem in a short time, enabling a chain of associations to run between participants and encouraging a spirit of playful competition.

The surrealist codification of procedure extended the domain of creativity on the level both of practices and of subjectivity. Other practices apart from art were held to contain creative potential, from psychological procedures to children's games. This expansion was paired with a generalization of creativity on the subjective level. If creativity is dependent on techniques of association, then it can no longer be restricted to the artist; rather, everyone is potentially capable of it. Surrealism systematically drew attention to groups who had previously been stigmatized as pathological – infants, primitive peoples, and the mentally ill – but who now appeared predestined for creativity since their chains of association were less rigid than those of the average Western adult.[24] The pathological or abnormal subject was then not only rehabilitated as normal but found to exemplify the creative self; she was the very model of the artist.

Material and technique

In addition to the codification of creative procedure, the avant-garde milieus and, subsequently, postmodernism saw a shift of focus to the role of material in the creative process. At the heart of this development was a broadened understanding of what can validly be regarded as a material object of art. The focus of the aesthetic process shifted from ideas and meanings to the level of mere 'base matter', the materials to be worked. In the 1970s, the process was accelerated by which the strict boundary between artistic and quotidian objects was undermined by art investing profane entities with aesthetic quality. Body art and land art are just two examples of this tendency. Dada and surrealism had already incorporated everyday objects into artworks. Further, the use of materials in art was altered in particular by the systematic breaching of boundaries between artistic creation and the general production of artefacts. This affected in particular the boundary between artistic production and technological, industrial production. Such interferences between the artistic and the technological are to be found above all in two very different contexts: in the merging of art and technology in design, exemplified by Eastern European constructivism and Bauhaus in the 1920s, and in the serial work of minimal art in the USA in the 1960s.

Especially in the Soviet Union and the Weimar Republic, product and design art pushed aesthetic objects over the border of what previously counted as art, at the same time incorporating technology and collective work into aesthetic processes. The Soviet constructivists in the 1920s replaced the work-focused aesthetic connecting the artwork to artistic activity with the more basic nexus of object and labour.[25] Marx's concept of labour played a central role here by framing work in general as an act of creation of which art is merely a specific but not a privileged instance. Conversely, this model allowed artistic work to be understood as labour.[26] If all work is creative, then the realm of objects that can serve as artworks is extended indefinitely. On this principle, art could be freed from its function of producing meanings and concentrate instead on the shaping of its materials. It became 'production art'. As Ilya Ehrenburg wrote, 'art is the creation of objects.'[27] The concept of labour became universal, but labour had become technological and industrial. Production art was incorporated into the industrial, technological complex, engendering a hybrid of artist and engineer, an engineer-artist working in a collective, construed as 'the inventors of objects, the organizers of materials, the workers of form'.[28]

Soviet production art was short-lived. It was gradually displaced by agitprop in the course of the 1930s, surviving only in isolated pockets such as the field of textiles. It remains questionable in what way this production art was specifically aesthetic in distinction to engineering. A version of the materialist shift in art with a stronger amalgam of theory and practice occurred at the same time at the Bauhaus in Weimar and Dessau. This version took its point of departure from the artisanal practice of the German arts and crafts and workshop movements, transposing them onto the model of 'design' of everyday objects which would come to wield a powerful historical influence.[29] Bauhaus successively dissolved two distinctions that had been crucial to the bourgeois artistic field: the distinction between art and craft and the distinction between art and technology/industry. Accordingly, the training at the Bauhaus was built on a combination of artistic, artisanal and technological skills rendering obsolete the distinction between *artes liberales* and *artes mechanicae* and leaving *Bauen*, construction, as the blanket term for all the activity taking place there. Artistic practice was understood as always involving technical and manual skills in working with material, while manual work conversely involved artistic skills. The focus was therefore not on artworks as such but on any aesthetically designed object of utility, not on the ideal of a wholly different world but on the aestheticization of the practical world of things.

Artistic skills were explicitly understood as learnable. Johannes Itten developed a paradigmatic theory of contrast, form and colour intended to cultivate the sensibility for basic universal laws that can be applied to individual problems.[30] The programme also involved the systematic training of a tactile sense for different materials. The so-called *Werkkünstler*, the work-artist, was to be taught key aesthetic skills, thereby shifting the focus from the hunt for originality to the production of harmonious effects using standard patterns. In its second phase, Bauhaus moved away from craftwork to a focus on mechanically produced household objects. Design and production, inseparable in the classical concept of creativity, were thereby divided, and art, newly cast as design, came to resemble technical engineering. The distinction between the aesthetic and the technological then consisted in the aesthetic surplus gleaned from the application and variation of universal chromatic harmonies and forms, committing designers to a sense of themselves as technicians of forms.[31]

The interlocking of artistic and artisanal practice at the Bauhaus led finally to the transformation of art into design. In the post-Second World War period, this shift was manifest in the gradual expansion of Western design as an independent aesthetic industry.[32] However, the use of industrial materials in artistic production did not necessarily imply craft and design, as was demonstrated by minimal art in the 1960s, which can be regarded as the forerunner of postmodern installation art.[33]

At first sight, minimal art was concerned to produce not objects of utility but objects for aesthetic observation in traditional purpose-built exhibition spaces. However, minimal art did involve a different focus on the technical materiality of reproducible objects. It distanced itself from the visual illusionism of traditional visual art, concentrating instead on placing three-dimensional objects in space for the observer to take in by moving around them. These *specific objects*, as Donald Judd called them, were generally produced by industrial means, examples being Dan Flavin's fluorescent light tubes or Judd's coloured Plexiglas forms, incorporating materials not made by the artist and previously used in non-artistic contexts. Departing from the ideal of the original work, the artefacts of minimal art comprised series of identical objects. The creative act consisted in the spatial disposition of industrially made products alienated from their original purpose. The object of art was then no longer the individual work but rather the atmosphere provided for the viewer by the placement of the objects in a space, that space usually being a museum. The recipient was addressed not as a passive observer but as a mobile, sensuously multifaceted entity interacting within a space. The industrial artefacts were tasked with generating sensuous-affective, spatial atmospheres independent of their original practical purpose. While the light fixtures in Flavin's installations are not interesting in themselves, they have a capacity literally to cast the exhibition space in a different light by means of simultaneous chromatic contrasts and optical blending. The purpose of the art object was not to provide the occasion to decode a meaning locked inside it but, rather, to obtain an *affect effect* by virtue of the arrangement of the materials.

Minimal art thus laid down several important lines of transformation relating to the dissolution of the boundaries holding creative practice inside the artistic field: the emphasis on audience participation; the logic of appropriation and copy; and the aesthetics of installation and performance. These areas will be investigated in more detail in what follows.

Activating the recipient

In addition to the creative procedure and dissolving the borders holding in artistic objects, avant-garde and postmodern artworks activated the recipient. This reduced the difference between the producer and the recipient, redressing the imbalance between the creating, conceiving, inventive genius and the passive public. Artistic practice now addressed the public as a group of creative and active inventors of interpretations and producers of affects in their own right. Marcel Duchamp confirmed (albeit in somewhat traditional terms) this redistribution of the creative function from the author to the recipient when he wrote, 'All in all, the creative act is not performed by the artist alone; the spectator brings the work in contact with the external world by deciphering and interpreting its inner qualification and thus adds his contribution to the creative act.'[34]

It follows from this statement that art should be audience oriented (though not popular) inasmuch as it provokes cognitive and aesthetic processes. This audience orientation was still not taken for granted in the 1960s, as is illustrated by Michael Fried's critique of minimal art. Fried dons a modernist cloak to repeat the romantic critique of philistine mass consumerism, accusing postmodern art of minimalism of a theatricality tantamount to abandoning the struggle against capture by an audience.[35] Further, avant-garde and postmodernist audience orientation was a specific one. The audience was regarded not as a vehicle of entertainment or scandal but, rather, as a collection of individuals as self-reflexive and affected as the artists themselves, equally unpredictable in their legitimately autonomous reactions. The audience thus became the artist's accomplice.

A classic version of this focus on the active recipient can be found in Marcel Duchamp's work and the later conceptual art he decisively influenced. Pivotal to both was that the recipients must not remain inactive. They must perform their own creative work, decoding the piece and experimenting with it, producing a sensuous, emotional confrontation within the self. The activation of the recipient is closely tied to the reorganization of artistic production designed to include the expectation of reflective recipients. This state of affairs is clearly visible in Duchamp's installations and ready-mades.[36] An example is the piece *3 stoppages étalons* (3 Standard Stoppages, 1913), consisting of a wooden box with three lengths of wood and panes of glass. The work is the result of an experiment. Duchamp dropped three metre-long pieces of string on a canvas. The strings produce random forms, with new lengths diverging from the standard metre length. The wooden slats indicate the three new metre lengths. Duchamp essentially imitated a non-artistic practice, namely the scientific experiment, in which something new and unpredictable is brought into being by the experimental set-up. Yet the set-up was the result of a concept of the artist's with which the recipient was meant to engage – 'a box containing an idea'[37] – the thought being that units of measurement are conventional. In works of this type, the recipient is provided by the artist with elucidations, often in the form of a written commentary in the exhibition or in a catalogue, furnishing an Aha! moment. In contrast, Duchamp's ready-mades work differently. Here, there is no experimental set-up but, rather, pre-existent objects: a bottle dryer, a snow shovel or the celebrated urinal. Instead of creating something new, the artist *chooses* some given, profane object.[38] The artistic selection voids the object of its everyday meaning and displaces it to a new context. The work is no longer a made object but a context. It is not just the urinal but the urinal *in* the museum. It is the context to which contingent significations can be attached by the recipient.

By adopting elements from Duchamp's work, the conceptual art emerging in the 1960s became one of the most influential postmodern artistic forms internationally.[39] Concept art is installation art employing photographs, texts and objects, producing what could be called operations rather than works. Here too the novelty of the artwork lies not in the object and its production but in the artistic idea that the arrangement of artefacts is intended to transmit. As Sol LeWitt put it, 'Ideas can be works of art.'[40] The work is an intellectually stimulating idea, often simple and certainly not entirely original, for the viewer to work through and appropriate. For example, Hans-Peter Feldmann's piece *Alle Kleider einer Frau* shows seventy-two black and white photographs presented in grid formation with what is alleged to be the complete wardrobe belonging to a particular woman,[41] thus conforming precisely to the concept designated by the title. The quotidian items of clothing become museum exhibits; banal objects are transubstantiated into puzzling, even uncanny forms, body accessories without a body to fill them. The piece thus examines the relation between artistic and profane objects, while the recipient must perform the corresponding interpretative work of solving the puzzle. The reception is characterized not by a learning process but rather by a spontaneous Aha! effect on the part of the recipient, who is complicit in the work's authorship.

3.4 Creativity in Postmodern Art

Methods of appropriation: the relatively new

A number of practices emerging in postmodern art since the 1960s led to self-doubt and a readjustment of the claim of artworks to originality and radical novelty. The notion of the inventive genius and the distinction between original and copy have been rejected for a number of different reasons. Rosalind Krauss has undertaken a critique of the myth of discontinuity or rupture.[42] However, this deconstruction of the claim to originality should not be misunderstood as implying that postmodern art has abandoned artistic novelty. Novelty simply becomes relative and more subtly shaded, which in turn renders it all the more *potent*.

Good examples of these alternative production methods outside of the paradigm of originality are pop art and Andy Warhol's screen prints, the serial reproduction of industrial forms in minimal art that we have already seen, and *postproduction* and *appropriation art*, both of which make use of found cultural objects, for instance mass media photography.[43] All of these cases can be subsumed under the label 'appropriation', since the basic mode of production is always the same. The aim is not to add an artefact created *ex nihilo* to the world of existing things but rather to respond to the world of things and meanings by means of things found in it. The artist is then a 'plagiarist' for whom everyday culture has become an 'immense encyclopaedia from which he draws'.[44] These acts of appropriation always involve a reassignment of meanings because the everyday world is the beginning, not the endpoint, of the artistic process. Novelty does not spring from the originality of the genius but emerges from the repetition of the given and the past.

Three different appropriation methods can be distinguished, each representing variants of what *relative novelty* in art can mean. The first version involves recourse to already existing objects. This applies to Duchamp's ready-mades and to Alan Kaprow's later environments with their junk objects. Novelty consists here in the selection of objects or in their displacement to a new context, whether this displacement is commented on or not. The second variant is the serial production of identical forms. Here, objects are indeed produced but as a result of an industrial process. Moreover, they can be standardized objects produced in series like any commodity; they need not be the artist's original invention. This applies to the multiples of minimal art. The novelty resides here in the spatial disposition of familiar objects and in the resulting creation of atmosphere.

The third variant is the reproduction of technical images such as photographs. This group includes Warhol's classic screen prints, in which images of celebrities are reworked, as well as the reproductions and 're-enactments' of familiar photographs of Sherry Levine, Cindy Sherman and Elaine Sturtevant. The reproduction operates here as a context-shifting quotation that amplifies the distance to the original. In this group, the photographic sources are already technical reproductions, what Derrida might call 'copies without originals'. Warhol, for example, exploited standard methods from his work as a commercial illustrator to obtain estrangement effects with the chromatic exuberance of his screen print reproductions.[45] Elaine Sturtevant's post-production art elected a different method. In the photograph *La rivoluzione siamo noi*, she takes on the role played by Joseph Beuys in his self-portrait photograph of the same name from 1972,[46] wearing the same clothes and imitating his energetic striding towards the viewer. The subtle difference to the original reveals the latter for what it really is. The novelty of the post-production artwork thus consists in the reinterpretation of the original, which is shown up to be a cultural stereotype.

From the work to the event: the aesthetics of installation and performance

Several attributes of postmodern art can be found in the installation and performance art movements that began emerging in the late 1960s, the first impulses of which were provided by happenings and Allan Kaprow's environments.[47] The main effect of these movements was to replace the artistic work by the artistic event.[48] Instead of producing a durable, transportable artefact, the artist generates a unique situation, a spatial and temporal performance with people or things as the performers. Aesthetic objects no longer needed to be fixed or permanent. The performance itself was the work, which thereby came closer to the everyday world outside of art.[49] After all, social practice itself is ultimately always performative in that it produces reality by means of the staging of bodies and objects. By substituting the artistic event for the artwork, postmodern art made relevant the framing conditions of practice in general, its embeddedness in space and time, that the classical work of art had artificially bracketed.[50] Performances and installations integrate site-specific circumstances. The space in which they take place as a specific location is an integral component. Moreover, performances, and many installations, are not repeatable. They are temporary events, dependent on the participation of an audience constituted in a particular way and gathered for this one occasion.

Audience involvement plays an elemental role in constituting the event of installation art and, to a still greater extent, performance art. Since the 1960s, the art discourse itself has continued to investigate this anti-consumerist and anti-auratic audience participation. As Beuys wrote, 'Every man is a plastic artist.... Everyone will be a necessary co-creator.'[51] The audience is expected to participate in the creation of the event. In some installations, this occurs interactively – for example, when the roles of actor and viewer are reversed, or by involving mutual touch. The activation of the recipient is thereby turned up a notch higher. This goes further than the activation of audience interpretation in conceptual art, heightening the contrast to the traditional model of the aesthetic space in which the observer is freed of the need to act. It now activated the viewers' bodies, forcing them to decide how the performance would continue or how the installation would function. This systematically both undermines and highlights the border between the experience of art and the performance of non-artistic practices. The accompanying destabilization of the frame is often mediated by affects.[52] The viewers' disgust and pain at the sight of an act of self-wounding which really occurs rather than being merely represented – such as in the performances of Marina Abramović – is no longer the type of catharsis experienced in a theatre situation in which the audience is freed of the necessity to act. Such an experience occupies the median strip between everyday life and artistic events.[53] In the context of performance art, the recipient as participant develops a heightened aesthetic awareness, an attitude that could be described as *diffused concentration*. In contrast to traditional theatre, with its linear, psychological dramatic development, every seemingly negligible detail of a performance can become relevant, while the action provides no criteria for selection. This causes the competent recipient to develop a sensibility for the apparently banal. What Simmel refers to as a 'protective organ', characteristically developed by modern inhabitants of cities for personal interaction, is then lowered by a dilation of sensitivity.[54]

The replacement of the work by the aesthetic event and the activation of the aesthetic disposition of the audience through performance and installation art also transform the artist-subject. Artists now mutate from producers of works into initiators of atmospheres.[55] Their main purpose is to generate a perceptual and affective space, the effect of which always remains unpredictable. The creation of atmosphere is a fundamentally intermedial and synesthetic task for which all potential effects are deployed; there is a mixing of visual and aural impressions, physical motion and film, props, audience influence on spatial order, and the shifting of start and finish markers. The work of creative design is geared towards an audience-oriented total artwork with the individual artist often replaced by a whole artistic collective with its own proper name, for example in post-dramatic theatre.[56]

3.5 Postmodern Artist-Subjects

The artist as arranger

Since the 1990s at the latest, scattered changes in artistic practices have been visibly converging to generate a new type of artist-subject. The artist and the artistic collective are now above all *communication-oriented arrangers of aesthetic processes*. The bearer of an artistic 'skills profile' replaces the exclusive figure of the original artist. This skills profile, combining symbolic, affective, intellectual and media competencies, resembles structurally the competency profile of professionals in other 'cultural industries' that developed in aesthetic capitalism in the last quarter of the twentieth century.[57] Art is therefore a micro-reflection of the characteristics of the more general, professional, creative subject performing aesthetic labour.

As an arranger, the artist is concerned primarily with selecting, modifying, combining and presenting elements from the social and cultural world, both contemporary and past. As Burgin wrote in 1969, 'The artist is apt to see himself not as a creator of new material forms but rather as a coordinator of existing forms.' The artist thus becomes a 'manipulator of signs', as Hal Foster points out.[58] The activity of the arranger requires a skilful handling of diverse social and cultural contexts. An arranger must be familiar with the inventory of high culture and with global contemporary popular culture. The frequent claims that postmodern art is an art of context, such as those made by Peter Weibel in his essay of the same name from 1971, and by Nicolas Bourriaud, with his notion of 'relational aesthetics', are expressions of the primacy of this universal competency in symbols and semiotics.[59] Contextual art reflects on its spatial, institutional and social embeddedness, making it into its thematic content. Relational aesthetics is an art form that does not create novelty in the strict sense but consists rather in references to social and cultural spaces that have already come about, insinuating itself into the *social interstices*, shining critical light on the surrounding structures by means of artistic representation.

The artist as socio-cultural arranger is many-faceted. She is a quasi-academic *researcher*, a *self-commentator*, a *curator*, an *atmosphere generator* and an agent of political, cultural *intervention*. Artistic practice in modernity had frequently incorporated material research as preparation work, but postmodern art also methodically integrates into the production process quasi-scientific, pseudo-scientific and journalistic practices such as collecting, observing, documenting and archiving.[60] These methods are employed not for the sake of securing objectivity but more as subjective research, such as in Christian Boltanski's personal archives. Further, postmodern artists have their own way of assimilating skills from art history and from theory. Theoretical self-commentary becomes part of the artwork and a necessary condition for self-contextualizing. Artists no longer count on art historians and critics to provide commentary but operate instead as artist-intellectuals supplying their own explanations of their work.

This situation is further illuminated by the fluid boundaries between artists and curators that have emerged since the 1970s.[61] The profession of the freelance curator was conceived in Germany in 1969 with the founding of the Agentur für geistige Gastarbeiter (Agency for intellectual migrant workers) by Harald Szeemann, who three years later would become the first programmatic exhibition director of the Documenta in Kassel. The curators see themselves as artists by virtue of their activity as arrangers and intellectual commentators, as 'exhibition auteurs', thereby eliciting a counter-offensive by artists assuming curatorial tasks. The artist-curator resembles the figure of the director; she is an artist-subject of the second order. No longer concerned with the artistic arrangement of material, she is now interested in arranging pre-existing artworks and artistic contexts in the three-dimensional space of the museum as well as in intellectual space. Her aim is to generate a spatial, atmospheric and intellectual context, part of which is the coordination and communicative networking of people, media and patrons. As in performance art, the work itself consists in the temporary curated presentation. The permanent, reproducible artwork is replaced by the organization of a temporary cultural event. The activity of the postmodern artist is often collective and the activity of the artist-curator is always collective. Andy Warhol's Factory can be seen as a blueprint for this species of collective creativity machine that stimulates and interconnects the creative activities of various agents.[62]

The job of atmosphere manager is elementary to the task portfolio of artist-curators and performance artists in particular, as well as to postmodern artists more generally. The arrangement of signs intersects here with the inducement of affects. As sign arranger and self-commentator, the artist is also both a discourse manager and a generator of atmospheres. The purpose of arranging things and human bodies in space is to affect the audience, to produce what Harald Szeemann referred to as a 'walk-through event structure'.[63] This kind of affect management requires mastery in a range of media (photography, film, computer, theatre, dance, music, installation, etc.) as well as an ability to design holistic atmospheric spaces.

Finally, the postmodern artist-subject has frequently assumed the role of an agent of 'interventions'.[64] Her task is to attract attention to the artistic event and to the *problem* it examines. In the extreme, this skilful mobilization of interest can itself make up the core of artistic production, such as in Christoph Schlingensief's artistic events.[65] The successful intervention requires the artist to analyse the context in which art exerts influence and develop a conceptual strategy for exerting such influence. He must choose the right place and the right moment, mobilize the right audience, media and critics and prepare his own commentary. This sort of intervention goes further than the public art scandals of the avant-gardes. While both are audience-oriented, the intervention is intended not to scandalize but to draw positive attention and awaken public awareness and reflection.

All in all, the postmodern artist's profile is characterized by a combination of skills associated partly with the aesthetic material and partly with the audience. The whole social economy of signs, narratives and affects, together with the sum of utilizable media, becomes potential material for art. The arrangement of this material is welded to the skilful mobilization of audience attention. The institutional transformation that has been gaining ground in the global artistic field since the 1970s facilitated just such a professionalization of the artistic management of audience attention. An expectation of unexpected events has been generated by the global institutionalization of social contexts dedicated to presenting *new* art (biennales, art fairs, art festivals, and curated, temporary exhibitions in a rapid-growth global museum landscape). The institutionalization also heats up the competition for the scarce resource of audience attention divided among artistic products and artists.[66]

The artist as performer

In the postmodern context, the artist-subject, as arranger and transmitter, becomes both professional and mundane. However, this is only one side of the story. Since the 1980s in particular, a renewed affective investment in the figure of the artist can be observed, though in modified form. The representation of the artist in the nineteenth-century cult of art was divided into the established, yet therefore less innovative, artist-prince, the original but already deceased creative genius, and the controversial anti-artist (bohemian artist, scandal artist, secessionist, dandy, etc.). By the 1940s a new type had begun to emerge, first assuming a distinct shape with Pablo Picasso or Jackson Pollock: the artist as a mass media star, combining aesthetic originality with celebrity in his own lifetime.[67] Joseph Kosuth and Andy Warhol can be regarded as later postmodern incarnations of this artistic figure. Since the 1990s this pattern has spread in the context of a system of artistic stars, encompassing painters, performance artists, film directors and authors.

In the postmodern artistic field, the recognition of the artist's public persona begins to separate from the interest in his work.[68] The older model of the artist was based on the connection between the artist and the work, while now the artist is represented by herself and others according to an internal media logic. In extreme cases, the reception of the artworks and the artist can be entirely separated. The key issue is no longer that the artist has produced a work, although this remains a necessary condition, but that she permanently presents herself *as an artist*, projecting an identifiable look, comportment, and way of engaging with media, as well as adopting a set of behaviours outside of the production of art, be they private, political or commercial. The mass media are the means by which this permanent public presentation of the person is made possible.

A further factor that emerged in the 1960s is the replacement of the dealer-critic system in the visual arts, which had once secured the special status of art critics passing judgement on works, by the dealer-collector system.[69] Now, the collectors decide the success of an artist, making the artist's self-presentation for a popular, non-specialized audience more influential. In the mid-1960s, the conceptual artist Joseph Kosuth was one of the first exponents of this, managing to present himself in the media, despite the inaccessibility of his works, as a dandy-type rebel and a business-savvy intellectual. Andy Warhol perfected the attainment of recognizability with his self-presentation as a fixture of New York celebrity culture and an object of global media attention.[70] Postmodern artists since Kosuth and Warhol are dependent on the *visuality* of performance, the presentation of media images of themselves in order to establish a distinguishable individual identity.

The cultivation of artistic persona independently of the artworks harks back to an element of the earlier artistic field: the self-stylization of the artist in bohemian culture. There, as we saw, the interest in

the artistic shaping of works had already shifted to the public demonstration of lifestyle. On the other hand, the postmodern artist-subject
is no longer part of an identifiable counter-culture but, rather, belongs
to the global 'creative class'. Her self-stylization therefore follows a
different pattern. It strives to form a recognizable and appealing
individual style distinct from the other individual styles within the
artistic field. The production of an individual style draws on and
recombines elements from the historical pool of signs for the artistic
that has been building up since the eighteenth century, among them
the figure of the bohemian artist, the artist-prince, the political artist,
the artist-engineer, the introverted outsider or the extroverted masculine artist.

This logic of difference inherent to the task of developing an individual style as a media personality can be illuminated by comparing
three apparently diverse contemporary artists: Pipilotti Rist, Markus
Lüpertz and Christian Boltanski.[71] The Swiss concept artist Rist stages
herself in mass-media organs such as *Vogue* and *Emma* as an unconventional type experimenting with diverse forms of femininity, among
others by means of clothing. At the same time, she stresses the fact
that she does not work alone but rather as the leader of an artist
team. Lüpertz, in contrast, appears as a living anachronism with his
post-romantic borrowings from figures such as the artist-prince, the
narcissist and the dandy. Finally, Boltanski consistently refuses any
form of self-representation claiming authenticity, using his art instead
to reflect on precisely this problem. He makes free play of his own
biography with collections of documents and interviews, keeping
himself invisible behind them. The question is not whether the postmodern artist is more typically modelled after the media-oriented
creative artist Rist, the neo-genius revivalist Lüpertz or the self-
deconstructivist Boltanski. All three are exemplary of the postmodern
artistic field in that each is able to hold their own in the contest for
attention by generating an individual self-presentation. The important
factor is not the content of the presentation but, rather, securing a
distinctiveness from other artists in the field by means of a specific
combination, nuance or innovation.

In contrast to the artist in the bourgeois artistic field, the postmodern artist-subject ceases to represent herself as dangerous, fascinating, resistant to general imitation, and fundamentally foreign to
the prevalent culture; rather, she acts as a node within a broader
mass-media system extending far beyond the arts and made up of
creative stars displaying desirable characteristics.[72] The postmodern
artist is an ideal self that can be imitated, a subject capable of both
self-styling and creative work. She synthesizes two features that were

incommensurable in the bourgeois artistic field. Her work and her person both set new aesthetic standards *and yet* she obtains immediate social recognition.[73]

3.6 Art as a Blueprint of Late Modernity

In the course of the twentieth century, the artistic field went centrifugal. The domain of what counted as an artistic object overflowed its borders to seep into events and artefacts not previously regarded as art. The practices and skills of the artist-subject expanded to embrace the competencies of the arranger and the atmosphere generator. The recipient, finally, came to be addressed as co-creator. By going centrifugal, art has breached the borders separating it from other social fields, set up networks and begun to inhabit border zones. As a result of breaching borders, objects and skills are being imported into art from other social practices – the techniques and objects of the mass media, the methods of the sciences and natural objects. The networks allow different fields to act on one another, such as art and advertising or art and urban planning. Border zones have been growing up in which disciplines such as architecture and design have come to be attributed polyvalently to art as well as to other fields. Whereas the bourgeois artistic field was concerned chiefly with securing its borders as an autonomous zone, centrifugal art is now driven by the contrary interest of methodical networking, border dissolving and generating interstitial zones between inside and outside.

We have seen in detail how fundamental processes of border dissolution have been occurring in the postmodern, centrifugal artistic field. Throughout these processes, the artistic field has retained the structural floor plan it had acquired in early modernity, though reproducing it in more radical forms. The specific sociality of art still rests on the four columns: the production of aesthetic novelty by the artist as a creative subject (now expanded to include the collective); the orientation towards specific aesthetic objects; an aesthetically focused audience; and the institutional management of attention directed at these artistic works and events. Like its bourgeois precursor, the centrifugal artistic field continues to constitute a form of the social directed at the permanent production and reception of aesthetic novelty.

However, a paradoxical state of affairs has emerged around the primacy of aesthetic novelty. Since the time of the avant-garde movements, and most prominently in postmodernism, the artistic discourse has consistently dismantled the myth of the new, the myth of novelty in art and of the artist as original creator. As we have seen, this deconstruction translates into corresponding artistic practices involving conscious combination, arrangement, reinterpretation and appropriation.[74] However, this self-disenchantment has not caused the orientation towards surprise, foreignness, the unconventional and the 'tradition of the new' to disappear from the artistic field.[75] On the contrary, the disenchantment of the creative artist extends and deepens the ability of the artistic field to generate surprise and otherness. If the new is no longer equated with total ruptures committed by artistic geniuses or a radical avant-garde, then a widened spectrum of phenomena can count as *relatively* new. Aesthetic novelty can be produced with less inhibition when rearrangements and appropriations, even those of popular and media culture, are classified as artistically interesting.

The loosening of criteria of novelty and interest has made it easier for the social regime of the new to become perpetuated in more robust form. This simultaneously moderated and radicalized understanding of creativity has altered the approach to 'old' aesthetic objects, which are no longer simply rejected as obsolete but rather pressed into the service of new creation by recombination and appropriation. When the interpretation and rearrangement of the old, as well as of contemporary popular culture, become legitimate creative procedures, then art gains access to a huge reservoir of new activities. The dissolution of borders between genres and media, the admission of chance operations and the toleration of a plurality of styles have similar effects. The loosening of the braces restraining the components of the artistic field thus enables the rise of the regime of pure, unbound aesthetic novelty as the producer of surprise transcending the confines of bourgeois art.

The altered relation between artists and recipients has contributed significantly to anchoring the dominance of aesthetic novelty. In the bourgeois artistic field, the 'art for art's sake' logic of the author and the populist logic of the audience were first opposed then supplanted by the scandal-making of the early avant-garde. Now, the centrifugal artistic field reverses the logic of scandal into a paradoxical logic of the expectation of surprise. In postmodern art, the audience is addressed no longer as the representative of conservative, middle-class taste in the spirit of *shocking the bourgeoisie* but, rather, as the democratic, co-conspiratorial community of active, creative and open recipients. It is now taken unreservedly for granted that the audience *wants* to be surprised by aesthetic novelty.[76] Art thus finds itself in the situation of striving to fulfil the need to be affected by the unfamiliar, the perplexing and the disturbing. The antagonism between the logic of the audience and the logic of the producer is dissolved in the complicity between artists and audiences in the regime of aesthetic perplexity.

The changes to the internal structure of the artistic field as well as to the status of art within society at large over the twentieth century have occupied sociological analysis continually since the 1920s and often motivated it to cultural critique. However, it would at first have seemed unthinkable that the artistic field could become an exemplary blueprint and pacemaker for general social change. Theodor W. Adorno's theory of the culture industry predicted that large chunks of the art scene would be colonized by consumer capitalism, and Arnold Gehlen predicted a post-bourgeois autonomous 'art of reflection' that promised the audience 'relief' rather than education and emancipation.[77] Both prognoses were made before the emergence of centrifugal art and the establishment of the creativity dispositif. The predictions of postmodern authors in the 1970s and 1980s that the aesthetic would expand from postmodern art into other spheres would seem more compatible with the current state of affairs.[78] However, these authors regard the process of border dissolution in art primarily in terms of the undermining of the distinction between high and popular culture while adopting the perspective of the recipient or consumer finding aesthetic enjoyment outside of art. They tend to equate the dissolution of borders with the disappearance of art, an approach which Jean Baudrillard deplored as 'transaesthetic'.[79] These theories are for this reason less useful than they at first seem in explaining the postmodern artistic field as a model case of the creativity dispositif. An alternative is offered by Luc Boltanski and Eve Chiapello. Their approach consists in identifying not only aesthetic *reception* as formative for broad segments of society, particularly in post-Fordism, but also aesthetic *production*, creative work.[80] Nevertheless, in their *The New Spirit of Capitalism*, Boltanski and Chiapello are interested not in the structure, genesis and practices of the artistic field but, rather, in 'artistic critique' – i.e., in the critique of capitalism and alienation in aesthetic discourse since 1800.

In a different way than the theorists of postmodernity, Boltanski and Chiapello suggest that art must be understood as a fundamental structural model for the sociality of late modernity. In its beginnings in the nineteenth century, the artistic field was fixated on purely aesthetic practices. It was thus structurally incompatible with the rationalist fields of bourgeois modernity and could therefore assume a compensatory function. In the last quarter of the twentieth century it then became an exemplary blueprint or 'format' for the creativity dispositif as a whole. How is this to be understood? Formats are here understood as various forms of sociality: social practices, discourses, types of subjectivity, and subject–artefact relations. Exemplary social formats are formats that assume model character, both normatively and affectively, outside of the social space where they initially hold sway. Exemplary formats thus become the objects of imitation and diffusion, in processes of translation, rather than verbatim replication, between social realms. Different social entities can become bearers and mediators of this diffusion of exemplary formats: discourse, media images, mobile subjects and mobile artefacts.[81]

The centrifugal artistic field provides one such blueprint format for practices, discourses, forms of subjectivity and subject–object constellations for the creativity dispositif outside of the arts. Its exemplary function covers the artist as subject and extends to a creative practice aimed not at rational purposive production or standardizing of behaviour but, rather, at the production of aesthetic novelty. It also covers the codification of creative procedure. The format enables objects and events which offer themselves not as instruments but as modes of aesthetic enjoyment to acquire exemplary relevance. This relevance applies to the education of audiences seeking aesthetic experiences and surprises and creatively involved in appropriation. It is also to be found in the institutional arrangements oriented primarily towards the problem of managing attention to novelty. Like all historically significant exemplary formats, centrifugal art effects a functional de-differentiation across all of society, assimilating to one another practice forms from different social fields regardless of what specialized task they fulfil.[82]

Within the framework of postmodern art and the creativity dispositif, the artistic field and the model of the artist have shifted from the margins to the cultural centre of society. This process can be read off another change in the field: the transformation of its affective map. While the bourgeois artistic field was an emotional combat zone criss-crossed by intense positive and negative affects, the centrifugal artistic field is almost entirely devoid of negative affects.[83] The view of the artist and art as pathological, which had still been present well into the 1920s, has been ended by the normalization of the creative self promoted by psychological discourse, by the popular star system and by the aesthetic economy with its model of the creative worker. The antagonism between bohemians and bourgeoisie, which had retained a clear line of conflict into the 1970s, also appears to have resolved into a state of complicity between the creative subjects on stage and those in the auditorium. On the other hand, the positive affects that had characterized the artistic field from the beginning continue in centrifugal art, though deprived of some of their intensity and aura because of the decline of exclusivity as properties of art and the artist. A further positive affect to emerge is the admiration not only for artists' aesthetic productivity and originality but for their social success, consisting not least in the attention directed at their person and therefore constituting an admiration at the fact of being admired.

The dissolution of the borders between and around artistic practices in the context of the creativity dispositif poses the problem of how to maintain a clear-cut distinction between art and its social environment. What remains of art's particularity when aesthetic social forms have spread into other areas of society and placed them under the regime of aesthetic novelty? This problem accompanies the transition from bourgeois to centrifugal art from the beginning. It finds itself in the reflection of what art is, which has been ubiquitous since the 1920s,[84] as well as in the cultural critique of the artistic, the lamentation over the inflation of art, and the demand that art go back to being political.[85] Cultural critiques of art often assumed a bourgeois or modernist model of artistic autonomy. Yet it does not follow from the reciprocal structural assimilation of the artistic field and other social areas that the regime of aesthetic novelty outside of art is inevitably filled with the same forms and contents. On the contrary, there are indications that the centrifugal artistic field reacts to the aesthetic and creative tendencies surrounding it by developing – whether explicitly or implicitly – strategies of distinction. In this way, new differences can develop between the aesthetic forms of reception from other areas (design, media, creative work, nature) and what counts as the sensuous-affective experience of genuinely artistic objects and events.

The most important strategy by which centrifugal art distinguishes itself from non-artistic aesthetic practices consists in directing audience reception in such a way as to nurture an attitude of aesthetic reflection. The audience is encouraged to go beyond its sensuous-affective stimulation and excitement and to reflect on it from without. Centrifugal art thereby promotes second-order operations – artistic operations taking account of the conditions of their own possibility.[86] A clear example of the promotion of aesthetic reflection is the conception of the typical audience experience of postmodern performance art as a *threshold* experience.[87] When an installation or a performance on stage elicits claustrophobia or disgust, then the uptake of the artwork consists not only in these feelings but also in the subjective reflection on the conditions by which they came about. By the same token, centrifugal art often leads to negative sensuous-affective reactions and so distances itself from the orientation towards the positive, pleasurable aspect of aesthetic experience dominant outside of art. This aesthetic of negativity, the precursor of which is to be found in an aesthetic of ugliness, aims at producing reflexive experiences of confusion and malaise. A further postmodern strategy employing aesthetic reflexivity is the politicization of the aesthetic. Here, the artwork takes the whole of society as its narrative or imaginary point of reference and deliberately provokes controversy. Correspondingly, postmodern art forms distinguish themselves from the aesthetic outside of art by systematically engendering audience polarization.[88]

With the ascent of the creativity dispositif, the aesthetic reflexivity developed by centrifugal art can adopt both self-reflection and social commentary by addressing itself to the general structure of the regime of aesthetic novelty. Art is then the place where the creativity dispositif observes itself. Precisely this sort of reflection of the social form of art in particular and the social regime of aesthetic novelty in general took place in the avant-garde and postmodernism and continues to take place today. It is a reflection on the artist's claim to creativity, on the status of the audience, on what makes an object or event artistic, and on the mechanisms by which institutions, canons and markets manage attention. This reflection by art on its own basic conditions is carried out not only in discourse about art but also in artistic objects and events themselves. These acts of reflection are preparatory to a secondary reflection on the structures of the creativity dispositif as a whole. Since the artistic field is in many ways the archetype for the creativity dispositif, it suggests itself as the appropriate location for questioning its mechanisms. Centrifugal art then assumes the role of society's observer of itself. But this occurs not only because modern art had always laid claim to disclosing the totality of society and human experience through art; it takes place above all because it had always been the medium for exploring the kind of social form exemplified by creativity and the aesthetic audience that now reveals itself capable of extending to the whole of society. It is no great exaggeration to claim that not until society has become like art can art teach society about itself.

However, although centrifugal art promotes this aesthetic self-reflection of the basic conditions of the creativity dispositif, it does not thereby free itself from them. Centrifugal art remains the agent of a boundless social regime of aesthetic novelty and the normalization of the creative self. The contents or forms of art can imply critical examinations of these conditions all they like. Such critical artistic events produced by artists with comprehensive intellectual and medial skills for an audience interested in perplexity still perpetuate the everlasting cycle of aesthetic novelty. They fall into line with an aesthetic of perplexity in which even the acts of critique obey the law of aesthetic surprise.

4

The Rise of the Aesthetic Economy

Permanent Innovation, Creative Industries and the Design Economy

4.1 Resolving the Paradoxes of the New

If we were to adopt the point of view taken up by Max Weber in his seminal *Economy and Society*, the last thing we would expect of modern capitalism would be to see it systematically promoting creativity. According to Weber, the main structural feature of capitalism is not the mobilization of innovation and creativity but regularity and standardization.[1] Weber regards Western capitalism's mode of goods production in the early twentieth century as one of the most prominent instances of what he calls formal, bureaucratic or technical rationality. He characterizes the modern economy as 'enterprise capitalism' based on rational-purposive rules for organizing production and labour towards the final aim of maximizing economic efficiency. Enterprise capitalism is thus distinguished fundamentally from the fluid, unpredictable, adventure capitalism of pre-modern societies. In enterprise capitalism, the enterprise introduces the division of labour, hierarchic direction and planning, and a calculable interaction among people and between people and things. In this model, the modern economy resembles a machine, a bringer of objectification and disenchantment. In Weber's analysis, its dominant agent is the administrator and technician, and the accompanying personality type it both needs and produces is the disciplined, expert, unemotional professional.

Weber's pointed interpretation of the advanced capitalist economy as a hyper-regulated rational machine is no mere sociological speculation. It is confirmed by the detailed historical and sociological analyses of the processes by which 'organized capitalism' (Hilferding) developed within large corporations in the United States and Western Europe in the late nineteenth and early twentieth centuries.[2] The managers of this enterprise capitalism were guided by a model of the organization, essentially derived from engineering, as a smoothly running *system* comprising standardized elements (people, things, rules and habits of conduct). The example of Frederick Taylor's 'scientific management' is merely the tip of the iceberg. The coordinated specialization of the mass of employees and workers under the leadership of what can be termed the manager-engineer extends into the whole organized matrix. The economic practices are not directed towards producing novelty. Once they have been set up, they systematically generate repetition in the form of the social and technical rules of organization meant to ensure the production and distribution of standardized capital and consumer goods.

Weber's interpretation is not unchallenged. Marx, whose analysis of capitalism half a century previously is the most important alternative, draws an entirely different picture. It is the image of an unlimited power of economic innovation, which would move Joseph Schumpeter a century later to speak of 'creative destruction'.[3] For Marx, the most salient feature of the economy of the West is the never-ending process of pure capital accumulation and the generation of surplus value.[4] This process relies on the maximal exploitation of whatever forces of production are available at any particular time in a bourgeois society freed from the constraints of tradition. Capitalist economy is distinguished from all forms of pre-modern economy by its extraordinarily dynamic use of new, productivity-increasing technologies and by its exploitation of new means of generating surplus value. As well as the maximal exploitation of labour, capitalism develops strategies for finding new markets. According to Marx, the self-propelling capital accumulation continually undermines previous economic and legal structures and ways of life, replacing them with a comprehensive capitalization of life and work – 'all that is solid melts into air'.[5]

At first glance, Marx and Weber seem to provide contradictory accounts of the economic practices of the second half of the nineteenth century and of capitalism in general. For Weber, capitalism leads to an extreme closure of the social, an eternal recurrence of the same under a rationalist principle of efficiency optimization, which in turn tends to strangle novelty. For Marx, in contrast, capitalism represents an opening, an endless dynamics of innovation, a radical, unprecedented abandonment of the past. On the Marxian view, capitalist economy has always been creative, while Weber frames it as a rigid force for standardizing behaviour. How can we best deal with this opposition?

The discrepancy between Marx and Weber is partly on account of the fact that the two theorists are dealing with topics that broadly overlap but do not fit exactly at all points. Weber is focusing on the internal structure of enterprises and their organization of labour, while Marx is concerned primarily with the operations of the market, which take place above the level of the individual organizations. There is also a difference of historical perspective. The organized capitalism with which Weber was confronted around 1900 is not identical with the industrial capitalism Marx was writing about in the mid-nineteenth century.[6] But even in relation to the high-capitalism phase of big enterprise, such as became established most prominently in the USA and Germany in the last quarter of the nineteenth century, the theories do not actually contradict each other. It is reality that turns out to be contradictory. If the two theories are superimposed, they produce two complementary perspectives on two *paradoxes of novelty* in high capitalism, which characterize the period from the end of the nineteenth century to the late 1960s.

The first paradox of novelty is that between the internal structure of economic organizations and the external effects of their activities. As Marx correctly pointed out, high capitalism unintentionally produces a large number of new and unpredictable social and cultural phenomena *outside* of economic institutions, such as the objectification of everyday life, the undermining of the gender binary, the emergence of new social inequalities, and the resulting political counter-tendencies. However, this dynamic of unpredictable consequences around the economic sphere is counterbalanced by a maximum of calculability *inside* economic organizations in the form of Weber's formal-technical rationality, made possible by the standardized production of goods. The structure of repetition inside the specialized and hierarchic organizations and the incalculable external effects of the economic sphere are two parallel and interdependent phenomena.

These organizations are themselves structurally divided into two, which produces a second paradox of novelty. Although there is some space inside organizations for the production of novelty, it is strictly confined to the technical, systematic task of research and development. Within the economic organization of modernity, technical innovation is pursued in a separate department away from the routine operations of production and administration.[7] The history of technology and the sociology of technology have shown that technical innovations in nineteenth-century industrial capitalism were largely the result of random discoveries made by scattered individuals taken up just as randomly by the economy until the advent of high capitalism, when it became one specialized task among others within economic organizations.[8] With the aid of this arrangement, capitalism, even in its strictly organized form (which since the 1920s has closely resembled state socialism) can be innovative while nevertheless retaining the bureaucratic repetitiveness of productive, administrative work. This is precisely the dual paradox of novelty in the economy of organized modernity: a structure of repetition and reproduction inside the organization is accompanied by unintended social effects outside of the economy, while, at the same time, inside the organization this same structure of repetition lives side by side with specialized departments for technical innovation.

The culture of the economy in its bureaucratic version in organized modernity is thus guided by a cultural model of technology.[9] This culture of technology, as manifested in the discourse of 'scientific management' and the – affirmative or critical – notion of the economy as a machine, presupposes the identity of social and technical progress and is presided over by an overall ideal of a machine-like, matter-of-fact, efficient regulation of society. The technological model thus tends towards both order and change at the same time – or, more accurately, towards technical transformation within an ordered, systematic framework. Antonio Gramsci used the term *Fordism* to refer to this symbiosis of high capitalism and technology in the form it assumed in the USA in the 1920s.[10] This system of standardized mass production proclaims a prototype of society as a well-ordered organization into which the individual is fitted like a part in a machine. At the same time, Fordism presupposes mass consumption across a broad middle class as the complement of mass production – the affluent society, its prosperity assured by consumption. In the cultural imaginary of Fordism, technology forms a triad with the objectified collective and affluence.[11]

Fordism and organized capitalism are in many respects a thing of the past. Their usurpation by a new form of capitalism has been broadly documented in sociology since the 1980s. Claus Offe and Lash and Urry diagnosed this new form as disorganized capitalism, while Marxist authors have cultivated the term post-Fordism.[12] In *The Second Industrial Divide*, Piore and Sabel have elaborated how, in the 1970s, the old Fordist economies of scale began to be replaced by an economy of speed based on constantly changing goods for limited consumer segments. On the level of labour organization, the emergence of 'flexible specialization'[13] weakens the division of labour and strict hierarchies constitutive of bureaucratic enterprise capitalism. They are replaced by a new form of self-employment and, increasingly, post-bureaucratic forms of work, such as communicative networks between organizations, project work based on the de-specialization of work steps within teams working within limited time spans, and the intrapreneur, the entrepreneur internal to the organization.[14]

The now established diagnosis that we are living in a post-industrial society is taken further to show that the late modern economy is an economy of knowledge. This affects the content and techniques of work, in that work with information and ideas – promoted by digital information technologies – takes up increasingly more space for more workers.[15] Finally, on the level of the forms of economic subjectivization, Nikolas Rose and others have spoken of a 'new enterprise culture' shaping the individual as an entrepreneurial self, with an entrepreneurial attitude not only towards selling goods but also towards developing a personal skills profile for marketplace survival. The complement to this labour-force entrepreneur is the active consumer pursuing an individual lifestyle with diverse symbolic goods rather than devoting themselves to Fordist mass consumption.[16]

The current 'disorganized' capitalism is thus distinguished from organized capitalism in several ways. From the point of view of a theory of the creativity dispositif, these processes of radical marketization, the acceleration of the exchange of goods, the digitalization of knowledge and globalization are, however, not the heart of the post-Fordist economy. They are certainly important features, but post-Fordist economy is first and foremost an *aesthetic economy* on which the other features are causally dependent. This book is forwarding the claim that the current economy cannot be understood in rational or cognitive terms because its main processes are not rational or cognitive but, rather, sensuous and affective – processes of the aestheticization of the economy. The aesthetic economy shifts capitalism's orientation towards the production of novel goods away from its fixation on technical invention and dissolves its borders in two ways: first, the aesthetic economy depends more on permanent innovation on the cultural level of organization and individual skills; and, second, it seeks these innovations increasingly outside of technology in aesthetic novelty – that is, in the production of new signs, sense impressions and affects. The creativity dispositif is certainly not held up by the economy alone. Moreover, the economy is too heterogeneous to be understood as an aesthetic economy through and through. Nor, by the same token, is the economy entirely post-Fordist (just as, previously, it was not entirely Fordist or formal-rational). Instead, the aesthetic economy is driven by a specific set of expanding forms of work, the market and consumption.

Since the late 1990s, the so-called creative industries and the so-called *creative economy* have become both the hard core and the avant-garde of the post-Fordist economy, receiving special political care and attention in the form of subsidies.[17] The creative economy in the narrower sense encompasses a range of branches from media to consulting, research and development, entertainment, architecture, advertising, music, design, the internet, public relations, exhibition management, fashion and tourism. The emphatic semantics of creativity and the creative economy employed in the public discussion on the topic give merely a first hint of what is to come. Which features of these new economic practices emerging in the 1970s and 1980s allow them to be understood as constituting an aesthetic economy fundamentally distinct from the formal rationality of Fordism?[18] Four characteristics can be identified.

1   Innovation, the production of new processes and objects, becomes a permanent task determining a large part of the activities of companies as a whole, whereas it had previously been the special problem of research and development. This means that innovation becomes temporally and socially generalized and applies both to products and to the development of the organization itself. Inside the organization, innovation is at first a technical matter, but it is increasingly seen to demand the *cultural* reform of routines, practices and employee skills. The focus on innovation there is not yet sensuous and affective, not yet aesthetic in orientation, but provides an important precondition for the universal regime of novelty in the aesthetic economy.

2   In work practice, the production of novelty becomes increasingly symbolic, perceptual and affective. The broad and expanding field of the creative industries is concerned mainly with creating powerfully attractive goods and services endowed with new meanings, functioning as signs producing surprising and enjoyable sensuous and emotional experiences. This type of economic operation can be superficially associated with notions of the information society, with idea creation and management. However, its focus is less on ideas in the sense of cognitive insights than on meanings coupled with material bearers (words, images, sounds, buildings, ways of acting) and sense perceptions and emotions – i.e., on aesthetic objects and events. The growth of symbolic goods is bound up with the aesthetic intensification of their sensuous and affective properties and applies as much to situations and events as to objects. These kinds of work are thus directed to the creation of signs, perceptions and affects – to aesthetic innovation.[19] This creative work is therefore aesthetic work.

3   The work practices in aesthetic capitalism are borne along by a culture of motivation based on a neo-romantic model of work and profession which identifies satisfying work with creative work, supplanting the repetition of technical or administrative processes with the variable and challenging production of new and especially of aesthetic objects and events. This creative work can and should produce a personal transformation. Innovative enterprises with their symbolic, aesthetic modes of operating require people with creative motivation. These workers should have an emotionally charged, enthusiastic self-image and approach to work.

4   An economy based on innovation and creation must treat consumers as aesthetic subjects. The new consumers are interested less in material goods than in goods and services providing sensuous and affective experiences. Businesses must develop a sensibility for the aesthetic needs of their customers. In the aesthetic economy, the consumers themselves are regarded and regard themselves as creative, as people not merely buying and using goods but actively producing meanings, experiences and emotions and melding them together into an individual lifestyle. Enterprises no longer see themselves primarily as self-guided centres of production, because they are fundamentally dependent on the unpredictable attention of an aesthetically oriented consumer public.

Developing itself along these four lines, the aesthetic economy dissolves the dual paradox of novelty that had dominated organized capitalism. At the same time, the aesthetic economy gives a strong aesthetic bias to the focus on innovation. *Aesthetic capitalism* causes the two Fordist brakes against the incessancy of novelty to give way: the separation of social transformation from a bureaucratic structure of repetition inside the company and the separation between company routine and special divisions for technical innovation. In an economy based on permanent aesthetic innovation, these separations are no longer sustainable.

The aesthetic economy did not come about suddenly. A simple juxtaposition of Fordism (organized capitalism) with the completely different social formation of post-Fordism (disorganized capitalism) that replaced it around 1980 would suggest such a rupture, but this account would make the emergence of new forms of work and consumption inexplicable. Nor can the aestheticization of the economy simply be understood as a mere reaction to the economic and financial crisis of the early 1970s, as the commodity markets became glutted.[20] Even if it were true that the crisis demonstrated the limits of Fordist economy, cultural factors were still required to enable a transformation of economic practice.[21] A look through the genealogical or archaeological magnifying glass reveals that aesthetic economic practices had already been developing in and around the Fordist, formal-rational economy itself in the early twentieth century. Where can the practices and discourses be localized that orient the economy towards permanent innovation, creativity and the aesthetic? In this chapter we will explore in detail four different contexts of particular relevance.

1   The first context is the reaction from middle-class or 'bourgeois' society against the emerging bureaucratic and economic rationalism at the turn from the nineteenth to the twentieth century. Two very different but complementary examples of this are the cultural niches that attempted to promote the normality of aesthetic work and permanent innovation respectively against the rising mainstream: the British arts and crafts movement and the late bourgeois discourse of the entrepreneur in German economics (section 4.2).

2   A second important context that contributed to the reform of rationalist economic culture is US management theory since the 1950s. Here, in opposition to the dominance of bureaucracy, there was a call from two different quarters for enterprises to deal with the challenge of permanent innovation: first, the discourse of personality and organization and, second, the innovation economy (section 4.3).

3   A third decisive factor for the establishment of an aesthetic economy was provided by the early 'creative industries'. The creative economy is not a recent invention. Scattered segments of the economy dedicated to the production of meanings and feelings had been sprouting up since the 1920s. Three branches have proved especially influential over the long term: fashion, advertising and design. They can be understood as microcosms of the aesthetic economy inside Fordism, which came to assume a leading role in economic change in the course of time (section 4.4).

4   In order to understand better how the aesthetic economy came to be established, it is worthwhile finally to look at two further complexes that have been developing since the 1980s: so-called postmodern management theory, which interprets the enterprise as a cultural and emotional phenomenon, and the interdisciplinary design economy, for which design is a paradigm case of the contemporary economy in general (section 4.5).

Although without these historical practices and discourses the genesis of the aesthetic economy would be almost incomprehensible, they at first appear unrelated to one another. However, they turn out to be connected by two lines of development. One line is the view of economic actors and organizations as fluid and endowed with a natural power of innovation (entrepreneurial discourse, personality and organization theory, innovation economics). The other line adopts aesthetic work as a model for the production of consumer objects and images (arts and crafts, advertising, fashion, design). In general, in order to understand the genesis of the creativity dispositif, we need an alternative history of the modern economy. The main stream of this history cannot be narrated as a process of formalization and rationalization or of the spread of the market. Instead, economic rationality was subordinated over time to its apparent cultural other – that is to say, to the aesthetic, to the affective logic of creative production and aesthetic reception. Now, at the end of this process, the opposition between the economic and art, which had prevailed in bourgeois and organized capitalism, has dissolved, and economic and artistic practices have developed similar structures.

4.2 Pockets of Bourgeois Opposition Against Organized Modernity

Arts and crafts

In 1851 the first world exposition took place in London's Crystal Palace. It was an opulent presentation of objects, furnishings and architecture made possible by methods of industrial mass production especially prominent in England at the time. Examples of craftwork from British colonies and from Britain's own pre-industrial past were also shown for the purpose of contrast. While the exposition was seen by the majority to celebrate successfully the technical superiority of industrial society, it also met with strict rejection by a small group. In his article 'Wissenschaft, Industrie und Kunst', Gottfried Semper claimed the industrial products were of inferior quality.[22] In Semper's view, the working of the materials and the finish, as well as the aesthetics of their disposition in space, represented a regression from pre-industrial production.

This critique of industrial capitalism from the point of view of work quality and aesthetics rather than that of social injustice was at first a minority position. It was most at home in Great Britain, where it was coupled with a critique of civilization, for example in the case of Matthew Arnold, and its home address was the arts and crafts movement.[23] This movement constituted a pocket of resistance against standardized industrial production and promoted an alternative understanding of work and manufacturing. The writings of John Ruskin, combining art history with ethical considerations, provided a first thrust.[24] William Morris, concerned more closely with practice, joined together with other co-combatants in Great Britain and later the United States to follow Ruskin's impulse, leading to the establishment of small craftwork collectives specializing in furnishing and architecture.

The ideal of the arts and crafts movement is already declared in its name. Its aim is to dissolve the distinction between work and art by a return to the traditions of craftwork. This implies taking down the notion of a gulf between art and the aesthetically inferior craftwork that was central to modern aesthetics. The movement developed a new way of working in which craftwork is regarded as a legitimate art in its own right requiring both attention to the material and intellectual effort. Arts and crafts was importantly characterized by an historically exceptional notion of the relation between the creator, the object and the aesthetic user that transposed the late eighteenth-century triad artist–work–recipient from the arts to the realm of work and production. This was made clear when William Morris stated that the movement was about objects 'made by the people – for the people, as a joy for the maker and the user'.[25] Three points are worth noting about this statement. First, it locates the object in the centre point between producer and consumer; neither production nor consumption is given priority. Second, the producer and the consumer are not viewed as mere participants in the trade of goods but are brought into relation to the materiality of the object, as maker and user respectively. They are simultaneously individualized and democratized as 'the people'. Third, work and consumption are approached as affective processes, as producing joy; both the creation and the employment of the objects are intended to be sensuous and enjoyable.

This aesthetic triad of the maker, the object and the user implies a model of the maker as a craftsman-artist who 'expresses' himself in the object he or she has made. Work is then understood not as the technical application of rules but, rather, as the creation of a singular object by an equally singular individual. According to Ruskin, the individuality of the object is manifested precisely not in its perfection but in its irregularities, deviations and idiosyncrasies. The important thing is the identification of the maker with the production process. As Ruskin wrote, 'I believe the right question to ask, respecting all ornament, is simply this: Was it done with enjoyment – was the carver happy while he was about it?'[26] The skill of the craftsman-artist is thus universal and is practically available to anyone. Their 'inventive-ness' is a general human property that just needs an environment with aesthetically stimulating artefacts. It is this prerequisite which industrialized England no longer fulfilled. The arts and crafts move-ment addressed user and maker alike as individuals with sensuous-affective needs to be fulfilled by the things produced and used. The consumer also demands an authenticity in household goods that is lacking in mass production.[27]

The arts and crafts movement was opposed to the seemingly unavoidable hegemony of mass production in industrial capitalism. At the time, this must have appeared hopelessly marginal and struck the public imagination as antiquated. In retrospect, however, it can be seen as a space for cultural experiment that helped to prepare the aesthetic economy by promoting the aestheticization of work processes, objects and users. The movement fell back on a romantic notion of aesthetic creation but removed it from the exclusive context of the original genius and broadened the definition to include any work of creating objects performed by anyone. In addition to the aestheticiza-tion of the use of everyday objects, this led to the kind of post-romantic aestheticization of work formulated in different versions since the early nineteenth century by Fourier, Marx and Emerson.[28] The arts and crafts movement was built on a three-way antagonism, restricted to a subculture of producers and consumers who resisted absorption by the capitalist economy. The movement was anti-industrial, anti-capitalist and anti-aesthete. It rejected industrial and technical stan-dardized production and preferred individual and unique items. It was principally distrustful of the market and commercial interests and favoured non-commercial cooperation. Finally, the movement was opposed to the aestheticism of the period. While aestheticism was oriented towards the allure of the new as a purely aesthetic impulse and on changing styles, the arts and crafts movement sought deeper aesthetic satisfactions outside of the cycles of fashion. Arts and crafts objects were intended for long-term use and should fulfil a universal criterion of simplicity.[29]

The 'divinatory' entrepreneur as innovator

As we have pointed out above, although the arts and crafts movement began as a seemingly outnumbered defensive action against the domi-nance of industrial capitalism, it would turn out in the long run to be an influential experimental space that used pre-Fordist and anti-Fordist means to make the post-Fordist creative economy at all think-able. A second, entirely disparate cultural context shortly after 1900 was surprisingly complementary to arts and crafts in terms of the genealogy of the creativity dispositif. This second context is the late bourgeois economic and political discourse of the entrepreneur. Its main centre was Germany and its main exponents were Schumpeter and Sombart, as well as von Mises and Knight.[30] The discourse of the entrepreneur in no way corresponded to the mainstream thinking of the time but was, rather, a minority view opposed to a managerial revolution that was becoming increasingly powerful, especially in the USA and Germany, and which favoured large bureaucratic corporations. Schumpeter and the others responded to the corporation by advancing the solitary figure of the entrepreneur. In the eyes of management and public debate in the context of organized capitalism as it was developing in the early twentieth century, the entrepreneur was an antiquated figure.[31] His appearance in economic discourse is nevertheless of interest to us here because it was the first systematic attempt to make a role model of an economic form of human subjectivity, the essential feature of which is its propensity to create novelty.

To the extent that the entrepreneur figured at all in economic thought before 1900, he was understood as a person investing capital or assuming a leadership or surveillance function. Adam Smith defined the entrepreneur as a provider of capital (land, money or work), whereas representatives of the French tradition such as Jean-Baptiste Say defined him in terms of his function of coordinating labour.[32] The figure of the entrepreneur first entered economic debate as the cultural other to the figure of the manager. The manager was the agent of planning and technical steerage, while the entrepreneur was introduced as the creator of unpredictable novelty. As such, 'he is the only type who has been able to maintain at least relative immunity from subjection to the control of rational bureaucratic knowledge.'[33]

In his *Theory of Economic Development*, Joseph Schumpeter takes as his point of departure the difference between economic circulation and economic development.[34] This circulation, the eternal return of the same, analogous to the circulation of human blood, is for Schumpeter the normal default setting for an economy and as such requires no further explanation. All the more in need of explanation are the instances of economic collapse. For Schumpeter, these shifts in the balance originate in production, not in the actions of consumers. Production improves incrementally while fundamental innovations are the exception in capitalist economies and can become established only in the face of resistance. Innovations are attained by combination – not by producing novel objects but by intelligently arranging extant 'materials and forces'. The new does not come from nothing but, rather, consists in 'combin[ing] these materials and forces differently'.[35]

For Schumpeter, the entrepreneur is the agent of these new combinations. This conception has an affinity with the notion of the new as a rearrangement of the old in the art of the avant-garde and postmodernity.[36] Recombination can operate in different spheres: the production of a new type of commodity, a production method, the discovery of new markets, or the restructuring of a business. The creation of novelty is therefore not limited to the production of a new object, such as by technical innovation, but can also include the change of social or technical rules or the relationship of the enterprise to the market. Schumpeter presupposes as a general rule that the problem of novelty is the task of the individual rather than of the enterprise (whereas the innovation economy will later adopt the opposite view). Novelty requires a specific personality type.

According to Schumpeter, this personality type possesses three qualities: a new way of seeing, wilful self-assertiveness and a strong emotional relation to the activity. Opportunities for technical or other revolutionary change are not in short supply; on the contrary, novelty is always in abundance. The real problem is not to discover the possibility but to make it a reality. This also permits a distinction between the inventor and the entrepreneur: the inventor develops something new, while the entrepreneur deploys it in the organization and in the market. This requires receptiveness for new revolutionary ways of seeing as well as 'effort of will', a 'great surplus of force',[37] in order to assert this new way of seeing in the organization and in the market. A further typical character trait of the entrepreneur is the ability to cope with uncertainty – a trait which Frank Knight would later see as the entrepreneur's crucial feature.[38] Making novelty successful is thus for Schumpeter not an achievement primarily of perception or cognition but, rather, of energy, will and the desire to succeed. It is this emotional aspect that distinguishes the entrepreneur from the 'rational machine' with its managers and employees. The entrepreneur experiences a 'joy of making, of the creation of novelty as such',[39] but also a sporting ambition to win at any cost. Yet for Schumpeter these emotional qualities are strangely contrasted to the entrepreneur's outward blandness, his unattractiveness in the public eye of his time.

The entrepreneur's focus on creating a *work*, in the broader, non-artisanal sense, is also emphasized by Werner Sombart.[40] The work is the enterprise itself, which is 'like a corporeal living creature'[41] and thus the issue of the entrepreneurial 'need to make real'. While the entrepreneur is understood here in analogy to the artist-genius, Sombart is careful to point out the vast difference between the two, drawing instead a parallel to a different type – that of the discoverer and conqueror. While the artist creates a work for its own sake, the entrepreneur is concerned with its success. Tellingly, Sombart renders the entrepreneur as hyper-masculine while feminizing the artist. It is the entrepreneur now who is endowed with the markings of the earlier artistic genius. The entrepreneur is a 'divinatory nature' with a 'brilliant power of intuition'.[42] He therefore occurs not only in the business world but also in other fields. He is more than a mere salesman, in whom Sombart sees only a useful and skilled calculator. For Sombart, the entrepreneur is an innovator.

In essence, the late bourgeois discourse of the entrepreneurial innovator casts him as an exclusive and emotionally charged figure. The entrepreneurial leaning is, on the one hand, postulated as an anthropological constant and, on the other, as a quality evenly distributed among the human race.[43] From this it follows that the *pronounced* entrepreneurial quality is a rarity, neither innate to all humans nor even learnable. For Schumpeter, even someone disposed to being entrepreneurial cannot act entrepreneurially all the time because he will always fall back on his comfortable old routines. The innovative bent of the entrepreneur cannot transform itself into routine. The entrepreneur so conceived resembles the artist of traditional discourse in being an original creative genius. Yet, despite this exclusivist tendency in the entrepreneur discourse, its main objective is to establish the necessity of innovation to the proper functioning of capitalism. Innovation is not conceived as restricted to the technical, to research and development, but includes also the revolution of business organization and market success. Consequently, Schumpeter sees in the managerial revolution the end of capitalism. The entrepreneur turns out to be a counter-cultural figure that is likely to vanish along with bourgeois culture.

The arts and crafts movement and the late bourgeois discourse of the entrepreneur can be viewed in conjunction. In complementary ways, they both insist on the necessity of aesthetic work and permanent innovation against the dominance of formal rationalism. Arts and crafts tends in the direction of aesthetic production away from the market, while entrepreneurship builds on a strictly market-oriented model of innovation to which aesthetic work in the proper sense is fundamentally foreign. Yet, in both cases, creation and innovation are endowed with enormous affective intensity. Both movements rely on pre-modern figures such as the craftsman and the conqueror. Finally, both contain models of creative production, either in the opposition to industry, the market and aestheticism for arts and crafts or the praise of the heroic entrepreneur against the modern organization. Both discourses contain parallels to the constraints imposed on the figure of the artist in the bourgeois artistic field inasmuch as the entrepreneur resembles the creative genius, while the arts and crafts movement presents itself as a subculture in the mould of the bohemians. Despite these limitations, both cultural niches end up providing impulses towards a long-term reformation of the economic field along the lines of creativity. They are the beginnings of two strands that will intertwine: the management-oriented strand of innovation and the strand of symbolic-sensuous creation.

4.3 Permanent Innovation as a Management Problem

'Personality and organization' and the problem of motivation

The emergence and spread of formal rational business administration in Weber's sense in the USA and Germany from the late nineteenth century was guided from the beginning by a new form of knowledge with the label *management*. When economic activity is no longer undertaken first and foremost by individuals or families but, rather, by organizations and collectives, then management comes to mean a form of knowledge and of government, of overseeing and controlling the collective. According to the theory, management is the attempt to acquire and rationally deploy knowledge of how administration works for the purpose of optimizing efficiency.

Yehonda Shenhav and David Noble have shown that the emergence and spread of management theory beginning in the 1880s in the USA was an open and controversial process. Management initially emerged as a subdiscipline of engineering, approaching the problem of successfully operating an organization as a purely technical matter.[44] The first managers were, accordingly, engineers. This early management theory was determined in large part by the practical problems of the new large-scale industries such as rail, machine and shipbuilding and, later, the chemical and auto industries. The previously mentioned 'scientific management' developed by Frederick Taylor is just one particularly influential variant among many, all of which conceive the organization in analogy to a technical system made up of standardized parts.[45] However, since the 1920s, and increasingly since the 1950s, management theory has gradually discovered 'creativity' as a real and necessary factor of the organization. The point of departure for this consideration was the identification of a problem of motivation as crucial to modern business. By neglecting the fact that a business needs motivated employees, the machine approach incurred unwanted effects such as inefficient work and inner resignation. The motivation problem is taken up by the human relations and later the human resources schools. Both regard the relation of the organization to the personality of the individual co-workers as key. This focus leads in turn to the 'personality and organization' theory of management.

From the 1920s, the *personal management movement* began making empirical studies of worker satisfaction and motivation. The studies of industrial psychology by Hugo Münsterberg and Walter Dill Scott and the so-called Hawthorne interviews were seminal examples.[46] The latter demonstrated that simply paying more attention to workers meant that their output showed sustained improvement. The Hawthorne interviews provided the first impulse for the human relations school in management theory.[47] Against the behaviourist, engineering model of the worker as a kind of black box, this school discovered workers' inner psychic life and sought ways to influence it positively. The relation between the individuals and the organization was considered here primarily in terms of the relations between individuals, the most important parameter being social recognition and harmonious interaction. The purpose of human relations reforms was consequently the cultivation of a strong group ethos within the organization.[48]

The human relations school occupies a genealogical turning point. With its firm conviction that the organization is an ordered entity which must avoid any divergence from the norm, it belonged to the same discursive space as scientific management, to which, however, it saw itself opposed. At the same time, the emphasis of human relations on the psychology of organization members made it a transition to the human resources school of the 1950s. The latter no longer reduced people to harmonious social beings but framed them instead as insatiably striving for self-fulfilment at the workplace. The organization had to take this need seriously in order to be able to solve the motivation problem.[49]

The breakthrough for the human relations movements came in 1957 with Chris Argyris's *Personality and Organization*.[50] The new perspective on the organization developed there by Argyris was based largely on contemporary psychology, in particular the self-growth psychology of Abraham Maslow and others.[51] Argyris took this psychology at its word, accepting as scientifically proven that the human psyche strives for creative self-expression. According to Argyris, a stream of energy is in motion in the psyche, flowing towards 'goals of self-actualization or enhancement'.[52] People do not attempt to avoid tension but, rather, seek the positive form of tension associated with reshaping their environment. Argyris distinguishes joy, as the productive disequilibrium between need and reality, from pleasure, as a condition of energetic stasis. The individual desires constantly to change and develop himself in different fields, including work. However, the emphasis of human relations on harmony makes it unsuitable for fulfilling this desire. The self-growth conception of the individual inevitably leads to an antagonism between the individual and the organization, with its specialized and hierarchic structure. This tension reveals itself as the real cause for the motivation problem and thus for the failure of organizations to operate at maximum efficiency.

What is needed is therefore a new post-bureaucratic organizational form. Douglas McGregor made the influential distinction between such a form, calling it 'Theory Y' in opposition to the older organization type termed 'Theory X'. How such an alternative organization is to be structured was left unclear by both McGregor and Argyris. While Argyris merely suggested that the task of the future organization consists in 'helping individuals grow and become more creative',[53] he later deployed system theory vocabulary to argue that the organization should be structured as an 'open system'; it should be open to the individuals who constitute it and are themselves systems. This openness presupposes a reduction of task specialization within the organization and the expansion of individual workers' skills. McGregor pointed to the necessity of the role of the supervisor, whose function is not control but consultation. The skills of the workers were regarded as resources for the organization whose self-development is to be fostered by a 'management by self-control'.[54] Finally, Argyris developed the blueprint for an energetic co-evolution of the individuals and the organization – for 'individual growth' and 'organizational growth'.[55]

Human resources theory thereby invented the notion that economic organizations require constant stimulation in order to run. It justified this claim with the psychological argument that it is the human need for self-transformation and creativity itself which demands this dynamic stimulation. If the organization attempts to quell these needs, the result will be disastrous inefficiency. The human resources school, like the closely related 'positive psychology', was humanistic in its foundations, anticipating elements from the progressive counter-cultural critique of organizations emerging in the late 1960s. However, it combined this humanistic footing with a functionalist torso: if the organization is to work efficiently, it will have to solve the motivation problem. However, the aims of the organization itself, their connection to formal rationalism, were not a subject of debate for the human resources school. Market success was not explicitly given as the organization's reason for innovation; rather, it was the need to take care of its internal environment – i.e., the human souls. This is probably why the model of post-bureaucratic organization remains vague. The school was nevertheless influential enough to have implanted the notion of the employee as a creative self in management theory. This provided an important precondition for postmodern management discourse.[56]

The innovation economy and the problem of the environment

The personality and organization school was complemented by the management model of the innovation economy. This latter justified the need for permanent innovation not in psychological terms but in terms of the organization and its market environment. On this model, the real problem of organization is not one of motivation but one of *environment*. The trigger for innovation economics was the book *The Management of Innovation* (1961) by Tom Burns and George Stalker. Their study appeared within a broader context of scholarly work from the late 1950s critiquing formal-rational organizations.[57] Burns and Stalker, in contrast to the human resources school, regarded the organization as an emergent social structure with the inherent weakness that it doesn't conform to the formalist model – nor should it do so. They investigated the development of the British electronics industry, which had experimented somewhat unsuccessfully with traditional research and development divisions briefed to advance technical innovation, and their soberly written study arrived at a conclusion which was spectacular for the time: enterprises can be subject to the economic necessity of permanent innovation.

With a conception of business administration influenced by system theory, Burns and Stalker framed the organization as a sphere of internal complexity situated within an environment. However, their focus was not on the 'inner environment' of the employees' psyches, as was that of Argyris, but on the outer social environment comprising technological developments, competing enterprises and consumers. The decisive question was then whether these environments are stable or dynamic. Traditional management theory presupposed a stable environment, to which it attempted to apply the kind of formal rationalism Burns and Stalker referred to as the 'mechanistic management system'. In reality, however, market and technological environments often turn out to be instable. Accordingly, the task was to structure the organization in such a way as to make it sensitive to changes in the environment and able to recalibrate appropriately. As Burns and Stalker wrote, 'the organic form is appropriate to changing conditions, which give rise constantly to fresh problems and unforeseen requirements for action.'⁵⁸ What was required was not a one-off change but, rather, an organizational structure designed for the permanent 'management of innovation'.

Burns and Stalker now sketched the alternative of an 'organic management system', the main feature of which is its abandonment of the traditional organizational model of strict specialization and hierarchies. Innovation management presupposed that work processes no longer run along separate lines but, rather, are constantly coordinated with one another in changing ways. Instead of fulfilling specialized tasks, workers participate in developing the enterprise as a whole within a shifting environment. This demands of the employee a stronger, more emotional engagement and an overcoming of personal limits. Burns and Stalker, however, saw this as the Achilles' heel of the new model – in contrast to Argyris and later postmodern management theory. Innovation management finally turned out to be a permanent task for the whole enterprise not restricted to the research divisions. The question was then how to motivate employees to undertake this task.

We are once again at a crucial historical juncture. The work of Burns and Stalker marks the first tentative conceptual beginnings of an economics of permanent, non-technological innovation within the organization. This reconfiguration in management theory was predicated on a notion of differences between the system and its environment that oblige the system to adapt to environmental changes. Permanent innovation thus turns out paradoxically to be a process of adaptation. This new cultural context was opened up in *The Social Psychology of Organization* (1967), by Karl Weick,⁵⁹ who called for a view of organizations as fundamentally interpretive and processual. Jacques Derrida's *Writing and Difference*⁶⁰ was published in the same year and is subterraneously connected with Weick's book, the latter demanding we should speak not of organizations as structures but rather of *organizing* as a process. Organizations reproduce themselves, but this reproduction or *iteration* always implies difference. Reproduction therefore always harbours the potential for new events. Organizing is at core a communicative and interactive process in which the environment around the organization is interpreted. In Weick's constructivist version of the system–environment conception, the information about changing market conditions is not representation but, rather, the tentative interpretation of an environment that could be interpreted in other ways. For Weick, therefore, the new is in no way understood as restricted to technical discoveries. Instead, it results from the organization accepting new interpretations on the level of information processing. The organization must undergo evolutionary change. As

Weick wrote, 'evolutionary systems are creative systems.'[61] Creativity is thus distributed across the whole social system of the organization, no longer reduced to the skills of individuals.

The work of Tom Burns and Karl Weick provided impulses for a paradigm shift from organizational psychology and organizational sociology. They proposed that business organizations should be sensitive to the environment as a basic problem requiring permanent innovation on a non-technological level. Since the 1970s, the broad front of management theory had been shifting towards an innovation economy and towards innovation management. However, the prevalent notion of innovation is ambivalent. On the one hand, models of post-bureaucratic management are elaborated but, on the other, the old, technology-oriented tradition is perpetuated, most frequently with the so-called linear models based on predictable and technologically induced processes. In this context, a four-phase scheme is frequently employed in which *discovery* in laboratories performing basic research is followed by *invention* in applied research, *development* in research and development divisions, and, finally, the *diffusion* of the product. Ideally, the four phases follow chronologically and the four contexts are kept institutionally and spatially separate.[62]

In juxtaposition to this, the so-called non-linear models of innovation economics that began accumulating in the 1980s retained Burns and Weick's principles of permanent, institutionally unrestricted innovation. These models picked up already existing organizational practices and sharpened them. They often worked with charged metaphors, such as Stephen Kline and Nathan Rosenberg's model of innovation as a chain operating in the tension between the market and technical development. However, this latter model is concerned with managing uncertainty by connecting all the steps in a process of innovation along a continual chain running forwards and backwards in feedback loops. The point of departure for developing novelty is not the technology itself but, rather, the problems that emerge from the organization's routines. The 'rugby' model of innovation developed by Hirotaka Takeuchi and Ikujiro Nonaka using the example of Japanese companies such as Honda and Canon does away entirely with the expectation that innovation occurs in ordered steps, instead assigning innovation tasks to an ambitious, interdisciplinary, independent project team. Finally, Andrew van de Ven's 'firework' model compares innovation in enterprise to a journey with alternating sluggish and rapid phases.[63] While these non-linear models proposed innovation as a discontinuous process, the question has arisen as to which structural conditions need to be in place to enable permanent innovation. The common solution in innovation economics is anti-bureaucratic, network-like structures connecting different organizations and their information flow, as well as dense 'communities of practice' sharing implicit knowledge. Networks and communities of practice, as relatively egalitarian systems of communication, are supposed by these models to facilitate the diffusion and recombination of knowledge necessary for innovation.[64]

Both the personality and organization theory and innovation economics recommended abandoning the bureaucratic rationalism of the organization while invoking the necessity of permanent innovation. They justified permanent innovation, on the one hand, psychologically with reference to the need of employees to change and, on the other, by the organization's need to adapt to a changing outer environment. However, the two theories would prove to be merely intermediate stages on the way to a matured form of aesthetic economics. They called for innovation on a permanent basis but limited creativity to technical or organizational innovation and thus did not develop a distinctly *aesthetic* notion of novelty. In retrospect, it can be seen clearly that one factor was missing before the aesthetic economy could emerge and spread. That factor was the 'creative industries'.

4.4 The Establishment of the Creative Industries

The term 'creative industries' emerged in the 1990s. We will be using it here as a deliberate anachronism to refer to an earlier period. Since the advent of Fordism in the 1920s, there already existed economic practices concerned primarily with producing symbols and sensuous impressions rather than things. Earlier versions of this kind of symbolic economy go back to bourgeois modernity and the luxurious culture of the aristocracy.[65] In industrial capitalism, the symbolic and sensuous economy was initially marginal. However, three early forms of the later aesthetic economy were already beginning to develop: fashion, advertising and design.

Fashion, advertising and design would at first seem mere supplements to the mass production of investment and consumer goods. Design provides an added aesthetic value for objects that are in essence technical and functional, while advertising is the attempt to promote the sale of these already complete goods, principally with the aid of visual representations. Fashion, in the rarefied, aesthete form of haute couture, would appear to be a mere relic of post-aristocratic luxury consumption. This subordinate relation was dramatically reversed between 1920 and 2000. All three branches were transformed from marginal adjuncts to dominant economic forms, becoming blueprints of the aesthetic economy. At first, they developed largely independently of one another but followed a common overriding pattern. During an initial formation phase in the 1920s, the three branches began to accrue aesthetic potential but one that was systematically limited. The 1960s then saw a transformation period. The youthful, style-oriented counter-cultures of this time unfurled their consumer potential, lending their weight to the historically decisive gear shift into a comprehensive aesthetic mobilization. In the 1970s, the third phase began, a period of consolidation, a 'creative revolution', breaking off from the counter-cultures to spread throughout society, catapulting the creative industries to the lead in aesthetic capitalism. In what follows, we will explore in more detail the gradual growth of the three branches as they form the nucleus of the aesthetic economy.

Fashion

Fashion is an ambivalent term.[66] On the one hand, it designates concrete products, either handmade or industrial – items of clothing mainly – whose function is to cover the human body. At the same time, fashion is a model for culture in general, an incessant, non-progressive series of alternating objects invested with connotations of newness and contemporaneity. The exemplary field of fashion in this second sense is *apparel*. Fashion apparel is the model case for objects, the primary value of which is symbolic or aesthetic, and the function of which is to facilitate self-styling and provide continual aesthetic novelty. There therefore exists a fundamental structural resemblance between fashion and the artistic field.

However, the effective reach of fashion was limited. Clothing first assumed symbolic and aesthetic uses in court society in the eighteenth century, especially in France. In the nineteenth century the European aristocracy was both the main recipient of fashion items and the main pacemaker of the fashion system. In the latter half of the century, the economic elite of the new middle classes rose in significance as consumers of fashion, especially in America, which relocated the fashion industry from the court to haute couture.[67] In Paris, Charles Worth and Paul Poiret emerged as the first fashion creators with celebrity status. Fashion thus transformed mere tailoring into an art. As such, it developed the ambition continually to create original items, thus providing an alternative to the market of industrial, standardized products. Fashion was therefore the first economically relevant form of trade in products attributed to individual original creators, parallel to the attribution of artworks to artists. Fashion articles from the hands of artist designers were initially tailored to the wishes of individual recipients in a way analogous to the practice of commissioning art in modernity.

However, the luxury fashion of haute couture was the exclusive possession of a social elite, and it was still a pre-industrial craftwork. Fashion was subject to what Georg Simmel described in 1905 under the impression of the *nouveaux riches* as fashion cycles. The elite adorned itself with fashion innovations as marks of distinction. These innovations would then trickle down in diluted form, producing imitations which were then responded to in turn by new variations at the top.[68] Fashion was therefore primarily a means to project power differences between social groups onto the female body. The play of signs and affects in haute couture was necessarily limited in scope by the insurmountable social boundary between classes. Couturiers strived to invest individual items of clothing and clothing styles with aesthetic individuality, but the wearers were preoccupied mainly with the play of class distinction. Further, haute couture excluded large sections of the population from the fashion cycle and was directed almost entirely at women. Finally, it was constrained economically and technically by the ideal of craftwork, to which industrial textile manufacturing was at first qualitatively inferior.

Haute couture thus bound fashion to a model of exclusivity. There were, however, opposing tendencies that anticipated future developments. The dress reforms for both men and women in the 1880s brought about for the first time an anti-fashion movement that challenged the monopoly of haute couture. Since the 1830s, the dandy had used the aesthetic products of exclusive fashion as an instrument of original stylization *as an individual*. Counter-cultural fashion tendencies were also prevalent among bohemians. Finally, after 1900 the artistic ambitions of haute couture designers to create unique items of clothing were challenged by product pirating in the form of growing numbers of illegal, convincing copies of their originals.[69]

After the First World War, and then increasingly after 1960, the fashion system was transformed in two ways. First, it went from a medium of exclusion to a medium of inclusion, before turning subsequently into a dynamic system of multiple styles directed no longer at a special class but rather at any active individual consumers wanting to be stylish.

Since the 1920s fashion had been becoming increasingly democratic, in that industrially produced clothing came to be recognized as high quality, and the middle classes were integrated into the fashion cycle. In this way fashion became a creative *industry*. The French designer Coco Chanel stands out as exemplary for the social opening of haute couture leading to the *aesthetic inclusion* of larger social groups, their sensitization for aesthetic standards. The transition to industrially produced clothing meant that the fashion designer was no longer a creator of unique items but rather provided the design for mass ready-to-wear products. Nevertheless, this radical change did not damage the fashion designer's originality status.[70] Between the wars, as fashion designers fitted film stars as well as working women, they accumulated greater symbolic capital as creative celebrities in their own right. This shift in the model of originality ran parallel to that of avant-garde art. Just as the technical reproducibility of art objects did not infringe the status of artists such as Duchamp and Warhol once the notion of original artwork in the strict sense had been discarded, now the fashion designer was attributed originality on the basis of her design notwithstanding the fact that the clothing based on that design was a mass commodity.[71]

However, the shift from exclusivity to inclusion in the fashion system was not the last chapter in this story. The fashion industry's discovery of street style among London subcultures around 1960 was a further event that would have far-reaching consequences. In artistic and student milieus in suburbs such as Soho, outside the established fashion industry, people were experimenting with clothing on a search for individual styles.[72] This kind of individualizing and experimental fashion had been seen before, among others in bohemian circles, but the London scene was broader based, absorbing a younger section of the population. This street style was taken up and developed further by the fashion industry. An important role was also played by the London art and design schools, which regarded fashion designers as artists. Mary Quant paved the way for this by opening up her boutique Bazaar in 1955. Street style was aimed initially at a young audience and was against haute couture, although, with Yves Saint Laurent's aggressive use of fragments of pop culture in the 1960s, street style elements also became part of haute couture and middle-class fashion. Since the 1970s, a broad aesthetic mobilization of lifestyle through fashion has been observable. This mobilization is exemplary of the aesthetic economy in general. It has three interconnected structural features.

1   The fashion industry has discovered the broad mass of active, individual consumers who cultivate an interest for individual aesthetic stylization. These consumers are addressed as autonomous creative individuals who do not copy pre-existent fashion templates but, rather, assemble their own combinations. Here, for the first time, divergence from the norm has gained power as a social standard outside of art. Youth culture, subcultures and urban art

scenes have become microcosms for this broader aesthetic activism. The appeal to the consumer as an individual elaborating her own style has extended also into the middle classes, affecting both women and men.[73] In contrast to the older class-based fashion system, the new pluralist fashion system relies not only on signs but also on affects, coupling fashion with individual identity. The personal *look*, a term cultivated by Mary Quant, has become the instrument of self-creation.

2　While earlier fashion cycles were based on class differences and driven by the taste for luxury, the cycles of the new fashion system with its plurality of styles are now structured by the more abstract difference between hip and square. The hip/square code, the distinction between cool, authentic style and conventional style, derived from youth subculture with its street style. It has been spreading outwards from there since the 1970s. The hip/square code wrought a modification upon the more general fashion system's new/old binary. No longer fettered by strict class divides, fashion can now operate in pure form: the *above/below* binary, which previously constrained the semiosis of fashion, has been superseded by the distinction between *original* and *conventional*. This distinction doesn't apply primarily to status groups; rather, it focuses on successful individuality (and is secondarily extendable to lifestyle groups). Now, whether it is intended or not, wearing anything at all implies an aesthetic choice as an indicator of individuality, a marker of conventionality or originality. There is now no such thing as absence of style. However, in contrast to the univalence of class fashion, the hip/square version necessarily remains contentious. As a consequence, the aesthetic styles in the new fashion system have since continued to multiply, persisting in parallel and in competition with one another.[74]

3　Although the fashion system since the 1970s has been contingent on the fashion empowerment of the middle classes, the figure of the designer has not lost significance. Rather, she has been transformed in a similar way to the postmodern artist, becoming an arranger and a celebrity.[75] Yves Saint-Laurent, Vivienne Westwood, Issey Miyake and Donna Karan are exemplary of the postmodern designer.[76] One type constantly combines different cultural impulses to form new styles. Belonging to this faction are Saint-Laurent, who in the 1960s appropriated accessories from protest culture and science fiction films and later experimented with citations from British colonial times, and Westwood, who went from punk culture to using African and baroque elements in her 1981 'Pirate' collection. The second type of fashion designer retains a style once it is developed and varies only the nuances. This second group includes the anti-design of Miyake, with its redolence of *neue Sachlichkeit*, and the reserved urbane femininity of Karan. Postmodern fashion designers can thus build on the status as creative star or celebrity that their profession had begun to attain in the late nineteenth century, staging themselves as media figures reminiscent of the mythical artist.[77]

At the penultimate juncture of transformation of the fashion system, the fashion industry is absorbed into the aesthetic economy as a whole at the melting point between fashion, art, the star system and commercial activity. Typical of the dissolution of these borders is the way the larger fashion companies since the 1960s have developed increasingly into general design and lifestyle corporations.[78] Fashion is becoming a component of the design of everyday objects, just as design has transmuted into a kind of fashion.

Advertising

Like fashion, advertising has its own origins which the rationalist conception of modernity would regard as impure. It began not at the court at Versailles but in the provincial American marketplaces with their popular entertainments. Jackson Lears has uncovered the disreputable roots of the advertising business, tracing them back to the eighteenth century among the carnival atmosphere of the marketplace – not as the site of abstract trade transactions but as a concrete location with sales stands.[79] Goods were not only sold here but were praised in elaborate performances. Clothing and jewellery were seductively staged, medicine and exotic objects persuasively demonstrated to the buying public. The economic market originated in the village fair.

Advertising first developed into a specialized profession after 1900, in close connection with the spread of Fordist mass production and mass consumption. Business administration now turned its attention to the selling of wares as a problem of systematic planning, with businesses setting up dedicated departments, followed in the 1920s by the first independent advertising agencies cropping up in larger numbers.[80] Advertising, understood as the public presentation of commodities intended to animate the buyer to purchase, was closely bound up with the emergence of the visual media technologies photography and film. From its beginnings, advertising was an aesthetic industry, deploying images to invoke sensuous-affective reactions and a sense of identification with the product. Advertising presented styles and mixtures of aesthetic qualities rather than things. Advertising design began deploying elements from aesthetic modernism in the 1920s.[81]

However, in its formative period, extending into the 1950s, the advertising industry was also a prototype of rationalist organization.[82] It was organized according to a strict division of labour and was regarded less as a creative than as a scientific enterprise. Claude Hopkins's book *Scientific Advertising*, which remained the standard work into the 1950s, made the claim that advertising need only apply general psychological laws discoverable by science in order to influence consumers.[83] The consumer was to be approached from an assumption of stimulus–response behaviourism that targeted feelings of shame and status worry mixed in with rational persuasion as to the usefulness and efficiency of the product. In the mass culture of the 1940s and 1950s, the advertiser typified William Whyte's conformist 'organization man'. He was 'the man in the grey flannel suit' in one of the big advertising agencies on New York's Madison Avenue, as played by Rock Hudson in the 1961 film *Lover Come Back*. Advertising did not enjoy an exclusively positive reputation at the time, as manifested by Vance Packard's critical vilification in *The Hidden Persuaders* of the trade as shadowy and manipulative.[84]

The profession advanced from a Fordist corporate operation into a genuinely creative industry in the course of the 1960s and 1970s. George Lois dramatized this change as a 'creative revolution'.[85] The prototype for the emerging form of the advertiser was the Doyle Dane Bernbach Agency, which opened for business in New York in 1949 under Bill Bernbach's leadership. Bernbach developed an anti-advertising style of advertising, parallel to anti-fashion and anti-design. His style upturned the science-emulating rules of the genre and developed the ideal of an all-pervading aesthetics in advertising which was taken up in the 1960s by the rapidly spawning smaller agencies. An example is his legendary Volkswagen advertisement, in which the simple, long unaltered VW Beetle was presented as extraordinary precisely on account of its familiarity. The VW is shown on a tiny scale in the campaign with the caption 'Think small'. The apparent disadvantages of the car are ironically reversed to become its strengths.[86] In a second ad from the campaign, the VW is cast in motor-show-like lamplight with the caption 'The '51 '52 '53...'60 '61 Volkswagen', instructing the reader that, unlike the models of other manufacturers, the VW stays the same over the years – ironically turning this staid conventionalism into a unique selling point. Why change something that is already perfect?[87]

The advertising models of the creative revolution from Bernbach and others shared a number of features in common. The prototype of the advertiser was now the artist rather than the administrator or the scientist. Advertising could no longer be standardized but had to invent original ideas. The transformation of advertising into a creative industry was predicated on organizational reforms: first, the post-bureaucratic abandonment of the division of labour and hierarchies in favour of creative project teams working independently to create whole advertising strategies on their own; and, second, the emancipation from the wishes of the client. Bernbach asserted the importance of the artist as a role model when he wrote, 'it is ironic that the very thing that is most suspected by business, that intangible thing called artistry, turns out to be the most practical tool available.'[88] Bernbach's colleague Howard Gossage corroborated this with the statement that the aim of advertising is to sell not products but ideas, and the ideas should be as extraordinary as possible.[89]

Gossage and Bernbach pointed to the same preconditions for creativity in advertising already familiar from postmodern art discourse: the cultivation of the capacity for everyday perception and discrimination and a sensibility for current semiotic trends. On their theory, the advertiser must cultivate an enthusiastic rapport with the cultural developments of his time, whether in popular culture, art or technology. The advertising of the creative revolution makes use of a variety of methods familiar from the arts and other creative domains, combining the seemingly incommensurable, developing subtle plays on words, deftly interweaving different media (such as in the use of cartoons in the 1960s) or integrating intertextual historical references.[90] Bernbach's advertising in particular resembled conceptual art in that it started with an idea that was then put into visible form, placing the observer before a puzzle to be resolved into an Aha! effect. The 'new advertising' addressed the consumer not as an empty object of manipulation or as a mere cost–benefit optimiser but as a self-reflecting individual who has matured beyond naivety.

While US advertising at first performed its creative revolution under its own steam, the second, decisive step was characterized – as it had been in fashion – by absorption of impulses from 1960s youth and counter-culture, which finally made advertising into a comprehensive agent of aestheticization. In this context, the hip/square binary from fashion has come to be a guiding distinction in advertising. At the same time, advertising has shifted its focus from presenting the *product* to staging a *lifestyle*. Despite its generally critical stance on consumption, the counter-culture produced an army of aggressive consumers with a pacemaker function, demanding unconventional, 'young' products differing from the norm.[91] It was also the counter-culture that developed the post-materialist outlook that the value of an object is more than its superficial utility: it should contribute to an authentic and sensuously satisfying lifestyle.

These aesthetic surges in advertising and youth culture have been spreading to society at large since the 1970s. Advertising is now directed at consumers at pains to sculpt a self-determined, aesthetically satisfying lifestyle. This causes the demonstration of the utility of a product to be eclipsed by the suggestion of the original lifestyle within which the product is enjoyed (or, at another remove, by the originality of the advertisement itself). In order to achieve the representation of an attractive lifestyle, the advertisement is especially concerned to exploit the sensuous and affective potential of visuals by creating images capable of arousing desire.[92] The best example of this aesthetic upsurge in advertising is provided by the Pepsi-Cola campaigns from 1961 and after. In the 'Cola Wars' with Coca-Cola, Pepsi attempted to distinguish itself, despite the lack of notable, perceptible differences between the two products, by resorting to the hip/square binary.[93] While Coca-Cola was presented as a mass, home-grown product, Pepsi styled itself in 1963 as young and unconventional, as an expression of vitality, youth, authenticity, emotion and activity, exhorting, 'Come Alive! You're in the Pepsi Generation'. In the campaigns since 1969, the leitmotif jingle 'You've got a lot to live, and Pepsi's got a lot to give' accompanied fast-paced colour-saturated scenes of highly charged activity featuring the Pepsi bottle in a supporting role only. What the advertisements were selling was this active nature-loving lifestyle among like-spirited contemporaries, with Pepsi as the perfect accompaniment.[94]

In the course of the creative revolution, the advertising industry has evolved from an aid to selling things into a machine for the creation of original images and texts. Advertisers have occasionally vied for consumer attention with shock effects – for example, in Oliviero Toscani's Benetton campaign from the 1980s and 1990s showing AIDS patients and war victims.[95] The person of the advertiser also mutates – from the man in the grey flannel suit into the aesthetically conscious 'now' generation. By the 1980s, as art-collecting British advertisers such as Saatchi & Saatchi stepped into the limelight, the industry was viewing itself in general as a creative branch at the forefront of the aesthetic economy.[96]

Design

We have already examined the arts and crafts movement and the Bauhaus as two important impulses for modern design. Design encompasses any activity in which everyday objects are made primarily or secondarily for their aesthetic qualities. As such, it is a form of aesthetic labour performed with various materials and therefore a prime example of aestheticization. Design turns previously non-aesthetic entities into aesthetic ones. Design as craftwork occurred in the modern era most prominently in the service of aristocratic culture, but the beginnings of modern design proper are to be found in the arts and crafts reform movement, with its critical stance on the loss of aesthetic qualities as a result of industrial production.

In the early twentieth century, two broad-based design movements entered into mutual rivalry, both employing industrial production methods. Ornamental art deco faced off against anti-ornamental modernism and functionalism, the latter reliant on the aesthetic force of technical and abstract forms.[97] A programme of aesthetic and technical reform, modernism was boosted by the Bauhaus after the First World War before being launching into international cultural hegemony from the USA as the international style in the 1930s. The international exhibition of modern architecture in the Museum of Modern Art in New York in 1932 marked the global arrival of the international style among the Western cultural elites in interior design, architecture, object design and graphic design. After the Second World War this modernism was the only one on offer in the West, becoming established in Germany at the Ulm School of Design, from which it spread internationally in electronic product design from companies such as Philips and Braun.[98] The functionalism is here not only aesthetic but utility-oriented, seeking the optimal form for any particular purpose. Yet, despite appearances, modernism did not dominate the scene unchallenged. In the 1930s, when design was put to work in the USA for the purpose of aggressive product promotion, for example in the automobile industry, it often resorted to aesthetic strategies drawing on the opulence of art deco. A stylistic prototype was the US designer Raymond Loewy, who founded his own design company in 1936 under the principle 'good style sells more product'.[99] Design served in this context to endow goods with added aesthetic value for the mass consumer. Loewy opted for spectacular anti-modernist forms such as streamlining for automobiles.

The gradual formation of the design industry in the first half of the twentieth century, in particular in industrial and product design, thus led to a fundamental aestheticization of the world of objects, albeit in *restrained* form. This restraint applied both to modernism and to art deco. Art deco was limited to an aestheticization of the surfaces of products which remained essentially technical but were given a post-production aesthetic finish, as Loewy's automobile demonstrates. The function of design for such products was to provide an added value, an aesthetic supplement for a basically technical product. In contrast, modernist design, in the tradition of the Werkbund and Bauhaus, built the whole product from the ground up as a synthesis of functional and sensuous aspects. But the play of meanings and affects into which the user is drawn by such modernist design objects was rigidified and thus restrained by the modernist notion that aesthetic qualities derive from utility – i.e., that form follows function, from which it follows that there is only one correct solution for any design problem.

This restraint or brake mechanism in design was finally overridden by a process analogous to that in fashion and advertising. It was the 1960s and 1970s counter-culture that made the decisive change. In this period, a critical anti-design movement directed against the dictates of modernism emerged internationally, coming mainly out of small, young design agencies.[100] An important part in this process was played by the traditional, artistic Italian agencies such as Archizoom, Superstudio and the group Global Tools, as well as British agencies such as Archigram, all influenced by the postmodernist art scene, the protest movement's critique of consumption and power elites and critical tendencies towards the sensuous reappropriation of urban life.[101] This faction also launched campaigns at the intersection of design and art in the attempt to increase awareness of design issues and present design as a task of generating social spaces for society as a whole, such as the 1969 project 'No-Stop City' by Archizoom.[102] These design objects made use of an ornamental, popular aesthetic (a prime example of this was Ettore Sottsass's Mickey Mouse table from 1972) often assuming the form of artistic sculpture.

In this period of transformation, radical design was driven by three tendencies present in similar form in fashion and advertising. The first was the discovery of the public, which was addressed as a community of emancipated consumers with their own aesthetic interests. Advertising approaches such as 'design ethnography' were concerned with different lifestyles and their everyday design.[103] Second, after the collapse of the modernist hegemony there emerged a play of differences, a florescence of new aesthetic styles, an exploration of the endless possibilities for combining disparate elements from high and popular culture. Third, design expanded the scope of its own assignment to incorporate the transformation of the entire world of artefacts. It was no longer understood as a niche within product design and now pursued the political project of reshaping the whole human environment to fulfil sensuous and practical needs. Of particular relevance to the history of discourse around this development in design are Robert Venturi's *Learning from Las Vegas*, an emphatic call for popular aesthetics and the use of analogy, symbol and image, and Victor Papanek's *Design for the Real World*, which appealed for holistic design open to a variety of interpretations.[104]

In this transformative phase, design began to explore a new approach which would become prevalent in the 1980s, when it freed itself from the critical stance of 'radical design'. Design has since assumed the status of a general discipline of the creative economy. The aesthetic worth of an increasing number of products has gone from being a marginal aspect to becoming their most conspicuous feature, making product semantics the core of the commodity.[105] This enables not only material goods but also whole environments and atmospheres to become objects of design. On the other hand, since the 1980s, design as a general discipline has propelled the dynamic, infinite play of novelty and difference for a public interested in becoming aesthetic by continually developing new styles (for example, 'neo-primitivism' or 'super-normal'), in a way similar to fashion. As a result, classic modernist design has become just one style among many.[106] The fascination of consumers for this unleashing of different design styles is manifest in the broad mass-media sensibility for design and for its institutionalization as a cultural good, in the establishment of design museums (the first of which opened in 1989) and design magazines (such as *Wallpaper*, founded in 1996), and the emergence of design publishers (such as the international Taschen-Verlag, founded in 1980). Since the 1980s, designers such as Philippe Starck and Terence Conran have emerged into public consciousness as appealing creative figures in the mould of successful artists. The designer has attained a symbiosis of aesthetic and economic skill.

However, design could only become an umbrella discipline of the creative economy by transcending product semantics to endow brands with an effective, long-term aesthetic identity, which is then ultimately extended to include the shaping of collective consumer identities, thus transforming itself into a form of aesthetic corporate consultancy.[107] The goal of design has become to secure brand distinction and establish affective consumer identification with the brand and its symbolism. A trigger for this general orientation towards the brand was Wally Olins's *The Corporate Personality*.[108] Branding is not necessarily limited to commercial enterprise but can also be applied to state or public institutions and to whole nations in need of a sensuous-affective revamping.[109] In this expanded context, design is no longer confined to the optical surfaces of single objects but begins also to incorporate spatial environments, extending finally to whole organizations and cultures.[110] This *internal design* within organizations – for example, the design of work environments, employee events and in-house ceremonies – is directed no longer at the customer but, rather, at the employees themselves, heightening their motivation and fostering a sense of identity. Design producers thus become design consumers when they are at work. A work environment that has been designed on every level has become a prerequisite for post-industrial labour.

Design has in this way become a paradigmatic practice for the methodical creation of emotionally satisfying all-round atmospheres, permeating increasingly into the sphere of management. This merging of management and design and the rise of a *design economy* is the last phase in the spread of the aesthetic economy. This topic will absorb our attention in the following section.

4.5 'Management by Design'

We have studied two strands of cultural development separately in order to explain their contribution to the genesis of the aesthetic economy. On the one hand, we looked at the reform of business administration in the personality and organization school and innovation economics. On the other hand, we saw the development of the three leading areas of the creative economy: fashion, advertising and design. The two strands can be seen to run independently of each other. We can speak first of an aesthetic economy when the two strands have run together and intertwined – a process which in retrospect reads like question and answer. The sense of the need to restructure businesses after Fordism is answered by the forms of labour in the creative industries. By turning labour into an aesthetic activity, the creative economy offers a solution to the problem, examined above, of motivation in bureaucratic organizations. By directly addressing consumers as aesthetic individuals, warming up their aesthetic sensibility by the play of different styles and experiences, the creative economy has recast permanent innovation as independent of technical development. It thus promises a solution to the second problem of bureaucratic organization: the problem of environment. Since the 1980s, management theory has clearly been developing along these lines in two distinguishable ways. First, the postmodern management theories developed in the 1980s by Tom Peters and others couple creativity with entrepreneurial spirit and, second, the management techniques of design economics propagate aesthetic work as the model of all post-industrial business.

The theories of Peters, Rosabeth Moss Kanter and Charles Handy took off from the idea of permanent innovation borrowed from innovation economics.[111] While this approach is predicated on a presumed tension between the organization's need to innovate, on the one hand, and employee inertia resulting from routine and security, on the other,[112] postmodern management takes up the central idea from personality and organization theory that every worker has a natural tendency towards personal development. By thus redefining the economic subject and the organization, post-bureaucratic management envisages an easy convergence of dynamic individuals with dynamic institutions. The worker is redefined as naturally innovative on two levels: as a creative individual striving for personal development and constantly new ideas; and as an entrepreneurial self, searching for challenging ways to assert himself and his ideas in a dynamic environment. From this point of view, Chris Argyris's self-realizing individual and Joseph Schumpeter's entrepreneur turn out to be the same person. In this spirit, Rosabeth Moss Kanter's management manual *The Change Masters* postulates the existence of a complementary relation between the organization's need to innovate and workers' naturally occurring creativity. A distinction is made between people and machines reminiscent of the *Lebensphilosophie* distinction between life and form, ascribing vital 'creative capacities' and 'idea power' to human beings striving for the chance to act out this power. Kanter joins this creative subject to the figure of the 'internal entrepreneur', reminiscent of Schumpeter's entrepreneur, but one whose entrepreneurship is now acted out *within* an organization.[113]

The symbiosis of the creative and the entrepreneurial self and innovative organization is made conceivable in the first place by management theory discarding all technocratic conceptions of the organization. Organizations are now conceived as cultural and affective processes in which the employee functions as an interpreting and emotional entity. The cultural aspect affects both the form and the content of the work practice – the creation of ideas, symbols, and consumer experiences – as well as the organizational background. This recasts the organization as primarily a cultural entity possessing implicit knowledge, routines, values and self-interpretations. Tom Peters, whose publications and activities as a business consultant have had an enormous influence on management theory since the 1980s, explicitly bases his approach on the antagonism between the 'rationality' of the old bureaucratic organization and the 'culture' of the new, dynamic organization.[114] Culture means two things here. The organization is cultural because it is concerned with the constant creation of ideas, signs and experiences. But there also exists an 'organization culture', the sum of values and identities that serve in the background of productive collective work. While on the one level culture is conceived as inherently dynamic and fluid, on the other level it is stable. In order for a business constantly to produce new creative ideas, it needs a secure framework of collective identities and values.[115]

In addition to the culturalization of economic processes, another central factor for postmodern management technique is the emotionalization of the organization and labour practices. The notion that employees strive for security is discarded. They are now assumed to be positively affected by – and indeed enthusiastic about – the energy and unpredictability of the business. These positive affects are linked mainly to the mobility resulting from the collective production of symbols as well as from the state of competition for markets. Enthusiasm results from the turbulence of the instantaneous event and the moment of creation. Kanter quotes employees of Chipco to this effect: '"It's like riding a bucking bronco." "It's like riding a roller coaster." "It's exhilarating." "It's fun." "There's never a dull moment." "Time flies here."'[116] Peters employs a strongly emotive vocabulary to depict the fascination and intensity of the organization in a permanent state of flux, a kind of 'carnival'.[117]

From this notion of business administration and the market environment as places of cultural and affective practice and the idea of the employee as a hybrid of creativity and entrepreneurship, it is a smooth transition to a management theory that demands aesthetic work as the basis of an advanced post-industrial economy. This universal extension of the model of aesthetic labour has taken place in 'design economics', which has been gaining prominence since the 1990s. The instant design agencies mutated into organization development operations they began to offer a total management foundation for successful businesses, which in turn adopts the design industry as their model. The motto of this symbiosis is *management by design.*

Tom Kelley's *The Art of Innovation: Lessons in creativity from IDEO* and Tim Brown's *Change by Design* – the guiding principles of which grew out of American business consultancy[118] – suppose that work in a non-bureaucratic project team, a creative, enthusiastic creative cell, is for every business an indispensable precondition for success. The business must also exploit consumers' natural resourcefulness and originality in their dealings with commodities and experiences: 'as consumers we are making new and different sorts of demands.'[119] 'Design thinking' as a management technique presupposes that every product and service can be made aesthetic by integrating symbols, percepts and affects. Kelley deploys buzzwords to demonstrate that the design economy aims not for nouns but, rather, for verbs; it is concerned not with objects that can change hands but with supplying consumers with a sensuous, emotional event. He dubs this project 'designing new experiences'.[120] In a management version of the aesthetic of presence, the symbolic meaning of the commodity is replaced by the sensuous, affective experience.[121]

The design economy presents artistic labour as a model instance of project work in post-Fordist business.[122] It is not the solitary artist who is the paragon here but, rather, the postmodern artist collective. What Roberto Verganti calls 'design-driven innovation' conjoins two forms of labour familiar from postmodern art: the attentive outward observation of the signs and affects current in the culture and the striving to programme inward spontaneity. Verganti deduces a set of postulates from the work of Italian design agencies such as Alessi, Memphis and Artemide, as well as Apple (and extends it to management in total),[123] according to which design-driven innovation must attentively follow global and local symbols and cultural trends in order to ferret out as yet unfulfilled needs. The designer as manager is an expert at this semiotic circulation, mining design schools, artists, cultural anthropologists, couturiers, market researchers, journalists, engineers, subcultures and inventive consumers for sources of cultural development.

In order to create aesthetic novelty in the context of this global circulation of signs and affects, management by design requires two technologies of the self borrowed from the work of artist collectives and transferred to project work in general: 'release' and 'artful collaboration'. Rob Austin and Lee Devin advise the aesthetic economy to imitate the work of actors and directors in a theatre ensemble. 'Release' means freeing up individuals from mental restraints. This has the effect of heightening focus and setting creative processes in motion. The assignment of the art director – whether in the capacity of manager or team leader – is to facilitate this release, which is thus revealed as an indirect means of control. 'Artful collaboration' is collective experimentation in which the unpredictable actions of participants are accepted by others as welcome occasions to react with their own ideas. Surprising behaviour is not considered disturbing, annoying or threatening but, rather, welcomed as material to be appropriated and elaborated further. As a form of aesthetic labour, management by design is an ambivalent activity with enormous affective intensity. As well as the emotional stimulation of novelty creation and mutual encouragement, it harbours the danger of failure and the sense of being overwhelmed by a challenge – the persistent, recurrent sense of doubt inherent to any creative process 'on the edge'.[124] Although they set out with the assumption of the universality of aesthetic work, Austin and Devin come to the more limited conclusion that not everyone is cut out for the emotional effort involved: 'it's not for everyone this artful work.'[125]

4.6 The Aestheticization of the Economy and Affective Capitalism

We have traced the genesis of the aesthetic economy from disparate contexts. We have seen that this genesis has been following a pattern, characteristic of the creativity dispositif in general, of intersection between a social regime of novelty and processes of aestheticization. A regime of novelty need not be aesthetically oriented any more than a process of aestheticization need be oriented towards novelty. The creativity dispositif constitutes the intersection of the two processes, and the genesis of the aesthetic economy shows in exemplary fashion how this intersection comes about. It has become clear that the radicalization of an economic regime of innovation and the aestheticization of the economy initially proceed independently of each other. Both tendencies are, each in its own way, distinct from formal, rational, organized capitalism, in which novelty was confined to technology and therefore non-aesthetic. In combination, the two processes present an alternative to the Fordist model of bureaucratic work and standardized consumption.

The two cultural strands that have finally been subsumed in the aesthetic economy initially ran parallel. The one strand consists of versions of an economic culture which attempted to break open the double paradox of novelty inherent in formal, rationalist economy in order to introduce a radical economic regime of novelty without being aesthetic in essence. The bourgeois, turn-of-the-century discourse of the entrepreneur that would later be reappropriated by neoliberalism aimed at energizing the economy and its agents, the entrepreneurs. The innovation economy in the 1950s and 1960s worked to restructure the enterprise into an entity capable of self-transformation in the face of a changing market environment. In neither of the two contexts was permanent innovation identified with aesthetic labour, but both nevertheless distanced themselves from an objectified and technical model of innovation. The entrepreneurial discourse framed the activity of the entrepreneur as emotionally charged, while the innovation economy began to experiment with notions of an 'organizational culture' amenable to innovation. In turn, the personality and organization discourse supplied the psychological accompaniment to the innovation economy, framing members of the organization as individuals striving for self-creation.

The aesthetic tendencies expressed in the arts and crafts movement and the early 'creative industries' emerged at the edge of the Fordist economy independently of these elements of management reform. In these movements the production of goods assumed the form primarily of aesthetic work on the production of signs, sensuous experiences and positive affects. All these contexts maintained connections to the artistic field. However, the aestheticization strategy of arts and crafts stood apart from the unending cycle of novel goods. Earlier design, especially in the context of Bauhaus and functionalism, tended to be incompatible with the sequence of one novelty superseding the last, seeking instead stable, reproducible aesthetic forms. Further, these early 'creative industries' were not unreservedly aesthetic; their mode of production remained under the influence of non-aesthetic factors. This applies, for example, to the orientation towards factual information in advertising and symbols for class distinctions in fashion. We have seen above how the appropriations by 1950s and 1960s youth culture, counter-culture and critical aesthetic discourse unleashed the aesthetic potential of fashion, design and advertising, leading these fields into the heart of a regime of aesthetic novelty. This enabled the creative industries to become a driving force behind the aestheticization of the post-Fordist economy.

The two strands of development – the general regime of economic innovation and the aestheticization of the economy – converge in the aesthetic economy, which has been unfolding since the 1980s, influenced as much by postmodern management theory propagating the upsurge of culture and emotion in organizations as by management by design. The aesthetic economy has now become a general design economy practising *aesthetic management*. Its innermost structure reproduces the blueprint of aesthetic sociality that had always been present in the artistic field. This aesthetic sociality consists of social practices for the production and reception of aesthetic experiences. It is an aesthetic of novelty, originality and surprise. Finally, it provides a social model, coordinating creators, creative practices and an aesthetically interested audience around aesthetic objects and aesthetic experience within a set of mechanisms for regulating attention.

The aesthetic economy built on this blueprint from the arts transverses the old front that once separated the economic and the aesthetic. The economy is no longer geared solely to the production of standardized goods; it is aesthetic labour, creative work for producing aesthetically new and singular things. Whether the objects produced are material or immaterial, what is of primary importance is their sensuous and emotional value, which transcends both their use value and their status value. The consumers are now an audience, hungry for sensuous and emotional gain and expecting surprise. The relation between the audience and the creators is regulated by the management of attention to sensuous stimulation and emotional promise, concentrated in the exhibition spaces of the urban experience-economy and advertising, and disseminated by mass media.[126]

The postmodern centrifugal artistic field gives rise to boundary dissolution tendencies among all four components of aesthetic sociality. Without the breakdown of these borders the aesthetic economy would not have been possible. In both areas – postmodern art and the aesthetic economy – the creation of novelty is the fruit of aesthetic labour, which is understood less as the creation of something original than as the rearrangement of signs, sensuous impulses and affects responding to developments in the culture. In both areas, the aesthetic objects are no longer exclusively material but increasingly include immaterial atmospheres. In both areas, the aesthetic labour presupposes an active audience. Finally, the management of attention is targeted at the new, while consigning the old to oblivion.

The organizational forms of the aesthetic economy in advertising and design, fashion, architecture, entertainment, the media and elsewhere thus constitute prototypes for what can be called *aesthetic apparatuses*[127] – institutional complexes for production, presentation and consumption, hybrids of aesthetic and non-aesthetic practices, the main purpose of which is to produce aesthetic events. These aesthetic apparatuses consist in large part of purposive-rational and normative practices and involve the selection of personnel, distribution, administration, market analysis, internal communication and negotiation. The crucial feature of these purposive-rational and normative structures is that they serve a sensuous-affective purpose: the production of new aesthetic events. These events are concentrated around aesthetic consumption, though they also occur in *aesthetic labour* itself. Aesthetic labour has thereby become a hybrid practice in which instrumental rationality and sensuousness for its own sake merge together. Work practices are generally purpose-oriented, aimed at producing goods or services for interchangeable recipients in order to gain a living or a profit. In aesthetic labour these goods and services have an aesthetic character in that they are intended to supply aesthetic experiences. At the same time, this type of creation work also characteristically involves perceptions and feelings experienced on their own terms.[128]

Disorganized capitalism has often been described as a basically flexible and reflexive economy of knowledge, a 'cognitive capitalism'.[129] It is based on the collection, processing and application of forms of theoretical and practical knowledge which have gained an unprecedented degree of accessibility and adaptability with the digital revolution. These knowledge-based activities are no longer confined to a few specialists in research and development. In contrast to earlier industrial society, cognitive capitalism depends on employees rigorously updating their qualifications and on well-informed consumers. Interpreting the post-Fordist economy as a knowledge economy casts light on transformations that have taken place since the 1970s within the organization of work affecting workers' technical qualifications. However, these transformations have previously been understood in terms that finally render cognitive capitalism no more than an advanced version of organized capitalism. The theory of cognitive capitalism successfully explains the radical spirit of permanent innovation within the current economy, yet it lacks the concepts to grasp the fundamental role of the aesthetic within innovation.

If we understand late modern society as characterized most prominently by the creativity dispositif, then we can elucidate the radical aestheticization of the economy resulting from aesthetic labour and aesthetic consumption. The aesthetic economy is concerned principally not with information but with the circulation of symbols, sensuous experiences and emotions. At heart it is not cognitive but aesthetic. The reflexivity of knowledge proves to be merely the instrument for perfecting both creative work and the aesthetic receptivity of consumers. The paradigm of this aesthetic economy is the *design economy*. Design then comes to encompass the strategic construction of arrangements of objects, ways of thinking, signs, sense impressions and affects for aesthetically cultivated users. Design can be applied to individual artefacts as well as to services, to electronic bearers of signs, and to whole spatial and virtual environments. The organizational form that provides the supporting framework for this kind of activity is aesthetic management. The important consequence of this is that the aesthetic economy is more than a symbolic economy or an economy of signs. Signs and symbols are indeed the elementary constituents of the aesthetic economy, but their prime function is to stimulate the senses and the emotion rather than merely to convey meaning.[130]

In *The New Spirit of Capitalism*, Luc Boltanski and Eve Chiapello sharply delineate how the model of project-based labour characteristic of disorganized capitalism is predicated on a motivation to work that has been changing since the late 1960s, especially in the academic middle classes, becoming influenced by the model of the artist as a non-alienated, expressive worker. They rightly point out that the alternative and counter-cultures of the 1960s and 1970s mark a pivotal point in history which ushered in a post-materialist labour ethos.[131] Yet Boltanski and Chiapello, too, fail to capture the structure of the aesthetic economy in its entirety. The aesthetic economy is not only aesthetic because it motivates people to work by framing work as a means of self-realization. It consists also in the specific *techniques* and *skills* of aesthetic labour, the ability to engage skilfully with symbols, perceptions and affects. Finally, it involves the consumers' new sensibilities and desires and the efforts the economy has made to adapt to them. The motivation to be creative alone would not have been sufficient to bring about the aesthetic economy as we know it today. What was needed above all was people's capacity to perform aesthetic work. Such skills are derived from the creative industries, which had been cultivating aesthetic techniques of object-making since the early twentieth century. Finally, Boltanski and Chiapello strangely fail to take account of the transformative effects consumers have had on the culture of work. The establishment of the aesthetic economy was conditional on enterprise discovering the existence of an audience whose desire for aesthetic goods and for creative self-realization in the act of consumption it could systematically observe and predict.

As we have established, a fundamental aspect of the aesthetic economy is its focus on affective intensity. The practices of aesthetic capitalism are those of *affective capitalism*. At the same time, they are oriented on creativity – i.e., on the production and consumption of aesthetic novelty. With his concept of affective labour, Michael Hardt demonstrates the presence of such emotional processes at the heart of the post-Fordist economy while nevertheless underestimating the relevance of affectivity.[132] In contrast, with the emergence of affective consumer communities, Nigel Thrift has discovered an equal measure of affectivity in the current economy on the side of consumption.[133] The evidence suggests that all these processes of affection and emotional excitation characteristic of the current economic field radiate out from the fixation on creativity, from the production and reception of novelty in aesthetic events. This affectivity is attached both to the labour and to the consumption side of creativity. It encompasses the enthusiasm arising from the production of novel symbolic, perceptual objects and atmospheres in aesthetic labour, the fascination for novel aesthetic objects and acts of consumption consisting in experiencing environments, and the individual consumer's fascination for the autonomous deployment of these products to the purpose of generating an aesthetic style. Different economic forms apart from capitalism certainly have their own specific affective structures, be they weaker or stronger. An emotional potential is inherent in symbolic exchange, in social distinction, in work with natural materials, in wealth, in comfort and in solidarity. But in aesthetic capitalism the affectivity is both more extensive and more closely allied to acts of production and consumption. This affectivity results from aestheticization. The process of aestheticization collapses production and consumption into each other. The production process itself always already implies consumption, since it involves sensuous, affective enjoyment, while consumption in turn involves the active production of experiences and styles. In the economy as in art, affection is an inter-objective rather than an intersubjective relation, a relation between people and things rather than between people, associated with the production of fascinating objects and their use by fascinated people.[134]

5

The Psychological Turn in Creativity

From the Pathological Genius to the Normalization of the Self as Resource

5.1 The Inkblot Test

The first psychological creativity tests were performed unwittingly by Hermann Rorschach between 1911 and 1922 in the psychiatric clinics at Münsterlingen, Berne and Herisau. A physician and psychiatrist who was strongly interested in the new psychoanalysis and in avant-garde art, Rorschach was the first to use inkblots systematically for testing patients.[1] Rorschach's inkblots were a set of ten randomly produced patterns with bilateral symmetry, including seven in black and three coloured. The inkblot forms can be interpreted in a variety of ways by patients invited to identify objects in them. Rorschach's third inkblot can be seen as a dancing dwarf with bloody feet or a doubled map of Antarctica. Inkblot eight could be the organs of a human torso with rats gnawing at the sides or a richly ornamented soup bowl. There are seemingly no limits to what can be imagined.

This sort of experimentation with inkblots was not Rorschach's invention. In 1857, Justinus Kerner published his little book *Klecksographien*, which introduced middle-class circles to the manipulation of inkblots as a parlour game.[2] The point of such games was to find the most original and entertaining interpretations of the blots, which the participants generated themselves. Rorschach, whose book *Psychodiagnostik* (1921) was directed at a wide audience, was interested in something entirely different. He was trying to ascertain not his subjects' originality but their degree of normality.[3] Whatever Rorschach's intentions were, his introduction of the inkblot as a rigorous and replicable test method was a remarkable advance in the development of psychology. Since around 1900, psychology had been gaining cultural influence as a new intellectual technology, thanks not least to the development of methods for clinical, comparative testing of mental abilities.[4] These tests were predominantly in standardized, written form and evaluated quantitatively. This approach was used, for example, for intelligence tests, which became widespread above all in the USA. Rorschach's test belonged in part to this psychological testing movement. Yet the openness of its results, which had to be determined qualitatively, made it significantly more individual than strictly standardized psychometric tests.

The aim of Rorschach's test was clearly stated. It was to be used in psychiatric clinics to distinguish 'normal' from 'ill' patients and to identify various illnesses. The evaluation was focused less on the contents of the patients' interpretations, as was psychoanalysis, and more on their form, on the general pattern of perception to which the individual interpretation belonged. The remarkable thing about Rorschach's procedure was the absence of predetermined standards of normality. The standards had to be generated by the test itself. A psychologist carrying out the inkblot test does not give the person being tested statements or images which would dictate right and wrong answers but uses instead the randomly generated images to have the subject arrive at an interpretation which is a priori open. This method unwittingly revealed psychic normality as a matter of convention. The purpose of the test was to ascertain whether or not the subject was capable of producing 'good forms'. Whether or not a form is good was determined by its frequency. As Rorschach wrote, 'Form answers given by a large number of normal subjects...were used as the norm and basis.'[5] The absolute distinction between healthy and ill was thereby translated into the gradual, qualitative distinction between better and worse. This was then determined quantitatively. The method thus turned out to be circular, equating healthy normality to statistical frequency.

In the course of Rorschach's assessment, the tester's interest and criterion changed in telling ways. The focus shifted to 'originality', which fell outside of the standard for psychic normality. Originality was regarded no longer as pathological but rather as valuable. Rorschach now added to his original distinction between healthy and ill, good forms and bad forms, introducing the distinction between 'stereotype' and 'original' answers.[6] The most common inkblot interpretations, for example animals, were defined as indicators for stereotypical thinking. Rorschach added the value-laden comment that such stereotypical responses, evincing neither 'originality of reasoning nor sense for practical things', indicated a mere 'proud but sterile technician of logic and memory'.[7] The normality the test was seeking thus proved to be merely conformist, while the original responses, the unusual and surprising interpretations, were regarded as more valuable. These divergent interpretations, which according to Rorschach's original premise indicated neurosis or other psychiatric tendencies, could now be evaluated positively as indicators of originality. Abnormal perception, which Rorschach initially interpreted as a sign of pathological psychic deviation, was now a mark of 'non-stereotyped' thinking. These original responses were initially evaluated by Rorschach in purely quantitative terms – i.e., as more seldom. But he later felt obliged to adopt an ad hoc qualitative distinction between good and bad original answers, although he offered no justification for this distinction. Rorschach seems to have given up the search for one when he wrote, 'In schizophrenics, most absurd and very appropriate answers are found following one another.' This shows that the distinction between worthwhile and worthless original responses did not coincide with the distinction between healthy and sick. Nevertheless, even Rorschach's estimation of the 'good' original responses remained ambivalent when he construed an excess of originality as indicating a *Weltfremder* – someone 'in the world but not of it'.[8]

Rorschach's dismantling of his own premises did not damage the career the inkblot tests enjoyed in the USA after the Second World War.[9] The Rorschach test, praised by Bruno Klopfer as the 'psychological X-ray' of personality psychology, was used en masse on returning soldiers, then later on schoolchildren, and finally also for career counselling and forensic psychiatric examination. In all these cases, the test was used to assess whether a subject was psychiatrically normal or abnormal. What is important to our context is the fact that the original Rorschach test implies two overlapping but contradictory theories of human personality: a psychology of the abnormal of the type that had emerged in psychiatry in the mid-nineteenth century and a psychology of personality types. The latter gradually uncovered a human ability to produce unusual perceptions and actions, concentrating its theories, tests and ultimately its therapies on this 'creative' aptitude, regarding creativity not as pathological deviance but rather as a sign of psychic health. The Rorschach test had begun as part of the psychological apparatus of abnormality. It then turned into a creativity test, which in turn provided the foundation of a psychology of creativity.

5.2 The Psychopathology of Genius

As well as being a set of theories and discourses, modern psychology can be understood as a complex of subjectivization techniques for determining, in a therapeutic context, what kind of psyche is normal and desirable and what kind is pathological and undesirable. The prehistory of psychology can be traced back to the early nineteenth century. Since around 1900, psychology has been an academic and clinical discipline in Germany, the USA, Britain and France, deployed by the state and by business, with its own specific vocabulary of the self and its own techniques for evaluating and changing the self. As Foucault has pointed out, the discursive, practical field of psychology has key significance as a 'truth game' within the modern human sciences.[10] It can be claimed that the culture of modernity was always focused if not fixated on the subject, interminably resetting the distinction between subjective interiority and the exteriority of objects and other subjects. If this is true, then twentieth-century psychology is the leading means by which the subjective inner world has become an object of scientific inquiry. At the same time, these scientific notions of the self have entered popular imagination, contributing to the development of corresponding technologies of the self.

The field of psychology – comprising scientific and popular psychology, psychotherapy, applied psychology, psychiatry and psychological tests – exercised a decisive influence on the formation of the creativity dispositif. In the previous two chapters we saw how the discourse and techniques of psychology had been taken up since the 1920s in the arts as well as in business administration. However, independently of these influences, psychology developed an increasing tendency to understand the self as something essentially creative. This reinterpretation of the modern self as a creative subject had practical consequences beyond psychological diagnosis and therapy. Since the 1960s it has continued to contribute to popular notions of what it means to be a well-balanced person and lead a satisfying life. This has been especially prevalent among the educated classes, who tended to be more open to the influence of psychology.

The process by which the vocabulary and technologies of the self of psychology went from *discrediting* the creative personality to *normalizing* it was not a linear development. The psychological discovery of creativity as both a human default setting and an ideal would appear at first to be an improbable turn of historical events. It is true that late nineteenth-century psychology, influenced by medicine and psychiatry, did take account of psychic phenomena associated with creativity under the label of genius and in the framework of the aesthetics of genius. Yet this psychology vehemently denigrated genius as pathological. The academic psychology of the first half of the twentieth century, which was either cognitivist or behaviourist in outlook, toned this verdict down, but it did so in favour of an empirical science of perception and behaviour in which creative phenomena were not systematically included.

The psychiatry emerging in the mid-nineteenth century as the forerunner of modern psychology was basically a psychology of the abnormal, taking its point of departure from mental illness and extending its interest from there to the wider field of 'deviant' behaviour.[11] The discussion of genius at the time can be localized in this context of the discussion of normality. The objects of the psychology of the abnormal were deviancies expressed involuntarily, such as automatic behaviours, the prime example of which was epilepsy. Foucault sees the strong discursive focus on sexuality in the nineteenth century as an important manifestation of this concern with normality and abnormality. What George Becker refers to as the 'mad genius controversy' between 1850 and 1910 can be understood as a second main strand in the psychiatry of the abnormal.[12] In chapter 2.3 we saw how this stigmatization of genius paradoxically tied into the aesthetics of genius. The latter had been predicated on the opposition between the creative power of the artist and the mediocrity of the masses. The psychological stigmatization of genius assumed this binary while reversing the values. Now, the majority was characterized as psychologically predictable while the genius was hazardously volatile. In psychiatry and in the psychological cultural critique, from Louis Lélut and Jacques-Joseph Moreau to Cesare Lombroso and Noble Royse, the heightened perceptual sensitivity of the genius was regarded no longer as an achievement but as the sign of a deficiency of reason.[13]

This psychiatric framing of genius characteristically involved treating creative achievements as a criterion of genius, although these same achievements were accorded only secondary importance in psychological analysis. The goal of this psychiatry was not to explore the faculties responsible for creative acts but, rather, to examine the whole personality of the genius from the point of view of psychological predictability. The explanations for the psychological imbalance of the genius ranged from neurasthenic constitution to biological degeneration. In 1890, Noble Royse claimed that the uneven distribution of psychic 'energies' predestined the eccentric genius to psychic and physical illness. Cesare Lombroso attributed to the genius an excessive affective sensitivity. Warren Babcock, finally, saw the genius as a special case of biological degeneration, with four functionally equivalent possible life paths. The genius will either die early from weakness, undertake a criminal career, suffer from mental illness or lead a life of artistic or intellectual success.[14] Interestingly, the presumption of the creative person's psychic instability in the late nineteenth century was increasingly coupled with sociological arguments, namely the reference to the anomic nature of the genius and to the lifestyle of the bohemians, with their lack of social integration.[15]

Parallel to the stigmatization of the genius in the second half of the nineteenth century, there emerged two countervailing tendencies, beginning within the proto-psychological field with somewhat dubious attempts to experiment with the notion of genius as normal. One tendency was phrenology, defended by the Fowler brothers as a practical study of the brain, which attained popularity in the USA in the 1830s.[16] Phrenology was essentially an early version of differential psychology, which presupposed the inviolable uniqueness of the individual, from which it followed that unusually pronounced human traits, such as intellectual or artistic abilities, were not to be regarded as pathological. The second tendency had a similar effect: Francis Galton's reflections on the heritability of genius, which he equated with being more intellectually gifted, investigated the descendants of 'geniuses' from the worlds of art, politics and science.[17] Galton's theory of inheritance led to a Darwinian privileging of cognitive giftedness as socially necessary. Galton developed racist, eugenic fantasies around the principle that the psychic instabilities in family lines must be tolerated if society wants to obtain socially useful, gifted individuals.

Galton and the phrenologists represent a biologically oriented countermovement to the stigmatization of genius. In both theories, the genius was no longer either degenerate or associated with creativity and artistry; rather, it went hand in hand with exceptional *cognitive* abilities. In what relationship cognitive capacities might stand to the creative capacity to produce aesthetic novelty remained for them an open question. The change in the concept of genius ushered in by Galton, by which genius was distinguished no longer by artistic creativity but by intellectual giftedness, turns out in retrospect to be a genealogical turning point. By transferring genius to the realm of intelligence, the figure of the genius could be voided of pathological properties and become instead a positive role model. In the context of intelligence research undertaken in the 1950s, the concept of creativity – a term which was by then being used explicitly – was unburdened of its associations with madness, going beyond what had been possible for Galton and the phrenologists, who assumed genius was innate, to become a normative aim in psychology. This de-escalated situation was a necessary precondition for the cultivation of creativity, understood as an aesthetic faculty on the model of the self-expressive artist, making creativity a positive goal in psychological practice.

In what follows, we will explore in more detail how, in the twentieth and into the twenty-first century, psychology has come to be concerned with the topic of creativity in a variety of forms and contexts. With a first wave in the 1910s and a second in the 1950s, several psychological contexts emerged independently of one another, all framing the figure of a creative self positively against the older discourse of pathology. Beginning in the 1910s, two intellectual schools at the edge of academic psychology – psychoanalysis and gestalt psychology – founded traditions enabling a rehabilitation of creativity. The strand developed by psychoanalysis was oriented on personality, while that of gestalt psychology was based on cognition. The theme of creativity was not taken up in psychological practice until the 1950s, when a psychology of self-realization and a psychology of creative intelligence took up the two respective strands. Finally, a general psychological programme for nurturing creativity in everyday life has been developing since the 1980s. The personality and cognitive strands intertwine here to make psychology one of the pillars of the creativity dispositif.

5.3 Creativity on the Margins of Academic Psychology

Psychoanalysis and creation: sublimity and rupture

Academic psychology at the turn of the twentieth century had been concerned chiefly with the empirical search for general laws of perception. Meanwhile, Sigmund Freud's psychoanalysis dealt with the question of the psychic structure of creativity, above all with reference to the classical figure of the artistic genius, with the subject occurring in scattered writings as a subordinate theme. Freud was the last person to propagate a strict opposition between normal and abnormal. His main text on the subject, *Leonardo da Vinci and a Memory of His Childhood*, explains the creative subject in terms of sexual sublimation.[18] Freud was not interested in the conditions of the possibility of individual creative acts; he instead wanted to explain how an exceptional, creative personality comes about. He discovered the origins of the creative personality in a separate region: creativity as the diversion of sexual energies into artistic, intellectual, creative joy. According to a popular misconception, Freud continued the pathology theory by equating art with neurosis. In reality, his statements are more nuanced. For Freud as for Babcock, the neurotic and creative personalities were functionally equivalent, yet with the decisive difference that Freud dismissed as naive the opposition between neurosis and normality.

Freud elucidated the mechanisms of this functional equivalence using the example of Leonardo da Vinci. Freud assumed a general connection between an elementary sex drive and inquisitiveness in early childhood, a kind of infantile sex research, which is later inhibited by the super-ego. After puberty, the bond between research drive and sexuality develops in one of three different ways: in the case of neurotic inhibition, due for example to excessive morals, both the urge for new experiences and the sex drive are restricted. In the contrasting case of 'neurotic compulsive thinking', inquisitiveness remains strong and uninhibited but becomes sexualized. Finally, in creative sublimation, the libido is not suppressed and so does not constantly rise from the unconscious to beset the ego but, rather, is sublimated beforehand into the artistic, intellectual desire for new insights and experiences. According to Freud, this type is the most balanced, as the example of Leonardo da Vinci shows, where there is no evidence of neurosis. What the theory calls 'creative power' is specified as curiosity and desire for novelty, for the concealed and surprising. Creative orientation is therefore for Freud clearly a *secondary* function of the libido, a substitute, a compensatory object for sexual desire.

Psychoanalysis after Freud developed from this point with various attempts to establish the *primary* relevance of the creative orientation in the psyche, tending to grasp creativity as universal and normal. An influential discursive shift was brought about by Otto Rank with his *Art and Artist: Studies on the Development and Genesis of the Creative Urge*.[19] After initially working along the lines of Freud's drive theory,[20] in his later work Rank accuses the master of misconstruing the human *urge* to create on account of his fixation on *drive*. Influenced by *Lebensphilosophie*, Rank presupposed the existence of a universal human creative urge. According to Rank, the human soul is not only subject to drives but also has its own will, no mere unconscious force but, rather, free and conscious, the expression of a primordial vitality of the self, striving to realize itself and shape the world. The will to shape is asexual and therefore cannot be explained away by sublimation.

By construing the creative urge as universal, Rank helped prepare the later self-growth psychology. At the same time, Rank's framing of the relation between creation and drive is deeply rooted in the nineteenth-century thinking of Schopenhauer and Nietzsche. In Rank's version, the objects of creative action and this action itself remain oddly inscrutable. Nevertheless, Rank's account culminates in a systematic separation of the general creative will and the narrower modern type of the artist, implying an 'ideology of the personal artistic type'.[21] Instead of unfolding creative striving, the modern artist had constricted it. According to Rank, the artist had always suffered from renunciation, had ground himself down in the opposition between work and life as between two mutually exclusive alternatives. Now the aim was to free the creative will from creative ideology and thus from art itself. As Rank wrote, 'A man with creative power who can give up artistic expression in favour of the formation of personality – since he can no longer use art as an expression of an already developed personality...will remold the self-creative type and will be able to put his creative impulse *directly* in the service of his own personality.' The possessor of such creative power will pursue a 'voluntaristic art of life'.[22] Rank thus takes up and rejects the old pathology discourse. For him, the modern artist was indeed a pathological case, though not because he had transformed life into art in a non-bourgeois way – rather, because he did not take the transformation far enough, persisting in separating his work from everyday practice.

Rank's fixation on a specific personality form leaves the structure of the creative process itself unspecified. Lawrence Kubie's newer version of the psychoanalytic concept of creativity takes the creative process as its focus.[23] After the Second World War, psychoanalysis became the dominant form of psychological therapy in the USA, while the pathology discourse dissipated. In this context, Kubie took up the distinction between creativity and neurosis, though not reverting to Rank's theory of the will; instead he postulated the creative process as a special form of perception and interpretation, or, more precisely, as a special form of engagement with symbolic orders. According to Kubie, we learn everyday forms of behaviour by more or less automatic imitation, which is then subjected to reflective control in order to establish routines. But at the points of transition between preconscious imitation, reflective control and reautomatization, the various feelings, thoughts, perceptions and behaviours become separated from one another. These 'dissociations' would turn out to be preconditions for both neurosis and creativity. In the case of neuroses, dissociations manifest themselves in compulsive repetition, such as the repetition of affects that have broken loose from the situations in which they initially arose. In the case of creativity, dissociations are the precondition for various elements coming into connection in new and surprising ways.

According to Kubie, the motor force for this process is neither the unconscious libido nor the conscious will. The decisive factor is instead the intermediate level of the preconscious. The preconscious loosens the otherwise rigid attribution of symbols. This is what makes creativity possible in the first place. As Kubie wrote, 'It is the preconscious type of symbolic function which frees our psychic apparatus (and more specifically our symbolic processes) from rigidity.'[24] The basic concern of social practice is thus how to deal with repetition. Repetition is not pathological in everyday routine, but in neuroses, which for Kubie are ubiquitous, it threatens to turn into compulsive behaviour to which the subject becomes affectively tied. Creative acts make it possible to break out of such compulsive repetition. Kubie was in this sense a forerunner of post-structuralism, replacing the special problem of the artistic genius with the general assumption of the importance of playfully breaking out of routines. His description of this process of loosening the symbolic order through the preconscious made borrowings from the creativity models of the artistic avant-garde.

Gestalt psychology and productive thinking

Psychoanalysis is focused on the internal structure of the psychic apparatus and the differences between personality types. In contrast, gestalt psychology, developed mainly in Germany from the 1910s to the 1930s, was centred less on individual personality and investigated instead specific actions and thought processes as events occurring independently of personality type.[25] Like psychoanalysis, gestalt theory provided an alternative to the academic psychology of the time, which was sensualist and increasingly behaviourist. Gestalt theory was concerned chiefly with investigating what Max Wertheimer called 'productive thinking', everyday processes of problem-solving. The concern is not with creativity in the sense of a creative potential assumed to be striving for expression in the individual but, rather, with the constructive responses provided in practical coping with problems. The production of novelty in this context is not free of the compulsion to act, as it was in the model of the artist, but is a constructive reaction within the performance of rational purposive action. Gestalt psychology thus renders the activity of creating novelty quotidian and anthropologically universal. The paradigm is not art but experimental science.

The gestalt psychology propagated by Max Wertheimer, Karl Duncker, Wolfgang Köhler, Kurt Levine and others was directed against Wilhelm Wundt's psychology of perception. Their critique was largely directed against Wundt's 'elemental' approach, which they replace with a holistic, gestalt-oriented perspective. While Wundt operated with analysable basic elements in perception, the gestalt psychologists advanced the claim that meaningful perceptions consist in gestalts or global wholes.[26] The founding document of gestalt psychology proper, Wertheimer's article 'Experimental studies on seeing motion',[27] provided the point of departure for the emerging interest in moving images from the beginnings of cinematography. Wertheimer attempted to prove experimentally that the sequence of images produced perceptions of movement despite the lack of a corresponding movement in the object perceived, thus bringing out independent gestalt structures.

The question that now arose was connected with the mechanism of the transition from an old to a new gestalt. Cognitive patterns may be largely applied routinely, but in practice situations frequently occur requiring new gestalt structures to be processed. Recurring sense perceptions are then processed differently. The most important concept in gestalt psychology is correspondingly that of *restructuring* or *multistability*. Wertheimer criticized previous philosophical explanations of the experience of novelty as deficient.[28] One school had understood novelty as a process of formal logic in the tradition of the Aristotelian syllogism, where the new is deduced from known premises. According to Wertheimer, this approach failed to take account of the constructive character of perception, suggesting a seamless, calculable transition from the old to the only relatively new. The other approach had followed Humean associative psychology, interpreting the new as an ultimately random conjunction of percepts. This account failed to take seriously the problem-solving character of *productive thinking*. The most salient feature of the emergence of novelty is for the gestalt psychologists a non-predetermined gestalt transformation progressing towards an adequate perceptual grasp. The gestalt shift, as an elementary process of restructuring or multistable perception, what Köhler called *Gestaltmetamorphose*, in which the content of a perception is transformed from one figure into another, is regarded by the gestalt psychologists as a more likely explanation than the Aristotelian or the Humean of how successful coping with practical problems works, how we deal with perceived hindrances or pressures by changing their perceptual interpretation.

Although the gestalt transformations are cognitive acts, the gestalt psychologists also describe them as sensuous and emotional processes, by which sensuous perceptions are rearranged. Gestalt transformations are not inner, mental reflections but rather changes of pattern resulting from the connections between data from individual senses. It is therefore not surprising that the most common gestalt shifts are phenomena of *mental images* switching back and forth. The restructuring and recentring that take place in these cases are not free of affects. Friedrich Sander, for example, investigated how the production of these new patterns is driven by feelings of unease.[29] The affects are attached not to novelty as novelty but, rather, are concerned with resolving the practical situation. An emotional tension prevails, striving to resolve itself into the 'good gestalt' in which all perceptual elements cohere.

As mentioned previously, gestalt psychology was the attempt to develop a vocabulary for explaining all the processes of productive thinking without recourse to the concept of subjectivity. The agent of a practical coping situation is not the subject with its unpredictable and often inhibiting properties striving towards resolution but, rather, the self-propelling gestalt structure itself, 'the structural dynamics of the situation'.[30] This aspect of gestalt psychology has a parallel to the new description of creativity provided by the artistic avant-garde, according to which the new comes about of its own accord and the subjects are not the masters of the process. However, in contrast to the models and practices of artistic creativity, gestalt psychology insists over and over again on the rational and intentional character of gestalt shifts. Interestingly, in the conclusion of *Productive Thinking*, Wertheimer admits the incompleteness of his account of the production of novelty as an act of problem-solving in the course of which an unstable starting position is brought to a stable and satisfying conclusion.[31] To identify a problem in an apparently unproblematic situation is already to think productively, to bring about a shift in perception without being confronted with a practical problem. Processes of gestalt shift can also occur in play or experimentation without external cause. In both constellations Wertheimer therefore allows for the existence of a quotidian production of new patterns of perception independent of problem-solving and the pressure to act.

Gestalt psychology paved the way for the cognitive turn in psychology in the late 1960s. It valorized creativity as a useful and desirable quality by understanding it as a general human problem-solving capacity. Yet gestalt psychology remained confined to a narrow field of research. The psychology of creativity received a greater thrust in the 1950s from self-growth psychology and intelligence research, which raised creativity to an aim of individual and social technologies of the self. Both schools perpetuated the split between psychoanalysis and gestalt psychology, personality psychology and cognitivism.

5.4 Creativity as a Psychological Necessity

Self-realization and self-growth psychology

The significance of self-growth psychology for the transformation of the popular vocabulary since the 1950s can hardly be overestimated.

Initially a US-based movement, operating also under the names humanist psychology, positive psychology and human potential movement, self-growth psychology developed the influential model of a human psyche that wants, can and should attain self-realization, chiefly by means of individual advice and therapy but also through education and business consultation. Among the central figures of the movement were Abraham Maslow, Carl Rogers and Rollo May, at a greater remove also Erich Fromm, Gordon W. Allport and Fritz Perls.[32] Self-growth psychology grew up in the USA in the 1950s in the gap between academic psychology, with the latter's predominantly behaviourist bent, and therapy-oriented psychoanalysis. With the foundation of the American Association for Humanistic Psychology in 1962 and the *Journal for Humanistic Psychology* a year later, self-growth psychology became institutionalized. From the beginning, it was closely associated with new forms of therapeutic practice, such as Rogers's client-centred talking therapy and Perls's gestalt therapy.

Self-growth psychology brought the same kind of three-stage cultural transformation seen in other social areas, such as the creative industries of advertising and fashion.[33] An incubation phase in the 1950s was followed by a phase of counter-cultural radicalization in the late 1960s, then a period of hegemony that has continued from the mid-1970s to the present day. In the post-Second World War period, humanistic psychology was a form of cultural critique directed against social conformism. Taken up by the student movement and the counter-culture generally, it came to be infused with radical elements by figures such as Herbert Marcuse and Timothy Leary, thus ensuring it popular appeal. Finally, it lost its counter-cultural status to become the spearhead of a new, dominant therapy practice catering broadly to the psychologically sensitized and educated middle classes.

Self-growth psychology certainly did not invent the idea of self-realization. This had been the achievement rather of German and British idealism.[34] Direct references to romantic and idealist discourse are, however, scanty in the self-growth psychology literature. The most prominent reference is Herbert Marcuse's explicit borrowings from Schiller's model of the 'ludic drive' or 'play impulse'.[35] Despite this long historical run-up, the process by which the concept of expressive subjectivity was taken up, turned into science and then processed into a universal form of therapy in the field of psychology began with its absorption into the self-growth movement. The decisive turning point within the psychological field was the shift from a psychology of pathology and normality to what Frank Dumont has called a 'wellness model of human nature'.[36] The personality models of the psychiatric, psychoanalytic and behaviourist schools had shared a common concern with the problem of explaining and overcoming psychic pathologies. In contrast, the personality theory of positive psychology was not focused as previously on healing patients but, rather, on the qualitative improvement of the average person. The result of this shift of perspective was a sudden upturn in the number of people needing psychotherapy and advice. Psychological work no longer required disturbing psychic symptoms or divergence from the norm. Psychology could get to work straightaway attaining gradual improvement for anyone, whether they were normal, conformist or simply behaving inconspicuously. This constituted a structural change in the psychological techniques of subjectivization. Instead of search and destroy missions on undesirable psychic conditions, psychology was now there to mobilize potentially unlimited psychic capacities for improvement and enhancement. This form of psychology is liminal rather than limiting. The individual is supposed to strive towards an imaginary maximum of psychic maturity and wellbeing that she will never finally reach.

This transformation of the function of psychology had been under way in the USA since around 1910, initially in popular self-help literature offering guidance for the attainment of professional success, personal popularity or success in marriage and childrearing.[37] The background of self-growth psychology was the critique of average conformist behaviour levelled by authors such as David Riesman, William Whyte and Douglas McGregor in the 1950s.[38] This conformist, so-called social adaption-type behaviour had actually been a positive aim of US social psychology in the 1930s and 1940s in education, business consulting and elsewhere, providing the model for popular self-help literature.[39] Whereas social psychology had operated with the distinction between social conformity and antisocial divergence from the norm, self-growth psychology now spilt the field up differently, distinguishing between what Maslow called 'self-actualizing people' and the rest, those inhibited in their natural tendency to self-realization.[40] This ideal of self-actualization is closely intertwined with a concept of human creativity. In their model of the actualizer, Maslow, Rogers and others employed a two-pronged strategy involving typology and universality. The actualizing self is distinguished from the conformist personality type in the tradition of differential psychology, while all human beings are regarded as inherently capable of self-realization. The concept of self-realization leads thus to a clinical imperative for people actively to develop their own potential.

What exactly then is self-realization? As a psychological model, self-realization implies two elements: first, the unfurling of some inner core of individual potential pushing against outside resistance and, second, an aesthetic transformation of everyday perception. The first is *'man's tendency to actualize himself, to become his potentialities'*.[41] This can be summarized in the imperative 'What a man *can* be, he *must* be. He must be true to his own nature.'[42] This notion of self-growth as the unfolding of an authentic inner self is to be applied to an individual's whole biography. The second element, everyday attitude, Maslow terms *Being motivation* as opposed to *Deficiency motivation*, identifying it with a permanent striving for 'peak experiences'.[43] While the more common Deficiency motivations are directed to rational ends, to fulfilling social expectations, and to compensating for the deficiency, Being motivation is directed towards purpose-free experience of the moment in all its intensity. These two diametrically opposed personality types correspond respectively to the opposed poles of the rational purposive act and the perceptual act for its own sake. Those capable of self-actualization are able to transform more aspects of their everyday lives into such perceptual acts performed for their own sakes. Specific types of experience are predestined for this self-purposiveness, such as 'the parental experience, the mystic, or oceanic, or nature experience, the aesthetic perception, the creative moment, the therapeutic or intellectual insight, the orgasmic experience, certain forms of athletic fulfilment, etc.'.[44]

These 'peak experiences' are understood by Maslow as fundamentally distinct from average perceptions in instrumental action in that they involve total concentration on the object of perception for its own sake, are more complex and less selective, and take place without fear of the unknown and disturbing. This state equates to what Carl Rogers calls 'openness to experience'.[45] With the concept of peak experiences, Maslow and the other authors of self-growth psychology provided a new articulation of what in classical aesthetic discourse was purpose-free aesthetic experience, with the difference that this type of experience was now entirely integrated into everyday life, which thereby increasingly assumed aesthetic character. Positive psychology therefore represented a programme for the comprehensive aestheticization of everyday life, for permeating everyday life with *'the peak-experience... felt as a self-validating, self-justifying moment which carries its own intrinsic value with it.'*[46]

The broader, more fundamental notion of self-realization as aestheticization of the lifeworld and the narrower notion of the biographic unfolding of human potential both entail a concept of creativity extended to life as a whole.[47] On this understanding, creativity is not confined to isolated productive or cognitive, problem-solving acts alone. It is involved in the permanent transformation of everyday, selective, 'thin' perception into total, 'thick' perception. The life of the self-actualizer is defined by precisely this revolution of all areas of existence. 'Self-actualizing (SA) creativeness', which Maslow distinguishes from the merely specialized 'special talent creativeness' of artists and inventors, consists in this fundamental capacity to develop a new, aesthetic, perceptual comportment for creating objects and situations with surprising properties and recognizing such properties in the everyday world. Perception must be free of fear, and it must be non-schematic in order for surprising details to be noticed. Along these lines, Rollo May defined creativity as the ability to encounter a world in such a way as to accept it as it is instead of wanting to reshape it.[48]

The first-generation self-growth psychologists proffered their theories with a rhetorical gesture of freeing the self from its chains. The central distinction between people with Deficiency motivation and those with Being motivation was regarded as inherently asymmetrical. The first type follows social expectations, while the second type is the ideal the self would naturally gravitate towards if it were only free to do so. As self-growth psychology became more popular in the late 1960s, the self-actualizer became the model of psychological programmes, which sought to establish it as a normative ideal embodying a maximum of aesthetic, creative activity of which all human beings are innately capable. Every human being *ought* to attain this state and at the same time is presumed to *want* to attain it, whether consciously or not. It is not of crucial significance in what way the individual develops their creativity in detail, as this may vary from case to case, as long as some transformation of the structures of perception and the conduct of life towards the general ideal of the creative self takes place.

The normalizing tendency inherent in self-growth psychology is apparent in John Curtis Gowan's *The Development of the Creative Individual*.[49] Gowan adumbrates a psychological model of the developmental phases of the creative self. He reformulates Piaget's and Erikson's cognitive, moral development psychology in self-growth terms to frame the creative self and creative self-realization as the real aim of human development. On these terms, creativity intrinsically involves the transformation of fearful disorder into pleasurable complexity. Following Erikson, the decisive phases in the ontogenesis are the third, prior to school age, and the sixth, the period after adolescence. According to Gowan, social problems arise from the fact that the majority of people fail to climb up successfully through these creative phases, wasting away on the lower rungs. As he wrote, 'failure to become creative... is to fail and fall short of full development.'[50] This assertion reverses the classical psychology of the abnormal.

Instead of attributing neuroses and psychoses to excessive genius or creativity, Gowan explains them as extreme cases of retardation, of being frozen in a pre-creative, fear-laden state governed by rigid rules. His developmental psychology of the creative self culminates in a broad programme for psychological therapy and advice and a call for 'aid in the development process for full adulthood'.[51] This aid is supposed to lead to a new form of permanent, broad-based psychological support, helping everyone to climb the rungs of the ontogenetic ladder of creativity.

Creativity and intelligence research

In September of 1950, Joy Paul Guilford held the inaugural address at the 58th congress of the American Psychological Association at State College in Pennsylvania. The title of his lecture was 'Creativity'.[52] He lamented the negligent failure of previous psychological research to address the preconditions of creativity and denounced this state of ignorance as a liability for contemporary US culture. As a high-tech economy competing in a global market, the USA needed to exploit its creative resources to the maximum. Five years after the end of the Second World War, the necessity of attaining technological superiority over the Axis powers was still a fresh memory heightening awareness of the beginning political and economic rivalry with the Soviet Union. According to Guilford, the path to the highest economic and technological achievements begins in people's brains, in the seat of creativity. This prompted him to ask, 'Why do we not produce a larger number of creative geniuses than we do, under supposedly enlightened, modern educational practices?'[53]

Psychology is here once again conceived as an institution for the promotion of psychic resources rather than as a means of combating mental suffering. Like self-growth psychology, Guilford's cognitivist creative psychology was aimed at tapping into and exhausting creative potential. While self-growth psychology sought to produce holistic personalities free of the regard for social expectations, Guilford emphasized the social utility of psychology, framing creativity as a cognitive capacity for problem-solving on the model of the scientist and the inventor, not the artist.

In the 1950s and 1960s, Guilford and the cognitive creativity psychologists were also interested in the question of the holistic personality, albeit in the context of intelligence research. This had been the most influential version of differential psychology in the first half of the twentieth century, concerned not only with personality types but also with individual differences in abilities. Intelligence research

at the beginning of the century had been focused on school performance problems among children and youth until Alfred Binet and
William Sterns covered the field with their 'intelligence quotients'. In
the 1920s, with extensive series of tests undertaken by Lewis Terman,
intelligence research began honing its interest in exceptional cognitive
talent.[54] Terman referred explicitly to the classical figure of the genius,
recasting it as the 'exceptional talent'. He employed a concept of
intelligence restricted largely to the mathematical and language skills
relevant for success at school and predetermined as statistically nor-
mally distributed. Terman wanted to rehabilitate the exceptional
cognitive talent that had been discredited by the discourse of genius
as pathology, making it not a property of dubious outsiders but rather
the qualification profile of a professional social elite. His investigations were built up around long-term studies allegedly demonstrating
a dependence between exceptional talent at an early age and later
professional success, as well as between successful exceptional talents
and character stability and moral fortitude. However, in Terman's
widely received concept of intelligence, creativity is not dealt with as
a separate theme. Instead, it is subsumed as a component under general
cognitive intelligence, or 'general ability g'.

This was the point of attack for the movement of cognitivist creativity research, which began with Guilford and reached its climax
in 1966 with the *Torrance Test of Creative Thinking*.[55] Creativity was
now to be understood as an autonomous bundle of skills, the exact
relation of which to mathematical and lingual intelligence could not
be determined in advance by theory. Previous research, it was claimed,
had neglected the diversity and complexity of human intelligence.
Creative psychology diverged from previous research with a model
of multiple types of intelligence, which accorded creativity a higher
status than mathematical and lingual intelligence. Creativity was
thought to be equally susceptible to standard empirical testing as
cognitive intelligence had been. In order to isolate creative intelligence,
Guilford introduced a decisive distinction, which would have far-
reaching ramifications, between 'convergent thinking' and 'divergent
thinking'. Previous intelligence research had taken for granted that
intelligence was equivalent to convergent thinking, the ability to
perform logical operations correctly. To Guilford, this was mere
reproductive thinking useful for doing well in school. Creativity, in
contrast, was divergent thinking, the ability to develop unconventional
points of view, to digress from the beaten track of established
solutions.

This concept of creativity can be quantitatively as well as qualitatively defined. A purely quantitative definition is to be found in Frank

Barron's book *Creativity and Psychological Health*, which defined the most original answer as the one given most seldom.[56] The qualitative notion of creativity oscillates between a general identification with the ability to make new patterns and associations and a more specific ability to solve practical problems. Ellis Paul Torrance's large-scale *Torrance Test of Creative Thinking* included both elements, thereby leading to a contradiction between theory and practice. Torrance defined creativity instrumentally as an ordered 'process of becoming sensitive to problems, deficiencies, gaps in knowledge, missing elements, disharmonies, and so on; identifying the difficulty; searching for solutions, making guesses, or formulating hypotheses about the deficiencies; testing and retesting these hypotheses and possibly modifying and retesting them; and finally communicating the results.'[57] At the same time, the test series was designed to measure the kind of experimental, ludic thinking that goes beyond problem-solving. In the lingual part of the test the subject is asked to conceive unusual uses for everyday objects or to invent a story to go along with a given image.

Since the 1950s, parallel to these creativity tests, work had been done on developing practical techniques for fostering creativity. In this period, Alex Osborn developed the method of brainstorming as a creative technology.[58] Osborn understood the production of new ideas as a team effort and developed a questionnaire for setting in motion the generation of ideas. As in the experiments of the surrealists, Osborn's version of the art of creativity aimed to avoid inhibiting factors within the group, especially mutual sanctioning, and to increase mutual stimulation. The creativity techniques developed by William Gordon with his 'Synetics' group at Harvard tended in a similar direction. Here, too, a heterogeneous group was regarded as a condition of creative stimulation. This programme borrowed its imperative for promoting creativity from the artistic avant-garde. As Gordon wrote, the Synectic process involves 'making the strange familiar' and 'making the familiar strange'.[59]

As it gained ground, cognitivist creativity psychology was confronted with a problem of demarcation which reflected a difficulty involved in the practical aim of fostering creativity.[60] On the one hand, the aim of creativity psychology was to assert creativity as positive for society. On the other hand, the theory was forced to distinguish between desirable and dubious types of creative new ideas, since unreservedly demanding divergent thinking of any kind could turn out to be dangerous. Richard Crutchfield's distinction between conformist, creative and counterformist personalities is illuminating in this context.[61] The opposition between the creative and the conformist types endows the argument with a culture-critical thrust. The creative type – in contrast to the unfortunately dominant conformist – is capable of divergent thinking by virtue of strength of self. Here again, creativity need not correlate with mere cognitive intelligence, which is inclined to correlate with conformity. On the other side of this opposition, Crutchfield distinguished the possessor of creative ability from the 'counterformist'. Both the creator and the counterformist produce new, unusual ideas, but the ideas of the counterformist lack durability. The counterformist contradicts the majority on principle, seeking 'difference for difference's sake'. The results are pseudo-creative acts that make him, for example, 'the fashionable favourite of high society'.[62] Crutchfield associates the counterformist with conspicuously aesthetic, artistic character, with bohemian culture and with the bohemians' preference for the bizarre.

In the mid-1960s, Philip Jackson and Samuel Messick also saw the necessity of distinguishing productive from unproductive creativity. They admitted novelty and unusualness as necessary features of creative acts but regarded them as insufficient on their own. As Jackson and Messick wrote, 'somehow the mere oddities must be weeded out.'[63] True creativity must fit the social context, although, as the authors also admit, the creator turns out to be superior to the critic in the long run. Jackson and Messick adhere to their distinction even in the case of a highest creative step, such as an artwork capable of affording continually changing interpretations. They wrote, 'it is necessary to distinguish between condensation [the unity and coherence of meaning] on the one hand and chaotic complexity on the other.'[64]

As soon as creativity is seen as worthy of didactic and political nurturing, then the problem of the paradox of originality arises. We already saw a version of this paradox in the social field of art:[65] the true worth of a novelty cannot always be judged by its contemporaries; yet it must be judged if creativity is to be an aim of pedagogical, educational and vocational training measures. This necessity has frequently caused cognitive creativity psychology to switch from a vocabulary of the psychological and the cognitive to a vocabulary of the social, to the concern with the certification of creativity by an audience often consisting only of the psychologists themselves. At the same time, however, these public observers will inevitably interfere in the attempt empirically to gauge exceptional creative talent, to measure creativity as a cognitive structure in the human soul in a way analogous to how logical intelligence is measured. For example, when Crutchfield's counterformist takes the audience strategically into account and attempts to convince it of his creativity, then this is an unacceptable influence on the experiment. Cognitive creative psychology was therefore forced continually to adopt new approaches in order to separate what it saw as true creativity from merely apparent creativity, which is either too focused on the audience (the fashion conterformist) or not focused enough (the absurdity of the mad or the curious).

5.5 Creativity as Norm: Psychological Theories of Creative Practice

We have seen that the elaboration of creativity as a theme in psychology after the Second World War divides up into two complementary fields. Self-growth psychology was centred on the therapy of the private self, while cognitive creativity psychology was concerned with the diagnosis and promotion of creative skills useful in vocations. There is a deal of evidence to suggest that these two programmes of subjectivization have begun to converge and support each other since the 1980s. This convergence has contributed significantly to the perception of the creative self as the necessary cornerstone for a creative society. The result is what can be referred to as a *psychology of creative practice*, within which creativity becomes the centre of a whole psychological programme for the conduct of life and the performance of everyday practices on the model of a creative *habitus*, a collection of embodied schemata and strategies enabling the subject permanent and seemingly natural enjoyment of the perception and production of novelty and self-experimentation. The psychological theory of creative practice integrates the ideal of the creative self in a pragmatic of private and professional everyday life. Three main imperatives are characteristic of these technologies of the self: the transformation of everyday perception; the development of everyday creative techniques for all, extending the ideal of the artist to make it universally inclusive; and the fixation on creativity as a social strategy in the competition for attention.

Since the 1980s, there has been a growing tendency in 'positive psychology' to remodel the large-scale project of self-realization of individuals into a more constant transformation of attention in everyday life. The creative self shifts its aim from Maslow's high-flying peak experiences to Mihály Csíkszentmihályi's more quotidian flow experiences. Karl-Heinz Brodbeck situated his work in this context when he claimed that 'creativity is quotidian. Every seemingly insignificant act conceals a creative aspect which needs to be discovered. To put it briefly and paradoxically, you become creative by deciding to become creative.'⁶⁶ The decisive thing here is to start not with the human subject but with the flow of action within changing situations. From this point of view, creativity requires 'mindfulness', attunement to the uniqueness of the situation. Creativity will come about of its own accord if only given the chance; it is the natural being of everyday things when we let them be. Furthermore, there already exists an abundance of everyday techniques for opening up our perceptual capacities in this way.

Mihály Csíkszentmihályi, who was initially guided by a classical interest in the conditions for creative work by artists, discovered the phenomenon of flow as the core of this kind of everyday creative state. Flow is a dilation of perception paired with concentration on a particular task and a feeling of timelessness and satisfaction.⁶⁷ What is most noteworthy about this state is that it undermines the classical aesthetic distinction between purposive action and purpose-free perception. On the one hand, flow-like behaviour is not behaviour freed of the need to act. Indeed, it involves positive engagement with a challenging task requiring concentration. On the other hand, according to Csíkszentmihályi, this action is experienced as 'autetelic experience': an intensification and a heightening of complexity of perception as a whole takes place and is enjoyed for its own sake. This is the 'optimal experience'. The flow state occupies the exact middle between the poles of 'boredom' and 'anxiety'; it is a pleasurable form of concentration, combining receptivity and security. Creativity therefore resides not in the results of action but in altering the constitution of perception. As such, creativity is an umbrella skill. The creative habitus is capable of transforming the most banal acts into challenging situations.

The aim of these creative technologies, the objects of proto-psychological therapeutic practice since the 1990s, is the total transformation of the conduct of everyday life. Whereas brainstorming provided only methods for generating ideas, these creative technologies tend towards the permanent transformation of everyday life. In their self-help literature the artist is featured explicitly as a model, ultimately in the guise of the postmodern artist, the arranger of everyday semiotic and perceptual processes. The dissolution of the border between work and the private sphere, characteristic not only of artistic professions but also of the creative industries, provides the cultural background for this kind of permanent creative self-development. Twyla Tharp's creativity manual *The Creative Habit: Learn it and Use it for Life* provides an example.⁶⁸ On Tharp's account, professional creative work becomes a general labour of developing creativity as a personal resource that neither comes about by chance nor originates in talent, nor is obtainable by any one specific technique. Instead, creativity is an attitude of constant receptivity, a disposition to be always scanning the environment for new stimulants. As Tharp writes, 'everything feeds into my creativity.'[69] The creative self ought to develop a reflexive relation to its whole biography. The author advises all readers to draft a 'creative autobiography' using appropriate self-examination, along the lines of questions such as, 'What is the first creative moment you remember?...What is the best idea you've ever had? What is your creative ambition?' Everyone ought to develop their own creative code, the latent existence of which Tharp regards as beyond doubt. Keri Smith's advice book *How to Be an Explorer of the World* goes in a similar direction.[70] Smith takes up the enthnographic tendencies in postmodern art and recommends that everyone adopt the attitude of a collector, approaching everyday objects and situations as 'explorations'. Whether or not this experimental habitus, methodically supported by field notes, has a specific purpose, such as a project of the creative professions or art, is not explained in the book. Smith suggests simply that the experimental attitude serves the purpose of everyday practice.

Finally, a further change made by practice-oriented creativity training has been the systematic integration of the intersubjective context into creative effort. Intersubjective refers here not to the collective production of ideas – although this is also persistently being recommended by this type of training – but to the social recognition of creative achievements as new and valuable from the point of view of *audiences.* This focus on the audience is to be found in Robert Sternberg's investment theory of creativity.[71] For Sternberg, the capacity for free association, which creativity psychology had always emphasized, was just one creative skill among many. Three other dispositions are at least equally as important: the capacity to observe accurately events in the market of ideas; the ability to convince others of your own ideas; and, finally, the self-confidence to dissent. The creative self is consciously in search of unfamiliar ideas, which meet with resistance and harbour 'growth potential'.[72] The creative self takes risks and 'invests' in unusual ideas in the market of ideas when it expects by their aid to become part of the avant-garde. In contrast to Crutchfield's critique of the counterformist, who sets trends but whose creativity is inauthentic and problematic, Sternberg provides a positive model of creative individuals schooled by the contest for attention. When creative achievements are still new and controversial but have the potential to win recognition later – although this is never guaranteed – then creative enterprise and resourcefulness are needed to place bets on the right ideas that may turn out in the future to secure a popular certification that is now lacking. As well as this ability to predict future developments in the ideas market, creative individuals must possess the readiness to undertake the work necessary to convince people of the validity of their own ideas. Successful creative individuals are not now introspective artist or scientist types but rather canny self-marketers. The third and most important prerequisite is the decision to *want* to be creative. The creative individual must be willing and able to stand up against the majority. If they are not prepared to risk controversy, they will never attain recognition as an innovator.

Unlike Csíkszentmihályi, Sternberg is not proposing basing all of life on creativity. He is concerned instead with creative achievements in professional life (although his model of creativity certainly seems applicable to other fields such as the private market for recognition as a creative self). This model, which is notably diagnostic, therapeutic and normative all at once, frames the ability to think divergently by means of associations and analogies in a way reminiscent both of the artist and of the *entrepreneur of ideas* from the turn-of-the-century entrepreneurial discourse.[73] Ludwig von Mises's concept of speculation and Joseph Schumpeter's concept of the 'entrepreneurial will', which both reappear in neoliberal discourse in the context of the entrepreneurial self, are now applied to cultural ideas instead of to commodities and integrated into the model of successful creative habitus. This economic version of the creative self is at the same time a social version. The successful creative person sees through the social game of the audience certification of creativity, pursuing instead a strategy of critical otherness and *delayed acceptance*. Sternberg's response is an education programme, with the title 'Developing Creativity: 21 Ways to Decide for Creativity',[74] for training people to have the self-confidence to assume the risk of creative divergence, to calculate their chances and to endeavour to increase them by convincing others of their creative prowess.

5.6 Conducting the Conduct of the Creative Self

The transformation of the psychological complex, which turned the stigmatization of creativity as pathological into its active promotion, can be interpreted on a Foucauldian model. Admittedly, Foucault offered only fragmentary statements on the genealogy of Western psychology.[75] His writings on the pathology of abnormal forms of subjectivity are concerned mainly with the prehistory of psychology in the nineteenth century, concluding with psychoanalysis around

1900.[76] However, in order to trace the evolution of the psychological complex from the mid-nineteenth century to the present, a distinction can be extended that was introduced by Foucault in his later work in connection with other subjects: the distinction between *discipline* and the *conduct of conduct* as two different forms of control or government.[77] Applied to psychology, the two are distinguishable not merely in terms of the modes of governing the self but also in terms of notions of normality, difference and affectivity. Discipline is a mode of governing that is either negative and restrictive or positive and regulatory. Discipline denies the subject legitimate self-determination. It views inner impulses and leanings as a potential source of disturbance to be either ignored or eliminated. Discipline grasps the subject not as a self-organizing system that constructs its own world but as what Heinz von Foerster has referred to as a 'trivial machine' that can be shaped from the outside. The view of geniuses as pathological, excessive and unpredictable in thought and deed, which had been common in the nineteenth century, can be understood as a precursor to the psychology of discipline. This psychology rests on notions of limitation and exclusion and a distinction between normal, predictable behaviour and abnormal psychological and physical excess. It is interested above all in subjecting the abnormal type to treatment or excluding it, but it is also concerned with the search for signs of abnormality and divergence in everyday conduct.

This psychology of discipline begins with a focus on psychological exceptions before expanding from there into a discipline of the majority, whose behaviour is to be positively regulated. Both US social psychology, with its model of social conformity established in the 1920s, and behaviourism, which rapidly gained ground after the Second World War, can be understood as examples of such strategies, which, instead of merely presupposing the predictability of majority behaviour, seek actively to generate it by means of socialization informed by psychology.[78] The final aim of the disciplinary gaze is to normalize behaviour. This is a first-order normalization – i.e., it is directed mainly at visible conduct, while the inner world of the subject is a black box, left out of the picture, since it appears to offer no systematic resistance to being normalized. Normality is understood as inconspicuous and conformist behaviour. In an ideal world, everyone would behave in the same way. Therefore, individuality shows up as 'deviant behaviour'. Psychological discipline can ultimately be interpreted as a response to the question – arising from the rapid growth of industry, migration, cities and big business – of how a society is to ensure people behave in a predictable way. Discipline strives for the formation of social character, which was a chief task for the organized modernity of the first half of the twentieth century.[79]

This context makes it clear how massive shifts in thinking had to take place before the idea of creativity could become a positive point of reference within the psychological complex. The human soul had to come to be seen as auto-dynamic, as possessing a life of its own. Post-disciplinary psychology is naturally not content merely to recognize and unreservedly accept the self-organization of the soul. It wants to *influence* the soul, at least indirectly. This in turn presupposes an innate human capacity for shaping the self and the world. This capacity is precisely the prerequisite for a post-disciplinary form of governing, a conduct of conduct, which began looming in the early twentieth century in psychology, before picking up speed in the 1950s.

However, the question arises in which vocabulary this internal dynamic of the soul can be described and which technologies of the self follow from such a description. Psychoanalysis can be interpreted as a first version of this psychology of self-government. Psychoanalysis posited a theory of the self as a conglomerate of conflicting entities, with the aim of psychoanalytic therapy being to enable the soul to reflect on itself. However, the individual strands of creativity psychology (to which late psychoanalysis belongs) follow a different path. The soul here is not primarily a battlefield but rather a structured ensemble of *resources*, which can be exploited to enable intelligent action and to produce novel and satisfying perceptions and activities. Gestalt psychology, late psychoanalysis, empirical intelligence and creativity research, and self-growth psychology all view the auto-dynamic soul as productive and vital. Disciplinary psychology approached the soul with the intention of limiting and regulating it, while psychoanalysis demanded that the soul reflect on itself. In contrast, creativity psychologists are concerned primarily to *boost* and *heighten* the soul. This *psychology of the self as resource* assumes the creative self as the default setting, thereby helping to reinforce the creative dispositif in diagnosis and therapy.

For the first time, the psyche is no longer regarded as essentially dangerous; rather, it is viewed as a benevolent and kind entity which can be made the object of a correspondingly benevolent reinforcement and support.[80] The late modern psychology of the resource self is thus seen not merely as a therapy but also as a form of consultation. Its aim is to secure active, problem-solving individuals seeking to intensify experience rather than socially predictable subjects.[81] Ensuring motivation and quality of life and securing social innovation become leading ideas in the late modern psychological complex. Humans are seen as having a natural tendency to change themselves. Unlike disciplinary governing, affectivity and emotionality are regarded as positive resources, as sources of motivation for self-development.[82] The psychological conduct of creative conduct cannot dispense altogether with a criterion of normality, but it has developed a normalization of the second order, regulated by what can be termed an *identity in difference*. Since the soul is auto-dynamic, individuals will develop in different ways. This is acceptable as long as they conform to the general, identical category of the creative self, as long as they are truly capable of personal development and healthy self-growth and develop their own 'creative biography'. The subject is regarded as normal when it develops its individuality and expands its consciousness. This template of the creative self is contrasted to a conventionalism according to which the individual was to fulfil outside expectations rather than concern himself with developing his inner potential. Since the 1990s, a second distinction connected with the emerging hegemony of the creativity dispositif has opposed the successful to the failed creative subject. The successful creative subject skilfully obtains social recognition for creative achievements, while his opposite lacks the requisite entrepreneurial capacity for idea creation.

The psychology of the resource self that has dominated therapeutic and consulting practice since the 1980s takes elements from both the strands of creativity psychology prevalent in the preceding decades: the cognitive pragmatic strand of gestalt psychology and the intelligence research and the personality psychological strand of late psychoanalysis and self-growth psychology. The instrumental rational concept of creativity as a problem-solving faculty and the aesthetic, expressive model of creativity as the expansion of everyday experience for its own sake become intertwined here despite contradicting each other. The ideal is now the subject capable of combining her own desire for creative, aesthetic self-development with the necessity of solving problems in everyday life, work and social interaction. The goal of positive creative psychology then becomes a pragmatic aestheticization of the conduct of life in which the creative practice is both an end in itself for the expressive subject *and* a means to the end of professional and private success. It follows inevitably that the successful creative self is not only non-conformist and experimental; she also aims to obtain recognition from an audience for her creative achievements.[83]

6

The Genesis of the Star System

The Mass-Media Construction of Expressive Individuality

A culture guided by the ideal of creativity will inevitably develop a corresponding notion of human individuals as creative subjects. There are two main ways this concept of the creative subject is formed and disseminated: first, by means of practices aimed at training creative skills and, second, by means of representations of creative subjects as appealing role models. As we saw in the previous chapter, the psychology of the self as resource, with its consultancy and therapy practices originating in the 1970s, continues to contribute significantly to the training of everyday techniques and motivation in the worlds of work, business, administration and education, nourishing the private and professional realization of the creative self. Since the beginning of the twentieth century, an apparently unrelated but in fact complementary process has been taking place: the widespread representations of creative subjects as 'celebrities' or 'stars' in the mass media, especially in visual form. Beginning to radiate out from the USA around 1900, these representations are evidence of a new interest in the display of celebrated individuals in visual and text form.[1] Only a select few from very specialized professions are capable of becoming stars. They tend to be characterized by strong 'expressive individualism'. Their apparent uniqueness and cultural productivity can be realized and expressed both in works and in the presentation of a public image.[2] Modern stars turn out to be the successors of the figure of the artist. They are the objects of an aesthetic public gaze. They are not people with whom the public communicates or has dealings in any way except as objects of an aesthetic – i.e., a sensuous, affective regard which is enjoyed for its own sake.

Three different ways of attributing creativity to a star can be distinguished: first, as the producer of a work (the work star); second, as the creator of their own self (the personality star); and, third, as the creator of a work consisting in physical performance (the performance star). All these three star types attract attention from a public who regards them as having produced something new, unusual or original. This creative achievement is perceived as an aesthetic event, as a sensuous, affective end in itself. The creative product of the work star is the aesthetic object, whether artistic or not, while its author figures as the work's fascinating representative. In the case of the personality star, the star's body and biography mesmerize the public as the original product of an act of self-creation. In the case of the performance star, the audience focuses on the star's own bodily performance, whether on the screen or the concert stage, as the 'work' itself, beheld in the process of its coming about. As a star, the creative character is extroverted rather than introverted, seeking audience certification of their success as a producer of aesthetic novelty.[3] The expansion of the star system to encompass movie actors, pop groups, painters, directors, architects, comedians, talk-show hosts and chefs reinforces the creativity dispositif by increasing the popular appeal of the creative subject as an ideal. The star becomes the template of an ideal self[4] because her achievements as an expressive individual consist in the public attention she receives, her attainment of a higher degree of social recognition.

6.1 The Mass-Media Regime of Attention

The growth of popular interest in the creative star marks the most recent stage in the development of the subject-oriented regime of attention.[5] Early commentaries on the development of the star system, the best known of which originate from the Frankfurt School, include Adorno and Horkheimer's examinations of the culture industry, Benjamin's notion of the secondary aura of the film star, and Leo Löwenthal's analysis of the 'idols of consumption'. These theories tended to frame the star system as a feature of mass culture in strict opposition to bourgeois culture.[6] We will set aside here this assumption that mass culture represents an historical rupture. We will argue instead that the star system originates further back, resulting from the transformation of the regime of fame, the truly novel aspect of which was the emergence of the ideal of the artist. Leo Braudy has elucidated how the modern and late modern conditions of fame fundamentally differ from those of antiquity, the Middle Ages and the early modern period.[7] Fame can be understood as the growth of intense, enduring public attention and acknowledgement directed at exceptional individuals. The classical form of fame from antiquity to the early modern period was associated mainly with political, military and church leaders. In contrast, the modern version of fame prevalent since the Renaissance was tightly bound up with the individual works of artists. In the twentieth century, fame was metamorphosed into *stardom*, broadening out to include diverse versions of expressive individuality appearing in a variety of media.[8]

The characteristic form of the modern star is in stark contrast to the earlier political paradigm of fame. In traditional societies, fame tended to depend on birth and on the offices of political power, neither of which correlated significantly with achievement.[9] The connection of fame to public office tended to exclude private life from fame's ambit. In contrast, with the artist, a new paradigm, a modern form of fame develops, whereby public attention is directed at the extraordinary achievements of individuals without regard to their original social rank. These achievements are then not connected with political power but, rather, involve the production of artefacts such as artworks, which would formerly have been insufficient to provide fame. As we have seen, the view of the artist as expressing herself, her inner ideas and imagination, in a concrete work makes her a prototype of the self-creating expressive subject.

In the late nineteenth century, as the cult-of-genius version of the myth of the artist began subsiding, the entire culture of fame shifted to the media star as the new exceptional, expressive individual. There are two sides to this shift. First, attention was now directed to the star's public *and* private life. Second, the star was both exceptional and mundane. Stars are represented by the mass media as essentially public figures. At the same time, however, their artistic or professional achievements are not the only matters of concern. Their personal relations and interests, their dress, also become integral parts of their public image. Celebrities are suitable as ideal role models because they are not defined by professional and artistic achievements alone. They can be presented in the round as total personalities. They are quotidian in that their work and their personality represent cultural types (Marlon Brando as the lonely rebel, the Rolling Stones as angry young men).[10] Yet they are made exceptional by the fascinating idiosyncrasies of the works they produce, by their performance or their personality, which escape conformity to any familiar type and thus come to be invested with an aura.[11]

The modern form of fame in general and the figure of the star in particular are both contingent on a basic structural condition. The star is embedded within mass-media representation and is thus a result of the revolution of media technology. While the representation of the artistic genius since the Renaissance was at first closely tied to the mass medium of printing, the constitution of the star since the end of the nineteenth century has been informed not only by the growth of periodical printed matter and star journalism but, more importantly, by the emergence and dissemination of the technical, reproductive media of photography, recording, film, television and, more recently, the internet. The apparently trivial fact cannot be overemphasized that the mass media have the effect of placing masses of people over long periods in the position of receivers, of members of an audience who, instead of actively engaging with or generating events, are merely involved in their cognitive, aesthetic, sensuous observation.[12] If modern society is typified by the widespread growth of an *audience function* in a variety of social fields, then the aesthetically interested audience is one outgrowth of this development.[13] Further, if the audience is an important precondition for the emergence of the creativity dispositif, then the mass media clearly assume a function of pacemaker for the development of the dispositif. From their very beginnings, the mass media are placed in a structurally analogous position to the social field of art, with which they are also interconnected, in that both fields address human beings primarily as recipients.[14] The star as the object of admiration presupposes the emergence and expansion of this observer position of the audience.

In a related sense, the mass media provide a technological precondition for the emergence of the creativity dispositif in general and the system of the creative star in particular. They do so by virtue of an inherent *preference for novelty* of the cognitive and aesthetic variety.[15] There is a reason for this preference. The technical capacities of the text- and image-based mass media allow them to provide audiences with an overabundance of signs and sensuous impulses. They open up a whole new sphere of possibilities for mediated perception and communication as a supplement to direct perception and face-to-face communication in everyday dealings. This surplus engenders competition between media and non-media events as well as between different media events, with all parties vying for audience attention. Accordingly, the mass media develop strategies for attracting attention. The most important strategy – the production of events that can be presented as novel – is so fundamental that it is almost never examined. This preference for novelty is expressed in 'news' as well as entertainment, new hit records, new publications, and the parade of ever-changing, unusual celebrities. This endows the mass media with a systematic tendency to age quickly.

The systematic preference for novelty goes hand in hand with a second, apparently countervailing tendency: the production of symbolic *markers* capable of securing more enduring public attention. These markers (popular television series, central political themes, classic authors, etc.) must be sufficiently productive of symbols to provide constantly new and surprising events despite their more permanent character. A third characteristic of the mass-media preference for novelty is affectivity. The purely cognitive acquisition of information – for example that involved in the daily news – is also an instance of media novelty. However, the late nineteenth century saw the spread of a media regime of novelty based primarily on sensuous stimulation and affective excitation, on aesthetic surprise for its own sake.[16] It was hoped that the production of *affective* stimulation – whether excitation, shock or milder affects of surprise or interest – would be able to attract and hold attention to media events.

At the heart of this mass-media regime of aesthetic novelty is the representation of stars. People become stars by distinguishing themselves from 'ordinary' individuals in some relevantly interesting way. The star system constantly catapults new celebrities into public awareness, setting them apart by some new divergence from the norm and promising a constant stream of new works and events in their wake. Despite their recognizability, stars are not fixed subjects but, rather, 'epistemic objects', constantly transforming themselves in such a way that their audience can never quite pin them down.[17]

Stars are thereby able to establish themselves as symbolic markers, securing attention over a long period while at the same time maintaining interest in their person by consistently producing new events or works. The star is an aesthetic event. In the context of the mass media, especially the audio and visual, the representation of people as opposed to things or abstract entities has accrued an enormous inherent power to generate sensuous, emotional excitation: 'names make news'. This applies to stars in particular, who come to be perceived by the public as fascinating objects of identification. It also applies to a lesser degree to notorious figures like terrorists or mass murderers.[18]

The affective stimulation afforded by the presentation of stars is heavily dependent on the media revolution that replaced writing culture with audio-visual culture.[19] This transformation altered the conditions for the representation of human beings. Stars figure only secondarily on the textual level, in magazine articles, biographies, etc. Their natural habitat since 1900 has been the medium of technically reproduced images, motion pictures and sound recordings. Formerly, the medium of writing tended to represent people in their psychological interiority. Now, the audio-visual media train us to regard people primarily in terms of their perceptible surface.[20] The star was able to become a fascinating ideal self in large part because of her ability to be the subject of sensuous experience through the widespread mass-media presence of her image, and also her voice, so that the performance of her body becomes the subject of an aesthetic gaze.[21] It can justifiably be claimed as a general fact that the media star system has been training modern society since the 1920s to approach human beings as perceptible bodies with faces and voices. Driven by audio-visual culture, the form of the ideal subject has shifted from interior 'character' to the fascinating exterior 'personality'.[22] On the level of the affects, the relation between the observer and the star image oscillates between two modes: objectification and identification. In the first mode, the libidinous investment in the star can turn the latter into a fascinating and almost sacral object of adoration. In the second mode, this investment can tip over into identification, 'the transformation that takes place in the subject when he assumes an image',[23] with the recipient now assuming the place of the star and taking her as a role model for shaping his own self.

In what follows, we will undertake a step-by-step genealogy of the mass-media star system and how it has been helping to establish the creativity dispositif. We will begin with the emergence of the artistic star in the second half of the nineteenth century in the USA. We will then turn to the movie star system that began to develop in the 1920s and the music star system since the 1950s. Finally, we will see the expansion and generalization of the star system that has been occurring since the 1980s.

6.2 The Artistic Star as Performing Self

The figure of the star first emerged in the cultural context of the USA in the second part of the nineteenth century. At this time, publicly exposed individuals began to be transformed into objects of spectacle. Artists in particular became the centre of a new regime of visibility. However, this regime did not operate by means of control and division along the lines of the Panopticon studied by Foucault.[24] Instead, it engendered identification and affective stimulation. As we have seen, since the advent of the modern myth of the artist, the artist has occupied the attention of a bourgeois audience convinced of the existence of an inextricable link between the work and its author. Since the Renaissance, artist's biographies and autobiographies, artist portraits and, in its own way, art criticism had all served the interest in the artist by reinforcing the conjunction of work and individual.

Interest was particularly directed at figures of the past regarded as classical, establishing retrospectively the fame of their works.

The first contours of a genuine system of artistic stardom began to emerge in the second half of the nineteenth century in the USA, especially around literary figures such as Walt Whitman and Mark Twain, but also extending to Charles Dickens and Oscar Wilde, who were more or less appropriated as American authors in the course of their American lecture tours.[25] At first glance, this phenomenon may appear to be a mere extension of the general public interest in authors generated by the artistic field. However, the gradual establishment of the star system was contingent on factors originating outside of the bourgeois artistic field and endowing the star with the property of pronounced public visibility. These factors undermined the boundary between high culture and popular culture. This caused public attention to be drawn to stars as performing selves, who are simultaneously quotidian and exceptional.[26] Three such factors can be distinguished.

1   In the last third of the nineteenth century, before the development and dissemination of audio-visual media, the USA print media were already inventing what Ponce de Leon has called *celebrity journalism* and *human interest journalism*, genres of mass-media information and entertainment concentrating public attention on prominent individuals and so turning them into stars.[27] Human interest journalism operates largely with text but also uses combinations of text and photography. Initially a product of non-bourgeois popular press oriented towards spectacular news and novelties, the genre developed subtler versions of itself based on nuanced personality description, such as in the magazines *Vanity Fair*, the *New Yorker* and, later, *Life*. Other related journalistic genres also developed, chief among them the interview, the home story and the photo feature. This type of journalism is interested in the connection between professional achievement and private life. It is premised on the claim to penetrate to the expressive personality *as it really is*. Its typical prey was always some prominent individual whose professional achievements were relevant to the public and who could also demonstrate a non-conformist personality – as one handbook from the 1920s revealed, 'a person who does things in a unique, original way'.[28] Human interest journalism implied a general ideal model of an expressive subject whose creativity entered into their personality and biography, not just their 'work'. Artists such as Mark Twain and George Bernard Shaw became 'favourites' of turn-of-the-century personality journalism, but also politicians,

scientists and entrepreneurs such as Theodore Roosevelt, Albert Einstein or Henry Ford were elevated to prominence.

2   The media visualization of the body of the celebrity turned artists into performing selves independent of any works in the form of objects. They became representative of a personal, embodied style that the public could imitate.[29] In the middle of the nineteenth century, focus shifted to visual artists and writers, who, since the 1880s, could be made more manifestly present through the medium of photography, while the written presentation concentrated correspondingly on the description of outward mannerisms and idiosyncrasies. The American painter James Abbott McNeill Whistler was exemplary of this new typecast artist. Whistler's recognition was of course partly because of his work. At the same time, however, he was one of the first artists in the USA to make a concerted effort to direct media attention to events in his private life and to his eccentric appearance and appearances. Authors such as Walt Whitman and Oscar Wilde had already used the medium of press photography before Whistler to transmute their outward appearance into spectacle and become representatives of the bohemian or dandy styles.[30] Characteristic of these forms of image-building is once again the combination of the exceptional and the everyday. On the level of pictorial representation, the artist star is able to become a unique, seemingly impeccable object of desire. At the same time, as the representative of a style, he is (in opposition to the producer of works in the traditional sense) suitable for imitation by the viewer, who can appropriate his accessories, poses or other features.

3   A model of the public developed in the USA that contributed to the establishment of the early star system. This model was legitimized in an ambivalent way, illustrated by a popular genre cultivated in particular by authors since the mid-nineteenth century: the lecture tour. While the lecture tour was precisely not a media event, it was based on the visible presence of the body and the artist's voice intoning before a live audience present in the same space. Authors such as Dickens, Beecher-Stowe, Emerson, Whitman, Twain and Wilde all made successful use of this format.[31] Before the advent of film, the lecture tour was the only way for stars to make themselves perceptible as moving bodies and speakers before a larger audience. However, the real significance of the lecture tour is revealed against two aspects of the cultural background: first, the republican model of the public sphere, in which the community is mirrored in the fame of some personality; and, second, an entertainment model of the audience.

As David Blake[32] has pointed out, fame became accepted currency in America after the Revolution. Individual striving for fame was no longer understood as egoistic; rather, it was considered as a form of service to the democratic public. The public saw itself mirrored in the exceptional achievements of this individual from its very own midst. The admiration for famous personalities dovetailed with a self-confirmation of the public as a democratic community. This American model of the public can be termed a *political* model, in that it involved a collective representation of the charismatic individual in question. In this context, Walt Whitman was able to understand the cult around his person during his lecture tours as strictly democratic. His poetic achievements were then a service to American society and his appearances were the expressions of those latent powers slumbering in each and every individual.

However, the lecture tour also manifested an aspect of the public that is focused primarily on spectacle, on beholding the exceptional for its own sake. This version of the public developed in the mid-nineteenth century in the context of American entertainment culture, an important founding father of which was the circus entrepreneur P. T. Barnum.[33] Barnum presented living curiosities and orchestrated spectacles, transforming talent, animals and atmosphere into attractions. At the circus, the audience no longer admired itself through its political stars but, rather, admired the star as the producer of exceptional things and the supplier of sensuous attractions. The lecture tour itself becomes a kind of travelling circus, falling under the influence of this second incarnation of the public as the community of seekers of pleasurable observation. The early star, who presented himself in lectures, is thus ultimately both at once: a representative of the masses and a spectacular object of observation. In both senses, the bodily presence of the star is the object of an admiration legitimated by the culture.

The ambivalent model of the public as democratic and spectacular representation, the visualization of the star and his personal style, and celebrity journalism provide the framing conditions for the displacement of the original European myth of the genius by the US version of the artistic star. At the same time, the field of the performing selves capable of attaining stardom in the late nineteenth century extends beyond the artist.[34]

6.3 Creative Performance

Creative achievement was traditionally attributed to different types of artists, whether authors, painters or composers, for having brought works into being. As the artist was gradually transformed into spectacle in the late nineteenth century, creativity was still seen as bound up with the authorship of works, although tendencies to frame creativity as personality (for example in celebrity journalism) and as performance (for example in the lecture tour) were already present. Things began changing in the 1920s, and then more rapidly again in the 1950s, with the rise of the film actor and pop musician as exemplary embodiments of twentieth-century stardom. These artists were attributed creativity above all as performing artists on the basis of an aesthetic of presence.[35] The work of the performing artist is identical with the artist's staging of their own body. Unlike writers, painters or composers, performing artists do not disappear behind their work. Film actors and pop musicians are present bodily in the performance or execution of their work, albeit often via media. The aesthetic experience of the audience is directed towards the performance of the star rather than towards an aesthetic object in the narrower sense. In other words, in performing art, the artist shapes herself creatively and presents herself to an audience as the object of her own creation.

The older concept of creativity as contingent on works remained influential in some segments of the star system in the twentieth century, as it has in the twenty-first. But there is much evidence to suggest that the star system was able successfully to disseminate the ideal of the expressive subject to a mass audience on account of the institutionalization of creative performance, mainly in film and music.[36] From the perspective of the cultural history of subjectivity, the recognition of the aesthetic achievement of actors and musical performers is an unusual turn of events. Both were regarded as mere interpreters, inferior to the artists who create the original works they execute.[37] Actors and musicians were then able to change from marginal types to prototypes of culturally recognized aesthetic creation as a result of the technical methods of reproducing performance in film and music. Yet this change was more significantly dependent on a corresponding change to the concept of creativity; creativity consisted no longer in the work but in the aesthetically exciting performance of the performing self.

Film stars

Along these lines, the Hollywood film industry provided the institutional framework for the gradual mutation of movie actors into stars. Richard deCordova has elaborated the many preconditions for the establishment of the movie star.[38] The earliest films around 1900 were regarded by audiences as mainly technical, visual spectacles, in which the players themselves were of little interest. This changed with the growing awareness of the movie star, of actors who were known by name and whose identity for the audience persisted across different films. Florence Lawrence is often credited with being the first such movie star. The movie star bore a structural resemblance to the stage star, but the latter lacked one necessary ingredient. The private life of the film performer had yet to become the object of media interest, which interest was in no small part fired on by the film industry itself. The movie star came to be staged as a *total* personality, encompassing her performance both in film and in life.[39] The display of the star's private life fascinates the viewer with its combination of opulence and crisis. The movie star swims in luxury and sets trends, but her life story is ever haunted by catastrophe.[40]

The movie star becomes the prototype of creative performance by appearing in film and elsewhere not only as someone playing a role and embodying a type but also as a self-shaping expressive subject in her own right. An important part in this development was the method acting developed by Lee Strasberg from Russian avant-garde theatre of the 1940s. The method was first taught to stage actors, who were encouraged to take up experiences and emotions from their own lives in order to embody the part in the moment of playing.[41] Every small gesture, every facial expression, every inflection of speech, every disposition of the body in space can be individually shaped by the actor. The method allows actors to forge their own character portrayal while also seeming to funnel real-life experience into the performance.

The most prominent actor trained in the method was Marlon Brando. Brando is exemplary for the way the figure of the actor has become a powerful symbol for independent expressive individuality since the 1950s.[42] Brando's stardom is founded in large part on the idiosyncrasies of his performance, which produces continual surprise and manifests his self-created individuality. His long silences, his intense gaze, the refined stutter technique, the provocative exhibition of his own well-made body and the unpredictability of his motions all contributed to the suggestion of his individuality. Brando's highly individualized and emotional acting affects the audience in the instant of viewing while at the same time embodying the attractive social type of the 'wild young man'. Further, the audience perceives Brando not only as a performance star but also as a celebrated personality in his own right away from the cinema, yet whose personal qualities are closely tied to his screen performance.

Although method acting was a specialized theatrical task, since the 1950s it has influenced the subjectivization of American and European movie actors. This subjectivization by method acting extends beyond the type of the glamorous star from between the wars to make the film actor a prototype of distinctively individual performing creativity, for which the presentation of the body is the object of creative effort and design. When the performance is sufficiently strong, the star's off-screen personality is reduced to derivative significance, although it must still be visible. For the star to become an object of identification in the fullest sense, her off-screen life must be publicly displayed. The star quality of the person is nevertheless dependent on their film performances being regarded as exceptional.[43]

However, a further variant of the appealing creative subject began crystallizing in the movie world from the 1950s, which somewhat curtailed the importance of the movie star. This new creative subject was the director, growing out of the *cinéma d'auteur* of the French Nouvelle Vague and 'New Hollywood' or 'American New Wave'.[44] The film director has since come to be regarded as an artist in their own right. More importantly, the director now represents the prototype of a postmodern creative subject, attaining star status by authoring surprising combinations of diverse materials: narratives, symbols, persons, places, spaces, objects, camera styles, music.[45] Directors earn star status not as creative performers (except in the case of those who are also actors) but as creators of works in the broader, postmodern sense: in this case because they are creators of atmospheres. Figures ranging from Ingmar Bergman to Alfred Hitchcock, Wim Wenders and the Cohen brothers combine work creativity with a mass-media personality style; they are members of an additional group of global creative celebrities who have emerged from within the mass media.

Pop stars

Pop music was a further area that made a decisive contribution to the establishment of the modern figure of the star.[46] The 1950s were also the central historical turning point for pop music. Like the actor, the pop star provided a model for creativity as star performance coupled with the additional elements of the production of works and the creativity of personality.

In the post-Second World War period, the pop star was the focus of an initially young but increasingly aging population. The pop star is the producer of aesthetic novelty on all three levels. *First*, the core of the star quality of the pop musician is their physical, vocal performance in live concerts and on recordings. This performance is offered as an individual and novel achievement, calculated to be distinguished as much as possible from what audiences had previously been familiar with. The pop singer's performance includes both the recording of their voice, as a vestige or trace of the body,[47] and the live concert. Pop music and pop stars possess an affective power of attraction rooted most deeply in this sensuous presence of the body and the voice. *Second*, the pop system and the pop star strive for aesthetic novelty in terms of harmonics and melody. In this respect they are thoroughly consistent with classical music. Pop and rock stars are thereby also work stars, at least when they write their own music. Pop music characteristically attempts to increase the number of newly composed music titles, accelerating their distribution and aiming always 'to break and remake codes'.[48] *Third*, the musical star is also a personality star. A large part of the aesthetic novelty of the pop star is their personality as a whole. Of crucial significance to personality is the aesthetic style, manifested in clothing and body movements.[49] At the same time, a pop musician's individual style becomes the model for the collective aesthetic style of their (mainly youthful) audience.

The popular music that preceded latter-day pop music grew up in US cities in the late nineteenth century.[50] Its beginnings were in live music from music halls and theatres. At that stage, it was already performed by prominent interpreters whose song sheets were published for a middle-class audience. Composition and performance were strictly separated. The new songs were routinely composed by anonymous 'tunesmiths', while the singers, who were familiar to the audience, were distinguished above all by technical proficiency. As the song sheets were gradually replaced by gramophone records, the figure of the private listener emerged alongside that of the concert attendee. The technical reproducibility of music increased the sizes of audiences while also extending music into the private sphere of the listener. Modern and late modern pop and rock music in the proper sense emerged in the mid-twentieth century in the context of a set of structural changes, prepared above all by the subcultures of black urban music in the 1920s and 1940s. This made it possible for the pop star to become a popular creative subject disseminated by mass media with a structural resemblance to the artist and at the same time a figure with whom the audience could identify. Johnny Ray and Elvis Presley were among the first stars in this system, which rapidly increased in complexity in the 1960s.

The first of the above-mentioned structural changes was the transformation of the live concert. The pop star appearing on stage is defined less by technical precision than by the individual performance experienced by an audience affected by the singularity of the event.[51]

Presley's erotic singing voice and body motions on stage were revolutionary, setting the style for the long term. Now, pop musicians were not only singers or instrumentalists; they were total artworks for the stage. The musician could attain stardom through the specific structure of the pop and rock concert as a multi-sensory performance, atmospherically dense and improvised for an audience that becomes a collective participant. While the production of music recordings entails the loss of the interactive character of concerts, by concentrating the artist's voice and the instrumental accompaniment, the recording is intended to make the expressivity of the pop and rock artist tangible in the individual sound. The recording is more than just the particular song; it is an individual performance of voice and instrument, delivered to listeners to be experienced in private.[52]

The second prerequisite for the establishment of the pop star was the aesthetic stylization of the star's body through diverse accessories, drawing on diverse youth and subcultures and reinjecting impulses into them. Pop stars have been massively influential stylistic innovators of whole lifestyles, comprising clothing, facial expression, manner of speech, and body posture. These stylistic innovations presuppose an audience actively interpreting and emitting signs, to which the musicians react in turn. The aesthetic stylization of the body and the extra-musical personality become the themes of mass-media focus on the pop star. The pop star is more capable than the movie star of presenting themselves as an ally of youth and subculture, as an agent of cultural divergence and as a creator of aesthetic novelty that is not only culturally different but counter-cultural.[53]

Finally, since the late 1950s, two further structural features of the modern pop and rock star have been developing. First, there has emerged the subject form of the singer-songwriter. The second feature is the function of the concert as a crowd gathering, viewable via media. Following in particular the assimilation of folk traditions, some musicians began performing their own compositions and lyrics (prominent examples being Bob Dylan, John Lennon and Paul McCartney, and Brian Wilson).[54] The legitimate artistic status of the musicians was thus further heightened by the presence of a work in the classical sense, thus making musicians into work artists. A final characteristic of the pop system is the self-referential nature of stardom resulting from the media presentation of the *audience*. The presence of huge crowds at live concerts is itself the object of media presentation. This figure of the crowd is ironically parodied in the 1964 Beatles film *A Hard Day's Night*,[55] in which the four musicians are harried by swarms of teenagers. Despite early cultural critique directed against crowds of fans allegedly suffering from hysteria, this focus on fans increased the power of audience identification with the stars. Audience attention is attracted most powerfully by those objects already at its centre. The result is the culture of the attraction *of attraction*.

The British pop group The Beatles illustrate paradigmatically this feature of the pop star in the 1960s and the many levels of their 'creativity'.[56] This case shows the inner tension at work in the pop star system between the development of types securing audience access and aesthetic individuality invoking the myth of the artist. The Beatles began in 1959 as a type of precursor boy band before reinventing themselves in the mid-1960s as an artistic rock group. They developed an appealing group style imitable by a young audience, deploying mod haircuts, androgynous posturing and uniform suits, all of which brought them high public visibility for their concert tours and television appearances. Thanks to their unique sound and their unusual, ludic, yet casual stage presence, their live performances were received by critics and audiences alike as a demonstration of high aesthetic quality. In this first phase of the band, the tendency to represent a type prevailed over idiosyncrasy. The Beatles stood for a fresh and uncontrived experience of music and style, with their air of being workaday, uncomplicated local boys from Liverpool supplying teenagers with popular dance music – a persona the aesthetic novelty of which wore off within a few years.

At precisely this point in the mid-1960s, The Beatles managed to transform themselves. They retained continuity with their former identity while starting down a new path of aesthetic experimentation both on the musical and on the personality level. Beginning with the album *Revolver*, they successfully made the transition to 'avant-garde' music with the value of surprise, combining rhythm and blues with other music styles such as folk, electronic and classical, managing thereby also to attract the interest of art critics. This technically more demanding music forced them to pass from concert performance to studio performance. Ultimately, the media spectacle of the four band members' after-work personalities (such as their voyage to India or the marriage of Lennon and Yoko Ono) assumed a character of self-discovery, absorbing appropriate motifs from the newly forming counter-culture. They also executed ironic parodies of their own star status, such as with the cover of *Sgt. Pepper's Lonely Hearts Club Band*. The Beatles thus transformed themselves in the second half of the 1960s from a relatively fixed object into a mobile object of aesthetic projection for the audience. The Beatles and their products were characterized by an unpredictable mutability, making them a source of aesthetic novelty up to and beyond their final break-up.

6.4 The Expanding Star System

The movie star and the pop or rock star are the most prominent elements of the twentieth-century star system and have the effect of aestheticizing social perception in two ways. First, the perception of the star is informed by an interest in the sensuous and affective aspects rather than in information. Second, in their work, their personality and, especially, their performance creativity, stars function as expressive individuals constantly producing aesthetically relevant objects. Meanwhile, the mass-media audience takes in the stars' presence, training themselves to see people in general with a primarily aesthetic gaze, perceiving them in their expressive and creative potential as appealing role models. This aesthetic sensitization of the audience by the star culture of film and music thus provides a powerful impulse for the establishment of the global creativity dispositif. Within this context, film and music have become central elements of the global creative industries.

The star system attained its mature, late modern structure in the 1980s within the framework of the creativity dispositif. There is significant evidence to suggest that it has since spread throughout the whole culture, strengthening its influence, while the star has become less dependent on expressivity and creativity. This has increased the number of subject types capable of attaining stardom in the mass media and thus lessened the importance of movie and music stars. These late modern stars generally conform to the model of the expressive creative subject, often reinforcing the paradigm of the performance star. The further expansion of the star system and the growth of the performance star can be seen most typically in the areas of television (such as the talk-show host) and sport (in the European context, most prominently in soccer). Sporting celebrities appear at first to belong to a whole other register of heroes and victors, but sport turns out in time to be the locus of a popular 'aesthetics of presence'.[57] It can be argued that the rising popularity of soccer since the 1990s is due to this aestheticization. Its appeal is based on the aesthetic qualities of the game and the players' capacity for stardom (with David Beckham here the most prominent example); it is due not least to the players' individuality and aesthetic, stylistic quality and the presumed genius of their game, combined with qualities of off-field personality. The soccer celeb is naturally anything but a work star. He is instead a performance star like the actor and the singer. The audience perceives the player as a moving body displayed in the execution of a performance regarded as creative.[58] Television celebrities, such as the talk-show hosts Oprah Winfrey and David Letterman, are performance stars of this sort. The star status of television personalities also relies on the fact that they can be observed in the act of bringing off an aesthetic achievement, specifically in the form of a verbal performance emphasizing the entertaining form of expression rather than content.

In addition to the performance stars, the old and new work stars (who are also always personality stars) enter the late modern star system. In our examination of the postmodern artistic field emerging in the 1980s we saw artists achieve a new type of prominence as celebrities. This applied especially to visual artists[59] but to writers and directors as well. Mention can also be made of cartoonists, street artists and related figures who were not recognized previously as artists. The rapport between the work and the personality of the postmodern artist is paradoxical. On the one hand, the work, whether recognized or controversial, is the condition of stardom. On the other hand, the mass-media interest is directed only secondarily towards the work and primarily towards the self-creation of an artistic personality with a distinct, individual style.[60] Yet the individual artist is merely one node among many in a comprehensive, multitudinous star system. Qualitative differences in judgement between creative achievements, for example those implied by the high-pop distinction, are increasingly flattened out in favour of the unified measure of quantity of attention. Other professionals located outside of the arts in the broader aesthetic economy contribute to an expansion and diversification of the domains of the work star and to a lesser degree of the personality star. This is especially true of the areas of fashion, design and architecture.[61] Other professional fields are capable of leading to stardom to the extent that they can be understood as involving creative subjects producing works capable of being received on aesthetic terms; they are not seen as performing merely technical or cognitive tasks. In the humanities, for example, intellectual stars following in the footsteps of Jean-Paul Sartre have occasionally gained huge media attention. Entrepreneurs also turn out to be capable of stardom in the more exceptional cases where they have been able to style themselves as 'creative'. In the twenty-first century, Steve Jobs and Mark Zuckerberg have taken up this role.[62]

The star system has expanded in scope and diversified to include new types of subjects present in the media to whom can be attributed achievements in the creation of (primarily aesthetic) novelty, whether actors, singers, visual artists, comperes, athletes, fashion makers, designers, architects, intellectuals or creative entrepreneurs. These perceived aesthetic achievements can take the form of films, songs, stage appearances, images, installations, spectacles, athletic activity, clothing, aesthetic utensils, recipes, buildings, urban design, theories or the stylization of personality. As such, most late modern star types operate within the framework of the expanding aesthetic economy. This expansion of the star system has been accompanied by two further developments. First, it has become easier to commute between different types of stardom and creativity. Second, media test genres for becoming a star have emerged. In the first instance, movements of commutation across the borders between these specialized subsystems can be observed. Given the right circumstances, symbolic capital in the form of attention and 'creative skills' gained in the one subfield can be transposed to another. Actors are painlessly transformed into directors, designers into writers of books, footballers into fashion models, intellectuals into film-makers. An example of the second case are the 'casting' shows for pop singers that have emerged since the beginning of the twenty-first century, in which stardom-prone individuals are systematically discovered, subjected to comparison with one another and trained.[63] Becoming a star thus comes to be based on a set of rational prerequisites. However, star training involves a paradox. It suggests that star skills can be learnt, whereas the public attention required to elevate someone to the status of a star can by definition be devoted only to a select few.

The expansion and diversification of the star system entrains its own countervailing tendency. It leads to a decoupling of public attention from publicly certified creative achievement. The originality of a work or performance, its status as a valuable and aesthetically interesting novelty, is fundamentally dependent on audience appraisal. Yet audience attention to media celebrities can become separated from the real ability of the star to produce something *valuably* new in the public's estimation. This separation of attention from creative value is most apparent in two cases: the notorious or negative star and the pure personality star – that is to say, the pseudo-star. Since the emergence of the mass-media star system in the 1920s, the authors of spectacular acts of violence, especially serial killers and mass murderers, have received enormous public attention, sharing many attributes of star status.[64] The monstrosity of such acts breaks through the familiar membrane of the routine, causing the perpetrators to be regarded as exceptional personalities. Aided by the growing popularity of an aesthetic of evil and the uncanny, these perpetrators exercise a morbid, sensuous and affective allure on the public.[65] The notorious attain stardom in the most genuine sense of being the creators of aesthetic objects within a regime of novelty. The novel work they produce, consisting of their personality and their crime, is usually denied the attribute *valuable* or *exemplary* from the very same public that acknowledges their stardom. Negative celebrities exhibit no socially acceptable creative skills and are nevertheless objects of intense fascination and often cumulative, enduring attention. They are successful at attracting attention despite having no recognized creative achievement to show for themselves.

More frequently, this separation of attention from creative worth applies in a less drastic way to the pure personality star. Since the emergence of the star system in the film industry, and then increasingly in television and through magazines such as *People* (since 1974), there has also come to exist a type of star who has created neither a specific work nor a special sort of performance. Their stardom resides instead entirely in the media presentation of their perceived personality.[66] This type of star can be termed a pseudo-star in distinction to a genuine star. The pseudo-star operates by the following mechanism. Blessed by the coincidence of some minimal divergence from the norm, whether positive or negative, media attention accumulates around the budding pseudo-star, making them into a durable symbolic marker drawing public interest to their private and professional life in a self-perpetuating upward spiral. The pseudo-star possesses a low degree of novelty and sensuous-affective excitation but a sufficient amount to establish prominence. The heart of this mechanism is the self-referential spiral of attention in which interest is increasingly channelled to some figure who for whatever reason has already been receiving sporadic attention.[67] The affects the audience feels towards such pseudo-stars are more ambivalent than those towards the star in the real sense and can turn sour. The pseudo-star is then no longer perceived as a fascinating ideal self but as an everyday person to be encountered with contempt and malicious glee. The audience becomes aware of the star's artificiality as a media invention, which undermines the legitimacy of their claim to fame.

The pure personality star and the negative star share an analogous discrepancy between achievement and success. Neither has produced a recognized creative object, yet both enjoy social success as the objects of durable public attention.[68] The star system thus contains the potential to undo the connection between the creative subject, the aesthetic object and the audience, shifting all the focus to the audience, which is susceptible of being affected by any and every novelty, whether it recognizes it as worthwhile or not. The star system thus makes possible a dispositif which simultaneously awards and withdraws distinction from the creators of aesthetic novelty.

7

Creative Cities

Culturalizing Urban Life

7.1 'Loft Living'

In 1970 *Life* magazine ran a richly illustrated special edition on New York with a brief text presenting the city to the magazine's middle-class readership. This is not the New York of Blake Edwards's *Breakfast at Tiffany's*, the luxurious centre of elegant partygoers indulging in idleness and seemingly free of the burden of paid labour. Nor is it the New York that filled the screen in Martin Scorsese's *Taxi Driver*, the grimy pit of violence, danger and facelessness. Holly Golightly would be as alien a presence in the city portrayed by *Life* as would Travis Bickle. Bearing the title 'Living big in a loft',[1] the article is an exposé of the unconventional, forward-looking New York lofts and their counter-cultural yet established artistic inhabitants, representatives of a milieu blending creative endeavour with gregarious leisure. A decisive feature of this artistic class is the type of space which acts as its stage. Here, the scene is set in former factory buildings transformed into studio apartments.

The article in *Life* introduces the attractive new loft lifestyle to a larger nationwide audience.[2] 'Loft living' in New York in the 1970s was initially a curiosity, but in the decades to come it wrought a deep structural transformation upon cities in North America and Western Europe. The spatial structures of the old industrial and administrative centres have since been progressively forced aside by forms of urban living and working, leisure and tourism, that continue to transform them into symbolic and aesthetic centres of culture, thus bringing about a *culturalization* of the city. In the course of this culturalization, cities are now being metamorphosed into sites for the permanent production of novel signs and atmospheres. They are becoming 'creative cities'.

This later development is already prefigured in the *Life* article, which introduces the 'creative city' as a new cultural ideal. The article is arranged around four large-format photographs. The first shows a typical Manhattan canyon filled with a traffic jam of trucks, framed by massive, shadowy, turn-of-the-century buildings rearing up above the caption: 'Behind these grubby façades lurks an artists' colony.' The second photo affords a peek behind the façade. We see an enormous, dimly lit hall with a collection of minimalist artworks – a combination of studio and apartment. The third large-format photograph shows life in a loft in all its spectacular glamour: a huge living space with massive, free-standing wood columns, a wooden floor polished as smooth as a mirror, the room spanned by a white wall bearing huge specimens of pop art and postmodern photography. In the foreground, on a suite of furniture made up of pieces of diverse styles thrown together sits a relaxed and stylish couple, while in the background a child traverses the vast expanse on a bicycle. The loft in the fourth photo is populated by party guests engaged in conversation. The space seems to serve as a studio workshop but is loosened up by an enormous red and blue cushion on which some of the visitors have draped themselves. The 'Japanese-born' host is enjoying a game of table tennis with one of the guests in the background. In the story he comments on the dimensions of the loft, asserting its bearing on his creative capacities when he says, 'If you live and work in very small apartments, your ideas get very small.'

Life in the loft apartments of New York's Soho district is endowed by the article with attributes which will turn out to be the blueprint for the transformation of urban space in the subsequent decades. American middle-class families after the war came to adopt an ideal of strict separation between living and working. They migrated out to the suburbs to commute into their offices in the city. Meanwhile, the New York artistic class adopted a model of keeping their inner-city living and working spaces close together or even combining them. Since the 1920s, New York's inner city had been home to artist colonies. In the 1950s individual artists had begun to use industrial buildings as spartan work and living spaces. Now, the *Life* article shows a loft-living art scene which is no longer restricted to a marginalized set of bohemians set apart from the established educated middle classes. The art scene had become the vanguard of a broader cultural shift: the middle classes themselves were becoming a 'creative class'. This role-model function was made possible partly by the growth of the artistic class. In the early 1960s, New York was home to just under 4,000 artists. By the 1970s, artists and workers from related fields numbered 50,000. Artists were thus ingested into New York's diverse creative economy. The photo set in *Life* demonstrates how the artistic scene managed to combine motifs from the counter-culture with the ideals of the American middle classes. In contrast to the mythic projection of Jackson Pollock as a heroic artist in Hans Namuth's short film,[3] the Soho artists in their studio homes are stylized as the representatives of a lifestyle which could serve as a legitimate model for a broader public. The combination in one space of creative, self-organized work, leisure and the private sphere, together with the non-conformist aesthetics of the spaces, is appropriated from counter-cultural prototypes. At the same time, however, the artists are framed as the representatives of an ideal, egalitarian nuclear family and successful participants in a professional interactive network. In stark contrast to the precarious existence in the artist's garrets of the post-war period, the new loft apartments are ostentatiously high class, yet renovated and furnished to make them resonantly authentic. In this way, the outsider artist is relieved from duty by the successful creative professional.

The loft space is more than just a backdrop for the lifestyle of creative persons. It is a constitutive condition for their creativity. The space is unusually large in comparison with that of other contemporary apartments and offices, and it is usually open plan rather than being subdivided along functional lines. The floors and ceilings are generally wood panelled, with the ceiling beams deliberately left visible. The look of the lofts is frequently characterized by their bare brickwork and iron fire escapes. The buildings have been appropriated from a previous epoch and subjected to a change of use.[4] These relics of the industrial age are thus transformed into bearers of a postmodern industrial aesthetic. Once industrialization has come to an end, its architectural vestiges are no longer associated with hard physical labour performed on faceless machines. The architecture is now experienced as the sign of an authenticity predicated on its continuous historical use and the perception of the building materials as natural. The postmodern aesthetic approach is to combine historical and contemporary elements, especially in the interiors. These former factory floors appear as though predestined for the realization of an individual style that draws on diverse historical sources and overthrows the design paradigm of the typical suburban family house.

The loft is particularly well suited to the production of 'atmospheres' of the kind of sensuous-affective moods the Japanese artist is invoking when he says, 'If you live and work in very small apartments, your ideas get very small.' According to Sharon Zukin, the loft provides space for the social drama of everyday life.[5] The concept of the social drama was first introduced by the urban historian Lewis Mumford in reference to the modern metropolis as a whole.[6] The interior layout of the lofts provides a private setting in which to play out the drama of the social by providing the atmosphere of spaciousness otherwise found only in representative public buildings. The capacious space exudes neo-aristocratic excess, satisfying late modern society's need for self-realization, while the unification of the open-plan space encourages a flexible and experimental usage, suggesting a 'holistic' lifestyle. The loft turns space into an object to be systematically enjoyed. It is not just a background but an exhibition venue for the varied lives of its inhabitants and their visitors.

The *Life* magazine feature 'Living big in a loft' marks an historical transition. It is the transformation of urban space brought about by agents who were neither quite the mainstream nor exactly the counter-culture.[7] This point of transition is indicated by the ambivalence of the images. The last photograph in the article shows a group of guests absorbed in conversation while their host plays table tennis in the background, suggesting a professional yet hedonistic social network. In contrast, the photo with the minimalist artworks awakes associations with some occluded underground culture far from the middle-class norm. Notably, the series of photographs is restricted to the interiors of the lofts, emphasizing the difference between inside and outside. The cosy interiors are opposed to the inhospitable public space outside. In the 1980s, a further development was to emerge in New York and elsewhere, as the aestheticization of space shifted from the interior to the exterior and became an object of systematic urban planning policy.

7.2 The Functional City and the Cultural City

In the modern world, the social becomes increasingly concentrated in urban spaces. Each historical version of modernity since the eighteenth century has endowed the city with its own characteristic type. The current, late modern phase of transformation to the globalized metropolis in the West and elsewhere began in the 1970s. It is perhaps exemplified most pointedly by the rise of lofts. Urban planning discourse has given this phase the programmatic title *creative cities*.[8] From a distanced, sociological point of view, it is this development which can be understood as the *culturalization* of the city, increasingly turning it from a functional into a cultural entity.[9] The culturalization of urban space constitutes one of the pillars of the creativity dispositif. The main feature of this transformation is the city becoming a production site for new signs, experiences and atmospheres. 'Creative city' is a value-laden term denoting a positive ideal, but in the context of a theory of the creativity dispositif it must be interpreted differently. The modern metropolis is not 'naturally' creative.[10] It is not endowed with an innate capacity for creativity that had been germinating all this time, waiting finally to break into flower. Instead, since the 1980s, cities have been actively shaped to make them capable of producing constant aesthetic novelty.[11]

Because of the overall significance of the phenomenon of the city for modern society, its culturalization is of particular importance for the creativity dispositif to assert its power. Cities are total social phenomena, not exclusively assigned to one functionally specialized system such as the economy, art or the mass media. They combine diverse social practices – such as work, home living, art or science – each of which has its place in whole forms of life. The particularity of the cities as social entities is that they distribute *space* and coordinate artefacts and people within that space. Cities generate a social materiality of their own which has a greater historical persistence than that of signs or actions.

Since the Chicago School of the 1920s, urban sociology has tended to understand the city primarily as a spatial arrangement of inhabitants and has inquired into the social inequalities between cities' individual residential areas. Along these lines, Louis Wirth defined the city by means of three features: size, density and population diversity.[12] However, in the light of the newer theory of the interplay of space and culture, we can develop a more complex view of the city.[13] As social entities, cities can be divided into three levels. On the first level, they are viewed not only as conglomerations of human inhabitants but also as systems of material artefacts; while they exist *in* space, as implied by the traditional concept of space as a container, they also *produce* space in the form of buildings, traffic routes, shaped natural environments (parks) and energy infrastructure (water, sewage, electricity). Cities are *social* complexes in an expanded sense of the term 'social', meaning that they are high-density networks of subjects as well as objects, people as well as things.[14] Second, these material entities and their spatial structures influence which practices inhabitants and users can perform within them, while at the same time being generated and shaped by their users. On this second level, the city *is* the way it is used. It consists precisely in the everyday modes of interacting with its material structures, which *produce* space by structuring it. Third, these practices involve processing specific signs, mental maps, images and discourses of the urban which endow the city with cultural meaning. If cities are to be grasped as total social phenomena, then it is in part by virtue of the way all these three levels interconnect. This invests them with cultural relevance and material continuity and durability.

Under modern conditions, urban development makes a significant contribution to the formation of the creativity dispositif in part on account of its close connection with politics. Urban space concentrates activities of state control manifested in representative architecture and public places, public housing projects, transport infrastructure, and the promotion or inhibition of public action. In cities, the exercise of political power is not restricted to the abstract imposition of laws and regulations and the manipulation of the flow of money. It also involves the shaping of material space. By addressing the role of cities in the genealogy of the creativity dispositif, we are able to see that a crucial development has taken place since the 1990s, whereby the state control of the lower, local levels of society has helped to secure and disseminate the creativity dispositif with its aesthetic imperative.

The gradual emergence of the culturally oriented city since the 1970s cannot be explained without reference to the *functional city* which preceded it and which represents its opposite.[15] Different versions of the functional city emerged throughout Europe and North America in the 1920s and 1930s. It can be regarded as the spatial equivalent of the Fordist 'organized modernity'[16] that had developed in contradistinction to the bourgeois city of the nineteenth century.[17] For these classic European cities from the seventeenth to the nineteenth century, the stark dualism between the city and the country was just as fundamental as the distinction between public and private space. These cities, with commercial capitalism as their *raison d'être*, characteristically concentrated important functional locations of bourgeois life at their geographical centre. In the second half of the nineteenth century, they became subject to large-scale urban planning projects, most prominently in Paris under Baron Haussmann. The bourgeois city soon found itself on the defensive, lacking the means to deal with the massive changes imposed on it by industrialization, by the influx of rural migrants, and by the emergence of the proletariat. By the end of the nineteenth century it was threatened with social disintegration.

The functional city was an effective response to the crisis of the bourgeois city. From the 1920s to the 1970s, it dominated the urban planning discourse both in the West and in the new socialist societies, having a transformative effect on the shape of the city.[18] Established economically on industry and administration, the functional city was a radical response to the problem of the organization of work and living for the masses. The solution was to create a new urban order based on the separation of work and living space, banning both from the inner city in order to maintain standards of living and quality of life. This made the regulation of both individual and public traffic the main design problem. The functionalist ideal of urban planning was the *series*, the capacity to reproduce a prototype, whether in the form of apartment blocks or single family homes. Functionalism was aesthetically inclined towards an anti-ornamental purism, extending into the extreme details of interior design – for example in Le Corbusier's 'Unité d'habitation', or housing unit. The functional city appeared in two versions. The European version was dominated by the concentration of people in apartment blocks, while the US version was suburban. Le Corbusier typifies the European version, while Frank Lloyd Wright represents the USA.[19]

The functional city and the Fordist economy began to enter a crisis of legitimacy in the early 1970s. Two phases of this crisis should be distinguished. First, there emerged the alternative model of a culturally oriented city occupying social niches. This was taken up within critical discourse among planners and architects, while it was realized in practice by the occupation of the inner city by counter-cultural elements and subcultures and by the post-material middle class. Since the 1980s, this cultural dynamic has become a goal of urban politics itself. The most conspicuous expression of this was the 'Towards an Urban Renaissance' programme initiated by the British Labour government in 1998.[20] Both the critical, counter-cultural urbanism discourse and culturally orientated urban planning have since been promoting an active culturalization of urban space to counter the perceived alienation and standardization of the functional city. These culturalization strategies encompass three elements: *semiotization*, *reflexive historicization*, and the sensuous, affective *aestheticization* of urban space.

What are culturalization strategies? Cities are always already cultural. Inhabitants and planners move through them with specific cognitive maps, they are charged with semiotic and symbolic character in everyday living, and different neighbourhoods exude different sensuous, affective atmospheres, however these are felt by different people. All this applies also to the functional type of city. The term 'culturalization' refers therefore specifically to a *reflexive* stance to urban culture that began to be adopted in the 1970s by city dwellers and visitors, as well as by the urban economy and public planners. This reflexive stance is geared to consciously increasing, intensifying and concentrating signs and atmospheres in the city. In the context of the late modern city, 'culture' has since become an unreservedly positive concept. 'Culture' is combined with the vitalist connotations of dynamism and movement that find expression in the label 'creative cities'. When cities endeavour to stylize themselves as creative, they are deploying a strategy of culturalization in order to mobilize and expand their cultural resources.

The culturalization of the city involves, first, *semiotization* – i.e., an increase and concentration of the symbolic qualities of urban spaces. The city comes to be understood as a generator of signs. The symbolic density of the culturally oriented city is opposed to the symbolic emptiness of the functional city. Culturalization involves, second, a reflexive *deployment of history*, a new appreciation and appropriation of the city's historical legacy that is made to harmonize flexibly with its current state. Third, culturalization involves *aestheticization* as the final goal of the entire process. Aestheticization is here to be understood in the narrower sense of the systematic heightening and concentration of sensuous, affective urban atmospheres with the aim of providing users with sensuous and emotional satisfaction independent of the city's practical functions. Both the semiotic and historical concentration turn out ultimately to be means to the end of this aestheticization. The aesthetic recoding and the aesthetic enrichment of the city are intended to contribute to the development of a satisfying atmosphere. Louis Wirth's seminal definition of the city containing the attribution 'high population density' implies that the culturalized city strives for a new type of density, not only a density of inhabitants and artefacts but also a *cultural density*, a new intensification, concentration and dynamism of signs, histories and atmospheres.

In what follows, we will attempt to retrace the genesis of this urban culturalization and its contribution to the establishment of the creativity dispositif. Critical urbanism emerged in the 1960s in opposition to functionalism. Since the 1970s a multidimensional movement of culturalization of urban space has been emerging, concentrated on aestheticizing the inner city, generating economic creative clusters, postmodern consumer spaces, and the gradual transformation of the city into a museum, or 'musealization'. Since the beginning of the new millennium, a cultural *governmentality* of the city has been emerging, promoted by the state and endeavouring to establish the 'creative city' as a place for the permanent production of aesthetic novelty.

7.3 Critical Urbanism

The revolt of the sensuous

The vision of the culturally oriented city was initially introduced by the urbanism discourse of the 1960s in opposition to the state-planned functional city. The culture movement was boosted by the student and protest movements and in turn laid the groundwork for diverse movements within subcultures, the counter-culture, the educated middle classes, and critical urban planners and architects, all of which began gaining force around 1970. These movements were geared towards a regeneration of those parts of the city that had fallen victim to the functional city, having either lost their functions or become dilapidated or depopulated. This regeneration involved reviving such neighbourhoods as residential, leisure and work areas. Even in this early phase, elements of critical urbanism entered into local government policy, for example in the form of the protection of heritage sites. The critical urbanism discourse is a complex of different demands for the utopia of an aesthetic, semiotic and historically rich city in the interests of its inhabitants and users. At least four strands can be distinguished within critical urbanism: a humanist culturalism, typified by Lewis Mumford and Kevin Lynch; a cultural revolutionary urbanism, such as was sketched by the French situationists; a middle-class vitalism, propagated most prominently by Jane Jacobs; and the urbanism of critical architects of the 1960s such as Aldo Rossi and Robert Venturi.[21]

The cultural historian Lewis Mumford and the urban planner Kevin Lynch both subscribed to an ideal of the city originating in the early modern period, from which they saw real cities in the post-war United States as having made a radical departure. They defended this ideal on humanist, anthropological terms, characterizing it by means of the aesthetic tropes of drama and the image. For Mumford, who had already levelled criticism at the transformation of the city in the late 1930s, cities must be organized around providing citizens with a 'theatre of social action' or 'social drama'.[22] The city is here the scene of a Goffman-like 'presentation of self in everyday life', providing its inhabitants with an intense and varied experience. As Mumford wrote, 'the city fosters art and is art.' For Mumford, the public performances of urbanity that intensify experience are not necessarily harmonious and peaceful, but they are contained within a clearly defined and compact spatial centre.

Kevin Lynch's metaphor for the ideal city is the well-made image.[23] Lynch assumed an opposite position to that of conventional urban planning – that of the user, a psychological, aesthetic being with emotional needs experiencing the city sensuously. This sensuous experience is primarily visual, and the ideal city provides the inhabit- ant with a constant supply of new 'emotional satisfaction'.[24] To answer the psychological question of how this satisfaction is to be attained, Lynch deployed the criteria *legibility* and *imageability*. Legibility is the city's capacity to be grasped as a coherent meaningful whole, while imageability is its ability to generate strong, memorable and positive images both in its parts and as a whole. The ideal city is able to make of its constitutive elements, its paths, edges, districts, nodes and markers, a sensuous impression that is 'visible, coherent and clear'.[25] The ideal city, paradigmatically the city of the Italian Renaissance, is for Lynch neither dynamic nor chaotic but, rather, aesthetically stable and classically harmonious.

Whereas Mumford and Lynch saw the aesthetic experience of the city as residing essentially in repetition and routine, the French situationists advanced a vehemently dynamic notion of urban experi- ence, which they placed within a broader social context.[26] In the 1970s, fashioned chiefly by Guy Debord and incorporating impulses from surrealism and Henri Lefebvre's urbanist theory, situationist thinking exerted a decisive influence on the relation between counter- culture and the city in locations such as Paris, West Berlin, Bologna and Zurich. The situationists' cultural revolutionary gesture was directed towards attaining a fundamentally new, sensuously and affectively satisfying situation of everyday life in the city. As Debord wrote, the aim is to 'reduce the empty moments of life' and 'to multiply poetic subjects and objects – which are now unfortunately so rare.'[27] The *dérive*, an everyday technique of purpose-free roaming in the city, is the most important tool in the situationist kit. For the *dérive*, the urban environment is a sensuous, affective and semiotic field of stimulation for the observer to submerse themselves in. Against the tedium of repetition, the city is here understood as the place of potential encounters with surprising 'otherness', with relics of historical events, with foreigners and unfamiliar milieus. Paris is the paradigmatic case. Both aesthetically minded users and an aestheti- cally usable urban space are needed for the city to be transformed into an aesthetic environment. The historically heterogeneous urban landscapes, in which distinct temporal and semiotic layers overlap, appeared to the situationists better suited to this than places of expres- sionless functional architecture. They opposed the everyday aesthetic practice of *dérive* to what Debord terms the *society of spectacle*. Whereas the society of spectacle was based on passive consumption, the situationists now proposed the autonomous creative appropriation of the city. Henri Lefebvre's influential extension of situationist thought sees interaction with the city as an encounter with an *espace vécu*, a lived space, a sensuously, affectively experienced space without a particular order, rather than with an *espace conçu*, a conceptually grasped, categorized space.[28]

The ideal of the city as a 'lived space' can be found in a somewhat more profane version in what is arguably the internationally most important piece of urbanistic critique from the 1960s, Jane Jacobs's *The Death and Life of Great American Cities*.[29] Jacobs saw US urban planning in her time as having fundamentally failed on account of its basic mistrust of the possibilities of urban space. According to Jacobs, this is true of the seeming opposites represented, on the one hand, by functionalist planning à la Corbusier, with its extreme density of living functions, and, on the other, by Ebenezer Howard's garden movement, with its ideal of the small town.[30] 'Urbanity' is for Jacobs a vitalist watchword. The most important condition of 'vitality' or 'liveliness' is diversity. Cities need a diversity of milieus, practices, architectural styles, impressions and experiences. Diversity is made possible by 'mixture of use' of houses, streets and quarters. Mixture of use is opposed to the functionalist and suburbanist vision of a strict spatial and functional separation between living, working and leisure. Big cities consist not of macro-units but, rather, are made up by the combination of smaller, specialized and highly individualized entities: specialist shops and cultural activities. Jacob thus provides a postmodern model of the city *avant la lettre*, cultural heterogeneity but as harmonious and idyllic rather than menacing, invoking 'wonderful, cheerful street life'.[31]

According to Jacobs, urban planning must therefore shift from a 'mechanical' to an 'organic' planning perspective. This view assigns important functions both to the revitalization of older quarters and to the modification of the look of streets to make for a maximum of visually appealing interruptions and irregularities. Every street should be as individual and unique as possible. Diversity cannot be planned in the strict sense but should occur naturally. This natural growth can be facilitated by creating the right conditions. As Jacobs wrote, 'most city diversity is the creation of incredible numbers of different people and different private organizations.... The main responsibility of city planning and design should be to develop...cities that are congenial places for this great range of unofficial plans, ideas and opportunities to flourish.'[32]

While Jacobs argues from the point of view of urban planning, the same conclusions were arrived at by those who were part of the critical architecture scene of the 1960s. The critical architects were

interested not only in individual buildings but, more importantly, in
the reorganization of cities as a whole. Functionalist architecture and
urban planning had attained international hegemony by 1928 at the
latest with the founding of the Congrès internationaux d'architecture
moderne, the International Congresses of Modern Architecture. From
its inception, scattered critique had been levelled against functionalism, in the post-war period prominently by Alvar Aalto and Oskar
Niemeyer.[33] However, the decisive blows against functionalist architecture were dealt by the planning projects of Robert Venturi and
Aldo Rossi.[34] Venturi aggressively extolled a programme for a semiotic
turn in built space, thus kick-starting the architecture of postmodernism under the principle that architecture unavoidably bears semiotic
and symbolic connotations that are decoded by the observer with the
aid of cultural knowledge. The international style, with its functionalist city, stood accused by Venturi of marginalizing this everyday
semiotic which now had to be revitalized. According to Venturi,
architecture should make use of the redundancies and contradictions
which are inherent to signs and stimulating for the common observer.
Architecture should be understood from the point of view of this user,
who will always prefer a common, everyday building to the heroic
monuments of modernism. At the same time, Rossi called for a radical
historical recontextualization of building. Individual buildings should
be incorporated into the social space of the city, into the 'historical
legacy' of the aesthetic and spatial structure as it stands. Rossi thus
paved the way for the heritage movement and its critique of the
blanket demolition of the historical inner city in the post-war period.
Despite their differences, Venturi and Rossi shared in common the
view that an appropriately contemporary architecture must be based
on the pre-existent semiotic, aesthetic and historical forms already
firmly planted in the city and in users' minds. Architecture thus has
the task of designing total atmospheric spaces. As Hans Hollein wrote,
'Architects have to stop thinking in terms of buildings only. Built and
physical architecture, freed from the technological limitations of the
past, will more intensely work with spatial qualities as well as the
psychological ones.'[35]

By turning its back on functionalist architecture and urban planning, critical urbanism diverged from the conception of novelty that
had been pioneered by Le Corbusier and urban modernism. From the
point of view of the international style, the modern city was a place
of maximum novelty, which, once attained, possessed universal value
and could only be replicated in this form. By attempting to develop
'final forms of expression – formal types – from new technical and

spatial conditions',[36] forms of expression that differ from the bourgeois historicist way of building, architectural modernism was able to set up a stark opposition between the novel and the old. At the same time, the novelties of this supposedly universal modernism came to appear aged to its users after just a few decades, with the eternal reproduction of the same housing blocks, satellite towns, car-friendly inner cities and factories. By calling for a revival of the historical, pre-functionalist building fabric, critical urbanism advances the old against the new without committing the fallacy of nostalgia. It supplants the model of static, technical (and political) novelty with a model of mobile aesthetic novelty oriented towards the autonomous sensuous and affective user. The revival of historical building fabric combined with the strongly symbolic content of contemporary architecture empowers the user to transform urban space into a space of lived experience, a place for practising *dérive*. The cultural legacy of the past therefore serves not so much the purposes of conservation as that of enriching the potential for semiotic and sensuous experience in the here and now.

7.4 Features of the Cultural City

As we have seen, critical urbanism provided the background for a revival of the historical inner city as a living and working space for subcultures and the art scene as well as for critical architecture and urban planning, a place in which historical building fabric and post-modernist architecture can blend. However, the further culturalization of Western cities extends beyond these tendencies. As in the other social fields that contributed to the rise of the creativity dispositif, critical urbanism's stance of opposition to hegemony inverted into a new form of hegemony. This systematic self-culturalization is mobilized by four collective *agents of culturalization*, which are at the same time agents of aestheticization and the individual aims of which conflict with one another: *first*, the urban art scene and subcultures seeking spaces for community and stimulation in the inner city; *second*, the post-materialist educated middle classes, often employed in the aesthetic economy, influenced by a universal creative ethos of self-realization and travelling to other cities as cultural tourists;[37] *third*, the locally or globally active enterprises of post-Fordist consumption and the creative economy, finding market locations for setting up creative clusters in the culturalized cities; and, *fourth*, state policies guided by the ideals of cultural regeneration and the creative city, which thereby constitute an important factor for economic development while also increasing the attractiveness of the city for inhabitants and visitors.

Urban culturalization mobilized by all four culturalization agents encompasses several intertwined processes: the expansion of aestheticized urban neighbourhoods, especially in the historical inner city; the establishment of an urban art scene; the spatial concentration of the creative economy in creative clusters; the concentration of places dedicated to the consumption of style and experience; the renaissance of urban high culture in postmodern form, characterized particularly by the rise of museums and cultural events; and the state subsidizing of spectacular monumental architecture.

Aesthetic neighbourhoods

A fundamental aspect of the transition from the functional to the cultural city is the aestheticization of the inner city and surrounding districts and their transformation into new living, working and consumer areas.[38] These neighbourhoods are generally characterized by historical building fabric from pre-functionalist times. In Germany and elsewhere, such buildings originate from around 1900; they are industrial buildings capable of being converted and, occasionally, historically older buildings from the early modern period. This historical building fabric is partly supplemented by post-functionalist architecture.

'Cultural regeneration' of inner-city areas – their being turned into residential areas – is the exact opposite of the model of the functional city. In 1925, Ernest Burgess proposed as a general rule that modern urban development led, first, to the spatial separation of living, working and commerce and, second, to residential areas being successively pushed off to the outskirts, while a belt of quarters with older architecture accumulates in the short term around the city centre, inhabited mainly by socially or ethnically marginal groups.[39] Supported by suburbanist politics on the one hand and an extreme concentration of state subsidized housing on the other, this prognosis of the decline of the historical inner-city quarters became a reality. However, when the artistic and alternative scenes and the new middle classes moved in, the process hit reverse. As early as the 1960s, inner-city districts with older buildings emerged into prominence as prized residential areas in locations such as New York's Soho or London's Islington. This movement swelled to a broad front in the 1980s in many Western cities. The main feature of such neighbourhoods is the way they combine living and working, gradually attracting specialized boutiques and restaurants, entertainment and culture in a way roughly equivalent to Jane Jacobs's model of mixture of use.[40]

The revitalization of the inner city as a mixed-use area has often been connected to the sociological concept of gentrification. The term was first used in 1964 by Ruth Glass in the context of London.[41] The gentrification theory posits the interchange of community groups with diverse social status. According to the theory, gentrification begins when those belonging to counter-cultures and subcultures move into vacated and underprivileged areas. This leads to social upgrading, which in turn draws in the middle classes. At a certain point, this begins to force out underprivileged groups and the less liquid segments of the counter-cultures and the artistic scenes themselves. Finally, the middle and upper classes rule the roost, consolidating their dominance with luxury renovations. This diagnosis is surely accurate in many cases, yet it presupposes a *cultural* motor driving the process which the theory does not explicitly account for. The deeper root cause of gentrification is the aesthetic, semiotic culturalization of the inner city by its new population, a process subsequently driven by media attention, the real-estate sector, local shops and local public intervention. The new inhabitants – whether they belong to the counter-culture or the post-materialist middle classes – populate only those quarters promising not just economic profit and social prestige but also semiotic, aesthetic appeal.[42] For the late modern city to become a site of gentrification, it must first have become an object of aestheticization. This culturaliza-tion of the historical inner city involves the three elements mentioned above: the rise of semiotics; the rise of historical reflexivity; and sensu-ous, affective aestheticization in the narrower sense.

The first phase of cultural regeneration is the *semiotic recoding* of the area and its historical building fabric. In this phase, the location is symbolically reinvested and put to new uses.[43] Recoding injects new signs into an area previously either burdened with negative connota-tions (dilapidated, dangerous, ugly, lacking in amenities) or empty of associations altogether. The foundational hip/square binary with which we have become familiar in the spheres of fashion, design and pop music since the 1960s is here seen at work in urban space. Richard Lloyd has suggested the phrase *grit as glamour* to describe one such recoding strategy deployed in Wicker Park in Chicago.[44] Taking up elements of bohemian aesthetic, the once shabby or faceless area is recoded as picturesque, bizarrely interesting and authentic, as *cool*, in marked distinction both to the suburbs, with their isolated single family homes, and to monotonous mass housing units. Historical industrial districts are especially well suited to recoding, since they seem to contain revivable traces of previous inhabitants and times past.[45] The recoding of the space leads its new inhabitants to approach its architecture with an aesthetic attitude. The historical building fabric is used for present purposes to generate affectively stimulating atmospheres. It is not enough for the built-up space to be historical. It must be *perceived* by the inhabitants as historical. This historical reflexivity has a paradoxical structure. Historical sites are interpreted as authentic while at the same time they are subjected to reappropriation; the past is both celebrated and at the same time unceremoniously given over to an alien purpose. Along these lines, former factories are turned into lofts or clubs, Wilheminian workers' housing is turned into apartments for the educated middle classes, and former mass residential areas from the turn of the century become centres of art, fashion and design. This aesthetic appropriation follows a typical, post-modern pattern,[46] combining 'retro fashion' – that is to say, the reappropriation of the past as the source of aesthetic satisfaction – and 'pastiche' – the mixing of disparate signs and usages of different times and spaces.

The rise of semiotics and reflexive historicity in inner cities merges with aestheticization in the narrower sense of the transformation of previous sensuously, affectively neutral or even repulsive locations into aesthetically enjoyable ones. In an investigation of cultural regeneration in the 1990s in two neighbourhoods in Barcelona, one historical and one industrial, Mónica Degen shows that both the everyday semiotic of the places and the everyday visual, auditory, olfactory and tactile interaction with the city as a whole had been transformed.[47] In the tradition of the vitalist metropolitan aesthetic, this sensuous experience of the urban favours concentration and variability of stimulus – as long as this takes place in a basically safe environment. The fact that neighbourhoods undergoing cultural regeneration at first still harbour ethnic minorities, those occupying the lower social rungs and other marginal groups is welcomed by the new inhabitants as a refreshing aesthetic enrichment of their daily lives. Social diversity provides semiotic, aesthetic variety, turning *grit* into *glamour*.[48]

The cultural regeneration of the historical inner-city quarters has brought with it a change in the way the city is perceived. Since the 1980s we have seen the emergence of a transregional, even global audience observing via mass media specific cities and neighbourhoods for their cultural value.[49] Cities had already been the objects of outside interest as places of state or church rule, trade or science. Now, however, they are increasingly evaluated for how much urban vitality they provide, how much diversion and intensity they furnish through their signs, history and sensuous atmosphere. Historical forerunners of this cultural way of perceiving cities and neighbourhoods are the artistic quarters in bourgeois society such as Montmartre in Paris or Greenwich Village in New York in the early twentieth century.[50] However, the aestheticized urban districts of late modernity burst the frame of the picturesque artistic quarter. Although they could at first be regarded as counter-cultural or alternative (as was the case in the 1970s and 1980s in Kreuzberg, Berlin), they have since become universally prized symbols of vitality. The aestheticized districts of culturally rich cities exercise a double attraction, drawing new inhabitants from other districts, regions or countries as well as tourists. Ideally, these places are perceived publicly as *buzz cities*, *places to be*, whether to live in or just visit.

To what extent do the culturalization and aestheticization of urban living space help to develop a regime of creativity? The answer is that both processes are led by an interest in aesthetic and semiotic novelty.[51] This interest assumes a different guise in each phase of local development within the broader *cycle of urban aestheticization*. In the first phase, that of occupation and reappropriation, an initial aestheticization transpires as the social space is recoded. Sense perceptions and moods are radically transformed despite the fact that no architectural changes have yet taken place. Now, the old quarters appear *new*, they are something to be *discovered*. In the second phase, the social space is transformed by the growing influx of new inhabitants, by renovation, new buildings, restaurants and galleries, giving the area a dynamic and unfinished look of work in progress. There is a constant bubbling up of new semiotic, aesthetic stimuli. In the third phase, the new building work and the influx of people begin to level off. The everyday aesthetic has shifted away from 'grit as glamour' and now often follows the pattern described by Mónica Degen as *designer heritage aesthetics*,[52] where dignified renovation is combined with postmodern architecture. The city celebrates a semiotic, sensuous diversity which has been voided of danger and disorder. The cycle of aesthetic novelty progresses on the surface level, with new cafes, galleries and boutiques sprouting up, while the district constantly develops new styles and types of shopping and entertainment experience without altering its deeper substance. This phase harbours the danger of *aesthetic saturation* and loss of momentum. This can cause the aesthetic process to wander off to other districts or cities, which then in turn reinitiate the cycle of recoding and subsequent processes.[53] This semiotic, aesthetic revival of previously uninteresting districts by furnishing them with a new identity becomes easier and easier as the total extent of aestheticized zones increases.

'Creative clusters'

The systematic rise of cultural and aesthetic novelty is also manifest in the post-industrial forms of labour which begin to occupy aestheticized districts. The aestheticization of historical inner-city areas since the 1970s is closely intertwined with the rise of the aesthetic economy. In opposition to the spatial specialization of the industrial, functional city, the economy of the cultural city is characterized by a concentration of diverse creative economic activities: design and fashion, advertising and consulting, music and entertainment, film and classical high culture, media and IT, lifestyle and experimental cooking, architecture, tourism, and the art scene.[54] Theories of post-industrial society have typically held that communicative, networked intellectual labour no longer required a fixed place – Melvin Webber spoke for example in 1968 of the coming of a post-city age.[55] However, the aesthetic economy turns out to take the opposite direction. If the work being done is genuinely aesthetic rather than technical (such as in IT) then it is highly sensitive to location. Although this work is integrated in transregional or global networks, it is concentrated in what the new economics of space has called *creative clusters*.[56]

Seen in the context of the prehistory of the creative economy, these processes of cluster formation are no surprise. Aesthetic work, for example craftwork, was mostly bound to local communities of practice where implicit specialist knowledge was transmitted. Studies of the *terza italia*, the craftwork tradition in north central Italy, provide an exemplary demonstration of the dependence of aesthetic work skills on space.[57] However, the urban clusters of the creative economy are not merely routine practice communities of proven tradition but also the spatial precondition for the production of successful aesthetic novelty. Three main circumstances seem to be responsible for this micro-logic of urban creativity.

First, the mixed-use, aestheticized urban districts provide a semiotic, atmospheric, stimulating space for creative workers and artists, inextricably interweaving the private sphere and work.[58] If aesthetic work always starts out with given signs and atmospheres, taking up impulses and processing them, then this is amply provided by the aesthetic districts of the metropolis with its higher frequency of encounters with otherness – whether in the form of other ethnic communities, subcultures or milieus, the atmosphere of built spaces, or concentrations of diverse offers of art or consumption.

Second, the creative clusters are condensed communication spaces for cultural entrepreneurs, or 'culturepreneurs', from a variety of fields. In the 1960s, for instance, a dense interactive network of cafes, clubs and galleries developed in parts of Manhattan, New York, generating interconnections within and between various branches of the creative economy. This cross-pollination of ideas between diverse individuals had been the driving force behind Andy Warhol's Factory.[59] Informal face-to-face communication seems to be more effective than indirect communication for transmitting ideas and providing new impulses. The pool of participants in a cluster is regularly augmented by new immigrants from the provinces feeding their own impulses into the system.[60]

Third, the creative clusters constitute strategic spaces affecting the generation of creativity in different ways. The cultural entrepreneurs cooperate with one another, but they also compete with one another. The closely woven space makes all participants' successes and failures immediately visible, which further heats up the race for novelty. In addition, the interactive space of the cluster helps individuals to make advantageous contacts, such as to door openers of other fields who can help them to attract attention to their ideas and thereby transform them into *successful* concepts.[61] The creative clusters are therefore dominated by what Mark Granovetter calls 'the strength of weak ties', the social usefulness of having a large number of semi-professional, semi-private contacts.[62] The aestheticized districts of the late modern city thus facilitate not only the production of creativity but also the conditions for the dissemination and social certification of the resulting creative ideas.

Consumer spaces and the tourist gaze

The creative city is a place not only for living and working in but also for consuming aesthetic objects and for what can be termed the *universal tourist gaze*. John Urry introduced the notion of the tourist gaze to describe the new mode of experiencing associated with modern tourism.[63] The late modern version of the individual tourist gaze is driven by the desire to encounter, for its own sake, the foreign, authentic, unusual, strange or harmonious in urban or natural landscapes. This tourist gaze is at heart an aesthetic gaze, regarding the city not as a means to an end but as an end in itself. There is much evidence to suggest that the tourist gaze is no longer restricted to tourism in the narrower sense. Now, it also includes the inhabitants of cultural cities themselves, in particular the post-materialist middle class occupying the aestheticized districts. It is in this sense that the late-modern tourist gaze can be understood as universal. Tourists not only visit foreign cities on the global urban tourism circuit but can also become visitors to their own city. With its fixation on the visual, however, the concept of the tourist gaze is too narrow, since the city is not only perceived with the sense of sight. Indeed, mobilization of all the senses is required to take in a city's atmosphere.

A prominent feature of the creative cities since the 1980s has been the diversification of consumer spaces. They have become a fixture of the ways cities are perceived by inhabitants and visitors alike and an important part of their everyday use. Consumer spaces offer the universal tourist gaze a wealth of varied objects of interest. There is nothing new about big cities being concentrated sites of consumption. In the early modern period, trading cities were the consumer nodes for the urban bourgeoisie and the aristocracy, while the late bourgeois metropolis at the close of the nineteenth century developed its own kind of spaces with luxury consumer capitalism in the form of opulent department stores and arcades. From the 1920s to the 1970s, the functional city, at least in its Western capitalist version, was admittedly part of the society of mass consumption. Nevertheless, the effects of Fordist consumer culture were limited by the standardization of consumption and the decline of the inner cities on account of the separation of living and working space.

The 1980s saw a fundamental transformation of consumer space in cities, the preconditions of which we saw also in the rise of the aesthetic economy.[64] These preconditions included the replacement of standardized mass consumption by lifestyle consumption, whereby individuals use goods to attain individual styles, and an expansion of the range of consumer goods beyond material objects to include cultural services and atmospheres. In the 'experience economy', the borders between consumption and entertainment begin to blur.[65] Lifestyle consumption and the experience economy are not spatially neutral. They occur more frequently in the inner city in cultural cities which have either transformed themselves into places of consumer experience or are specially built for that purpose.[66] In contrast to the traditional department store, postmodern consumer spaces are showcases for a diversity of objects and styles, demonstrating variation both inside the store itself – for example the sections for different brands in clothing departments – and in relation to one another. The ideal versions of this kind of space are the shopping mall and what can be called the *semiotic district*.

Semiotic districts consist generally of historical streets, often located within aestheticized areas, harbouring endless rows of diverse, independent businesses, mostly of the aesthetic consumption persuasion (fashion, design, art), with restaurants and smaller entertainment providers interspersed among them.[67] Neighbourhoods such as the Marais in Paris or Sodermalm in Stockholm often grow out of the subcultural fashion and design scene, forming whole 'designer streets' endowing public space with a semiotic and atmospheric quality. In contrast, shopping malls are enclosed, semi-public, semi-private, newly developed complexes of differently sized stores, mostly chain stores, offering a range of consumer goods. As George Ritzer points out, the malls provide an illustration of the 'Disney model' at work. This model had first been employed in Disneyland in 1955 in southern California to create a hermetically sealed environment for the purpose of generating an experience, coupling excitement with total lack of danger.[68]

In addition, since the 1990s, a third type has been established – the lifestyle centre – an attempt to combine features of the semiotic neighbourhoods with the malls.[69] Lifestyle centres are usually newly built complexes that differ from malls by having public streets pass through them. The earliest example of this kind of consumption-oriented 'city in the city' was the large-scale renovation of the harbour district in Baltimore from 1979. Other lifestyle centres are the Eastern Town Center in Columbus, Ohio, and Potsdamer Platz in Berlin. The centres seek to combine the appeal of semiotic neighbourhoods with that of the malls, blending variety with the security of moving within a monitored space. They provide a good illustration of how post-modern consumer spaces are constituted by having borders on two fronts. The one border keeps out standardized, homogeneous mass consumption, the charmless functionalism of public space, while the other keeps out the danger of a seething and uncontrolled metropolis.

Musealization

The creative city typically incorporates earlier popular culture as well as the old high culture in its culturalizing and aestheticizing strategy. The universal tourist gaze can pass with equanimity from the popular amusement of shopping to highbrow art appreciation. Under these conditions, the once bourgeois high culture of the late modern metropolis from the 1980s is reborn in a new form. Typical features of this renaissance are the rise of the 'festival' and the 'event'. Classic high culture was once usually subject to a principle of repetition. This applied equally to the theatre, the opera and the concert hall, with their fixed, in-house ensembles and repertoires, and to the museum, with its permanent historical collection. Now, a structure of constant change and short-term novelty rises to pre-eminence in the cultural marketplace. Theatre, film and music festivals are merely its most palpable manifestations.[70]

However, the most important transformation of high culture to have occurred in the 'creative cities' is the process of musealization. The museum was traditionally a centre of bourgeois culture which grew out of older aristocratic and newer bourgeois collections, a permanent, representative fixture of large Western cities since the early nineteenth century. By assembling an artistic canon and relics of national history, the museum helped to invest artworks with a certain aura and cast national history in spatial form.[71] The process of the musealization of urban space, which also began in the 1980s, has since brought about an enormous increase in the range of items regarded as worthy of aesthetic observation in museums. This widened category includes industrial historical sites and other objects from the industrial past, the nostalgic objects of a pre-industrial past (whether bourgeois, rural or aristocratic), relics of local personalities or natural history, relics of cultural minorities, mass-media objects with historical relevance (film, photographs, etc.), and objects displaying regional particularity. Like the border dissolution of the postmodern understanding of art, the expansion of the field of museum-worthy objects is governed by an aesthetic of the interesting.

Further, the classical form of the exhibitions with its dependence on atmosphere and linear narrative has increasingly been exploded.[72] *Musealization* leads to an attitude of historical reflexivity, which is a further general characteristic of the creative city. One of the elements of historical reflexivity is the logic of *indexical narrative* borrowed from exhibition culture. Indexical narrative makes objects without a priori aesthetic or historical interest into objects of note by referencing a broader narrative context. Invoking interesting lifestyles, the histories of minorities or individuals, they are able to transform even banal everyday objects into museum-worthy items.[73] Many of the new museums built since the 1980s are postmodern in that they reflect their own cultural conditions.[74] Their collections are often conceived and assembled according to a postmodern politics aimed at representing minorities and performing memory work.[75] Occasionally, typical museum themes are taken up and subjected to deconstruction and distortion by an exhibition practice informed by post-structuralism. This new approach to the museum first emerged in 1995 in the exhibition on the history of Sydney at the Museum of Sydney and the exhibition on the Spanish colonies in the Americas at the Museo de América in Madrid, which retold the histories in non-linear, fragmentary fashion. Postmodern museums are concerned more with interactive experiences, strategically targeting the senses and affects, than were classical museums – an approach familiar from postmodern art.[76]

This heightening of aesthetic values inside the museum is repeated on the exterior. Many of the newer museums have been built in a style that might be called *solitary architecture*, each project conspicuously individual and recognizable as the work of some 'signature architect'. The most prominent early example is the Centre Pompidou in Paris, by Renzo Piano and Richard Rogers. Such museum buildings function as symbolic markers independent of the items housed inside them, culturalizing whole neighbourhoods or even cities and making them identifiable as global cultural signifiers. The Guggenheim Museum in Bilbao, interbreeding the semiotics of the cosmopolitan and the regional, may be regarded as a paradigmatic success story of local culturalization by means of individualist museum architecture.[77]

7.5 The Governing of Culture

In the 1970s, the emergence of the semiotic city, the historically reflexive city and the atmospheric aestheticization of individual neighbourhoods and whole cities was supported by inhabitants and local economies. Since the 1990s, however, we have seen a systematic culturalization of urban space from government planning geared towards engendering creative cities. While the culturalization of the city by its inhabitants was often sporadic and fragmentary, state planning has been focused on developing the city and its perception as a whole. This transition from popular to political culturalization marks a turn in the genealogy of the creativity dispositif. Creativity has now become an object of government control.

Planning difference and atmosphere

The governing of the creative city is based on a planning discourse informed most prominently by the international consultants Richard Florida and Charles Landry. Florida's guiding principle is the necessity of securing economic growth, which in post-industrial times is especially dependent on the creative economy and its 'creative class'.[78] The uneven distribution of the members of this class within nations and globally is no accident. They gravitate towards creative cities such as San Francisco, Boston or Seattle.[79] Classical economics assumed that technology and human capital were the most important factors for the economic growth of a given region. Florida updates this view for the post-industrial period, substituting expert knowledge and creative human capital for the 'old' factors as necessary conditions for prosperity. Both new factors, however, are fleeting. According to

Florida, in order to attract 'technology' and 'talent', a city must also
provide a third element. It must become attractive for the creative
class and the creative economy by offering cultural diversity, openness
and 'high-quality experiences'. It would therefore seem that no larger
city can afford to miss out on becoming creative in order to compete
globally for the creative class. However, Florida does not explain
whether a city needs a specific spatial layout in order to be creative.
He instead associates the status of the creative city mainly with the
presence of a creative class.

Charles Landry, who can lay claim to having introduced the term
with his *The Creative City* (1995), makes more explicit reference to
the transformation of urban space.[80] Landry also takes the 'inter-urban
competition game'[81] as his starting point, yet he defines the ultimate
goal of the creative city ambiguously as improving quality of life and
solving social problems. His model of the creative city is closely tied
to the political method of 'cultural planning', emphasizing the importance of exploiting 'cultural resources'. Landry explicitly demands
that cities be perceived as cultural entities, with 'culture' functioning
as a blanket term covering a vast diversity of customs, ideas and
artefacts. According to Landry, every city has its own distinct cultural
legacy and should nurture its 'local distinctiveness'. Culturally oriented
urban planning should take its point of departure from such specificities, making them visible, heightening them and shaping them. As
Landry wrote, 'every city could be a world centre for something.'[82]
The term 'creative city' is therefore polyvalent and rich in connotations. From a sociological viewpoint, Landry's programme represents
an historically noteworthy attempt to institute a planning regime
geared to the comprehensive mobilization of culture on the three
levels discussed above: semiotic, historical reflexivity and aestheticization in the more specific sense. This planning project is not concerned
merely with the kind of 'cultural politics' brought into the German
discussion in the 1970s in the form of the demand for 'socio-culture'.[83]
It is in fact a total strategy for culturalizing cities. The aim is systematically to generate urbanity as a source of constant production and
intensification of new signs and symbols, historical reflection and
sensuous-affective atmosphere. These signs and atmospheres are to
be produced both by the creative economy and by the artistic scene,
both at consumer sites and in aestheticized neighbourhoods, both in
museums and at festivals by the solitary architecture of signature
architects, all providing the inhabitants and visitors with permanent
and constantly renewed 'urban experiences'. Since the late 1980s, this
vision of a total aestheticization of the city has been encapsulated by
the discourse of 'new urbanism', influenced by the classical discourse

of the metropolis and by critical urbanism. The beating heart of new urbanism is the concept of the urban experience. Its hope is 'to transform a city where everything was perceived to be dull into a city where everything is interesting.'[84]

The strategic culturalization of the city involves a politics of *cultural difference* for marking off one city from another. In contrast to the serial cities of functionalist, organized modernity, the strategic culturalization of the individual city is directed towards the production of divergences and specificities, underlining a city's uniqueness by making visible its differences to others. This urban place-branding picks up pre-existing elements of the city – its special sights and scenes, its natural landscapes and personalities, and makes them into an identifiable symbolic marker, reinterpreting them if necessary to generate positive identification.[85] This political concern for symbolic differences and individuality extends also to the targeted production of narrative, taking up urban myths told by inhabitants or visitors or creating new ones. Berlin is a perfect example of this. A creative city must always provide enough material for generating new, even contradictory, stories about itself.

This politics of difference cannot be seen as restricted to a set of advertising strategies, since it guides the real shaping of urban space.[86] In exceptional cases, neighbourhoods become what Guy Julier has called *designscapes*.[87] Designscapes are urban spaces that have been subjected to comprehensive design management, with old and new architecture, public spaces and cultural and commercial use adapted to one another in such a way as to provide inhabitants and visitors with a semiotically and atmospherically coherent experience of the city as a whole despite its internal heterogeneity.[88] The development of the Catalonian capital Barcelona since the early 1980s is arguably the best example of a culturally oriented recasting as a designscape.[89] The municipal and regional administration of Barcelona made a concerted effort to realize an urban identity wedding cosmopolitanism with regional peculiarities. The planners took up the city's architectural heritage while at the same time framing it as a culture and design capital, making an opening to the coast and introducing a series of new cultural institutions such as a museum for contemporary art and a national theatre. This politics of place-branding is confronted with an inherent paradox. The city must be identifiable and therefore semiotically fixed. Yet the same city must be capable of generating constantly novel semiotic and atmospheric experiences.

Culturally oriented urban planning is essentially focused on culturalization and aestheticization in the form of *atmosphere design*. We have already encountered this atmosphere management as an instrument of aestheticization in other segments of the creativity dispositif, such as postmodern art and the aesthetic economy.[90] To reiterate the definition given earlier on, the term *atmosphere* refers here to an affective mood produced by a spatial arrangement of people and things as perceived by the senses and interpreted with the aid of cultural schemes. *Aesthetic* atmospheres are atmospheres experienced for their own sakes. The culturally oriented city is most accessible to experience by its inhabitants and visitors through atmosphere. It is therefore the production of atmosphere which is the aim of inhabitants and government.[91] The culture of atmospheric design in the creative cities is directed towards producing the urban experience for its own sake, an experience of intense 'vitality' within a secure framework. This involves a preference for variety and difference of impression without risk-taking, making for an atmosphere of *domesticated dynamism and diversity*. The deployment of semiotics and historical reflexivity contributes to the generation of atmosphere and thus to the aestheticization of the city. Aestheticization fends off both the functional city with its boredom and emptiness, on the one hand, and the underprivileged city with its lack of security and regulation, on the other.

The limits of cultural planning

The culturally oriented urban planning of the creative city differs fundamentally from its functionalist counterpart. The terminology of social control and planning reveals how a programme of direct or *first-degree control* was pursued by the planning regime of the functional city, with its separation of living and working, the construction of mass accommodation, the rise of the suburbs and the adaptation of the city to the needs of vehicles.[92] This method of planning was reminiscent of the approach to an engineering task drawn up on a blank sheet. The hope was to be able to build a city from the ground up in an empty space, ideally exercising thereby direct control of how its inhabitants conduct themselves within it. The planner was envisaged as an entity capable of steering the city in any direction of choice. The planning regime of the culturalized city works differently. The culturalized city exercises *second-degree control* via urban planning, supervening on processes that have already been organized in advance of any state action. The planning regime for the creative city views its subject as a dynamic cultural whole. Urban culture, as a stream of signs, historical interconnections and atmospheres, already exists and constantly continues to be created by its inhabitants, users, workers and subcultures. The culturally oriented planning regime cited by authors such as Jane Jacobs, Aldo Rossi and Charles Landry sees the deterministic vision of total controllability as neither realistic nor desirable. Urban planning cannot generate out of nothing the dynamic cultural processes that make up a city. The task of regulation is rather to harness, steer and boost processes already at work.

As a specific form of what Michel Foucault has called *governmentality*, this urban control of the second order can be assigned the term *cultural governmentality*. For Foucault, governmentality is a way in which advanced liberal societies rule by *conduct of conduct*. The subjects to be governed are regarded as self-mobilizing, as a 'milieu' that predates all political intervention and can be indirectly influenced by means of incentives and disincentives.[93] In another segment of the creativity dispositif, in the subjectivization techniques of creative psychology that replaced the psychology of discipline, we saw that the conduct of conduct, or self-governing, is fundamental to the creativity dispositif.[94] A similar process can be observed to take place in the area of urban planning, with the old engineering model of planning being superseded by an indirect *creativity control* that approaches its object as innately creative and dynamic. In psychology, the programme of a simple discipline of the subject has come since the 1970s to be regarded as obsolete, since it ignores the transformative capacity of the individual. By the same token, urban planning has departed from the determinism of the functional city. Just as psychology understands the creative self as both naturally given and a positive aim, urban planning envisages the city as possessing an inherent dynamism which must be promoted. While the technocratic control of the functional city drafted plans 'in an empty, artificial space', culturally oriented governmentality attempts to 'to plan a milieu in terms of events or series of events'[95] in expectation of the vital self-mobilizing of urban reality.

This auto-dynamism of its object of control is for the governmentality of the city essentially *cultural*. Foucault left the question open to empirical research, which broader categories governmentality has employed since 1800 to deal with its object, the 'population'. He referred to three historical categories: life and nature, society and the market. In the creative city, however, there emerges a further category which turns out to be the most historically advanced form of governmentality: the governmentality of culture and the aesthetic.[96] This form of control totalizes culture, shutting out the unwanted non-cultural and the non-creative while at the same time presupposing them. It assumes that every city is creative and ought to be creative. Its 'outside' are those cities and neighbourhoods, together with their inhabitants, which are incapable of generating signs, historical reflexivity or aesthetic experience because they are incapable of attracting creative industries or because their architectural fabric does not impart an appealing atmosphere. Such cities, unable to fulfil the demand of cultural dynamism, provide the dull background against which the creative cities shine.

Nevertheless, the hegemony of the self-culturalization of the city and the planning regime of the creative cities has not been all smooth sailing. Since the turn of the millennium, countervailing tendencies and modulations have emerged, suggesting that alternative notions of culture, aesthetic and creativity may be relevant to urban development. On the one hand there are attempts to modify or eliminate creative cities altogether in the interests of sustainability. The visions of Jane Jacobs and Aldo Rossi of a sensuously satisfying, culturalizing city already involve an ecological critique of the functional, industrial city as exhausting the sensuous, affective resources of inhabitants and environment alike. Their version of the aesthetically satisfying city emphasizes equilibrium, dispensing with the notion of an endless process of modernization. This ecological critique can be directed against the governmentality of the creative city with its focus on stimulus intensification and economic growth.[97]

There have also emerged tendencies towards returning politics to creativity in the creative cities. Charles Landry's influential vision includes both a programme for the systematic self-culturalization of the city and the politicization of creativity. Landry employs the term 'civic creativity' to denote practices of social and political problem-solving in the service of city inhabitants.[98] Civic creativity thus serves both the aesthetic and the ethical purpose of improving the quality of life enjoyed by the users of urban space. All this points to a tension within the planning regime of the creative cities between cultural control in the service of the competition for attention and the interests of the users to enjoy enduringly satisfying urban experiences.[99]

8

Society of Creativity

Structures, Dissonance, Alternatives

8.1 Affect Deficiency in Modernity

'The Puritan *wanted* to be a person with a vocational calling; we *must* be.'[1] This somewhat sententious utterance was made by Max Weber at the conclusion of his genealogy of that disciplined and ascetic human self which went on to furnish the foundations for rational modernity. The culture of professionalism, calculability and duty that emerged within certain protestant sects in the sixteenth century was driven by strong religious motives, a search for redemption. Once this form of life had provided the psychological and cultural foundations for occidental rationalism and the capitalist economy in particular, it was wiped out almost entirely by the advent of secularism. According to Weber, occidental rationalism and capitalism continued to run around for some time like headless chickens. The values of profession, self-discipline and asceticism still reigned, if necessary by force, but they no longer generated meaning or provided fulfilment to a culture which had essentially lost its religion.

It is tempting to apply this account of the transition from self-motivation to coercion to the creativity dispositif. Did not a similar process occur around 1800 as purpose-free aesthetic practices and the creative power of the artist emerged as emotionally charged ideals, settling into a niche in artistic subculture? Did not this intensely affective inclination for creativity and the aesthetic in the twentieth century provide the impulse for the growth of increasingly capacious creative-aesthetic complexes? Do we not find ourselves now in the early twenty-first century facing a powerful creativity dispositif where the inner drive to create has drained out of us and been supplanted by an outward force coercing us to create and to seek aesthetic distraction?

A Weberian pessimism of this sort is tantalizingly simple, yet it cannot quite explain our current situation. The different segments of the creativity dispositif treated in the preceding chapters have shown how creativity has become the focal point of a whole catalogue of social imperatives. However, the creativity dispositif is more than a set of normative expectations. Its power and durability rest on both imperatives *and* desires to be creative. Of course, this desire to lead a creative life and attain aesthetic fulfilment, far from being natural and universal, has in fact been shaped by socio-cultural forces and internalized. The creativity dispositif derives its ubiquity from the positive affects and experiences it both gives rise to and draws sustenance from. It is this power that makes it so difficult to imagine an alternative to it. Here lies the difference to Max Weber's formal rationalism. The latter was an apparatus of coercion, disciplining body and soul and repressing the emotions. The creativity dispositif operates by means of practices and ideas of what a subject is which are inherently fascinating and exciting. It works with the ideal of an aesthetic life, the kernel of which resides in a comprehensive cultural structure of feelings and sensations in which the individuals participate.

This affective core is what makes the creativity dispositif so singular. Yet what is its role in the development of modern society? Dispositifs cannot be understood as 'evolutionary universals' (Talcott Parsons). Instead, they are historical and local phenomena responding to specific problems, to historical and local 'urgent need'.[2] What urgent problem is the creativity dispositif responding to? It is precisely the lack of affect in classical, especially organized, modernity. Modernity systematically supressed the affects which would otherwise have furnished those it socialized with motivation and fulfilment. The aestheticization processes embodied by the creativity dispositif are the attempt to overcome this suppression.

Classically modern society was not a homogeneous block. Rather, it consisted of two distinct historical configurations: bourgeois modernity and organized modernity. Each restricted in different ways the spectrum and intensity of socially acceptable affects. This caused them to suffer in the long term from a deficiency of motivation.[3] What we have referred to here as *bourgeois modernity* can be understood as the set of practices pertaining to the economy, the state, the family, science, and other areas developed in the eighteenth century against aristocratic society and agrarian traditionalism, and which determined the structure of European and US society in the nineteenth century. Its characteristic features were the market economy, parliamentary democracy, scientism and the patriarchal nuclear family. Its cultural foundation was the bourgeois form of life. The ideal of the bourgeois self was to practise self-reflection and exercise self-discipline. This ideal attained concrete form in the figures of both the dutiful ascetic and the self-made man. *Organized modernity* then provided a different model. Organized modernity was the result of the deep transformation of the economic and government practices that were formative for society in the first decades of the twentieth century. It opposed liberal bourgeois modernity, intensifying control, coordination and planning both within economic cooperation and by the state. In contrast to bourgeois class society, organized modernity was built on broad social inclusion and a mass consumer culture promising prosperity for all. David Riesman has described the ideal form of life of organized modernity as that of the 'other-directed character', who is peer-group oriented and strives for secure social status in the context of a normal biography.[4]

The preceding chapters have attempted to show how aesthetic practices leading to the creativity dispositif became set up in opposition to the structural properties of organized modernity. The Fordist economy, with its mass production, its hierarchical functionalist organization and standardized consumption, the psychology of social control, and the planning regime of the functional city are all constituents of organized modernity. Setting themselves off against this block are the aesthetic economy, the psychology of the resource self and the cultural city. The problem of organized modernity and also of bourgeois modernity, which continued to hold sway into the early twentieth century, was that it systematically produced a dearth of emotion. Aestheticization, and now the creativity dispositif, has been promising to alleviate this lack.[5] Affect deficiency was chiefly on account of the far-reaching de-aestheticization of social practices resulting from the rationalism inherent in both versions of modernity.[6] The rise of rationalism that took place within bourgeois modernity against the affective cultures of aristocratic society, popular rural and craftwork cultures and religion, particularly Catholicism, showed up in the trade economy, self-employment and the professions, as well as in the neutrality of bourgeois law, modern science's claim to objectivity, and the discipline and self-reflection of the bourgeois self. The wave of rationalism in organized modernity was manifest in the economic and state macro-structures in the model of formal rationality and the formation of the outward-oriented character which integrates itself into structures of social coordination. Both rationalization waves lowered the degree of excitation regarded as socially acceptable, favouring more emotionally neutral, disciplinary and socially coordinated mechanisms.[7]

The affect reduction brought with it a fundamental structural problem. It produced a deficiency of motivation. After all, what is the emotional incentive to participate in a rationalized form of life? What would incite anyone to *hear the call* and participate in institutions if not coercion? What motivates subjects to become actively involved? Where is the promise of emotional fulfilment? In short, what is there to make modernity appealing? Max Weber's assessment of modern society as a 'steel-hard casing'[8] can be understood as an astute insight into precisely this fundamental lack of motivation in modern, secularized, rationalized life. In reality, however, modernity cannot have been entirely devoid of affect. From its beginnings, it was armed with strategies for compensating its lack. In order to retrace these strategies in detail, a historical-sociological *affect cartography* of modernity would be required, which still has not been forthcoming.[9] For the purpose of a preliminary account, this affective structure of modernity appears to have been composed of three lines of force. In addition to processes of aestheticization, the most important zones of affective concentration in modern culture are constituted by religion and politics.

Religion had been the nucleus of socially accepted affectivity in pre-modern European society, and this nucleus has never quite disappeared entirely in modernity. Despite all the secular tendencies of modern culture, the potential for excitation through invocations of transcendence and sacred practices has remained a significant source of motivation and affect. The persistence of evangelical movements in the USA makes this palpably clear. The affectivity of religion, spanning a variety of forms from mysticism to aggressive millennialism, turns out to be for modernity what Raymond Williams has called a *residual culture* of persistent, enduring power, especially in bourgeois modernity and then again in late modernity.[10] An emphatically modern affect culture developed after the French Revolution in another context, that of the political. The politics of modernity was not limited to rational planning and cooperation. It housed affect cultures of considerable intensity associated with hopes of progress, emancipation and salvation, with nationalism, militarism, and fantasies of violence and destruction. The affectivity of the political in modernity was attached to the hope of perfecting the social collective here on earth.[11]

Social processes of aestheticization are therefore not the only areas in modernity where high concentrations of affects and motivations were generated. In addition to religion and politics, the aesthetic appears as one of three distinct social complexes for exciting emotions. While religion ties the affects to invocations of transcendence and the political ties them to the project of perfecting society, the aesthetic ties them to sensuous perception enacted for its own sake. Within this set of affective spaces, the process of aestheticization has gained intensity and influence into late modernity, finally becoming imprinted on affective culture in the West by means of the creativity dispositif.[12] The creativity dispositif presents itself as having permanently overcome the lack of affect in modern culture, a promise which religion and politics had been unable to fulfil thoroughly enough. Nietzsche's fundamental intuition that the aesthetic is the proper social alternative to the Western rationalist and moralist traditions proves to be both insightful and accurate despite its exaggeration and one-sidedness.[13] In the long term, the processes of aestheticization turn out to have been the most effective and powerful response to the purpose-driven and normative rationalization processes in modernity, with their lack of affect and motivation. The most powerful crystallization of these aestheticization processes is the creativity dispositif.[14]

8.2 The Basic Structure of the Creativity Dispositif

As we have seen, the creativity dispositif responds to the two versions of modernity, the bourgeois and the organized, by setting in motion the process of aestheticization. This process has two main parts: the coupling of aesthetic practices to the regime of novelty and the binding of the aesthetic to an ethos of production dependent on uptake by an audience. The individual chapters of this book have studied in detail how aesthetically oriented practices, discourses and forms of subjectivity have gradually developed in a variety of fields. Now, how do these fields relate to one another? Since they are not governed by a central planning agent they are not coordinated with one another from the outset. In retrospect, however, a complementarity emerges between them, a system of specialized division of labour capable of establishing the dispositif institutionally.

The artistic field assumes a key role in this complementarity. The field of modern art developed a blueprint for the creativity dispositif as a whole. Bourgeois art as it emerged in the late eighteenth century explored a social format fixated on cultivating pure aesthetic practices and forms of subjectivity freed of purposive rationality. It oriented the aesthetic firmly towards the ideal of novelty, originality and surprise, binding it to the couple of the artist and the audience. The ideal of the creative subject, the artist, came about precisely here. Subsequently, in the course of the twentieth century and beyond, the centrifugal art of the avant-garde and postmodernism extended the realm of what counts as legitimate artistic practice far beyond the exclusive bounds of bourgeois art and the cult of genius. The artistic field thereby provides the decisive impulse for the genesis of a social practice oriented towards aesthetic perception, experience and shaping of the self. It is evident that functionalist equivalents could not have been substituted for this impulse. However, the diffusion of this practice throughout society was first made possible by the capitalist economy, core segments of which turned into aesthetic economies in the course of the twentieth century. This has expanded the aesthetic beyond the narrow confines of art. The aesthetic economy has been submitted to an intensely affective regime of aesthetic novelty. This economy has developed in several steps. The paradigm of technical innovation was gradually replaced by a paradigm of organizational and finally aesthetic innovation.

The late modern economy has thereby led to the spread of new aesthetic *objects*. At the same time, the creativity dispositif presupposes the formation of creative *subjects* pursuing the ideal of creative self-shaping. It has become evident that this social fabrication of the creative subject presupposes in turn two other social fields: the psychology of creativity and the mass media with its star system. Since the 1970s, psychology, as a two-pronged – scientific and popular – agent of the fabrication of subjectivity, has propagated the view that the creative self is the healthy rule rather than the exception. This normal self is presumed to be striving for self-realization and perfection in the style of the ideal artist. The psychological complex has also been developing methods for individuals to train their creative abilities. While psychology has been applying technologies of the self to attempt *from within* to generate the creative subject, the mass media, in particular the audio-visual media, have supported the institutionalization *from without* by representing the cultural appeal of successful creative individuals. The mass-media star system in particular stages creative subjects as objects of identification, encompassing film and music stars as well as artists and figures from the creative industries. It is not the disciplined but, rather, the expressive individual who becomes the popular cultural ideal.

A final column of support to the creativity dispositif is added by the culturalization of Western cities, in particular by the aestheticization of atmosphere. This endows the culture of creativity with a *material* reality, a material and permanent form in built space organized to satisfy the wish for aesthetic novelty as 'urban experience'.

Moreover, the model of the creative cities makes the promotion and establishment of aesthetic novelty an aim of political control and planning.[15] All these individual social fields join together in this way to form a mosaic, each contributing to establish the creativity dispositif.

Aesthetic sociality

The creativity dispositif is highly productive. It is based on aesthetic sociality, a very specific form of the social, which promotes its dissemination. The emergence of a new form of the social presupposes that what we are calling the social is not a solid structure that stays the same in all contexts and at all times but rather something historically alterable. The social, *socius*, can comprise all imaginable connections between people, things and other entities. The question is what form the social takes in a given historical and local context.[16] It cannot be overemphasized that processes of aestheticization are neither antisocial nor indifferent to the social but actually produce their own form of it. We established that the particularity of aesthetic sociality consists of the way it conjoins four elements: subjects as creators, an aesthetic audience, aesthetic objects, and an institutionalized regulation of attention. These constituents form the four pillars of the creativity dispositif. There must exist practices geared to the production of aesthetic novelty and carried by individuals or collective creators. Across from the producers there must be an audience focused on the aesthetic appropriation of objects and events. These two elements, the producers and the audience, are yoked together by a third: the aesthetic object. Aesthetic objects are more or less material artefacts made and/or taken up and used with aesthetic intent. This triad of producer, audience and object is framed within an institutional mechanism, whether it be the market, the media or the state, concerned with managing attention. Within aesthetic sociality, the main problem is to decide which objects become objects of perceptual and affective attention. This aesthetic sociality is held together by an overriding regime of aesthetic novelty. The regime of aesthetic novelty is oriented towards the production and reception of events, each with its own sensuous, affective quality and each surprising, divergent from the norm and original.

Aesthetic sociality produced by the creativity dispositif is distinguished fundamentally from the familiar patterns which sociology discovered in classical modern societies but misidentified as universal. The two most important views have localized the social either in intersubjectivity and communication or in the chain of purposive rational action.[17] From the first perspective, the social is constituted by relations of communication, the circulation of signs, or the normative coordination of human interaction. The second view maintains that the social emerges from a chain of rational-purposive actions producing artefacts or exchange guided by self-interest.[18] The aesthetic sociality peculiar to the creativity dispositif can no longer be grasped by means of these classic notions from sociology. Four decisive changes have rendered obsolete the familiar models of sociality as interaction, production or exchange.

1   The centre of this social form is occupied by an historically exceptional amount of production, circulation and appropriation of sensuous perceptions and affects for their own sakes. Structures and practices of sensuous perception and the positive affects attached to them are no longer on the margins of the social but, rather, its very substance.[19] Aesthetic sociality is at core affective and sensuous.
2   The aestheticization of society is also associated with a valorization of the constitutive relevance of objects, specifically of aesthetic objects not assigned a specific purpose. Aesthetic sociality revolves around 'inter-objective' rather than intersubjective relations – relations between things and their producers or recipients – while the producers and recipients are indirectly connected with one another via the objects.[20]
3   There is a change to the form of the subject that is appropriate to this sociality. The communicator, the self-serving actor and the producer processing objects are replaced by the *audience-subject*, performing aesthetic reception and appropriation, the *creative subject*, producing new perceptions, signs and emotions, and an *aesthetic performing subject*, who is an object of aesthetic self-shaping enacted before an audience.
4   Action and perception here involve the dynamic self-transformation of social forms rather than the predictable replication of rules. Rule-guided action is replaced by creative action. The expectation of regularity is replaced by the expectation of surprise. Consequently, the repetition of social forms is replaced by the new norm of the dissolution and reconstitution of social forms.[21]

It has become evident that this aesthetic form of the social passes through three different states in the development of the creativity dispositif: it goes from being a *niche* to a *counter-culture* and from there to being a *form of social control*. These states differ in terms of the status of aesthetic sociality in society as a whole. First, aesthetic sociality develops an alternative niche to the rationalist mainstream, the direction of which it is unable to influence significantly. The arts and crafts movement existed in a niche of this sort. Aesthetic sociality then takes the stage as counter-culture in the instant in which it forcefully challenges the legitimacy of the establishment. A concentration of such aesthetic counter-cultures occurred in the 1960s with radical design, the psychology of self-realization, critical urbanism and counter-cultural music. Finally, aesthetic sociality assumes the form of governmental control when it grows beyond subculture to attain broader legitimacy and attempts systematically to control the production and reception of aesthetic events. This aesthetic or cultural governmentality can be found in creative psychology and in the urban planning of the creative city. This creative control is not exerted solely from above but is coupled to individual self-control and indirect control by institutional mechanisms. In the twentieth and twenty-first centuries, aestheticization has evidenced a strong tendency to move away from cultural niches and counter-culture towards forms of control. Where aesthetic niches and counter-cultures have continued to occur up to the present day, they are rapidly fed as impulses back into creative control.

Aesthetic mobilization

The creativity dispositif is a comprehensive force mobilizing individuals and society.[22] This mobilization has a seemingly unlimited transformative and dynamic effect, turning non-aesthetic entities into aesthetic objects in obeisance to the regime of novelty. The first sociological examinations of aestheticization emerged in the 1960s with the rise of mass consumption and the mass media and focused primarily on the spread of docile 'passive consumers' giving themselves up to the entertainment industry. However, this point of view, adopted for example by Guy Debord in *The Society of the Spectacle*,[23] does not adequately account for the creativity dispositif. In reality, people are now no longer tranquilized but rather *activated* as creative agents. Productive aesthetic practices are being *mobilized* and are now productive in terms of the senses, signs and affects rather than, as previously, in an industrial way. People and groups (organizations, cities) are made to activate and to mobilize themselves. The aim is to be stimulated aesthetically again and again *and* to be aesthetically productive. This mobilization is not directed any more at the sporadic production of individual works but at the performance of creativity, at creative production for its own sake. The purest form of creativity is then the production of the self. The body, soul and practice becomes the self's own aesthetic object.

Aesthetic mobilization has a paradoxical structure. The activation model endows the creativity dispositif with an aspect of *heightening* (*Steigerung*), while the aesthetic regime of novelty rests on a sequence of aesthetic stimuli that cannot be heightened.[24] How does this paradox come about? At the beginning of this book we distinguished three regimes of novelty that are important to modern society:[25] the regime of *novelty I*, in which the old, obsolete state of affairs is replaced by a new progressive state that cannot be superseded; the regime of *novelty II*, in which the movement of self-transformation becomes constant; and the regime of *novelty III*, consisting of an unending, non-progressive sequence of aesthetic stimuli of equal worth. The regime of novelty produced by the creativity dispositif in all its parts is founded on novelty as a stimulus. What counts for it is the production and reception of constantly new stimulus events, which should be as intense as possible, and the interest of which lies in their immediate presence. The aim is not to be *better* but to be *different*.

At the same time, however, a regime of novelty-as-heightening is at work within the creativity dispositif. This regime is the result of the imperative directed at individuals and social units activating them to increase their creativity. The heightening contains both the idea of a quantitative addition and a qualitative improvement. Further, it consists of two mechanisms of comparison. First, the individual or group takes their previous performance as the criterion for improving their creative ability and superseding their efforts so that the development never arrives at an endpoint. This is the aim of psychological creativity techniques and the control exercised by the creative city. Second, in the face of scarce resources of attention to novelty, creative individuals and groups are obliged continually to compare themselves with others and heighten their own creative performance in order to go one better. This leads to constant comparison among creative enterprises, creative cities, artists, stars, creative workers and those private self-shaping subjects who compete for attention on social networks. It is as though the creativity dispositif conjoins postmodern and modern culture. It merges the postmodern play of aesthetic events for their own sakes without progress or heightening with the modern mechanism of heightening productivity.

The aesthetic mobilization brought about by the creativity dispositif leads to a specific affect culture that conditions contemporary society. As we have demonstrated, the social diffusion of the orientation towards creativity in all manner of social fields would not have been possible without the promise of more intense social affectivity. Within the affective cartography of the creative dispositif we can distinguish four intersections of such positive motivations and states of excitement (with the corresponding negative emotions when expectations are disappointed): the creative activity, the aesthetic experience, the creative subject itself and creative spaces.

1   Creative activity, whether professional or private, recreational or as a form of life, holds out the promise of the enthusiasm of working on novelty and the fulfilment of being a free agent not bound by external rules and routines. The work of aesthetic novelty promises satisfaction in the concentrated 'flow' of simultaneously challenging and ludic activity and in beholding the resulting work, whether it be permanent or temporary. Since creative activity legitimates divergence from the norm, the individual can experience themselves as 'authentic', as though their actions proceeded from their own inner impulses.[26]

2   There is a promise of liberation from necessity that goes with aesthetic experience as sensuous experience for its own sake freed of external purpose. This experience can be had with everyday objects, with artworks, nature, the city, the body, another person – a partner, a child, a friend – or with a group. Experiencing aesthetic novelty promises vitality, the overcoming of the dreary eternal return of sameness. This experience of aesthetic novelty can be joined to positive creative activity.

3   The creative subject, perceived in others and, ideally, in oneself, is a fascinating object of identification. It is evident that no other figure in late modern culture can compete with the creative person, least of all the dutiful and conformist types from bourgeois and organized modernity. The creative subject, and the creative star in particular, is admired not only for successfully leading a life of perfect expressive individuality. They are admired also and above all *for being admired*. Successful creative subjects attract positive attention to themselves and find social recognition in the attention directed at their expressive individuality to the extent that they become an aesthetic object, for others and for themselves.

4   Creative spaces are organized to favour the creative activity, experience and nurturing of the creative self. Spaces are attractive in this way when they offer impulses for a variety of stimuli and encounters that would seem necessary to creative and aesthetic practices. We have seen how the culturalizing city in particular – situated between global culture with its hybrid 'flows' and the personal living and work environment – turns out to be a centre of crystallization for such a creative space.

The creativity dispositif as a whole thus engenders an affective culture of a special type, focused exclusively on *positive* affectivity. The affective cartography of the bourgeois artistic field had been an intersection of conflicting affects: the cult of genius and the pathology of genius; aesthetic utopia and the discipline of taste. In contrast, the creativity dispositif attempts to direct the affects at the seemingly unlimited positivity found in acts of forming, experiencing and admiring, in inspiration, facility and licence.

Attention to novelty

A social order based on creativity will inevitably revolve around the problem of attention. This applies, among other things, to the creative producer. Postmodern art and art theory and the newer creative psychology are agreed that creativity is not an innate capacity but, rather, unfolds on contact with the outside world with its diversity of stimuli. If this is true, then creative production results from a dispersion of attention. The individual must be attentive in order to let in a large number of different stimuli, signs and combinations, to allow them to show up in perception and to process them into something relatively new.

However, the problem of attention first expands to its true magnitude when the audience, the observer of the aesthetic novelty, enters the game.[27] In everyday social practice, the recipient is moved to direct their attention routinely to a narrow circle of phenomena. For an occurrence to be an aesthetic event, attention must be directed at it, it must *arrest* attention. This attention must then be held for a sufficient time for sensuousness and affectivity to develop their own dynamism and for the aesthetic episode to take place.[28] Now, in the creativity dispositif, attention is directed by the criterion of novelty. Events perceived by the observer as novel are given priority, remain longer in the torchlight of attention, and so have a greater chance of generating aesthetic effects.

In the bourgeois artistic field, too, managing audience attention was the central social problem. Now, in the creativity dispositif, the question of organizing attention becomes more urgent still, both because of the shift in social relevance from canonized novelty to the stimulation by novelty in the immediate present and because of the increase in the number of competitors for attention. As a general rule, a broad distinction can be made between two forms of attention management: *short-term attention* for events perceived as novel, interesting and original in their immediacy and *long-term valorization* of aesthetic novelty as culturally valuable. The social certification of novelty can occur in the short term when attention is held by an event, the immediate presence of which is felt to be surprising and noteworthy. When this happens then this event has succeeded in stimulating the senses and feeling before all the other aesthetic objects (artworks, design objects, stars, hopefuls) competing for attention. In contrast, the long-term certification of aesthetic novelty is conditional on a collective assessment, primarily by experts, subjecting the object to comprehensive comparisons with both present and past alternatives, testing its claim to novelty, leading perhaps to a canonization and recognition of the object as 'classic'.[29] This valorized novelty – classical artworks, classic design and fashion objects, classic urban districts and buildings, classic stars from the past – all thereby enter into *cultural memory*.

As we have seen, these canonizations also formerly exerted influence on the regulation of attention in the bourgeois artistic field. A relatively large portion of the attention of the bourgeois audience was consolidated by the continuous reiteration of the canon.[30] However, in the late modern creativity dispositif, the attachment of attention to classic and canonical items is on the downturn and the effect of cultural memory is weaker. Instead, there is a stricter focus of attention on contemporary and short-term novelty. This can be observed in the aesthetic economy, where, to the extent that past cultural items are appropriated at all, the classical is not just replicated but transformed into novelty by combination, in the style of retro, vintage or pastiche. Tendencies in contemporary art have a similar effect; there is an abundance of forms, such as performance art, installations, artistic events, curator art and festivals, which cannot be replicated at all but exist only in the immediate present. As a result of this loss of relevance of cultural memory and the associated loss of sensibility for what was once novel in the past, the occasions for comparison become fewer. It is easier to be surprised by the present when the past is no longer remembered. At the same time, the number of sensuous, affective events competing for attention increases as a result of the advancing aestheticization of social fields, the logic of heightening in aesthetic production, and the widespread availability of art in the media. Nevertheless, the recipient's capacity for attention is necessarily limited.[31] This places the recipient in the predicament of having to choose between different offers of items to be perceived while confronting the creative producer with the converse task of influencing audience attention. A cultural battlefield grows up around these efforts to obtain and retain attention in a society searching for aesthetic novelty.

8.3 Structural Framing Conditions: Economization, Mediatization, Rationalization

How has the creativity dispositif managed to assert its power? How could previously marginal aesthetic formats break out of the artistic field to spread throughout the culture? The most basic condition of this process of diffusion is the inclination towards creativity as a cultural response to the lack of affects in organized modernity. Additionally, however, the creativity dispositif could not have flourished without the homology and complementarity arising in the late twentieth century between aesthetic sociality and several other fundamentally modern forms of the social. Late modern society is not ruled by the aesthetic principle alone. The creativity dispositif may be comprehensive, but it does not exclude other structural features of modernity already familiar to sociology such as the formal *rationalization* of the social – i.e., the institutionalization of a rule-guided, means-to-ends rationality. It applies also to the *economization* of the social, understood as the assimilation of social interaction to the models of the market and capital. It applies lastly as well to the *mediatization* of the social – i.e., to the spread of media technologies that increasingly restructure communication and perception. Within the framework of a social theory of late modernity, the aestheticization of the social can be identified as one corner of a square of which the three other corners are occupied by formal rationalization, economization and mediatization.

Of course, even under the conditions of late modernity there exist social practices and forms of subjectivity that have remained largely untouched by aestheticization processes and determined instead by the non-aesthetic principles of rationalization, economization, cognitive mediatization and other criteria. These areas indicate the *limits of aestheticization*. There still exist practices subject exclusively to purposive, normative, rational imperatives – for instance, administrative practices for organization and scientific practices for testing hypotheses. There also exist forms of economic exchange without aesthetic relevance, such as the investment trade. Finally, there are media practices serving entirely to record and process information. Aestheticization and the processes of rationalization, economization and mediatization are therefore not necessarily always interconnected.

At the same time, however, there are recognizable structural commonalities between aestheticization and both marketization and mediatization. Moreover, even though such correspondences are lacking between aestheticization and formal rationalization, the two nevertheless stand in a relationship of potential complementarity. Marketization, mediatization and formal rationalization therefore provide the structural framework for the dissemination of aesthetic events. However, they help to spread only those aesthetic formats the basic structure of which is genuinely analogous or complementary to that of economization, mediatization or rationalization. Only these formats fit into the creativity dispositif.

Economization and aestheticization

The creative dispositif is in no way opposed to rationality. Nor is it anti-economic or anti-technological. On the contrary, it could not have become so expansive without recourse to typically modern forms of rationalization. One form to which this applies in particular is marketization. In a series of waves, modern society has seen the assimilation of large segments of social practice to market structures.[32] Markets are not reducible to individual interests but rather constitute their own sociality, by which objects that are principally comparable with one another compete for the favour of a public, which for reasons of scarcity can choose to consume only a limited set of objects. The market as a form of the social manifests in the exchange between providers and consumers; the consumer receives an object and the provider receives recompense. In its own way, the market therefore operates anti-traditionally. It demands that consumers make their own decisions, leaving uncontrolled the field of competition among objects. The commodity market is a special instance of the market as such. The interest of the participants in an exchange can also be directed at immaterial goods such as ideas or at other people offering themselves, for example on the labour or marriage markets.

The sociality of the market is radically objectifying. The things or people in demand appear as mutually comparable possible choices. This comparability is conditional on an attitude of distant appraisal towards the objects. There are many indications that the erosion of organized modernity after the 1970s coincided with a new wave of diffusion and targeted political promotion of the market as a social form.[33] This economization of the social inside and outside the economy (in municipal and social politics, science and education) inevitably brings with it a specific form of social rationalization and objectification that counters aestheticization.

However, a structural homology exists between the social form of the market and aestheticization in the form of the creativity dispositif. More than just a relation of exchange, marketization involves forming the social position of the audience to develop an attitude of interested attention to objects vying for its consideration. In other words, at the heart of both social forms, products are presented to an interested public and compete for attention. Further, the markets become energized the moment market society turns into capitalism – that is, into an economic regime in which the production and distribution of goods is systematically directed towards accumulating increasing amounts of more capital.[34] A common strategy of capital accumulation consists in constantly producing new types of goods to stay one step ahead of consumer satisfaction.[35] The capitalist version of marketization thereby promotes a specific social regime of novelty just as aestheticization does in the context of the creativity dispositif.

The triad of producers, objects and recipients fundamental to marketization was at first no more aesthetically oriented than was the regime of novelty that developed in commodity capitalism. The market audience can assess wares purely for their utility or status value, while by the same token the capitalist regime of novelty can limit itself to purely technical novelty. As we have seen, in the creativity dispositif, marketization or capitalist mobilization and aesthetic sociality converge and mutually reinforce each other. Here, market objects are of interest primarily as aesthetic objects. The regime of novelty thereby becomes a regime of aesthetic innovation. Both aestheticization and economization can draw profit from this state of affairs. On the one hand, market structures enable aesthetic sociality to become broadly diffused. Aesthetic practices can draw on markets, enabling large quantities of aesthetic objects to be produced and then targeted to the appropriate consumer audience. On the other hand, aestheticization compensates for the affect deficiency caused by capitalist marketization.[36] Participation in economic processes first becomes appealing when both work and consumption are coupled with aestheticization processes. Aestheticization provides economization with motivational fuel, animating people to engage in creative activities and to seek aesthetic experiences, creative people and places. Economization, with its inclination towards objectification, would have been hard put to provide this fuel on its own.

Mediatization and aestheticization

Technical mediatization functions as a second framing condition providing for a more unhindered spread of the aestheticization forms involved in the creative dispositif. Since the early modern era, social practice in modern society has been influenced by the growth of new media technologies: first book printing, then, from the mid-nineteenth century, electronic audio and visual reproduction, and finally, since the 1980s, digital media. These media technologies cannot be grasped as mere means for recording and disseminating items of communication. Media practices also develop their own forms of perception and communication. The mediatization of the social consequently involves a dissemination of practices which either employ media or depend on media technologies or are influenced by them.

The growth of the creativity dispositif was eased by the technical preconditions that mediatization had developed for its own regime of novelty – i.e., the technologies of book printing and the audiovisual and digital media.[37] Most importantly, mediatization delivers the technical means for a *sequential* production of bundles of signs – i.e., for texts, images, etc. over time. This applies to periodicals, newspapers and television series as well as to blog entries and other internet genres. Every new bundle of signs lays claim to novelty over and against previous bundles, as though breaking through the cycle of repetition and offering up a new item of communication or perception for the user's attention. On account of their sequential character, media have an inherent tendency to age. In addition, different bundles of signs appearing *simultaneously* strengthen the media regime of novelty. It is technically possible for several sequences of media products (magazines, publishers' programmes, television series, internet offers) to coexist at any one time, all asserting their newness in opposition to the past and to other concurrent communication and perception items on offer. Indeed, the number of simultaneously existing products is growing.[38]

The mediatization of society, like its economization, is not inevitably bound up with processes of aestheticization. The novelty offered by media can be purely cognitive or consist of information. Nevertheless, there exists a structural commonality between technical media and aesthetic sociality. Subject to a regime of novelty, the mass media set up the producer and the audience as the two main players, joined together by aesthetic objects such as texts and images. The way aestheticization and mediatization are coupled and mutually support each other should be grasped in analogy to economization. Aestheticization provides mediatization with a source of affect and motivation, thus alleviating the affect deficiency which would otherwise afflict media dedicated to the purely cognitive processing of information.[39] The fact that people experience media products today primarily as objects of sensuous, affective perception rather than as tools for communication gives them a strong motivation for continual media use.

Inversely, mediatization facilitates the social diffusion of aesthetic objects. Mediatization makes it first possible to arouse interest in aesthetic events, which are not themselves to do with the media in the narrow sense but which are transmitted by them, such as artistic events, new consumer products and aesthetic changes to urban space. Secondly, media technologies produce en masse bundles of signs that are experienced primarily as aesthetic, such as novels, films, recordings and television shows. Third, the aesthetic attitude of the user is transferred to other media products. Originally informative, cognitive products such as television discussions or the World Wide Web are experienced increasingly as sensuous, affective events rather than as matters of sober fact. We therefore observe an *aestheticization of the cognitive realm*.

Rationalization and aestheticization

The relation between aestheticization and the formal rationalization of the social has a somewhat different form. A basic feature of the order of bourgeois modernity, and to a greater degree still of organized modernity, is the way its social practice was orientated towards a rationality of means and ends – what Max Weber called '*gesatzte*' (lawful) rules. These rules can be employed at will towards a variety of different aims, promising their attainment with a maximum of efficiency, predictability and ease. This applies not least to modern organizations. As we saw in chapter 1.2, these processes of formal rationalization seriously weakened the aesthetic in different areas: in the economy, whether of the capitalist or socialist variety; in the state; in the sciences; and in the everyday 'methodical conduct of life' (Weber's term) in the culture of modernity.

This antagonism between formal rationality and aestheticization begins to break down in the creativity dispositif. Aesthetic sociality and rational purposive sociality are certainly structurally incommensurable. Rational purposive structures rest neither on the relation between producer and recipient nor on a regime of novelty. These structures can involve the eternal repetition of the same activities and need no audience. The creativity dispositif does not eliminate this structural difference but it does lead to a complementarity between the two social forms, already showing signs of the emergence of an *aesthetic rationalization*. Rational purposive formats develop which attempt to create the systematic preconditions for aesthetic labour and aesthetic experience. This applies for example to what I have termed the aesthetic apparatuses.[40] Included within this term are institutional complexes and organizations in the aesthetic economy, in the artistic field and in urban development which seek to ensure the constant and systematic production and distribution of aesthetic events. Elements of aesthetic rationalization occur also in those technologies of the self that are oriented towards systematically developing creative potential, such as are to be found in creative psychology. By means of these technologies, the *creative* form of life can reappear as a new form of the *methodical* form of life, the main aim of which is constantly to generate and exploit opportunities for aesthetic experience. Aesthetic rationalization manifests an inherent paradox. Strictly speaking, aesthetic novelty escapes rational purposiveness. Nevertheless, the systematic attempt is made to develop the conditions for it to occur, even when there remains a margin of unpredictability and resistance to control which contradicts the rational purposive programme. This coupling of aesthetic and rational purposive sociality is the reason why the creativity dispositif imposes an imperative of heightening. Formal rationalization basically pursues the aim of optimization. In the framework of the creativity dispositif, this is expressed in the striving for the optimization of aesthetic production and reception.

Formal rationalization has a variety of purposes. For this reason, the old antagonism between the rational and the aesthetic can change into complementarity. As long as the purposes are not aesthetically oriented, rationalization functions to weaken the power of the aesthetic. This situation is reversed the moment these purposes can be filled with aesthetic content, as in the case of the aesthetic apparatuses and technologies of the self. This means that formal rationalization and aestheticization are now in a relation of reciprocal support. Purposive programmes make it possible to render permanent the orientation towards the aesthetic and stabilize it institutionally. At the same time, the orientation towards the aesthetic and the creative provides a new motivational basis for the establishment of formal structures and the participation in them.

Limitation not colonization

Economization, mediatization and formal rationalization provide structural *framing conditions* for the dissemination of the creativity dispositif throughout society. However, the aestheticization of the social cannot be understood reductively as a mere effect or structural replication of the capitalist market economy, media technologies or formal rationalization.[41] Rather, aesthetic sociality is an autonomous form of the social. However, its dissemination throughout society is dependent on the structural homology to economization, mediatization and formal rationalization. Homology and complementarity do not entail the aesthetic being colonized or adulterated by the non-aesthetic character of capitalism, media technologies or formal rationalization. Instead, the homology enables a template or blueprint already contained in aesthetic sociality to be disseminated. Moreover, the inverse direction of dependence also becomes apparent when the processes of aestheticization turn out to be a necessary framing condition for the stability of the three other forms of sociality under late modern conditions. Economization and mediatization, and to a lesser degree formal rationalization, seem capable of long-term survival only if they focus on the production and reception of surprising and aesthetic events and thereby overcome the affect and motivation deficiency that threatens them in radical objectification.

Economization, mediatization and formal rationalization do not therewith wholly *determine* the form of the creative dispositif. Yet they do *limit* it. Strictly speaking, they limit not the creativity dispositif as such but rather the form of the aesthetic and the aestheticization that imposes itself on society. As we have noted several times, the creativity dispositif brings the fluid medium of the aesthetic and the variegated spectrum of conceivable aesthetic practices and episodes into a specific, rigid form subject to the regime of aesthetic novelty and the constellation of creator and audience. It is not the aesthetic as such which is structurally homologous and complementary to economization, mediatization and formal rationalization but, rather, the specifically modern aesthetic sociality that the creativity dispositif provides. From this it follows that economization, mediatization and formal rationalization help to spread only that form of the aesthetic that structurally corresponds to them or fits together with them. In this case, that means the form dominated by the relation between the producer and the audience and the regime of novelty. These three societal forms therefore contribute indirectly to a limitation of the structure of aesthetic practices – precisely that limitation which the creativity dispositif brings about.

8.4 The Dissonances of the Creative Life

Throughout all its component parts, the creativity dispositif makes creativity a universal focus. Every individual and every social practice can and must assume the positions of the creative producer and recipient. The ideal of a *creative form of living* dictates the comprehensive participation in the practices of the creativity dispositif. This ideal type prescribes the shaping of everyday practice, whether at work, in partnerships, parenthood, friendship, leisure, spirituality, the relation to the body, consumption, and media use – indeed, the whole of life according to aesthetic criteria. A life led throughout and maximally on these lines would certainly be a marginal empirical case. However, this model becomes a social reality in late modern society in the creative scenes around professions that are creative in the narrower sense. Moreover, the cultural appeal of the creative form of life extends further into the outer reaches of society.[42] The creativity dispositif and the creative form of life are therefore mutually dependent, yet the passage from the dispositif to a form of life demands a shift in viewpoint from the institutional and discursive logic of the dispositif to the everyday practical and biographical logic of the form of life.

From their first appearance in romanticism, aesthetically oriented forms of life were exposed to heavy philosophical and political critique.[43] This critique of aesthetic counter-culture was essentially rooted in the moral and political values of the dominant bourgeois classes. The critique loses its object in late modernity when the creative form of life becomes yoked to the creativity dispositif, because now the antagonism between bourgeoisie and the counter-cultures and subcultures has dissolved into the creative way of life. In bourgeois and organized modernity, the bourgeois form of life had promised social recognition and inclusion yet suffered from affect deficiency resulting from the focus on moralizing and objectification. Meanwhile, the aesthetic counter-cultures promised motivational satisfaction through expressive activity and the aesthetic form of life, albeit at the cost of social exclusion and discredit. The creative, aesthetic form of life peculiar to late modernity has replaced the irreconcilable opposition between bourgeoisie and counter-culture with a synthesis promising both the affective satisfaction of creative activity and aesthetic experience *and* social recognition and inclusion, the main criteria of which has now become the creative form of life itself.[44]

Since the 1990s, criticism has identified symptoms of dissonance and new states of deficiency within the creative form of life. The new critique comes not from outside it but rather from within the ranks of creativity itself. Participants in the creative scene have developed their own forms of cultural critique, pointing out the inherent contradictions resulting from creative and aesthetic practice.[45] At the same time, relatively new psychic and physical symptoms have emerged that can be interpreted as unintended reactions to the demands of the creativity dispositif, in particular depression, exhaustion and attention deficiency syndrome. These symptoms can be placed against the background of four structural features of creativity-fixated culture, which will be examined more closely in what follows: the compulsion to creative heightening; the discrepancy between creative achievement and creative success; the scattering of attention; and aesthetic over-stretching. These structural problems do not result from a colonization of the aesthetic by the economic or the rational but rather from the internal structure of the creativity dispositif itself.

Heightening creative achievement

Within the creativity dispositif, creative action is not a happy incident, an idiosyncratic escape or a random episode but, rather, an essential social desire and a social norm. No longer a random event, creativity counts as something everyone is obliged to achieve.[46] Activities that can be classified as creative because they involve production of aesthetic novelty are evaluated as indications for the creative character of their author.[47] Within the framework of the creative form of life, creativity is demanded at work as well as in personal relations. Partners and friends are selected on the basis of aesthetic achievement (the potential to excite, to produce experiences). The creative imperative also applies to the creative self's self-interpretation and narrative identity, with biographical success bound to creative achievement in both professional and private life.[48]

The coupling of the programme to universalize creativity with the expectation to be creative paradoxically causes creativity to be conceived as a capacity supposed to belong to everybody yet not attained by all. The dispositif deals with this disjuncture between description and prescription with the aid of the distinction between potential and realization. The demand to be creative calls on people to realize their innate potential by working on themselves. This universalization of creativity leads to a second social differentiation between creative and non-creative acts and people. If creative achievement secures social inclusion, then a deficiency therein will lead to social demotion and marginalization. The deficient must assume the responsibility for not having made proper use of their potential.

This achievement imperative is made more acute again by the imperative to supersede, which means creativity is not limited to the regulated fulfilment of stable demands, such as professional proficiency or personal solidarity. Instead, under the norm of divergence from the norm, creativity demands novel and interesting acts.[49] Each divergence is required to supersede the author's own previous acts and, more importantly, those of others. The demand for novelty is thus bound up with a demand for difference and distinction. This differs from the social demand for identical conduct in that the norm of divergence from the norm operates necessarily with comparison. Creativity presupposes an army of non-diverging conformists providing background contrast. This inevitably causes the criteria of the social recognition of creativity to become fluid. This in turn disconcerts the candidate, who is uncertain of whether they pass muster on the shifting terms.

The social marginalization associated with the assignation of a creativity deficiency has a special structure that distinguishes it from other forms of social expectation. Creative achievement is not just a different kind of proof of *external* achievement as is purposive rational or normative action. Instead, the deficiency of creative achievement is thought to reveal a deficient personality. In the semantics of late modernity, subjectivity is closely tied to the cultural values of individuality and authenticity, meaning that low levels of creativity signal low levels of individuality and authenticity. Human beings are regarded as essentially and innately creative and desirous of being creative. Consequently, a deficiency or absence of creative achievement not only leads to a withdrawal of social recognition but also indicates that the deficient individual no longer fulfils their own ideal of themselves, and their whole self-image is undermined. The person is then damaged not only in their social identity but also in their personal identity.[50] As long as people identify with the notion of a primordial creative desire, there is no legitimate escape, either outside or inside. The non-creative as the cultural outside or other of the creative form of life is the negative remains, the place of failure where there is no escape from the dominant norms.[51]

In the creative form of life, 'outer' social expectations and 'inner' desires are directed towards the same end. This carries with it both the promise of great meaning and satisfaction and a high risk of failure. The promise of a 'holistic' form of life in which aesthetic satisfaction and social recognition coincide is in tension with the risk of the loss of self-esteem for a self with a supposedly innate need for self-realization. Inferences drawn from social problems to psychological problems should be treated cautiously, yet there is good evidence to suggest that, since the 1980s, the increase in pathologies related to a sense of insufficiency such as depression, exhaustion and addiction are to be understood in terms of the demand for achievement and heightening made by the creativity dispositif.[52]

The discrepancy between creative achievement and creative success

The problem caused by the demand to achieve and to heighten or increase achievement relates to creative production. Meanwhile, there is a second source of potential dissonance in the relation between this creative practice and its audience. As we have seen, every creative activity within the creativity dispositif is related to an audience in the broadest sense of the term, required for certifying it as novel, interesting and original. In the ideal case, a creative practice regarded by its author as fulfilling the norms of quality will correspond to the perception, evaluation and positive affects of the audience and be successful in the marketplace. This ideal symbiosis of creative achievement and success is embodied by the type of the successful artist and other late modern creative stars.

However, the social criteria of achievement and success are not identical. The criterion of *achievement* is used to make normative evaluations of the skilfulness and quality of an activity. In contrast, *success* relates to the normative power of fact. An activity is successful when it is conducive to real social prestige (a component of which is economic success).[53] We saw how the bourgeois artistic field, the precursor to the creativity dispositif, was also characterized by a potential dissonance between the creator and the audience. It could happen that an author classified a work as original, while the audience failed to lavish the work with positive attention, thus producing the figure of the misunderstood genius. This disjuncture is inherent to the whole system of the creativity dispositif. Creative achievement and social success *can* correspond, but they do not correspond *necessarily*, since the certifying audience remains unpredictable. The social success of creativity is typically related to professional achievements of aesthetic work made for potential consumers, but it includes also the success or lack of success of the creative self as it competes for attention in the partner and friendship market.

In general, the marketization of the social tends to increase the importance of criteria of social success and detach them from criteria of achievement. People and things are successful in the market if they find takers, regardless of whether as a result of real achievement, chance or the whims of consumer appetite. However, the relation between producers and recipients goes beyond the commercial market. It has always included aesthetic sociality, even when this served state regulations or used public media. The real reason for the unequal recognition of creative achievement is to be found not in the economy but in the fundamental social structure of *aesthesis* itself. The artistic critique of the bourgeois artistic field was wrong to claim that insufficient audience sensibility is at fault for the failure to crown creative achievement with success. Instead, the dissonance is a result of the necessary limits of audience attention in the face of an excess of creative acts all competing for its favour. The audience cannot pay attention to every object of design, every television moderator, every person worthy of love or friendship, every blogger.

This discrepancy between creative achievement and success renders the problem of the insufficient recognition of creative achievement omnipresent throughout the creativity dispositif.[54] The dispositif thus produces its own version of the experience of social injustice. The simple operating principle of this injustice is that nothing secures more creative success than previous success, which was dependent usually on chance events within the economy of attention. By this mechanism initial incremental differences are reinforced until creative stars result. The group of creative stars constitutes then a kind of upper class within the social order of the dispositif.[55] In the case of the stars, achievement and success enter into symbiosis. This in turns poses the question of whether high degrees of success really stem from excellence in creative achievement.

Scattered attention

A third complex of experiences of dissonance pertains to the audience reception of aesthetic novelty. The creativity dispositif and the creative form of life depend on the assumption that users consuming aesthetic novelty, artistic events, media offers or urban experiences really derive the desired purpose-free, sensuous, emotional satisfaction. There is evidence to indicate that the exponential increase of novelties competing for attention leads to a higher risk of the failure of aesthetic experience and disappointment among recipients. The flood of stimuli threatens to make recipients dependent, shrinking their capacity for active concentration.[56]

Despite becoming codified in routine practices, aesthetic experience appears to be more unpredictable and susceptible to disappointment than purposive rational action. Successful aesthetic experience is dependent on learnt cultural schemata that also predetermine how different situations are experienced. The chief responsibility for success and failure is clearly borne by the structure of attention regulation. The social practice of attention oscillates between targeted attention that we direct ourselves and phenomena striking from without and drawing attention.[57] The first form is concentration, the latter distraction or scattering. Arguably, successful attention consists of a balance between the two poles. If the balance is disturbed, the danger of disappointment grows. In the extreme case, the individual attempts to control their own attention. This is typical of rational purposive action. Inversely, being carried along by the chain of stimuli leads to dependence. Successful aesthetic living combines the voluntary, active directing of attention to a phenomenon with passive attraction to certain of its properties.

An economic, artistic, media and urban dispositif systematically generating a large number of sensational events intended to arrest the recipient's attention risks disturbing the balance of attention, scrambling concentration and generating distraction. Two factors seem to be responsible for this. First, in the face of the storm of new impressions, less attention is directed at any one event. Second, the present moment is devalued in favour of future events promising more novelty and surprise. The recipient is consequently at risk of drifting passively from one phenomenon to the next. As a result, no event can fulfil its promise of satisfaction. Aesthetic pleasure shrinks to become the mere anticipation of pleasure. Surrounded by ever new stimuli, this promise of deferred pleasure threatens to replace real aesthetic enjoyment.[58]

The creativity dispositif contains a contradictory source of dissatisfaction. It seems there is at once too much and not enough novelty. The sense that there are too many offers of aesthetic perception can be experienced as overly taxing. At the same time, one starts to suspect that the sea of apparent novelty no longer really conceals anything new and original. The possibilities for creating something new in the arts, in design, in partnership, etc., have been exhausted and individual aesthetic events lack intensity. Complementary to these symptoms of depression and exhaustion, which can be read as a reaction to the demand to achieve and heighten, is the so-called attention deficiency syndrome. In some cases, ADS develops into a compulsive search for new perceptions for their own sake. It can therefore also be interpreted as a further, typical, contemporary sickness brought about by the creativity dispositif.[59]

Overstretching the aesthetic

Under the reign of the creativity dispositif, the process of aestheticization tends to extend unchecked into diverse social fields. This expansionist tendency can be traced back to the two factors mentioned above. The first factor is the affective stimulus of the orientation towards creativity, which compensates for modernist objectification and marketization. The second factor is the coupling of the aesthetic to the similarly expansive mechanisms of capitalist economization and technological mediatization. The overflow of the aesthetic into previously non-aesthetic social complexes turns the threatening scenario of classical modernity on its head. There, the aesthetic was potentially always exposed to rationalist colonization, whereas now, in the context of the creativity dispositif, the question is whether the colonization of the non-aesthetic threatens to take place – i.e., a devaluation of alternative social practices in favour of the one-dimensional criteria of the aesthetic.

In the philosophic debate, this point has been discussed mainly in connection with the dissolution of the ethical by the aesthetic.[60] Seen from a sociological point of view, many fields of social life display what could be called *aesthetic overstretching*. An example is the intensification of tendencies towards aestheticization in the mass media, personal relations and politics since the 1980s. In the mass media (print and audio-visual media and the internet), formats that were previously cognitive, serving to provide mainly political information, exhibit an increasing tendency to service a need for rapidly alternating perceptual, affective stimuli. As a result of this aestheticization of the media, sensational short-term themes gain in relevance over long-term analysis and commentary.[61] In the area of personal relations, an aestheticization of the private has been diagnosed. A series of authors have investigated the influence of the criteria of personal self-creation and shared consumer leisure time on the formation and maintenance of partnerships and friendships.[62] In the political field, Colin Crouch has spotted a 'post-democratic' constellation characterized by the transformation of politics into an aesthetic matter of personality and the transformation of political communication into a spectacle.[63] All in all, these processes of aestheticization stand in a relation of mutual support to processes of marketization. Sequences of signs in the media, partners and political agents all become aesthetic objects and objects of choice competing for limited resources of attention.

8.5 Alternative Aesthetic Practices

Societal dispositifs always have cracks and openings. Despite all the seductive tales of simple, linear progression, dispositifs in fact have a precisely traceable history of rise, transformation and resistance. They always come up against countervailing forces. Are alternatives to the creativity dispositif conceivable or perhaps already visible? Is the current culture's inclination for the production and reception of novelty as obligatory as it appears at first glance?

Artistic critique and social critique

How should aestheticization processes in society as a whole be evaluated? Luc Boltanski and Eve Chiapello have identified two traditions of critique in modernity: artistic critique and social critique.[64] For the purposes of applying this distinction to our context, the artistic critique can be understood to measure social practice in terms of its ability to realize aesthetic values. Artistic critique was confined to the margins in bourgeois and organized modernity but has now turned positive and stands at the head of the creativity dispositif. Social critique, the most important alternative critical tradition in modernity, judges social practice in terms of criteria of social justice. However, it can also be understood more broadly: social critique operates with diverse normative criteria aimed at attaining forms of social life based on transparent, universal participation in political decision-making, equal chances for development and economic participation, and morally guided mutual care among individuals. The reservoir of modern critique thus provides alternatives to the criteria of the aesthetic, even though the power of this social, moral critique to shape society is subject to fluctuation over time. Social critique, in this broad meaning of the term, can hinder the overstretching of aestheticization, helping to limit it and to learn to limit itself by holding up the values of deliberative democracy in politics, factual information in the media, the ethics of care for others in personal relations, and the model of a social city in urban planning. It follows from the above that the social and moral have their own imperatives and can in no way be reduced to the aesthetic.[65]

However, if the social critique of over-aestheticization were to seek to discredit the aesthetic altogether or reduce it to the kind of limited autonomous sphere represented by bourgeois art, then it would fail to comprehend the real significance of the aesthetic in modern culture. As we have seen, the project of aestheticization and creativity is to be understood as a reaction to the experiences of alienation caused by the rationalization and objectification at the heart of modern society.[66] The cultural model of a creative and enjoying *homo aestheticus* is a response to the motivation deficit resulting from objectification. However, the political, legal and moral procedures advocated by social critique are low in percept and affect; they are not ends in themselves but, rather, means to ends and therefore essentially incapable of alleviating the deficiency. Further, the aesthetic is not only incapable of being subsumed under the social and morality; the aesthetic is the more primary motivation. Therefore, the relation between aesthetic criteria and social criteria in the narrower sense for the shaping of human practice can be understood as a relation between the centre and its framing conditions. The older and newer demands of social critique for political participation and control, for civil rights, equal opportunities and moral care for others, can be understood as representing the necessary social conditions for the kind of self-realization promoted by aesthetic practices, with their auto-dynamic, experimental, sensuous, affective interaction with things, people and environments. For this reason, the self-containment of aesthetic practices resulting from the social critique of over-aestheticization does not negate aestheticization and its significance as a motivational force in late modernity. Self-containment would limit the extent of aestheticization, but the aesthetic would remain at the centre of a genuinely post-traditional form of life.[67]

The question now is what an aesthetic relation to the world could consist of. It should be emphasized again that the creativity dispositif is not identical with aestheticization as a whole but is one specific version of it among many past, present and future varieties. If the creativity dispositif produces new experiences of dissonance and deficiency in the way described in the last section, then the question is particularly urgent with regard to alternative aesthetic and creative practices. How can these practices be conceived and where can they already be found? In general terms, it can be said that the alternative aesthetic practices would have to modify the specific structure of the aesthetic found in the creativity dispositif. They would have to provide an alternative to the producer–recipient constellation and to the radical regime of novelty. This question of alternative aesthetic practices leads in two directions. First, it points to creative practices that are not directed at an audience and consequently find themselves situated outside of the attention market and the logic of heightening. These practices can be termed practices of *profane creativity*. Second, an *aesthetic of repetition* is called for, incorporating aesthetic practices not actively involved in the regime of novelty but oriented instead towards routine and repetition. Must aesthetic practice be inextricably tied up with the desire for novelty and for audience recognition and attention? If it is true that the creativity dispositif potentially alienates the aesthetic, forcing it into a corset, then the aesthetic should not be constricted further but rather allowed to reshape and stretch itself.

Profane creativity

If creativity consists of the generation of aesthetic novelty, then there is no reason why that process should be pressed into the framework of an individual or collective producer proffering novelty for audience attention and recognition. The producer–recipient model of creativity leads in the end to a highly particularized cultural pattern represented by the modern artist, whose originality must be certified by an audience. Although the creative subject has broken the bounds of the artist to become universal, this older model of creativity still enforces comparison and distinction between the creative and non-creative, the original and non-original. Creativity has become generalized, but at the same time the audience model dictates that it must always be *rarified*. Creativity remains the exception, rising from a background of conformity, despite the variability of what counts as new and interesting. Despite its own claim, this model is unwilling to take the final step towards a radical universalization of creativity. Creativity retains a structure of expectation with the possibility of failure, fitting in easily with the long list of demands made on people in modernity. Yet the demand to be creative is more unpredictable than other demands, since it is contingent on the fickle whims of the audience. An alternative to this kind of creativity generated by the creativity dispositif could be called *profane creativity* – a form of creativity that has liberated itself from the audience, from comparison and from heightening.[68] Unlike a *heroic* model of creativity based on the ideal of the artist, *profane* creativity is a phenomenon already present in everyday practices and networks and therefore not dependent on an audience. Profane creativity is to be found in everyday, isolated, seemingly banal actions which can be performed without an audience, such as occur in interpersonal practices where, crucially, the producer–recipient divide is surmounted by a meeting of *participants* and *co-players*. If creative practice is relieved of the judgement of an external audience, then it is enough for the participants to experience it as new and different, rendering bird's-eye-view comparative criteria superfluous. Profane creative practice is always *locally* situated, producing delight and discovery for the participants in the here and now. Profane creativity has no recipients, yet nor is it producer-based. It takes place in the sequence of practice and within networks of subjects and objects.[69]

Once our eyes have been opened to it, we discover profane creativity freed of the demand for originality and audience certification everywhere. Tim Edensor has elaborated one such 'vernacular creativity' in late modern cities. From the point of view of the artistic model of the creative class, these practices would not appear worthy of the label 'creative' because they provide nothing of interest for an audience.[70] They are not professional, nor are they supported by the culturally interested middle classes, nor do they take place in the creative neighbourhoods; rather, they blend seamlessly into suburban or socially precarious areas. A case in point is provided by Mess Hall, an experimental, local cultural centre in Chicago examined by Ava Bromberg. Mess Hall is a space for diverse cultural activities undertaken by local amateurs, not planned for presentation to audiences but focused on shared practice.[71] In this context, creativity is not a scarce commodity competing for attention but a public good always already available in ready amounts, present in every musical, culinary, craft or communicative act. In this example, the distinction between creative acts and routine practices thus breaks down.[72]

We can distinguish between four forms of profane creativity: improvisation, experiment, idiosyncrasy and the hermeneutic web. *Improvisations* are inventive acts resulting from the demands of practical action characterized by the blending of purposive rationality and free play. *Experiment* entails methodically freeing practices from routine – treating routines as material for play. *Idiosyncrasies* are the particularities in the way individuals act; they can condense into individual taste and mental and bodily habitus.[73] *Hermeneutic webs* are uniquely individual semantic and narrative processes, woven by individuals and groups and charged with affective meaning, such as narratives of self.[74] All these practices combine the process of aesthetic production with receptive aesthetic experience.

Profane creative practice is nothing new in the Western creativity dispositif. On the contrary, the creative practices that gradually formed independently in diverse social fields before flowing together to form the dispositif would have been inconceivable without profane creativity, especially in the early phases. Improvisation and idiosyncrasy were formative for the arts and crafts movement. The subcultural fashion industry that developed in London's Soho district in the 1950s started off as a practice of style-conscious do-it-yourselfers. The same applies to the colonization and regeneration of fallow urban areas – the *culturalization from below* that affected many Western neighbourhoods in the 1970s and 1980s. However, as soon as the residual or counter-cultural creative formats mutate into forms of governmental control, they begin to perfect modes of production and establish markets of attention. At this point, profane creativity flips over into heroic creativity and becomes performance.[75]

The practice of profane creativity is neither a social expectation nor an internalized desire. Instead, in profane creativity, social recognition and self-esteem are independent of expectation and desire. Creative acts escape evaluation from outside and so do not have the character of services performed for others or before an audience. Nor is this profane practice fuelled by a supposed 'will to creativity'.[76] On this expanded understanding of creativity, the pronounced constellations of recognized original production in front of an audience do not go under altogether but rather swim like islands in a sea of profane practice.

Everyday Aesthetic of Repetition

A second alternative to the dominance of the creativity dispositif, an everyday aesthetic of repetition, is differently slanted than profane creativity, opposing hyperactivity of all sorts. In the face of the institutional compulsion of aesthetic novelty and tendencies to attention scattering in the creativity dispositif, the question becomes urgent as to why aesthetic practices and episodes should be governed by a regime of novelty. This query goes against Max Bense's theory of information. According to Bense, in order to avoid becoming redundant and uninteresting, every piece of information must contain novelty and variation. This applies especially to aesthetic information.[77] It can be argued against Bense that aesthetic experience is not cognitive transmission and so by no means requires absolute novelty or original experiences. The aesthetic regime of novelty can thus be countered by an aesthetic of repetition in favour of reproducing aesthetic practices to call forth identical perceptions and emotions. In this way, the concentration on aesthetic objects and environments should be able to calm the mental stream that accompanies rational purposive action rather than overheating it. A comprehensive aestheticization of this type would integrate the focused perception and experience of objects and environments into everyday practice. Thus, in the aesthetic of repetition, aesthetic satisfaction is based not on excitation but on the experience of immobility and calm.

As a general rule, at least in the realm of predictable aesthetic episodes, the aesthetic, like anything social, is manifest in *practices*, in routine, repetitive and customary activities.[78] Practices performed collectively can assume the form of rituals. This basic structure of repetition is as much a part of primarily receptive aesthetic practices as it is of primarily productive practices. For instance, once someone has acquired the habit of watching films, this attitude can be assumed again and again. The same applies to appraising fashion or going for walks, and this will apply equally to a new film, a new piece of clothing or a new city. By the same token, the techniques of musical composition, writing and architectural design are all based on repetition, even when the piece or design is novel. Ideally, routine in aesthetic practice means mastery and effortlessness. The aesthetic of repetition takes this up and sees the aesthetic satisfaction of auto-dynamic perceptions and emotions not in the supposedly new product but in the skilful repetition.

It is no coincidence that this alternative aesthetic model situated outside of the regime of novelty has already been elaborated and applied in non-Western, non-modern cultural contexts. While avoiding the trap of exoticism, François Jullien, for example, has studied the ancient Chinese aesthetic of 'blandness',[79] which eschews diversity and variety in taste and calls instead for the constant repetition of 'that which constantly unfolds'. This type of aesthetic practice is not dependent on the comparison between different aesthetic stimuli but rather hones the experience of indifference and the undifferentiated. As Jullien writes, 'flavor provokes attachment, and insipidity provokes detachment.'[80] Ancient Chinese visual art, music and literature were designed to enable producer and recipient alike to repeat over and over the same aesthetic experience of pure sensuousness and moderate emotion. The bland painting of Ni Zan, for example, works with extremely sparse objects and a muted colour scale such that the painter is finally always painting the same landscape.[81] This aesthetic practice resembles the way Zen Buddhist meditation is designed to let the passage of mental images through in order to concentrate on an object in a state of pure perception. The object, finally, can be replaced by any everyday practice. The art of ancient China and Japan is not based on a notion of novelty in the Western sense but, rather, is about reworking prototypes.[82] The Western distinction between art and craft, innovation and reproduction, seems to melt away here, with artistic activities in the narrower sense and everyday aesthetic techniques such as calligraphy and the tea ceremony all proceeding in the same way.[83]

However, it would be short sighted to localize the everyday aesthetic of repetition only outside of the West. Upon closer observation, the practices and discourses which prepared the creativity dispositif contain aesthetic criteria that favour repetition over originality. This was already the case for the sense of natural life in romanticism.[84] Likewise, as we saw, some factions of critical urbanism in the 1960s called for the cultivation of an urban space characterized by recognizability and sensuous, emotional coherence.[85] Modern art and popular media culture have also worked not only with criteria of surprise but also with a countervailing tendency to appropriate and reappropriate classic aesthetic objects from film, design, literature and music. Finally, in the psychology of self-realization, Csíkszentmihályi's concept of flow experience stipulates long-term concentration on a single activity as an aesthetic end in itself.[86]

The concentrated repetition of aesthetic practices is therefore irreducible to a binary opposition of conformity and autonomy. It must instead be understood as an activity requiring distracting stimuli to be blocked out in order to enable intense concentration on single objects or on the act of repetition itself. The everyday aesthetic of repetition is thus not anti-rational but develops its own version of formal rationality. This is a rationality of the *exercise*, seeking a satisfying and measured level of intensity that cannot be superseded or heightened but instead requires to be maintained.[87] While the model of profane creativity promotes a democratization of creativity, the aesthetic of repetition promotes a tranquillization of the aesthetic. In this way, both can help to render the aesthetic more quotidian, which is what the creativity dispositif had strived for but failed to reach.

* * * * *

Will this weakening of the creativity dispositif and the spread of other versions of aestheticization (self-containment of the aesthetic, profane creativity, and the aesthetic of everyday repetition) find support in the future? This must remain an open question. Now, in the early stages of the twenty-first century, the creativity dispositif seems robust and stable and still expanding, both in the West and globally. Social practice and the cultural imagination continue to be strongly oriented towards creative production, self-creation and the perpetual experience of aesthetic novelty.[88] Different social structures conspire to stabilize and expand the dispositif: global aesthetic capitalism anchored in urban centres, especially in the design and experience economy; technological mediatization, more recently especially in digital form, institutionalizing sensuously, emotionally charged novelties; a state politics that sees the creative cities and their exploitation of creative resources as providing growth parameters for the future; and, finally, a private culture of the self that perpetuates with astonishing perseverance the model of expressive self-realization. These structures make the creative form of life seem like the most progressive form of life, even when what it promises is unattainable for many individuals and whole social groups. There is much evidence to suggest that the creative form of life, which first developed as a specifically Western cultural pattern, will continue to expand its range of appeal beyond the West to populations who have until now been excluded from it.[89]

The taming of the creativity dispositif would depend on forms of critique going beyond traditional political and social critique to advance new aesthetic criteria. Again, the prejudice must be combated that questions of the aesthetic, the sensuous and emotional alienation are politically secondary, mere 'first-world problems' or just private concerns. My concern in this book has been to show how aestheticization processes in the framework of the creativity dispositif have real and profound effects on the structure of society. They are the motor for contemporary society's seemingly endless uncontrolled dynamic of heightening. If what we understand as *the political* consists of exposing societal fixations and offering alternatives, then the task at hand is to thematize these aestheticization processes in the form of the creativity dispositif as a political issue (in addition to the closely intertwined and only seemingly inevitable processes of economization and mediatization). We should not make a blanket declaration of war on the aesthetic and the regimes of novelty and the audience, because we would then run the risk of moral fundamentalism, anti-modern conservatism, or the idyll of the private self. Instead, what is needed are strategies for the self-containment of the aesthetic and of the regimes of novelty and the audience. The self-containment strategies called for in late modern culture are, in the broadest sense of the term, *ecological*. They need to be deployed in the aesthetic economy and in urban planning, in the use of media and in the private culture of the self.[90] The aim will be to counter over-aestheticization by locally reinforcing the ethical and the social, responding to the idling cycle of the regime of novelty by cultivating tranquillity and concentration while sidestepping the constant audience observation and the demand for originality by multiplying the chances for withdrawal from the gaze of the other.

Perhaps we have been too fixated on our creativity and at the same time not creative enough.

Notes

Preface

1 Richard Florida, *The Rise of the Creative Class: And How It's Transforming Work, Leisure, Community and Everyday Life*, New York: Basic Books, 2002; John Howkins, *The Creative Economy*, London: Penguin, 2002.
2 Angela McRobbie, *Be Creative*, Cambridge: Polity, 2016; Terry Flew, *The Creative Industries: Culture and Policy*, Los Angeles: Sage, 2012; John Hartley (ed.), *Key Concepts in Creative Industries*, London: Sage, 2013; David Hesmondhalgh and Sarah Baker, *Creative Labour: Media Work in Three Cultural Industries*, London and New York: Routledge, 2011.
3 Erika Fischer-Lichte, *The Transformative Power of Performance: a New Aesthetics*, New York: Routledge, 2008; Hans Ulrich Gumbrecht, *Production of Presence: What Meaning Cannot Convey*, Stanford, CA: Stanford University Press, 2004; Gernot Böhme, 'Atmosphere as the fundamental concept of a new aesthetics', *Thesis Eleven*, 36 (1993): 113–26.
4 Rajendra Roy, Anke Leweke et al., *The Berlin School: Films from the Berliner Schule*, New York: Museum of Modern Art, 2013.
5 Ulrich Bröckling, *The Entrepreneurial Self: Fabricating a New Type of Subject*, Los Angeles: Sage, 2016; Hartmut Rosa, *Social Acceleration: A New Theory of Modernity*, New York: Columbia University Press, 2013; Joseph Vogl, *The Specter of Capital*, Stanford CA: Stanford University Press, 2015.

Introduction

1 Richard Florida, *The Rise of the Creative Class: And How It's Transforming Work, Leisure, Community and Everyday Life*. New York: Basic Books, 2002.
2 On this question, see Gerald Raunig and Ulf Wuggenig (eds), *Kritik der Kreativität*, Vienna: Turia & Kant, 2007; Peter Spillmann and Marion von Osten (eds), *Be Creative! Der kreative Imperativ*, Zurich: Museum

für Gestaltung, 2003; Ulrich Bröckling, *The Entrepreneurial Self*, London: Sage, 2015 (chapter 6: 'Creativity', pp. 101–17).

3 On the concept of creativity generally, see Günter Blamberger, *Das Geheimnis des Schöpferischen oder: Ingenium est ineffabile?*, Stuttgart: J. B. Metzler, 1991; Hans-Ulrich Gumbrecht (ed.), *Kreativität – ein verbrauchter Begriff?*, Munich: Fink, 1988. On the history of the idea of creativity as imagination, see James Engell, *The Creative Imagination: Enlightenment to Romanticism*, Cambridge, MA: Harvard University Press, 1981.

4 See Angela McRobbie, '"Jeder ist kreativ": Künstler als Pioniere der New Economy?', in Jörg Huber (ed.), *Singularitäten – Allianzen: Interventionen 11*, Vienna and New York: Springer, 2002, pp. 37–59; Cornelia Koppetsch, *Das Ethos der Kreativen: Eine Studie zum Wandel von Arbeit und Identität am Beispiel der Werbeberufe*, Konstanz: UVK, 2006.

5 The theme of flexible specialization was treated early in Michael J. Piore and Charles F. Sabel, *The Second Industrial Divide. Possibilities for Prosperity*, New York: Basic Books, 1984; on organization innovation, see Andrew H. Van de Ven, *The Innovation Journey*, New York: Oxford University Press, 1999.

6 See Richard Rorty, *Contingency, Irony, and Solidarity*. Cambridge: Cambridge University Press, 1989, pp. 96ff. (chapter 5: 'Self Creation and Affiliation: Proust, Nietzsche and Heidegger').

7 See Paul Leinberger and Bruce Tucker, *The New Individualists: The Generation after The Organization Man*, New York: HarperCollins, 1991; Daniel Yankelovich, *New Rules: Searching for Self-Fulfillment in a World Turned Upside Down*, New York: Random House, 1981.

8 On this term see Charles Landry, *The Creative City: A Toolkit for Urban Innovators*, London: Earthscan, 2009.

9 The concept of *modernity* refers to the social formation that has developed and reproduced itself since the latter half of the eighteenth century, at first in the West and then globally. The prefix *late* is not intended to suggest that modernity is about to reach its end. On these concepts, see also Peter Wagner, *A Sociology of Modernity: Liberty and Discipline*, London: Routledge, 1994.

10 Regarding these aesthetic opposition movements, see Andreas Reckwitz, *Das hybride Subjekt: Eine Theorie der Subjektkulturen von der bürgerlichen Moderne zur Postmoderne*, Weilerswist: Velbrück Wissenschaft, 2006, pp. 204ff., pp. 289ff., and pp. 452ff. On the term *counter-culture*, see Theodore Roszak, *The Making of a Counter Culture: Reflections on the Technocratic Society and on its Youthful Opposition*, Garden City, NY: Doubleday, 1969.

11 See Talcott Parsons, *Societies: Evolutionary and Comparative Perspectives*, Englewood Cliffs, NJ: Prentice-Hall, 1966.

12 Daniel Bell, *The Cultural Contradictions of Capitalism*, New York: Basic Books, 1976; Luc Boltanski and Eve Chiapello, *The New Spirit of*

Capitalism, London: Verso, 2005 (especially chapter 7: 'The Test of the Artistic Critique', pp. 419–82).

13 On post-structuralist ontology, see among others Bruno Latour, *Reassembling the Social: An Introduction to Actor-Network-Theory*. Oxford: Oxford University Press, 2005; Gilles Deleuze and Félix Guattari, *A Thousand Plateaus: Capitalism and Schizophrenia*, Minneapolis: University of Minnesota Press, 1987. For a contrasting account, see Hans Joas's attempt to develop a philosophical anthropology of human creativity: *The Creativity of Action*, Chicago: University of Chicago Press, 1996; and, in a similar vein: Heinrich Popitz, *Wege der Kreativität*, Tübingen: Mohr Siebeck, 1997.

14 This perspective on creativity is inspired by Michel Foucault's view of the genealogy of modernity. Foucault himself, however, never took account of this phenomenon. He tended instead to see the aesthetic on the model of the antique aesthetic of exis*ence as the other or the alternative to the dispositifs of modernity. For a critical take on Foucault's notion of aesthetics and creativity, see Fabian Heubel, *Das Dispositiv der Kreativität*, Darmstadt: Wissenschaftliche Buchgesellschaft, 2002.

15 On various models of creativity in early modernity, some outside of art, see Joas, *The Creativity of Action*, chapter 2, 'Metaphors of Creativity', pp. 70–144. Also noteworthy in addition to the aesthetic model of expression are the production, revolution, life and intelligence models.

Chapter 1   Aestheticization and the Creativity Dispositif

1 On the distinction between medium and form, see Niklas Luhmann, *Theory of Society* [1997], vol. 1, Stanford, CA: Stanford University Press, 2012, pp. 116ff.

2 See Paul de Man, *Aesthetic Ideology*, Minneapolis: University of Minnesota Press, 1996.

3 On this wide ranging discussion, see Terry Eagleton, *The Ideology of the Aesthetic*, Oxford: Blackwell, 1990; Wolfgang Welsch, *Grenzgänge der Ästhetik*, Stuttgart: Reclam, 1996; Karlheinz Barck et al., 'Ästhetik/ ästhetisch', in Barck et al. (eds), *Ästhetische Grundbegriffe*, vol. 1, Stuttgart: J. B. Metzler, 2000, pp. 308–83.

4 See, for example, Erika Fischer-Lichte, *The Transformative Power of Performance: A New Aesthetics* [2004], New York: Routledge, 2015; Hans Ulrich Gumbrecht, *Production of Presence: What Meaning Cannot Convey*, Stanford, CA: Stanford University Press, 2004; Gernot Böhme, *Für eine ökologische Naturästhetik*, Frankfurt: Suhrkamp, 1989.

5 A programme of this kind might cite Walter Benjamin as an authority. It is undertaken in more concrete detail in the phenomenology of the senses and in media theory. See Walter Benjamin, 'The work of art in

the age of its technological reproducibility: second version' in *The Work of Art in the Age of its Technological Reproducibility, and Other Writings on Media*, Cambridge, MA: Belknap Press, 2008, pp. 19–55; Gernot Böhme, *Aisthetik: Vorlesungen über Ästhetik als allgemeine Wahrnehmungslehre*, Munich: Fink, 2001; Marshall McLuhan, *The Gutenberg Galaxy: The Making of Typographic Man*, New York: New American Library, 1962.

6   See also Martin Seel, 'Ästhetik und Aisthetik: Über einige Besonderheiten ästhetischer Wahrnehmung – mit einem Anhang über den Zeitraum der Landschaft', in Seel, *Ethisch-ästhetische Studien*, Frankfurt: Suhrkamp, 1996, pp. 36–69.

7   Seel provides a simple and tangible example. The way pedestrians wanting to cross the road take note of traffic lights is sensuous and perceptive but not aesthetic. The perception becomes aesthetic when they are struck by the different colours as a play of lights; see ibid., pp. 46f.

8   The terms are deployed in this sense by Gilles Deleuze and Félix Guattari in *What is Philosophy?* [1991], New York: Columbia University Press, 1994, pp. 164ff. On the connection between perception and affects, see also Böhme, *Aisthetik*, pp. 29ff.

9   On the concept of the affect, see Brian Massumi, *Parables for the Virtual: Movement, Affect, Sensation*, Durham, NC: Duke University Press, 2002, pp. 23ff.

10   On the praxeology perspective, see Andreas Reckwitz, 'Toward a theory of social practices: a development in culturalist theorizing', *European Journal of Social Theory*, 5/2 (2002): 243–63; Theodore R. Schatzki, *The Site of the Social: A Philosophical Account of the Constitution of Social Life and Change*, University Park: Pennsylvania State University Press, 2002.

11   See Immanuel Kant, *Critique of the Power of Judgment*, Cambridge: Cambridge University Press, 2000; Émile Durkheim, *The Elementary Forms of the Religious Life*, New York: Macmillan, 1915 (Book III: The Principal Ritual Attitudes, pp. 297–447); Benjamin, *The Work of Art in the Age of its Technological Reproducibility*; Charles Baudelaire, 'The painter of modern life' [1863], in *Selected Writings on Art and Literature*, New York: Penguin, 1972, pp. 390–435; François Jullien, *In Praise of Blandness: Proceeding from Chinese Thought and Aesthetics* [1991], New York: Zone Books, 2004.

12   On this aspect see, for example, Wolfgang Iser, 'Von der Gegenwärtigkeit des Ästhetischen', in Joachim Küpper and Christoph Menke (eds), *Dimensionen ästhetischer Erfahrung*, Frankfurt: Suhrkamp, 2003, pp. 176–202. The more recent discussion of aesthetics has seen repeated attempts to contrast semiotic and hermeneutic aesthetics against sense-affect aesthetics. However, this is a spurious alternative. Aesthetic practices always contain a semiotic dimension to the extent that significations can be attributed to perceptual phenomena. In the course of the analysis I will nevertheless work with the distinction between aesthetic

(in connection with the senses and affects) and semiotic – for example, in chapter 7 in reference to the phenomenon of creative cities – but this is merely an operative distinction.

13 See Bruno Latour, *We Have Never Been Modern*, Cambridge, MA: Harvard University Press, 1993.

14 The concept of aestheticization is not without controversy in the history of concepts. Aestheticization referred for a long time to a phenomenon seen as problematic – by both the 'right' (see Carl Schmitt's introduction of the term in *Political Romanticism* [German: 1919], New Brunswick, NJ: Transaction Books, 2011 (German edn: p. 16)) and the 'left' (see Benjamin, *The Work of Art in the Age of its Technological Reproducibility*, p. 42). See also the rehabilitation of the concept, albeit with a different accent, in Wolfgang Welsch, 'Ästhetisierungsprozesse – Phänomene, Unterscheidungen, Perspektiven', in *Grenzgänge der Ästhetik*, pp. 9–61; Rüdiger Bubner, 'Ästhetisierung der Lebenswelt', in Walter Haug and Rainer Warning (eds), *Das Fest*, Munich: Fink, 1989, pp. 651–62.

15 Marx also launches a critique of de-aestheticization in his early Parisian writings. Durkheim and Simmel, too, are concerned with the role of the aesthetic. Durkheim sees it in the ritual affects of archaic societies that seem also necessary for modernity, while Simmel recognizes most clearly the aestheticized elements of urban modernity.

16 See Jean-François Lyotard, *Discours, figure*, Paris: Klincksieck, 1985; Jean Baudrillard, *Symbolic Exchange and Death*, London: Sage, 1993.

17 See Thomas Nipperdey, *Wie das Bürgertum die Moderne fand*, West Berlin: Wolf Jobst Siedler, 1988; Pierre Bourdieu, *Distinction: A Social Critique of the Judgement of Taste*, Cambridge, MA: Harvard University Press, 1984, pp. 9ff. Bourdieu tends to reduce bourgeois aestheticism to a mere distinction strategy.

18 The connection between the development of media and the transformation of perception has been studied extensively and controversially since the 1960s. See Marshall McLuhan, *Understanding Media: The Extensions of Man*, Cambridge, MA: MIT Press, 1994; André Leroi-Gourhan, *Gesture and Speech*, Cambridge, MA: MIT Press, 1993.

19 Karl Marx, *Capital: A Critique of Political Economy*, Vol. I, Part I, New York: Cosimo Classics, pp. 81ff.

20 On Fordism, see Antonio Gramsci, *Selections from the Prison Notebooks*, New York: International, 1971, pp. 279–318; on postmodern consumer culture, see, among others, Mike Featherstone, *Consumer Culture and Postmodernism*, London: Sage, 1991.

21 See Latour, *We Have Never Been Modern*.

22 On the sensuous, affective appropriation of objects see, among others, Karin Knorr Cetina, 'Objectual Practice', in Theodore R. Schatzki et al. (eds), *The Practice Turn in Contemporary Theory*, London: Routledge, 2001, pp. 175–88. For a different emphasis, see also Tilmann Habermas, *Geliebte Objekte: Symbole und Instrumente der Identitätsbildung*, Berlin and New York: Walter de Gruyter, 1996.

23   See, among others, Eva Illouz, *Saving the Modern Soul: Therapy, Emotions, and the Culture of Self-Help*, Berkeley: University of California Press, 2004; for an historical account, see also Charles Taylor, *Sources of the Self: The Making of the Modern Identity*, Cambridge: Cambridge University Press, 1989.

24   See Raymond Williams, *Marxism and Literature*, Oxford: Oxford University Press, 1977, pp. 121ff. On the alternative criteria, see chapter 8.5 in this book.

25   On the theorizing of novelty in postmodern culture see Boris Groys, *On the New* [1992], London: Verso, 2014. See also Till R. Kuhnle, 'Tradition/Innovation', in Karlheinz Barck et al. (eds), *Ästhetische Grundbegriffe*, vol. 6, Stuttgart: J. B. Metzler, 2005, pp. 74–117.

26   On the recipient as receiver, see Karl Bühler, *Theory of Language: The Representational Function of Language*, Philadelphia: John Benjamins, 1990, pp. 35ff.; on the semantics of the consumer, see Don Slater, *Consumer Culture and Modernity*, Cambridge: Polity, 1997, pp. 33ff.; on the audience, see Rudolf Stichweh, *Inklusion und Exklusion*, Bielefeld: Transcript, 2005, pp. 13ff.

27   See Wolfgang Iser's aesthetic of reception (which is, however, still trained on the model of the reader): 'Die Appellstruktur der Texte', in Rainer Warning (ed.), *Rezeptionsästhetik*, Munich: Fink, 1994, pp. 228–52. On postmodern consumer theory, see Slater, *Consumer Culture and Modernity*, pp. 131ff.

28   See Niklas Luhmann, *Political Theory in the Welfare State*, New York: Walter de Gruyter, 1990, chapter IV (pp. 155–66).

29   This concept of the audience is borrowed from theatre, though without the element of co-presence.

30   See Reinhart Koselleck, *Futures Past: On the Semantics of Historical Time* [1979], New York: Columbia University Press, 2004. See also the *Querelle des anciens et des modernes* (Quarrel of the Ancients and the Moderns) as the first modern instance of an *éloge* to novelty: Charles Perrault, *Parallèle des anciens et des modernes en ce qui regarde les arts et les sciences* [1688–96], ed. Hans Robert Jauß, Munich: Eidos, 1964.

31   For a version of this argument, see Rosalind Krauss, *The Originality of the Avant-Garde and Other Modernist Myths*, Cambridge, MA: MIT Press, 1985.

32   See Werner Rammert, 'Die Innovationen der Gesellschaft', in Jürgen Howaldt and Heike Jacobsen (eds), *Soziale Innovation*, Wiesbaden: Verlag für Sozialwissenschaften, 2010, pp. 21–51.

33   Art is therefore not restricted to novelty III but has always also yielded versions of novelty I (classicism) and novelty II (avant-garde).

34   On the subject of the logic of supersession, see Gerhard Schulze, *Die Beste aller Welten: Wohin bewegt sich die Gesellschaft im 21. Jahrhundert?*, Munich: Hanser, 2003, pp. 81ff. It will, however, become clear that novelty II is still present even in the creativity dispositif; see chapter 8.2 in this volume.

35 On the level of discourse, this constellation of the new is well known to have been in large part prepared by Charles Baudelaire. See, among others, Walter Benjamin's interpretation in 'On some motifs in Baudelaire' [1939], in *Illuminations* [1968], New York: Schocken Books, 2004, pp. 155–200; also Marshall Berman, *All That is Solid Melts into Air: The Experience of Modernity*, London: Penguin, 1988, pp. 131–71.

36 On the semantics of the interesting, above all in Friedrich Schlegel, see also Konrad Paul Liessmann, *Ästhetische Empfindungen*, Vienna: Facultas Universitätsverlag, 2008, pp. 101ff.

37 See Michel Foucault, *Security, Territory, Population: Lectures at the Collège de France, 1977–78*, Basingstoke and New York: Palgrave Macmillan, 2007, pp. 83ff; Jürgen Link, *Versuch über den Normalismus: Wie Normalität produziert wird*, Opladen: Westdeutscher Verlag, 1999.

38 See Max Bense, *Aesthetica: Einführung in die neue Ästhetik* [1965], Baden-Baden: Agis, 1982, pp. 208ff. and 276ff. It should be added that this applies to aesthetic information in the sense of a modern, occidental aesthetic of originality presupposed by Bense. On alternative conceptions of the aesthetic, see chapter 8.5 in this volume.

39 A leaning towards this interpretation is evident in both Fredric Jameson (see idem, *Postmodernism, or, The Cultural Logic of Late Capitalism*, Durham, NC: Duke University Press, 1991) and, in a different way, the representatives of governmentality studies (see Nikolas Rose, *Governing the Soul: The Shaping of the Private Self*, London: Routledge, 1990).

40 For more detail on this process of interlocking between aestheticization, economization, rationalization and medialization, see chapter 8.3 in this volume.

41 In the past, the French term *dispositif* has usually been translated as *apparatus*. However, 'apparatus' has the disadvantage of connoting something mechanistic and unchanging. We have therefore preferred to leave the term in the original French. See Michel Foucault, 'The confession of the flesh [1977]', in *Power/Knowledge: Selected Interviews and Other Writings 1972–1977*, ed. Colin Gordon, Brighton: Harvester Press, 1980, pp. 194–228.

42 *Format* is taken here as a generic term for different social entities, such as practices, discourses, subject–object relations and modes of subjectivization.

43 Foucault, 'The confession of the flesh', p. 195; translation altered.

44 Michel Foucault, 'Nietzsche, genealogy, history' [1977], in *The Foucault Reader*, ed. Paul Rabinow, New York: Pantheon Books, pp. 76–100, here p. 84.

45 See also Judith Butler, *The Psychic Life of Power: Theories in Subjection*, Stanford, CA: Stanford University Press, pp. 83–105 (chapter 3: 'Subjection, resistance, resignification: between Freud and Foucault').

Chapter 2 Artistic Creation, the Genius and the Audience

1 The term 'modern' is being used here in a sociological not an art historical sense and means the constitution of society since the eighteenth century, not the artistic modernism of 1900. Further, in this chapter, repeated reference is made to art as a *social field*. This does not follow the specific meaning of the term as used by Pierre Bourdieu but, rather, denotes generally any complex of specialized, differentiated social practices.

2 An aesthetic object is understood here not in Roman Ingarden's phenomenological sense (see *The Literary Work of Art: An Investigation on the Borderlines of Ontology, Logic, and Theory of Literature* [1931], Evanston, IL: Northwestern University Press, 1973) but, rather, with reference to Bruno Latour's concept of the quasi-object.

3 Howard Becker, *Art Worlds*, Berkeley: University of California Press, 1982.

4 For this perspective, see, among others, Georg Lukács, *The Theory of the Novel: A Historico-Philosophical Essay on the Forms of Great Epic Literature* [1914/15], Cambridge, MA: MIT Press, 1971; Robert Winston Witkin, *Art and Social Structure*, Cambridge: Polity, 1995. For a critique of the dominant sociology of art, see also Nathalie Heinich, *Ce que l'art fait à la sociologie*, Paris: Minuit, 1998.

5 For one such approach, see Max Weber, 'Religious rejections of the world and their directions' [1920], in *From Max Weber: Essays in Sociology*, New York: Oxford University Press, 1946, pp. 323–59; Pierre Bourdieu, *Rules of Art: Genesis and Structure of the Literary Field* [1992], Stanford, CA: Stanford University Press, 1996; Niklas Luhmann, *Art as a Social System* [1995], Stanford, CA: Stanford University Press, 2000.

6 See Talcott Parsons, *The Social System* [1951], London: Routledge, 1991, p. 259.

7 See Charles Batteux, *Les Beaux Arts réduits à un même principe*, Paris, 1773. Excerpts available in English in 'The fine arts reduced to a single principle', in *Aesthetics*, ed. S. Feagin and P. Maynard, Oxford: Oxford University Press, 1997, pp. 102–4.

8 On the artist in general, see Jörg Völlnagel and Moritz Wullen (eds), *Unsterblich! Der Kult des Künstlers*, Munich: Hirmer, 2008; Martin Hellmold et al. (eds), *Was ist ein Künstler? Das Subjekt der modernen Kunst*, Munich: Fink, 2003.

9 See also Nathalie Heinich, *The Glory of Van Gogh: An Anthropology of Admiration*, Princeton, NJ: Princeton University Press, 1997.

10 See Jochen Schmidt, *Die Geschichte des Genie-Gedankens in der deutschen Literatur, Philosophie und Politik 1750–1945*, vol. 1, Darmstadt: Wissenschaftliche Buchgesellschaft, 1985; Edgar Zilsel, *Die Entstehung des Geniebegriffs: Ein Beitrag zur Ideengeschichte der Antike und des*

Frühkapitalismus [1926], Hildesheim and New York, 1972; Hans Brög, *Zum Geniebegriff: Quellen, Marginalien, Probleme*, Ratingen: Henn, 1973.

11 The aesthetic of genius adopts elements of the individualism of Renaissance art. This reference to the history of ideas is a classical topos. See Alessandro Conti, *Restauro*, Milan: Jaca Books, 1992.

12 Alexander Gerard, *An Essay on Genius*, London, 1774, p. 8.

13 Shaftesbury refers to the poet as 'a second *Maker*: a just PROMETHEUS, under JOVE'. See Anthony Shaftesbury, 'Soliloquy, or, advice to an author', in *Characteristicks of Men, Manners, Opinions, Times* [1711], Hildesheim and New York: G. Olms, 1978, p. 207.

14 On the concept of inclusion, see Rudolf Stichweh, 'Inklusion in Funktionssysteme der modernen Gesellschaft', in Renate Mayntz et al. (eds), *Differenzierung und Verselbständigung*, Frankfurt and New York: Campus, 1988, pp. 45–116.

15 On this classical sociological distinction between *ascribed* and *achieved* qualities, see Parsons, *The Social System*, pp. 180ff. However, the institution of art academies since 1800 opposed the genius aesthetic and the cult of art by claiming that art can be taught.

16 This totality can be understood as 'nature', as 'history' or, later, as 'existence'. Hölderlin refers to it as the 'all-unity of life'. See Jochen Schmidt, *Die Geschichte des Genie-Gedankens*, pp. 404ff.

17 See Jochen Schulte-Sasse, 'Einbildungskraft/Imagination', in Karlheinz Barck et al. (eds.), *Ästhetische Grundbegriffe*, vol. 2, Stuttgart: J. B. Metzler, 2001, pp. 88–120; James Engell, *The Creative Imagination*, Cambridge, MA: Harvard University Press, 1981.

18 Jean-François de Saint-Lambert (ascribed), 'Genius', in Denis Diderot, *Encyclopedia of Diderot & d'Alembert Collaborative Translation Project*, vol. 7, Ann Arbor: University of Michigan Library, 2007 (orig. pubd as 'Génie', *Encyclopédie ou Dictionnaire raisonné des sciences, des arts et des métiers*, 7: pp. 582–4, Paris, 1757).

19 On the quasi-object, see Bruno Latour, *We Have Never Been Modern*, Cambridge, MA: Harvard University Press, 1993, pp. 51–5 ('What is a quasi object?').

20 For a systematic account of the differences between various genres of art, see Ursula Brandstätter, *Grundfragen der Ästhetik: Bild, Musik, Sprache, Körper*, Cologne: Böhlau, 2008, pp. 119ff.

21 On Karl Philipp Moritz's concept of the 'schönes Kunstwerk', the work of fine art, see 'Über den Begriff des in sich selbst Vollendeten' [1785] [On the concept of internal perfection], in Moritz, *Werke*, ed. *Horst Günther*, vol. 2, Frankfurt am Main: Insel, 1981, pp. 543–8. On the concept of the artwork in general, see Wolfgang Thierse, 'Das Ganze aber ist das, was Anfang, Mitte und Ende hat' [But the whole is what has a beginning, a middle and an end], *Weimarer Beiträge*, 36 (1990): 240–64.

22 Johann Wolfgang von Goethe, 'Upon the Laocoon' [1796], in *Essays on Art*, Boston: James Munroe, 1845, pp. 26–41, here p. 27.

23   For an overview, see Jürgen Habermas, *The Structural Transformation of the Public Sphere: An Inquiry into a Category of Bourgeois Society* [1989], Cambridge: Polity, 2011, pp. 27ff.

24   On the development of the political public, see ibid. On the public sphere of science, see Rudolf Stichweh, *Zur Entstehung des modernen Systems wissenschaftlicher Disziplinen*, Frankfurt: Suhrkamp, 1984.

25   For a detailed analysis, see Edgar Zilsel, *Die Entstehung des Geniebegriffs*.

26   On the growth of the market for literature, see Reinhard Wittmann, *Buchmarkt und Lektüre im 18. und 19. Jahrhundert: Beiträge zum literarischen Leben 1750–1880*, Tübingen: Niemeyer, 1982. On the art market, see Martha Woodmansee, *The Author, Art, and the Market: Rereading the History of Aesthetics*, New York: Columbia University Press, 1994.

27   On bourgeois reading habits, see Matthias Bickenbach, *Von den Möglichkeiten einer 'inneren' Geschichte des Lesens*, Tübingen: Niemeyer, 1999; on listening to music, see Peter Gay, *The Naked Heart: The Bourgeois Experience – Victoria to Freud*, New York: W. W. Norton, 1996, vol. IV, pp. 1ff.; on the museum, see Tony Bennett, *The Birth of the Museum: History, Theory, Politics*, New York: Routledge, 1995. For the artwork to become a maximally independent aesthetic object it requires above all a *space* prepared in such a way as to heighten aesthetic intensity and minimize non-aesthetic distractions and ulterior uses. Concerts and stage performances consequently take place in bourgeois concert halls and theatres. Here, in contrast to concerts and theatres at court, seating arrangements and the dimming of the auditorium are calculated to reduce communication among the audience. In the case of literature, reception is not public, but here too the appropriate spatial setting of the typical bourgeois house, with its reading room or private library, favours silent reading in contrast to gregarious reading out loud in court circles.

28   On the origins of literature and art criticism, see René Wellek, *Geschichte der Literaturkritik 1750–1830*, Darmstadt: Luchterhand, 1959; Albert Dresdner, *Die Kunstkritik: Ihre Geschichte und Theorie*, Munich: Bruckmann, 1915.

29   See Ernst Kris and Otto Kurz, *Legend, Myth, and Magic in the Image of the Artist: A Historical Experiment* [1934], New Haven and London: Yale University Press, 1979.

30   See Erika Fischer-Lichte, *Kurze Geschichte des deutschen Theaters*, Tübingen: Francke, 1999, pp. 81–115.

31   Processes of economization and medialization were thus built into the very framework of the artistic field from the start. This is investigated more systematically in chapter 8.3.

32   Johann Joachim Winckelmann, *History of the Art of Antiquity*, Los Angeles: Getty Research Institute, 2006. See also Rudolf Heinz, *Stil als geisteswissenschaftliche Kategorie*, Würzburg: Königshausen & Neumann, 1986. On the relation between the concept of style and the orientation on novelty, see Luhmann, *Art as a Social System*, pp. 130ff.

33 The individual style is here closely bound up with the establishment of the function of the author. See Michel Foucault, 'The discourse on language' [1971], in *Archaeology of Knowledge*, New York: Pantheon, 1972, pp. 215–37.

34 See Ulrich Schulz-Buschhaus, 'Klassik zwischen Kanon und Typologie', *Arcadia*, 29 (1994): 67–77; and Aleida Assmann and Jan Assmann (eds), *Kanon und Zensur: Beiträge zur Archäologie der literarischen Kommunikation II*, Munich: Fink, 1987.

35 See Winckelmann, *History of the Art of Antiquity*.

36 See Annemarie Gethmann-Siefert, 'Das Klassische als das Utopische', in Rudolf Bockholdt (ed.), *Über das Klassische*, Frankfurt: Suhrkamp, 1987, pp. 47–76.

37 On taste, see Friedrich Schümmer, 'Die Entwicklung des Geschmacksbegriffes in der Philosophie des 17. und 18. Jahrhunderts', *Archiv für Begriffsgeschichte*, 1 (1955): 120–41.

38 For a general overview, see Walter Grasskamp, *Museumsgründer und Museumsstürmer: Zur Sozialgeschichte des Kunstmuseums*, Munich: Beck, 1981.

39 In the twentieth century, it became possible with the reform movement in museums to include exhibits up to the immediate present, subjecting the collection to constant updating.

40 See Edgar Zilsel, *Die Geniereligion: Ein kritischer Versuch über das moderne Persönlichkeitsideal mit einer historischen Begründung* [1918], Frankfurt: Suhrkamp, 1990.

41 Ibid., p. 108.

42 See Franz Roh, *Der verkannte Künstler*, Munich: Heimeran, 1948.

43 Johann Gottlieb Fichte, *Friedrich Nicolai's Leben und sonderbare Meinungen*, Tübingen, 1801, p. 111.

44 This line of critique begins with prominent authors such as Goethe and Kant. See Kant, *Critique of the Power of Judgement* [1790], Cambridge: Cambridge University Press, 2000, pp. 186–9 (§§46–7).

45 Friedrich Schlegel, *On the Study of Greek Poetry*, Albany, NY: State University of New York Press, 2001, p. 30.

46 In visual art, Gustave Courbet is seen as the first artist consciously to deploy scandal. Oskar Bätschmann, *The Artist in the Modern World*, New Haven, CT: Yale University Press, 1997, pp. 122–30.

47 The best study of the subject remains Helmut Kreuzer, *Die Boheme: Analyse und Dokumentation der intellektuellen Subkultur vom 19. Jahrhundert bis zur Gegenwart* [1968], Stuttgart: J. B. Metzler, 2000; see also Wolfgang Ruppert, *Der moderne Künstler*, Frankfurt: Suhrkamp, 1998, pp. 189ff.

48 On lifestyle as a sociological concept, see Georg Simmel, *Philosophy of Money* [1907], London and New York: Routledge, 2004, pp. 433ff.

49 See Kreuzer, *Die Boheme*, pp. 154ff.

50 This does not imply that the bohemians actively undertook to develop a theory but, rather, refers to the way the bohemians consciously assert

themselves as a radical group which feels itself confronted by a larger social power.

51 Henry Murger, *Scènes de la vie de bohème*, Paris, 1851 (*The Bohemians of the Latin Quarter* [1851], London: Vizetelly, 1888); see also Honoré de Balzac, *Un prince de la bohème*, Paris, 1892 (*A Prince of Bohemia* [1844], New York: Sheba Blake, 2014).

52 Edward Young, *Conjectures on Original Composition: In a Letter to the Author of Sir Charles Grandison*, London, 1759, p. 42. On Young, see also Günter Blamberger, *Das Geheimnis des Schöpferischen oder: Ingenium est ineffabile?*, Stuttgart: J. B. Metzler, 1991, pp. 60ff.

53 Friedrich Schiller, *Letters upon the Aesthetic Education of Man in a Series of Letters* [1795], Raleigh, NC: Hayes Barton Press, 2005, p. 19.

54 Ralph Waldo Emerson, 'The Poet', in *Essays and Lectures*, New York: Library of America, 1983, pp. 447–68, here p. 448.

55 Karl Marx, *Economic and Philosophic Manuscripts of 1844*, New York: Dover, 2007, p. 108.

56 See Friedrich Nietzsche, *Human, All Too Human: A Book for Free Spirits* [1878], Cambridge: Cambridge University Press, 1986; and *Thus Spoke Zarathustra: A Book for All and None*, Cambridge: Cambridge University Press, 2006.

57 This cultural critique of the artist as pathological was prepared by philosophy; see above all Søren Kierkegaard, *Either–Or, Part I & II* [1843] (*Kierkegaard's Writings*, vols III and IV), Princeton, NJ: Princeton University Press, 1988.

58 See Hanna Hohl, *Saturn, Melancholie, Genie*, Stuttgart: Hatje, 1992.

59 See Louis F. Lélut, *Du démon de Socrate*, Paris, 1836; Jacques-Joseph Moreau [Moreau de Tours], *La Psychologie morbide dans ses rapports avec la philosophie de l'histoire, ou De l'influence des névropathies sur le dynamisme intellectuel*, Paris, 1859. On the stigmatization of the genius as pathological in psychology, see chapter 4.2 in this volume.

60 See Max Simon Nordau, *Degeneration* [1892], Memphis: General Books LLC, 2012.

61 Efforts to cast the artist as pathological also feed into the myth of the artist. Their supposedly abnormal character and amorality can be adopted by artists in their own accounts of themselves as marks of the suffering of the chosen, as a morbid difference to the philistines around them, and also as symptoms in their own psyches of society's ills (see Eckhard Neumann, *Künstlermythen*, Frankfurt: Campus, 1986, pp. 155ff.). Psychic peculiarities can also fascinate the public. An example of this interest is the image of Van Gogh as it has evolved since his death in 1891 (see, among others, Matthias Arnold, *Vincent van Gogh: Werk und Wirkung*, Munich: Kindler, 1995, pp. 808ff.). Here, the moralizing is removed from the pathology to reveal it as interesting.

62 On the figure of the other in cultural theory, see Ernesto Laclau and Chantal Mouffe, *Hegemony and Socialist Strategy: Towards a Radical Democratic Politics*, London: Verso, 2001.

63   Luhmann, *Art as a Social System*, p. 22.
64   For a critique of Bourdieu along these lines, see also Heinich, *Ce que l'art fait à la sociologie*.
65   See Gilles Deleuze, *Spinoza: Practical Philosophy*, San Francisco: City Lights Books, pp. 124ff.
66   Art can therefore be interpreted as a response to the lack of affects in bourgeois, bureaucratic modernity. See chapter 8.1.
67   Arthur Schopenhauer, *The World as Will and Representation* [1819] (*The Cambridge Edition of the Works of Schopenhauer*, vol. I), Cambridge: Cambridge University Press, 2010.
68   Sigmund Freud's concept of melancholic identification is used differently by Judith Butler. See Butler, *The Psychic Life of Power: Theories in Subjection*, Stanford, CA: Stanford University Press, pp. 132ff. (chapter 5: 'Melancholy gender/refused identification').

Chapter 3   Centrifugal Art

1   Hans Namuth and Barbara Rose, *Pollock Painting*, New York: Agrinde, 1980 p. 47.
2   Namuth and Rose, *Pollock Painting*, contains the photographs and commentaries by Rose Namuth and Rosalind Krauss. On the contemporary effect of the photos, see Allan Kaprow, 'The legacy of Jackson Pollock', *Art News*, 57 (1958): 24–6, 55–7. On Pollock's art historical significance, see Leonhard Emmerling, *Jackson Pollock*, Cologne: Taschen, 2003.
3   Hans Namuth and Paul Falkenberg, *Jackson Pollock*, film, Museum at Large, USA, 1950, 10 mins.
4   See Fredric Jameson, *Postmodernism, or, The Cultural Logic of Late Capitalism*, Durham, NC: Duke University Press, 1991, pp. 6ff.
5   Alexander Liberman, *The Artist in His Studio*, New York: Viking Press, 1960.
6   Quotation from the film *Pollock Painting*.
7   Harold Rosenberg, 'The American action painters', *Art News*, 51 (1952): 22–3, 48–50.
8   Melanie Franke (ed.), *'Ich kann mir nicht jeden Tag ein Ohr abschneiden': Dekonstruktionen des Künstlermythos*, Cologne: DuMont, 2008 [exhibition catalogue].
9   See chapter 5 and Andreas Reckwitz, *Das hybride Subjekt: Eine Theorie der Subjektkulturen von der bürgerlichen Moderne zur Postmoderne*, Weilerswist: Velbrück Wissenschaft, 2006, pp. 452ff.
10   See chapter 4.
11   On the transformation of the role of the artist, see Verena Krieger, *Was ist ein Künstler? Genie – Heilsbringer – Antikünstler*, Cologne: Deubner, 2007; Michael Wetzel, 'Autor/Künstler', in Karlheinz Barck et al. (eds), *Ästhetische Grundbegriffe: Historisches Wörterbuch*, Vol. 1, Stuttgart: J. B. Metzler, 2000, pp. 480–544; Matthias Michalka and Beatrice von

Bismarck (eds), *The Artist as...*, Nürnberg: Verlag für Moderne Kunst, 2006.

12 On the erosion of bourgeois taste and the new syntheses of academic and popular taste, see Bernard Lahire, *La Culture des individus: dissonances culturelles et distinction de soi*, Paris: La Découverte, 2004.

13 These institutional transformations have been well documented in sociology of art. For the museum, see Peter Galassi et al. (eds), *Making Choices 1929, 1939, 1948, 1955*, New York: Museum of Modern Art, 2000.

14 For an allied interpretation of the avant-garde as more than just a preparation for modernist aesthetics of autonomy, see Peter Bürger, *Theory of the Avant-Garde* [1974], Manchester: Manchester University Press, 1984; Richard Sheppard, *Modernism – Dada –Postmodernism*, Evanston, IL: Northwestern University Press, 2000. The concept of 'postmodern' art serves here as a crutch; see Leslie Fiedler, 'Cross the border – close the gap', in *Collected Essays*, Vol. II, New York: Stein & Day, 1971, pp. 461–85; Charles Jencks, *The Language of Post-Modern Architecture*, New York: Rizzoli, 1977.

15 Viktor Shklovsky, 'Art as technique', in Julie Rivkin and Michael Ryan (eds), *Literary Theory: An Anthology*, Oxford: Blackwell, 1998.

16 Max Ernst, 'What is surrealism?' [1934], in Lucy R. Lippard (ed.), *Surrealists on Art*, Englewood Cliffs, NJ: Prentice-Hall, 1970, p. 134.

17 Bernhard Holeczek, 'Zufall als Glücksfall: Die Anfänge eines künstlerischen Prinzips der Avantgarden', in Holeczek and Lida von Mengden (eds), *Zufall als Prinzip*, Heidelberg: Braus, 1992, pp. 15–24.

18 See Beate Bender, *Freisetzung von Kreativität durch psychische Automatismen: Eine Untersuchung am Beispiel der surrealistischen Avantgarde der zwanziger Jahre*, Frankfurt am Main: Peter Lang, 1989, pp. 73–103. See also André Breton's programmatic 'Manifesto of surrealism' [1924], in Breton, *Manifestoes of Surrealism*, Ann Arbor: University of Michigan Press, pp. 1–48.

19 See Bender, *Freisetzung von Kreativität*, pp. 167–86.

20 See Robert L. Herbert (ed.), *Modern Artists on Art*, 2nd edn, New York: Dover, 2000, pp. 126–40.

21 Ralf Convents, *Surrealistische Spiele*, Frankfurt am Main: Peter Lang, 1996.

22 See chapter 5.4.

23 For example, the participants agree that each of them should imagine a specific object, such as a crystal ball, and then proceed to answer a series of twenty-six questions without any coherent connection between them: '1. Is it diurnal or nocturnal? 2. Is it favourable toward love?' – up to no. 26: 'What crime does it correspond to?' Denise Bellon et al., 'Experimental research: on the irrational knowledge of the object: the crystal ball of the seers' [1933], in Penelope Rosemont (ed.), *Surrealist Women on Art: An International Anthology*, London: Athlone Press, 1998, pp. 70–3, here p. 71.

24 Hans Prinzhorn's studies of the paintings of mentally ill patients, which prefigured art brut, provide a well-known example. See Hans Prinzhorn, *Artistry of the Mentally Ill: A Contribution to the Psychology and Psychopathology of Configuration* [1922], Vienna and New York: Springer, 1995.

25 See Verena Krieger, *Kunst als Neuschöpfung der Wirklichkeit: Die Anti-Ästhetik der russischen Moderne*, Cologne: Böhlau, 2006.

26 See Aleksandr Bogdanov: 'Every kind of creative activity – in technology, in socio-economics, politics, everyday life, in science and in art – is a kind of work' (in David Quigley, Carl Einstein. *A Defence of the Real*, Vienna: Pakesch & Schlebrügge, 2006, p. 225). 'There is not, nor can there be, a strict boundary between creativity and simple labor' (in Evgeny Dobrenko, *Aesthetics of Alienation: Reassessment of Early Soviet Cultural Theories*, Evanston, IL: Northwestern University Press, 2005, p. 26).

27 Ilja Ehrenburg, *Und sie bewegt sich doch!*, Leipzig: Reclam, 1989, p. 165.

28 Boris Kušner, 'Die Organisatoren der Produktion', in Hubertus Gaßner and Eckhard Gillen (eds), *Zwischen Revolutionskunst und Sozialistischem Realismus: Dokumente und Kommentare: Kunstdebatten in der Sowjetunion von 1917 bis 1934*, Cologne: DuMont, 1979, pp. 123f., here p. 124; Maria Gough, *The Artist as Producer: Russian Constructivism in Revolution*, Berkeley: University of California Press, 2005, p. 106.

29 Magdalena Droste and Peter Gössel, *The Bauhaus, 1919–1933: Reform and Avant-Garde*, Cologne and Los Angeles: Taschen, 2006; Frank Whitford, *Bauhaus*, London: Thames & Hudson, 1984.

30 Johannes Itten, *The Art of Color: The Subjective Experience and Objective Rationale of Color* [1967], New York: J. Wiley & Sons, 2002.

31 In the case of László Moholy-Nagy, the most prominent exponent of industrial Bauhaus, this culminates in his characteristic red mechanic's suit.

32 On the development of the design industry, see chapter 4.4.

33 David Batchelor, *Minimalism: Movements in Modern Art*, Cambridge: Cambridge University Press, 1997.

34 Marcel Duchamp, 'The creative act', in Robert Lebel (ed.), *Marcel Duchamp*, New York: Grove Press, 1959, pp. 77–8 [transcript of Duchamp's talk at the session on the creative act, convention of the American Federation of Arts, Houston, Texas, April 1957].

35 Michael Fried, 'Art and objecthood', *Artforum*, 5 (1967): 12–23; http://atc.berkeley.edu/201/readings/FriedObjcthd.pdf.

36 On Duchamp's artistic practice, see Dieter Daniels, *Duchamp und die anderen*, Cologne: DuMont, 1992; Janis Mink and Marcel Duchamp, *Marcel Duchamp 1887–1968: Kunst als Gegenkunst*, Cologne: Taschen, 2000.

37 Ibid., p. 45.

38 Duchamp writes of the urinal: 'Whether Mr Mutt with his own hands made the fountain has no importance. He CHOSE it' (ibid., p. 67).

39 Daniel Marzona and Uta Grosenick (eds), *Conceptual Art*, Cologne and Los Angeles: Taschen, 2005; Paul Wood, *Conceptual Art*, London: Tate Gallery, 2002.

40 Sol LeWitt, 'Sentences on conceptual art', *Art & Language*, 1 (1969): 11–13, here p. 11, sentence 10.

41 The work was made in 1974 and is shown in Hans Peter Feldmann, *Alle Kleider einer Frau*, Toronto: Art Metropole, 1999.

42 Rosalind E. Krauss, 'The originality of the avant-garde', in Krauss, *The Originality of the Avant-Garde and Other Modernist Myths*, Cambridge, MA: MIT Press, 1986, pp. 151–70.

43 Romana Rebbelmund, *Appropriation Art*, New York: Peter Lang, 1999; Stefan Römer, *Künstlerische Strategien des Fake*, Cologne: DuMont, 2001; Nicolas Bourriaud, *Postproduction: Culture as Screenplay: How Art Reprograms the World*, New York: Lukas & Sternberg, 2002.

44 Sherrie Levine, 'Statement', in *Mannerism: A Theory of Culture*, Vancouver: Vancouver Art Gallery, 1982, p. 48 [exhibition catalogue].

45 See Klaus Honnef, *Andy Warhol, 1928–1987: Commerce into Art*, Cologne: Taschen, 2000.

46 The piece is an offset print on brown-tinted paper in an edition of sixty and dates from 1988.

47 For a general overview of this development, see Julie H. Reiss, *From Margin to Center: The Spaces of Installation Art*, Cambridge, MA: MIT Press, 1999; RoseLee Goldberg and Laurie Anderson Reiss, *Performance: Live Art Since the '60s*, London: Thames & Hudson, 1998; and, for an early theoretical reflection of an artist's own work, see Allan Kaprow (ed.), *Assemblage, Environments and Happenings*, New York: H. N. Abrams, 1965.

48 See Erika Fischer-Lichte, *The Transformative Power of Performance: A New Aesthetics*, London and New York: Routledge, 2008; Juliane Rebentisch, *Aesthetics of Installation Art*, Berlin: Sternberg, 2012.

49 This position is conceived as programmatic by Fluxus. See George Maciunas, 'Neo-Dada in music, theater, poetry, art' (1962), in *In the Spirit of Fluxus*, Minneapolis: Walker Art Center, 1993, pp. 156f. [exhibition catalogue].

50 On the relevance of place and context to art practice, see Peter Weibel, 'Kontext-Theorie der Kunst', in Weibel, *Kritik der Kunst, Kunst der Kritik: essays and I say*, Vienna: Jugend & Volk, 1973, pp. 65–9; on the once-only character of live performance, see Peggy Phelan, *Unmarked: The Politics of Performance*, London: Routledge, 1993, pp. 146ff.

51 See Goldberg and Reiss, *Performance: Live Art Since the '60s*, pp. 30ff. For the quotation, see Joseph Beuys, 'Not just a few are called, but everyone' [1972], in Charles Harrison and Paul Wood (eds), *Art in Theory, 1900–1990: An Anthology of Changing Ideas*, Oxford: Blackwell, 1999, pp. 889–92, here p. 891.

52 On the destabilization of frames, see Erving Goffman, *Frame-Analysis: An Essay on the Organization of Experience*, Cambridge, MA: Harvard University Press, 1974.

53 Fischer-Lichte, *The Transformative Power of Performance*, pp. 11ff. On Abramović, see Paula Orrell (ed.), *Marina Abramović + the Future of Performance Art*, London: Prestel, 2010.

54 Georg Simmel, 'The metropolis and mental life' [1903], in Gary Bridge and Sophie Watson (eds), *The Blackwell City Reader*, Oxford: Wiley-Blackwell, 2002, pp. 11–19.

55 For a systematic concept of atmosphere, see Gernot Böhme, *Atmosphäre: Essays zur neuen Ästhetik*, Frankfurt am Main: Suhrkamp, 1995. (Individual essays available in English: 'An aesthetic theory of nature', *Thesis Eleven*, 32 (1992): 90–102; 'Atmosphere as the fundamental concept of a new aesthetics', *Thesis Eleven*, 36 (1993): 113–26; 'Acoustic atmospheres: a contribution to the study of ecological aesthetics', *Soundscape: The Journal of Acoustic Ecology*, 1 (2000): 14–18; 'The art of the stage set as a paradigm for an aesthetics of atmospheres', *Ambiances* (2013), http://ambiances.revues.org/315.)

56 Examples here are the German artistic collectives Rimini Protokoll, She She Pop and Gob Squad.

57 Parallel to this development emerge countervailing strategies of demarcation between artists and commercial creative workers. See Karen van den Berg, 'Kreativität: Drei Absagen der Kunst an ihren erweiterten Begriff', in Stephan A. Jansen et al. (eds), *Rationalität der Kreativität?*, Wiesbaden: Verlag für Sozialwissenschaften, 2009, pp. 207–24.

58 Victor Burgin, 'Situationala [1969], in *Situational Aesthetics: Selected Writings by Victor Burgin*, ed. Alexander Streitberger, Leuven: Leuven University Press, pp. 7–14, here p. 9; Hal Foster, *Recodings: Art, Spectacle, Cultural Politics*, Seattle: Bay Press, 1985, pp. 99–115, here p. 100.

59 Peter Weibel, 'Context theory of art' [1971], in Weibel (ed.), *Beyond Art: A Third Culture: A Comparative Study in Cultures Art and Science in 20th Century Austria and Hungary*, New York: Springer, 2005, pp. 497–502.

60 In the mid-1970s, Günter Metken identified such 'ethnological' tendencies in French visual arts, which would become increasingly widespread. See Günter Metken, *Spurensicherung*, Cologne: DuMont, 1977; see also Hal Foster, 'An archival impulse', *October*, 110 (2004): 3–22.

61 See Beatrice von Bismarck, 'Haltloses Ausstellen: Politiken des künstlerischen Kuratierens', in Michalka and von Bismarck (eds), *The Artist as...*, pp. 33–47; Hans Dieter Huber, 'Künstler als Kuratoren', in Huber et al. (eds), *Kunst des Ausstellens*, Ostfildern-Ruit: Hatje Cantz, 2002, pp. 225–8.

62 See Nat Finkelstein, *Andy Warhol: The Factory Years, 1964–1967*, London: Sidgwick & Jackson, 1989.

63 See Denise Frimer, 'Pedagogical paradigms: Documenta's reinvention', www.artandeducation.net/paper/pedagogical-paradigms-documentas-reinvention/.

64 Anne-Marie Bonnet, *Kunst der Moderne: Kunst der Gegenwart*, Cologne: Deubner, 2004, pp. 135f.; Philip Ursprung, *Die Kunst der Gegenwart: 1960 bis heute*, Munich: Beck, 2010, pp. 45, 69.

65 On Schlingensief, see Catherina Gilles, *Kunst und Nichtkunst: Das Theater von Christoph Schlingensief*, Würzburg: Königshausen & Neumann, 2009.

66 On the institutional framework, see Pascal Gielen, *The Murmuring of the Artistic Multitude: Global Art, Memory and Post-Fordism*, Amsterdam: Valiz, 2010; Bonnet, *Kunst der Moderne*, pp. 86ff. On the interconnection between the increase of museums and the growth of creative cities, see chapter 7.4 in this volume.

67 On Picasso, see John Berger, *The Success and Failure of Picasso* [1963], New York: Vintage, 1989. On the prehistory of the artist as the performer of his own person in the mass media around 1900, see chapter 6.2 in this volume.

68 See Isabelle Graw, *High Price: Art between the Market and Celebrity Culture*, New York: Sternberg Press, 2010; Nina Tessa Zahner, *Die neuen Regeln der Kunst*, Frankfurt am Main: Campus, 2006; Wetzel, 'Autor/Künstler'.

69 Graw, *High Price*, pp. 120–3.

70 On Kossuth, see Blake Stimson, 'The promise of conceptual art', in Stimson and Alexander Alberro (eds), *Conceptual Art: A Critical Anthology*, Cambridge, MA: MIT Press, 1999, pp. xxxviiiff; on Warhol, see Zahner, *Die neuen Regeln der Kunst*.

71 For a detailed analysis, see Sabine Kampmann, *Künstler sein: Systemtheoretische Beobachtungen von Autorschaft*, Paderborn: Fink 2006.

72 This star character has become the object of self-ironic performances, such as, prominently, those of Andrea Fraser. See Nina Möntmann, *Kunst als sozialer Raum: Andrea Fraser, Martha Rosler, Rirkrit Tiravanija, Renée Green*, Cologne: König, 2002. On the star system, see chapter 6 in this volume.

73 The Young British Artists are representative of the globally successful artist. See Julian Stallabrass, *High Art Lite: The Rise and Fall of Young British Art*, London: Verso, 2006. This does not imply that there are no marginalized artists but, rather, that being marginal no longer legitimates them in the eyes of the audience. Marginality cannot now be claimed as a precondition for creativity as unknown genius was in the nineteenth century. On social precariousness among artists today, see Angela McRobbie, '"Everyone is creative": artists as pioneers of the new economy?', in Marc James Léger, *Culture and Contestation in the New Century*, Bristol: Intellect, 2011.

74 On the substitution of the avant-garde model of radical rupture by postmodern art, see Krauss, 'The originality of the avant-garde'.

75 This formulation is introduced in Harold Rosenberg, *The Tradition of the New*, New York: Horizon Press, 1959.

76 There are naturally social limits to the ability of the audience to absorb shock and perplexity. However, there is evidence for the hypothesis that the growth of the cultural 'omnivore' blithely mixing high and popular culture, the existence of which has been demonstrated by the sociology of art, helped to establish the expectation of surprise. The restrictions on bourgeois taste break down and the popular interest in sensation, fuelled by the mass media, spreads. See Richard A. Peterson and Roger M. Kern, 'Changing highbrow taste: from snob to omnivore', *American Sociological Review*, 61 (1996): 900–07.

77 Max Horkheimer and Theodor W. Adorno, 'The culture industry' [1944], in *Dialectic of Enlightenment*, New York: Herder & Herder 1972, pp. 120–47; Arnold Gehlen, *Zeit-Bilder: Zur Soziologie und Aesthetik der modernen Malerei*, Frankfurt am Main: Athenäum, 1960, pp. 201ff. (translated in part in Christoph Menke, *The Sovereignty of Art: Aesthetic Negativity in Adorno and Derrida*, Cambridge, MA: MIT Press, 1988, p. 171). On the concept of relief, see Arnold Gehlen, *Man in the Age of Technology* [1949], New York: Columbia University Press, 1980, pp. 1–23.

78 See Jean Baudrillard, 'The conspiracy of art' [1996], *Libération*, 20 May 1996, pp. 25–9; Jean-François Lyotard, 'Das Erhabene und die Avantgarde', in Lyotard, *Das Inhumane: Plaudereien über die Zeit*, Vienna: Passagen, 1989, pp. 159–87; Fredric Jameson, *The Cultural Turn: Selected Writings on the Postmodern, 1983–1998*, London: Verso, 1998.

79 Baudrillard, 'The conspiracy of art', p. 25.

80 Luc Boltanski and Eve Chiapello, *The New Spirit of Capitalism*, London: Verso, 2005; Gielen, *The Murmuring of the Artistic Multitude*.

81 The German bureaucracy that was Max Weber's empirical object in *Wirtschaft und Gesellschaft*, his study of bureaucratic rule, was the early twentieth-century blueprint of formal, rationalized organization that was adopted outside of the state, for example in business.

82 On this basic pattern of de-differentiation, see Andreas Reckwitz, 'Grenzdestabilisierungen – Kultursoziologie und Poststrukturalismus', in Reckwitz, *Unscharf Grenzen*, Bielefeld: Transcript, 2008, pp. 301–20; Eugen Buß and Martina Schöps, 'Die gesellschaftliche Entdifferenzierung', *Zeitschrift für Soziologie*, 8 (1979): 315–29. The process by which the artistic field with its regime of aesthetic novelty becomes a new blueprint for other social fields should not be misunderstood as having only one cause. There is not a single trajectory going from art as its starting point but, rather, a social web of various practices and discourses which in turn also influence art practice.

83 This does not exclude the conscious cultivation of negative affects towards artworks. On the contrary, the orientation of postmodern art towards perplexity or defamiliarization is often directed at producing negative feelings such as confusion or fear, which, however, are integrated into the artistic field. Rather than hindering the reproduction of the artistic field, they actually secure it.

84 This debate led to nominalist and institutionalist definitions of art, such as those by Arthur Danto and George Dickie. See Arthur Danto, 'The artworld', *Journal of Philosophy*, 61 (1964): 571–84; George Dickie, *Art and the Aesthetic: An Institutional Analysis*, Ithaca, NY: Cornell University Press, 1974. Nelson Goodman's art theory is interesting from a sociological point of view. He assumes a continuum between artistic and non-artistic forms of the aesthetic. Aesthetic objects that are distinguished by a heightened syntactic, by semiotic concentration, by plenitude and polyvalence, are socially accepted as art. The social distinction between art and non-art cuts through this continuum of gradual differences. The fact that criteria for aesthetic concentration and plenitude are not established for all time then turns out to be the cause for the controversial character of art. See Nelson Goodman, *Languages of Art: An Approach to a Theory of Symbols*, Indianapolis: Bobbs-Merrill, 1968.

85 See Fried, 'Art and objecthood'; Baudrillard, 'The conspiracy of art'. On the return to the political, see Pascal Gielen and Paul de Bruyne (eds), *Being an Artist in Post-Fordist Times*, Rotterdam, NAi, 2009.

86 This reflective function of art can naturally be attributed to the whole tradition of the modern, bourgeois, critical understanding of art from Kant to Adorno and Brecht.

87 Fischer-Lichte, *The Transformative Power of Performance*, pp. 174–80.

88 Rebentisch, *Aesthetics of Installation Art*, pp. 263ff.

Chapter 4 The Rise of the Aesthetic Economy

1 Max Weber, *Economy and Society: An Outline of Interpretive Sociology*, ed. Guenther Roth and Claus Wittich, Berkeley: University of California Press, 1978, pp. 63ff.

2 On this process, see Yehonda Shenhav, *Manufacturing Rationality: The Engineering Foundations of the Managerial Revolution*, Oxford: Oxford University Press, 1999; Alfred D. Chandler, *The Visible Hand: The Managerial Revolution in American Business*, Cambridge, MA: Harvard University Press, 1977; Maury Klein, *The Flowering of the Third America: The Making of an Organizational Society, 1850–1920*, Chicago: Ivan R. Dee, 1993.

3 Joseph A. Schumpeter, *Capitalism, Socialism and Democracy* [1942], London: Routledge 1994.

4 Karl Marx, *Capital*, vol. I [1867], London: Penguin Books, 1990.

5 Karl Marx and Friedrich Engels, 'The communist manifesto', in Robert C. Tucker (ed.), *The Marx–Engels Reader*, New York and London: W. W. Norton, 1978, pp. 469–500, here p. 476.

6 On the way Marx's theory was further developed, see Rudolf Hilferding, 'Democracy and the working class' and 'The organized economy',

in Tom Bottomore and Patrick Goode (eds), *Readings in Marxist Sociology*, Oxford: Oxford University Press 1983, pp. 146ff. and 246ff. Since the work of Werner Sombart, a consensus has reigned even among non-Marxist economic historians on the distinction between two historical phases – industrial and high capitalism – the latter identical with organizational capitalism or Fordism.

7 The complement to this organized capitalism on the level of society as a whole is 'organized modernity'. The term is used by Peter Wagner to denote a form of modernity which emerged in the economy, the state and culture around 1920 and remained dominant into the 1970s. See Peter Wagner, *Sociology of Modernity*, London: Routledge, 1994.

8 Werner Rammert, *Technik aus soziologischer Perspektive*, Opladen: Westdeutscher Verlag, 1993, pp. 162–76; David F. Noble, *Forces of Production: A Social History of Industrial Automation*, Oxford: Oxford University Press, 1984, pp. 42f.

9 For the USA, see Cecelia Tichi, *Shifting Gears; Technology, Literature, Culture in Modernist America*, Chapel Hill: University of North Carolina Press, 1987.

10 Antonio Gramsci, *Selections from the Prison Notebooks*, New York: International, 1971, pp. 277ff.

11 William H. Whyte, *The Organization Man*, New York: Simon & Schuster, 1956; David Riesman, *The Lonely Crowd: A Study of the Changing American Character* [1949], New Haven, CT: Yale University Press, 2001.

12 Claus Offe, *Disorganized Capitalism: Contemporary Transformation of Work and Politics*, Cambridge, MA: MIT Press, 1985; Scott Lash and John Urry, *The End of Organized Capitalism*, Cambridge: Polity, 1987; Amin Ash (ed.), *Post-Fordism: A Reader*, Oxford: Blackwell, 1994.

13 Michael J. Piore and Charles F. Sabel, *The Second Industrial Divide: Possibilities for Prosperity*, New York: Basic Books, 1984, p. 17.

14 Charles Heckscher and Anne Donnellon (eds), *The Post-Bureaucratic Organization*, London: Sage, 1994.

15 On the economy of knowledge, see Nico Stehr, *Wissen und Wirtschaften: Die gesellschaftlichen Grundlagen der modernen Ökonomie*, Frankfurt am Main: Suhrkamp, 2001. On digitalization, Manuel Castells, *The Information Age: Economy, Society, and Culture*, vol. 1: *The Rise of the Network Society*, Oxford: Blackwell, 1996.

16 Nikolas Rose, 'Governing enterprising individuals', in Rose, *Inventing Our Selves: Psychology, Power, and Personhood*, Cambridge: Cambridge University Press, 1996, pp. 150–68; Ulrich Bröckling, *The Entrepreneurial Self: Fabricating a New Type of Subject*, Los Angeles: Sage, 2016; Paul Du Gay, *Consumption and Identity at Work*, London: Sage, 1996.

17 John Howkins, *The Creative Economy: How People Make Money from Ideas*, London: Penguin, 2001; David Hesmondhalgh, *The Cultural*

Industries, London: Sage, 2002. On the expansion of the concept within the framework of state subsidy programmes, see the second *Creative Industries Mapping Document*, ed. Creative Industries Task Force, London: Department of Culture, Media and Sport, 2001, p. 5.

18 The concepts *aesthetic economy* and *aesthetic capitalism* are being used here synonymously, since the Western economy of the twentieth century has continued to be organized universally on a capitalist basis. The question of possible aesthetic tendencies in non-capitalist economies must be left unanswered here. In particular, pre-modern economies based on gifts and social trade restrictions involve significant sensuous-affective elements, which render them an alternative aesthetic social form outside of late modernity. On the other hand, one of the central problems for the Soviet-type state socialist economy (as opposed to the current Chinese version of state capitalism) seemed to be precisely its inability to become sufficiently aesthetic.

19 On the concept of aesthetic innovation, see Wolfgang Fritz Haug, *Critique of Commodity Aesthetics: Appearance, Sexuality and Advertising in Capitalist Society* [1971], Minneapolis: University of Minnesota Press, 1986, pp. 42f. A similar though somewhat inexact concept of work is found in Maurizio Lazzarato, 'Immaterial labour', in Paolo Virno and Michael Hardt (eds), *Radical Thought in Italy: A Potential Politics*, Minneapolis: University of Minnesota Press, 1996, pp. 132–47.

20 For one such primarily economical, historical interpretation, see David Harvey, *The Condition of Postmodernity: An Enquiry into the Origins of Cultural Change*, Oxford: Blackwell, 1989, pp. 173ff.

21 For a cultural analysis of economic practices, see Paul du Gay and Michael Pryke (eds), *Cultural Economy: Cultural Analysis and Commercial Life*, London: Sage, 2002.

22 Gottfried Semper, 'Science, industry, and art: proposals for the development of a national taste at the closing of the London Exhibition' [1851], in Semper, *The Four Elements of Architecture and Other Writings*, Cambridge: Cambridge University Press, pp. 130–67.

23 Eileen Boris, *Art and Labor*, Philadelphia: Temple University Press, 1986; Gerda Breuer, *Ästhetik der schönen Genügsamkeit oder 'Arts and Crafts' als Lebensform*, Braunschweig: Vieweg, 1998; Grace Lees-Maffei and Rebecca Houze (eds), *The Design History Reader*, Oxford and New York: Berg, 2010, pp. 53ff.

24 Especially important are John Ruskin, *The Seven Lamps of Architecture*, London 1849; and *The Stones of Venice*, London, 1851.

25 William Morris, 'The beauty of life' [1880], in *The Collected Works of William Morris*, ed. May Morris, London, 1910–15; vol. 22, London: Routledge, 1992, pp. 51–80, here p. 55.

26 Ruskin, *The Seven Lamps of Architecture*, p. 181.

27 This demand was in reality only to be found among the small reformist fraction of the upper middle classes to which the arts and crafts workers themselves belonged.

28   Herbert A. Applebaum, *The Concept of Work: Ancient, Medieval, and Modern*, Albany: State University of New York Press, 1992, pp. 409f., 429f. and 436f. On other romantic forerunners of the aesthetic consumer, see Colin Campbell, *The Romantic Ethic and the Spirit of Modern Consumerism*, Oxford: Blackwell, 1987.

29   All three antagonisms collapse in the further development of the movement. For example, the Liberty department store that opened in London in 1875 was a successful business selling high-quality household goods in the arts and crafts style but produced industrially and with changing seasonal collections.

30   Ulrich Bröckling, *The Entrepreneurial Self*, pp. 108ff.

31   Chester I. Barnard, *The Functions of the Executive*, Cambridge, MA: Harvard University Press, 1938; Reinhard Bendix, *Work and Authority in Industry: Ideologies of Management in the Course of Industrialization*, Berkeley: University of California Press 1956; Schumpeter, *Capitalism, Socialism and Democracy*.

32   Hans Jaeger, 'Unternehmer', in Otto Brunner et al. (eds), *Geschichtliche Grundbegriffe: Historisches Lexikon zur politisch-sozialen Sprache in Deutschland*, vol. 6, Stuttgart: Ernst Klett, 1990, pp. 707–32.

33   Weber, *Economy and Society*, p. 225.

34   Joseph A. Schumpeter, *The Theory of Economic Development: An Inquiry into Profits, Capital, Credit, Interest, and the Business Cycle* [1911], New York: Oxford University Press, 1961. See also Schumpeter, 'Unternehmer', in *Handwörterbuch der Staatswissenschaften*, Jena: Gustav Fischer, 1928, pp. 476–87.

35   Schumpeter, *The Theory of Economic Development*, p. 65.

36   See above, chapter 3.5.

37   Schumpeter, *The Theory of Economic Development*, p. 86.

38   Frank H. Knight, *Risk, Uncertainty and Profit*, Chicago: University of Chicago Press, 1971.

39   Schumpeter, *The Theory of Economic Development*, p. 93 (translation modified).

40   Werner Sombart, 'Der kapitalistische Unternehmer', *Archiv für Sozialwissenschaft und Sozialpolitik*, 29 (1909): 689–758.

41   Ibid., p. 701.

42   Ibid., p. 741.

43   On the quantitative distribution, see the footnote in Schumpeter, *The Theory of Economic Development*, p. 81.

44   Shenhav, *Manufacturing Rationality*; David F. Noble, *America by Design: Science, Technology, and the Rise of Corporate Capitalism*, New York: Oxford University Press, 1979.

45   Frederick Winslow Taylor, *Scientific Management* [1913], Minneola, NY: Dover, 1998.

46   Hugo Münsterberg, *Psychologie und das Wirtschaftsleben: Ein Beitrag zur angewandten Experimental-Psychologie*, Leipzig, 1912; for a summary, see Emil Walter-Busch, *Das Auge der Firma: Mayos Hawthorne-*

Experimente und die Harvard Business School, 1900–1960, Stuttgart: Enke, 1988.

47 Elton Mayo, *The Human Problems of an Industrial Civilization* [1933], New York: Viking, 1977.

48 Whyte, *The Organization Man*, Part I.

49 There is a smooth transition from human relations to human resources. In 1927, the Belgian socialist Hendrik de Man (Hendrik de Man, *Joy in Work* [1927], London: Allen & Unwin, 1929) identified the satisfaction of the ludic drive and the curious desire to construct as preconditions of productive work in organizations. More abstractly and modestly, Alexander Heron pointed out in 1948 that workers must be 'capable of producing ideas that can be used' (*Why Men Work*, New York: Arno Press, 1977, p. 175) in order to remain motivated. Chester Barnard's *Organization and Management* (Cambridge, MA: Harvard University Press, 1941) and Peter Drucker's *The Concept of the Corporation* (New York: John Day, 1946) also contained early critiques of repressive tendencies in technocratic and group-oriented corporations.

50 Chris Argyris, *Personality and Organization*, New York: Harper 1957, and *Integrating the Individual and the Organization* [1964], New York: Wiley, 2009; see also Douglas McGregor, *The Human Side of Enterprise*, New York: McGraw-Hill, 1960.

51 See chapter 5.4.

52 Argyris, *Personality and Organization*, p. 28.

53 Ibid., p. 212.

54 McGregor, *The Human Side of Enterprise*, p. 75.

55 Argyris, *Integrating the Individual and the Organization*, pp. 315ff.

56 Nikolas Rose, *Governing the Soul: The Shaping of the Private Self*, London: Routledge, 1990, pp. 103ff.

57 Tom Burns and George M. Stalker, *The Management of Innovation* [1961], Oxford: Oxford University Press, 2001; see also Michel Crozier, *The Bureaucratic Phenomenon*, Chicago: University of Chicago Press, 1964; James G. March and Herbert A. Simon, *Organizations*, New York: Wiley, 1958.

58 Burns and Stalker, *The Management of Innovation*, p. 121.

59 Karl E. Weick, *The Social Psychology of Organizing* [1969], Reading, MA: Addison-Wesley, 1979.

60 Jacques Derrida, *Writing and Difference*, Chicago: University of Chicago Press, 1978.

61 Weick, *The Social Psychology of Organizing*, p. 252.

62 Holger Braun-Thürmann, *Innovation*, Bielefeld: Transcript, 2005, pp. 30ff.

63 Stephen J. Kline and Nathan Rosenberg, 'An overview of innovation', in Ralph Landau and Rosenberg (eds), *The Positive Sum Strategy*, Washington, DC: National Academy Press, 1986, pp. 275–306; Hirotaka Takeuchi and Ikujiro Nonaka, 'The new new product development

game', *Harvard Business Review*, 64 (1986): 137–46; Andrew H. van de Ven, *The Innovation Journey*, New York: Oxford University Press, 1990.

64 See John Seely Brown and Paul Duguid, 'Organizational learning and communities-of-practice', *Organization Science*, 2 (1991): 40–57.

65 Werner Sombart, *Luxury and Capitalism* [1912], Ann Arbor: University of Michigan Press, 1967.

66 Malcolm Barnard, *Fashion Theory*, London: Routledge, 2007. Exemplary theories of fashion are provided by Roland Barthes, *The Fashion System* [1967], Berkeley: University of California Press, 1990, and Elena Esposito, *Die Verbindlichkeit des Vorübergehenden: Paradoxien der Mode*, Frankfurt am Main: Suhrkamp, 2004.

67 Bonnie English, *A Cultural History of Fashion in the 20th Century: From the Catwalk to the Sidewalk*, Oxford: Berg, 2007, chapter 1.

68 Georg Simmel, 'The philosophy of fashion' [1905], in *Simmel on Culture*, ed. David Frisby and Mike Featherstone, London: Sage, 1997, pp. 187–206.

69 Christopher Breward, *Fashion*, Oxford: Oxford University Press, 2003, pp. 65ff. and 159ff.

70 English, *A Cultural History of Fashion in the 20th Century*, pp. 30ff.

71 It is for this reason not surprising that between the wars the fashion scene and the artistic avant-garde began to overlap. Early examples of this are the designs by the avant-garde artists Elsa Schiaparelli and Madeleine Vionnet.

72 Breward, *Fashion*, pp. 182ff.; Diana Crane, *Fashion and its Social Agendas: Class, Gender, and Identity in Clothing*, Chicago: University of Chicago Press, 2000, pp. 132ff.; English, *A Cultural History of Fashion in the 20th Century*, pp. 80ff.; Ted Polhemus, *Streetstyle: From Sidewalk to Catwalk*, London: Thames & Hudson, 1994.

73 The new men's fashion magazine *Gentlemen's Quarterly* (GQ) proclaimed 'What we would like to see is men dressing more to the limits of their own personality and inventiveness' (February 1965, p. 84).

74 This means that anti-fashion movements such as punk, the extreme minimalist Japanese fashion (such as the *aesthetics of poverty* from Comme des Garçons) or seemingly obsolete retro forms can easily be reinjected into the fashion cycle, thereby involuntarily reinvigorating it. See English, *A Cultural History of Fashion in the 20th Century*, pp. 102ff.

75 See above, chapter 3.5.

76 Breward, *Fashion*, pp. 85ff.

77 Since Twiggy (Lesley Hornby), at the latest, models (previously referred to as mannequins) have been able to assume the status of creative celebrities in their own right. See Harriet Quick, *Catwalking: A History of the Fashion Model*, London: Hamlyn, 1997.

78 English, *A Cultural History of Fashion in the 20th Century*, pp. 138ff. Pierre Cardin and Yves Saint Laurent were the first fashion designers to bestow their names on a whole arsenal of everyday aesthetic objects.

79 Jackson Lears, *Fables of Abundance: A Cultural History of Advertising in America*, New York: Basic Books, 1994.

80 Ibid., pp. 189ff.; see also Stephen Fox, *The Mirror Makers: A History of American Advertising and its Creators*, Urbana: University of Illinois Press, 1997.

81 Roland Marchand, *Advertising the American Dream: Making Way for Modernity, 1920–1940*, Berkeley: University of California Press, 1985; Stuart Ewen, *All Consuming Images: The Politics of Style in Contemporary Culture*, New York: Basic Books, 1988, pp. 110ff.

82 Thomas Frank, *The Conquest of Cool: Business Culture, Counterculture, and the Rise of Hip Consumerism*, Chicago: University of Chicago Press, 1997, pp. 34ff.; for a documentary account, see also Martin Mayer, *Madison Avenue*, New York: Harper, 1958.

83 Claude C. Hopkins, *Scientific Advertising* [1923], New York: Snowball, 2010.

84 Vance Packard, *The Hidden Persuaders*, New York: McKay, 1957.

85 Frank, *The Conquest of Cool*, pp. 5ff.; George Lois and Bill Pitts, *The Art of Advertising: George Lois on Mass Communication*, New York: H. N. Abrams, 1977.

86 Bob Levenson, *Bill Bernbach's Book: A History of Advertising that Changed the History of Advertising*, New York: Villard Books, 1987, p. 28.

87 Frank, *The Conquest of Cool*, pp. 86f.

88 Levenson, *Bill Bernbach's Book*, p. 113.

89 Howard L. Gossage, *Is There Any Hope for Advertising?* [1967], Urbana: University of Illinois Press, 1987; repr. in *The Book of Gossage*, Chicago: Copy Workshop, 1995.

90 See the catalogue of Bernbach advertisements in Levenson, *Bill Bernbach's Book*.

91 See Frank, *The Conquest of Cool*, pp. 88ff.

92 Jean Baudrillard's analysis of the hypertext can be brought to bear here. See Baudrillard, *Symbolic Exchange and Death* [1976], London: Sage, 1993, pp. 50ff.

93 See J. C. Louis and Harvey Z. Yazijian, *The Cola Wars: The Story of the Global Corporate Battle between the Coca-Cola Company and Pepsi Co, Inc.*, New York: Everest House, 1980.

94 'Outdoors' (1970), a path-breaking example, is made up of a collage of white-water rafters, cyclists, a climber, campers at a campfire, and hikers (www.youtube.com/watch?v=gNdJN3tqVRw).

95 Pasi Falk, 'The Benetton–Toscani effect: testing the limits of advertising', in Mica Nava and Andrew Blake (eds), *Buy this Book: Studies in Advertising and Consumption*, London: Routledge, 1997, pp. 64–83.

96 Martin Davidson, *The Consumerist Manifesto: Advertising in Postmodern Times*, London: Routledge, 1992. On the transformation of the image of the advertiser, see Frank, *The Conquest of Cool*, pp. 111ff.

97   On the history of design in the twentieth century, see Lees-Maffei and Houze, *The Design History Reader*; Peter Dormer, *Design since 1945*, London: Thames & Hudson, 1993.

98   John Heskett, *Philips: A Study of the Corporate Management of Design*, London: Trefoil, 1989.

99   Dormer, *Design since 1945*, pp. 8ff. For the Loewy proclamation, see Raymond Loewy, *Never Leave Well Enough Alone*, New York: Simon & Schuster, 1951.

100 Dormer, *Design since 1945*, pp. 83ff., 101ff. and 120ff.

101 Andrea Branzi, *The Hot House: Italian New Wave Design*, Cambridge, MA: MIT Press, 1984; Peter Cook, *Archigram*, Basel: Birkhäuser, 1991.

102 Archizoom, 'No-stop city: residential parkings, climatic universal system', *Domus*, 496 (1971): 49–54.

103 Tony Salvador et al., 'Design ethnography', *Design. Management Journal*, 10 (1999): 35–41.

104 Robert Venturi et al., *Learning from Las Vegas: The Forgotten Symbolism of Architectural Form* [1972], Cambridge, MA: MIT Press, 2001; Victor Papanek, *Design for the Real World: Human Ecology and Social Change*, New York: Pantheon Books, 1971.

105 Guy Julier, *The Culture of Design* [2000], London: Sage, 2008, pp. 93ff.; C. Thomas Mitchell, *Redefining Designing: From Form to Experience*, New York: Van Nostrand Rheinhold, 1993. On product semantics, see Klaus Krippendorf and Reinhart Butter, 'Product semantics: exploring the symbolic qualities of form', *Innovation* 3/2 (1984): 4–9. An example of the new focus on design among corporations previously uninterested in aesthetics is the transformation of the household goods firm Alessi in the 1980s. An example for the tendency of environment design is the discovery of the 'office landscape' as an object of design. See Julier, *The Culture of Design*, pp. 75ff.

106 On these more recent developments, see Mateo Kries, *Total Design: Die Inflation moderner Gestaltung*, Berlin: Nicolai, 2010, pp. 46ff.

107 Bernd Schmitt and Alexander Simonson, *Marketing-Ästhetik: Strategisches Management von Marken, Identity und Image*, Munich: Econ, 1998.

108 Wally Olins, *The Corporate Personality: An Inquiry into the Nature of Corporate Identity* [1978], London: Design Council, 1978.

109 Dormer, *Design since 1945*, pp. 109f. One of the first examples of comprehensive revamping was the 1980s redesign of British Airways, a second the founding of Starbucks in Seattle in 1987, and a third the emergence of the epithet 'Cool Britannia' in Great Britain around 1996. On Starbucks, see Schmitt and Simonson, *Marketing-Ästhetik*, pp. 113ff.; on Cool Britannia, see John Ayto, *Movers and Shakers: A Chronology of Words that Shaped our Age*, Oxford: Oxford University Press, 2006, p. 233.

110 See Julier, *The Culture of Design*, pp. 191ff.; John Heskett, *Design: A Very Short Introduction*, Oxford: Oxford University Press, 2002, pp. 68ff.

111 Tom Peters and Robert H. Waterman, *In Search of Excellence: Lessons from America's Best-Run Companies*, New York: Harper &Row, 1982; Tom Peters, *Thriving on Chaos: Handbook for a Management Revolution*, New York: Knopf, 1987; Peters, *Liberation Management: Necessary Disorganization for the Nanosecond Nineties*, New York: Knopf, 1992; Peters, *The Circle of Innovation: You Can't Shrink Your Way to Greatness*, New York: Knopf, 1998; Rosabeth Moss Kanter, *The Change Masters: Innovation and Entrepreneurship in the American Corporation*, New York: Simon & Schuster, 1983; Kanter, *When Giants Learn to Dance: Mastering the Challenge of Strategy, Management, and Careers in the 1990s*, New York: Simon & Schuster, 1989; Charles Handy, *The Age of Unreason*, London: Business Books, 1989; for an analysis of this discourse see also Rose, *Governing the Soul*, pp. 103ff.

112 Jürgen Hauschildt, *Innovationsmanagement*, Munich: Vahlen, 2004, pp. 155ff.

113 Kanter, *The Change Masters*, pp. 23ff. A similar coupling of creativity and internal entrepreneurship is found in Peter F. Drucker, *Innovation and Entrepreneurship*, Oxford: Butterworth-Heinemann 2007, pp. 30ff. On the spread of entrepreneurship as a management technique, see Rose, 'Governing enterprising individuals'.

114 Peters and Waterman, *In Search of Excellence*, pp. 29ff.

115 The semantic sources on which Peters draws to describe the two functions of inner organizational culture are telling: he discusses the dynamics of ideas and signs with metaphors from the arts, games and experimental science, while the stability of the cultural background is backed up by concepts from religious faith.

116 Kanter, *The Change Masters*, p. 129.

117 Peters, *Liberation Management*, p. 15.

118 Tim Brown, *Change by Design: How Design Thinking Transforms Organizations and Inspires Innovation*, New York: Harper Business, 2009; Tom Kelley, *The Art of Innovation: Lessons in Creativity from IDEO, America's Leading Design Firm*, New York: Currency/Doubleday 2001. The agency IDEO, on whose work both manuals are based, opened in 1991 and is probably the best example of 'management by design'. For a similar example, see also Michael Shamiyeh, *Creating Desired Futures: Solving Complex Business Problems with Design Thinking*, Basel: Birkhäuser, 2010; Thomas Lockwood, *Design Thinking: Integrating Innovation, Customer Experience, and Brand Value*, New York: Allworth Press, 2009.

119 Brown, *Change by Design*, p. 177.

120 Kelley, *The Art of Innovation*, p. 214.

121 Brown, *Change by Design*, pp. 14ff. Brown cites an example from consultancy practice that illustrates this aestheticization strategy. Confronted with a consultancy task, IDEO decided that producing a technically new bicycle is not enough and realized the necessity of creating a new 'category of bicycling'. Other tasks include designing a

'food experience' rather than just comestibles and a 'checking-in experience' rather than just hotel accommodation.

122 Rob Austin and Lee Devin, *Artful Making: What Managers Need to Know about How Artists Work*, New York: Prentice Hall, 2003.

123 Roberto Verganti, *Design-Driven Innovation: Changing the Rules of Competition by Radically Innovating What Things Mean*, Boston: Harvard Business Press, 2009.

124 Austin and Devin, *Artful Making*, p. 123.

125 Ibid., p. 180.

126 Joseph Pine and James Gilmore, *The Experience Economy: Work is Theatre and Every Business a Stage*, Cambridge, MA: Harvard Business School Press, 1999.

127 On this concept, see chapter 1.3 in this volume. See also Pierre Guillet de Monthoux, *The Art Firm: Aesthetic Management and Metaphysical Marketing*, Stanford, CA: Stanford University Press, 2004.

128 The sociology of labour has studied this sensuous experience among creative workers. See Martin Baethge, 'Arbeit, Vergesellschaftung, Identität: Zur zunehmenden normativen Subjektivierung der Arbeit', *Soziale Welt*, 42/1 (1991): 6–19; Paul Leinberger and Bruce Tucker, *The New Individualists: The Generation after the Organization Man*, New York: HarperCollins, 1991, pp. 226–68, 352–87; Hans J. Pongratz and G. Günter Voß, *Arbeitskraftunternehmer: Erwerbsorientierungen in entgrenzten Arbeitsformen*, Berlin: Sigma, 2003, pp. 65ff.

129 This interpretation is derived from Daniel Bell. See Bell, *The Coming of Post-Industrial Society: A Venture in Social Forecasting*, New York: Basic Books, 1999; see also Stehr, *Wissen und Wirtschaften*. On the concept of cognitive capitalism, see Carlo Vercellone (ed.), *Capitalismo cognitive: conoscenza e finanza nell'epoca post-fordista*, Rome: Manifestolibri, 2006.

130 Scott Lash and John Urry, *Economies of Signs and Space*, London: Sage, 1994.

131 Counter-cultures must be seen in the broader context of the 1950s and 1960s, which saw similar cultural patterns with less radical demands such as the pop youth culture of the 1950s or critical bourgeois discourse such as organizational sociology (Argyris) or self-growth psychology. Taking account of this larger historical context allows a re-evaluation of the importance of 1968. For such an account, see Detlef Siegfried, *Time is on My Side: Konsum und Politik in der Westdeutschen Jugendkultur der 60er Jahre*, Göttingen: Wallstein, 2006.

132 Michael Hardt, 'Affective labor', *boundary 2/26* (1999): 89–100. Hardt refers here particularly to forms of labour with a strong intersubjective aspect, involving empathy with the customer, whether in the area of health or entertainment. See also Arlie Russell Hochschild, *The Managed Heart: Commercialization of Human Feeling*, Berkeley: University of California Press, 1983.

133 Nigel Thrift, *Non-Representational Theory: Space, Politics, Affect*, Abingdon: Routledge, pp. 29ff.

134 For an analogous approach to natural science and finance, see Karin Knorr Cetina, 'Sociality with objects: social relations in postsocial knowledge societies', *Theory, Culture & Society*, 14 (1997): 1–30.

Chapter 5 The Psychological Turn in Creativity

1 Ewald Bohm, *Lehrbuch der Rorschach-Psychodiagnostik: Für Psychologen, Ärzte und Pädagogen*, Berne: Huber, 1951.
2 Justinus Kerner, *Klecksographien*, Stuttgart, 1857.
3 Hermann Rorschach, *Psychodiagnostics: A Diagnostic Test Based on Perception* [1921], Berne: Huber, 1951.
4 See Michael M. Sokal, *Psychological Testing and American Society, 1890–1930*, New Brunswick, NJ: Rutgers University Press, 1990.
5 Rorschach, *Psychodiagnostics*, p. 23.
6 Ibid., p. 47.
7 Ibid., p. 37.
8 Ibid., pp. 63, 89, 146.
9 James Wood et al., *What's Wrong with the Rorschach?*, San Francisco: Jossey-Bass, 2003.
10 See Nikolas Rose, *Inventing Our Selves: Psychology, Power, and Personhood*, Cambridge: Cambridge University Press, 1996. For an alternative account of psychology as a field of negotiations over the definition of the self, see Eva Illouz, *Saving the Modern Soul: Therapy, Emotions, and the Culture of Self-Help*, Berkeley: University of California Press, 2008; Anthony Giddens, *Modernity and Self-Identity: Self and Society in the Late Modern Age*, Cambridge: Polity, 1991.
11 See Michel Foucault, *Abnormal: Lectures at the Collège de France, 1974–1975*, London and New York: Verso, 2003, pp. 156–66.
12 George Becker, *Mad Genius Controversy: Study in the Sociology of Deviance*, Beverly Hills, CA: Sage, 1978.
13 These proto-psychological works were often based on comparative biographical investigations. The first was Lélut's 1836 pathography of the recognized philosophical genius Socrates, followed by Moreau's 1859 empirical comparison of 180 exceptional artistic and intellectual figures, the majority of whom Moreau diagnoses as mentally disturbed, and Cesare Lombroso's internationally influential and controversial *Genio e follia*. Later follow-ups included N. K. Royse's scholarly *A Study of Genius* and the later, more carefully argued *Genie, Irrsinn und Ruhm* by Wilhelm Lange-Eichbaum; Louis F. Lélut, *Du démon de Socrate*, Paris, 1836; Jacques-Joseph Moreau, *La Psychologie morbide dans ses rapports avec la philosophie de l'histoire, ou De l'influence des néuropathies sur le dynamisme intellectuel*, Paris, 1859; Cesare Lombroso, *The Man of Genius* [1864], London: W. Scott, 1891; Noble Kibby Royse, *A Study of Genius*, Chicago, 1890; Wilhelm Lange-Eichbaum, *The Problem of Genius* [1928], London; Kegan Paul, Trench, Trubner, 1931.

14 Royse, *A Study of Genius*; Lombroso, *The Man of Genius*; Warren La Verne Babcock, 'On the morbid heredity and predisposition to insanity of the man of genius', *Journal of Nervous and Mental Disease*, 20 (1895), 749–69.

15 Becker, *Mad Genius Controversy*, pp. 38ff.

16 Michael M. Sokal, 'Practical phrenology as psychological counselling in the 19th-century United States', in Christopher D. Green and Marlene G. Shore (eds), *The Transformation of Psychology: Influences of 19th-Century Philosophy, Technology and Natural Science*, Washington, DC: American Psychological Association, 2001, pp. 21–44.

17 Francis Galton, *Hereditary Genius: An Inquiry into its Laws and Consequences*, London, 1869.

18 Sigmund Freud, *Leonardo Da Vinci and a Memory of his Childhood* [1910], *The Standard Edition of the Complete Psychological Works of Sigmund Freud*, London: Hogarth Press, Vol. 11, pp. 59–137, here p. 80.

19 Otto Rank, *Art and Artist: Creative Urge and Personality Development* [1932], New York: Agathon Press, 1968. Rank has been taken up more recently by Andrew Brink in *The Creative Matrix*, New York: Peter Lang, 2000.

20 Otto Rank, *Der Künstler: Ansätze zu einer Sexual-Psychologie*, Vienna: Heller, 1918.

21 Otto Rank, *Art and Artist*, p. 430.

22 Ibid.

23 Lawrence Kubie, *Psychoanalyse und Genie: Der schöpferische Prozeß* [1958], Reinbek bei Hamburg: Rowohlt, 1966.

24 Ibid., pp. 37f.

25 On gestalt psychology, see Herbert Fitzek and Wilhelm Salber, *Gestaltpsychologie*, Darmstadt: Wissenschaftliche Buchgesellschaft, 1996; Mitchell G. Ash, *Gestalt Psychology in German Culture, 1890–1967: Holism and the Quest for Objectivity*, Cambridge: Cambridge University Press, 1988.

26 An early anticipation of gestalt psychology is provided by Christian von Ehrenfels. His crown witness for the primacy of perceptual wholes over individual sense data is the faculty for recognizing a melody as one and the same despite key changes which alter all the individual notes. This ability, he claims, renders perception a productive act. See Christian von Ehrenfels, 'On "gestalt qualities"' [1890], in Barry Smith (ed.), *Foundations of Gestalt Theory*, Munich and Vienna: Philosophia, 1988, pp. 82–117.

27 Max Wertheimer, 'Experimental studies on seeing motion' [1912], in Wertheimer and Lothar Spillmann (eds), *On Perceived Motion and Figural Organization*, Cambridge, MA: MIT Press, 2012, pp. 1–92.

28 Max Wertheimer, *Productive Thinking*, New York and London: Harper, 1945.

29 Fitzek and Salber, *Gestaltpsychologie*, pp. 45ff.

30 Wertheimer, *Productive Thinking*, p. 238.

31 See ibid., pp. 242f.

32 On self-growth psychology in general, see Duane Philip Schultz, *Growth Psychology*, New York: Van Nostrand Rheinhold, 1977, and Martin Seligman and Mihály Csíkszentmihályi, 'Positive psychology: an introduction', *American Psychologist*, 55 (2000): 5–14.

33 See chapter 4.4.

34 Charles Taylor, *Sources of Self: The Making of the Modern Identity*, Cambridge, MA: Harvard University Press, 1989, p. 368.

35 Herbert Marcuse, *Eros and Civilization: A Philosophical Inquiry into Freud* [1955], Boston: Beacon Press, 1966, pp. 157f.

36 Frank Dumont, 'From illness to wellness models of human nature', in Dumont, *A History of Personality Psychology: Theory, Science, and Research from Hellenism to the Twenty-First Century*, Cambridge: Cambridge University Press, 2010, pp. 35–74.

37 T. J. Jackson Lears, 'From salvation to self-realization: advertising and the therapeutic roots of the consumer culture, 1880–1930', in Lears and Richard Wightman Fox, *The Culture of Consumption: Critical Essays in American History 1880–1980*, New York: Pantheon Books, 1983, pp. 1–38.

38 David Riesman, *The Lonely Crowd: A Study of the Changing American Character* [1949], New Haven, CT: Yale University Press, 2001; William H. Whyte, *The Organization Man*, New York: Simon & Schuster, 1956; Douglas McGregor, *The Human Side of Enterprise*, New York: McGraw-Hill, 1960.

39 William Graebner, *The Engineering of Consent: Democracy and Authority in Twentieth-Century America*, Madison: University of Wisconsin Press, 1987; Rose, *Inventing Our Selves*, pp. 114–49.

40 Abraham Harold Maslow, *Motivation and Personality* [1954], New York: Harper & Row, 1970; Maslow, *Toward a Psychology of Being*, New York: Van Nostrand, 1968; Carl R. Rogers, *On Becoming a Person* [1961], Boston: Houghton Mifflin, 1995.

41 Rogers, *On Becoming a Person*, p. 351 (emphasis in the original).

42 Maslow, *Motivation and Personality*, p. 46.

43 Maslow, *Toward a Psychology of Being*, pp. 83ff.

44 Ibid., p. 85.

45 Rogers, *On Becoming a Person*.

46 Maslow, *Toward a Psychology of Being*, p. 90 (emphasis in the original).

47 On what follows see ibid., pp. 151ff.

48 Rollo May, *The Courage to Create*, New York: W. W. Norton, 1975.

49 John Curtis Gowan, *Development of the Creative Individual*, San Diego: R. R. Knapp, 1972.

50 Ibid., p. 101.

51 Ibid., p. 109.

52 Joy Paul Guilford, 'Creativity', *American Psychologist*, 5 (1950): 444–54.

53 Ibid., p. 26.

54 Lewis Madison Terman, *Mental and Physical Traits of a Thousand Gifted Children: Genetic Studies of Genius*, Stanford, CA: Stanford University Press, 1925. For a critical examination of Terman's book, see Joy Paul Guilford, 'Creativity: yesterday, today, and tomorrow', *Journal of Creative Behaviour*, 1 (1967): 3–14.

55 Ellis Paul Torrance, *Torrance Tests of Creative Thinking*, Princeton, NJ: Personnel Press, 1966.

56 Frank Barron, *Creativity and Psychological Health*, New York: Van Nostrand, 1963, pp. 200ff.

57 Torrance, *Torrance Test of Creative Thinking*, vol. 1, p. 6.

58 Alex Osborn, *Applied Imagination: Principles and Procedures of Creative Problem Solving*, New York: Scribner, 1953.

59 William J. J. Gordon, *Synectics*, New York: Harper, 1961, p. 35.

60 Important steps in this process were the establishment of the Institute for Personality Assessment and Research in Berkeley in 1949 and of the Problem Solving Institute in 1954.

61 Richard S. Crutchfield, 'Detrimental effects of conformity pressures on creative thinking', *Psychologische Beiträge*, 6 (1962): 463–71.

62 Ibid., p. 469.

63 Philip W. Jackson and Samuel Messick, 'The person, the product and the response: conceptual problems in the assessment of creativity', *Journal of Personality*, 33 (1965): 309–29, here p. 313.

64 Ibid., p. 320.

65 See chapter 2.2.

66 Karl-Heinz Brodbeck, *Entscheidung zur Kreativität*, Darmstadt: Wissenschaftliche Buchgesellschaft, 1995, p. 2.

67 Mihály Csíkszentmihályi, *Flow: The Psychology of Optimal Experience*, New York: Harper & Row, 1990; *The Evolving Self: A Psychology for the Third Millennium*, New York: HarperCollins, 1993; *Creativity: Flow and the Psychology of Discovery and Invention*, New York: HarperCollins, 1996.

68 Twyla Tharp, *The Creative Habit: Learn it and Use it for Life: A Practical Guide*, New York: Simon & Schuster, 2003. Tharp is a well-known choreographer based in New York.

69 Ibid., p. 10.

70 Keri Smith, *How to Be an Explorer of the World: Portable Life Museum*, New York: Perigee, 2008.

71 Robert J. Sternberg, 'The development of creativity as a decision-making process', in Robert Keith Sawyer (ed.), *Creativity and Development*, Oxford: Oxford University Press, 2003, pp. 91–138.

72 Ibid., p. 94.

73 See chapter 4.2.

74 Sternberg, 'The development of creativity as a decision-making process', p. 118.

75 In two of his earliest works, Foucault spoke of a conflict in psychology between a scientistic paradigm and a hermeneutic, existentialist paradigm. See Michel Foucault, 'La Psychologie de 1850 à 1950' [1957], in, *Dits et écrits I, 1954–1975*, Paris: Gallimard, 2001, pp. 120–37; 'La Recherche scientifique et la psychologie' [1957], ibid., pp. 137–58; and 'Die wissenschaftliche Forschung und die Psychologie' [1957], ibid., pp. 196–222.

76 Michel Foucault, *Mental Illness and Psychology* [1960], New York: Harper & Row, 1976; *Abnormal: Lectures at the Collège de France, 1974–1975*; and *Psychiatric Power: Lectures at the Collège de France, 1973–1974*, New York: Picador, 2006. For a continuation of Foucault's account into the first third of the twentieth century, see Nikolas Rose, *The Psychological Complex: Psychology, Politics and Society in England, 1869–1939*, London: Routledge & Kegan Paul, 1985.

77 Michel Foucault, *Security, Territory, Population: Lectures at the Collège de France, 1977–1978*, New York: Picador/Palgrave Macmillan, 2009, especially lectures 2–4.

78 Graebner, *The Engineering of Consent*; Peter Miller and Ted O'Leary, 'Hierarchies and American ideals 1900–1940', *Academy of Management Review*, 14 (1989): 250–65; Ludy T. Benjamin, *A Brief History of Modern Psychology*, Oxford: Blackwell, 2007, pp. 93ff.

79 Peter Wagner, *A Sociology of Modernity*, London: Routledge, 1994. See also chapter 8.1 in this volume.

80 There is a connection here to what Charles Taylor has called the modern hegemony of benevolence, the origins of which he finds in eighteenth-century deism (Taylor, *Sources of the Self: The Making of the Modern Identity*, Cambridge: Cambridge University Press, 1989, pp. 261ff.). The psychology of the resource self shifts the locus of this fundamental kindness from God to the soul.

81 Boris Traue, *Das Subjekt der Beratung: Zur Soziologie einer Psycho-Technik*, Bielefeld: Transcript, 2010; Jens Elberfeld et al. (eds), *Das beratene Selbst: Zur Genealogie der Therapeutisierung in den 'langen' Siebzigern*, Bielefeld: Transcript, 2011. Since the 1980s, the psychological notion of a natural capacity for creative self-transformation has been increasingly substantiated by neurophysiology. See Marc Runco, *Creativity*, Amsterdam: Elsevier Academic Press, 2007, chapter 3. The popular appropriation of neurophysiology goes back to Roger Sperry's theory of left and right parts of the brain, locating creativity in the right half and logical capacities in the left. A more comprehensive approach is the notion of a creative brain in its totality. See Arne Dietrich, 'The cognitive neuro-science of creativity', *Psychonomic Bulletin & Review*, 11 (2004): 1011–26.

82 For this positive understanding of the emotions in more recent psychology, see Illouz, *Saving the Modern Soul*.

83 Both Robert Sternberg and Csíkszentmihályi emphasize this role of the audience in creativity (see Csíkszentmihályi, *Creativity: Flow and the Psychology of Discovery and Invention*).

Chapter 6   The Genesis of the Star System

1   On the genesis of the star, see P. David Marshall, *Celebrity and Power*, Minneapolis: University of Minnesota Press, 1997; Sean Redmond and Su Holmes (eds), *Stardom and Celebrity*, Los Angeles: Sage, 2007; Chris Rojek, *Celebrity*, London: Reaktion Books, 2001.

2   On the concept of expressive individualism as applied to US culture, see Robert N. Bellah et al., *Habits of the Heart: Individualism and Commitment in American Life*, Berkeley: University of California Press, 1985, pp. 142–63. Charles Taylor applies his concept of expressivity to post-romanticist Europe in *Sources of the Self: The Making of the Modern Identity*, Cambridge: Cambridge University Press, 1989, pp. 368–90 (chapter 21: 'The expressivist turn').

3   On the distinction between 'inner-directed character' and 'other-directed character', see David Riesman, *The Lonely Crowd: A Study of the Changing American Character* [1949], New Haven, CT: Yale University Press, 2001 (chapter 1).

4   On the star as ideal self in film, see Christian Metz, *The Imaginary Signifier: Psychoanalysis and the Cinema* [1977], Bloomington: Indiana University Press, 1982.

5   For an analysis of attention cultures, see Georg Franck, *Ökonomie der Aufmerksamkeit: Ein Entwurf*, Munich: Carl Hanser, 1998; Georg Franck, 'The scientific economy of attention: a novel approach to the collective rationality of science', *Scientometrics*, 55/1 (2002): 3–26.

6   Theodor W. Adorno and Max Horkheimer, 'The culture industry: enlightenment as mass deception', in *Dialectic of Enlightenment*, Stanford, CA: Stanford University Press, 2002, pp. 94–136; Walter Benjamin, 'The work of art in the age of its technological reproducibility: second version', in *The Work of Art in the Age of its Technological Reproducibility, and Other Writings on Media*, Cambridge, MA: Belknap Press, 2008, pp. 19–55, here pp. 31–4, especially p. 33; Leo Löwenthal, *Literature, Popular Culture and Society*, Englewood Cliffs, NJ: Prentice Hall, 1961.

7   Leo Braudy, *The Frenzy of Renown: Fame and its History*, New York: Oxford University Press, 1997.

8   Braudy finds a third variety, which was influenced by Christianity but which continued to be influential in modernity, in the audience-shy fraction of the artistic genius with its mistrust of the vanity of acclaim.

9   On the distinction between ascribed and achieved status, see Talcott Parsons, *The Social System*, Glencoe, IL: Free Press, 1951, pp. 180ff.

10   On how stars come to represent types, see Richard Dyer, *Stars*, London: British Film Institute, 2002.

11   On auratic individuality, see Roland Barthes, 'The face of Garbo', in *Mythologies* [1957], New York: Noonday Press, 1972, pp. 56–61; and, more recently, Jeffrey C. Alexander, 'The celebrity-icon', *Cultural Sociology*, 3 (2010), pp. 323–36.

12 For a sociology of audio-visual mass media, see Joshua Meyrowitz, *No Sense of Place: The Impact of Electronic Media on Social Behavior*, New York: Oxford University Press, 1985.

13 On the significance of the audience function for social theory, see Rudolf Stichweh, *Inklusion und Exklusion*, Bielefeld: Transcript, 2005, pp. 13ff. Stichweh, however, is not concerned with the aestheticization of the audience.

14 The activation of the audience in the postmodern artistic field since the 1970s is analogous to the activation of mass-media audiences by the internet.

15 See Niklas Luhmann, *The Reality of the Mass Media* [1996], Stanford, CA: Stanford University Press, 2000, pp. 15ff. For a more systematic account of the relation between the emergence of the media and the creativity dispositif, as well as of the problem of attention in relation to the dispositif, see chapter 8.3 in this volume.

16 This tendency has been criticized from many quarters. See, for example, Guy Debord, *The Society of the Spectacle* [1967], New York: Zone Books, 1994.

17 On the concept of the epistemic object in the context of science, see Hans-Jörg Rheinberger, *Toward a History of Epistemic Things: Synthesizing Proteins in the Test Tube*, Stanford, CA: Stanford University Press, 1997. Here, we are transposing the concept onto aesthetics.

18 On the latter, see chapter 6.4.

19 On the specific structure of the visual in media technology, see John Ellis, *Visible Fictions: Cinema, Television, Video*, London: Routledge, 1992. See also Marshall McLuhan, *The Gutenberg Galaxy: The Making of Typographic Man* [1962], Toronto: University of Toronto Press, 2002; Friedrich A. Kittler, *Literature, Media, Information Systems: Essays* [1997], London and New York: Routledge, 2012.

20 This is pointed out in Benjamin, *The Work of Art in the Age of its Technological Reproducibility*, pp. 27ff.

21 This gaze has been the subject of abundant interest in film studies. See Laura Mulvey, 'Visual pleasure and narrative cinema', *Screen*, 3 (1975): 6–18.

22 On this useful distinction, see Warren I. Susman, *Culture as History*, New York: Pantheon Books, 1985, pp. 271–85.

23 Jacques Lacan, 'The mirror stage as formative of the function of the I' [1949], in *Écrits: A Selection*, London and New York: Routledge, pp 1–8, here p. 2. On the distinction between *Objektbesetzung* (object investment, cathexis, occupation) and identification, see Sigmund Freud, *Three Essays on the Theory of Sexuality* [1905], New York: Basic Books, 1996.

24 Michel Foucault, *Discipline and Punish: The Birth of the Prison* [1975], New York: Random House, 1995, chapter 3, 'Panopticism', pp. 195ff.

25 We are treating here of the prehistory of the postmodern system of artistic stardom that was the theme of chapter 3.5.

26 The concept of the performing self is borrowed from the cultural history analysis by Sarah Burns, for whom it is fundamental to explaining a new type of subjectivity emerging in the USA in the late nineteenth century. Sarah Burns, *Inventing the Modern Artist*, New Haven, CT: Yale University Press, 1996, pp. 1–16, 221–46.

27 Charles Leonard Ponce de Leon, *Self-Exposure: Human-Interest Journalism and the Emergence of Celebrity in America, 1890–1940*, Chapel Hill: University of North Carolina Press, 2002; also Joe Moran, *Star Authors*, London: Pluto Press, 2000, pp. 15–34.

28 Harry Franklin Harrington, *Chats on Feature Writing*, New York: Harper, 1925, p. 56.

29 Burns, *Inventing the Modern Artist*, pp. 221–46; Philip Fisher, 'Appearing and disappearing in public: social space in late-nineteenth-century literature and culture', in Sacvan Bercovitch (ed.), *Reconstructing American Literary History*, Cambridge, MA: Harvard University Press, 1986, pp. 155–88.

30 This applies to the widely distributed photograph *Whitman and his Butterfly* from 1873, with Whitman sporting an imposing beard, a simple cardigan and rustic headwear, immortalized in pensive observation of a butterfly. It also applies to the photograph of Wilde on his 1882 American tour in New York sporting a velvet jacket and knee breeches, meditatively inclined on one elbow, a book in the other hand, casually draped over a luxuriant sofa. See *Walt Whitman, half-length portrait, seated, facing left, wearing hat and sweater, holding butterfly*, photographed by Phillips & Taylor, Philadelphia (http://hdl.loc.gov/loc.pnp/ppmsca.07141); *Oscar Wilde/Sarony*, photographed by Napoleon Sarony, January 1882, in Richard Ellmann, *Oscar Wilde*, New York: Knopf, 1988, p. 460. For the complete series of photographs, see www.oscarwildeinamerica.org/sarony/sarony-photographs-of-oscar-wilde-1882.html.

31 David Haven Blake, *Walt Whitman and the Culture of American Celebrity*, New Haven, CT: Yale University Press, 2006, pp. 197f.; Moran, *Star Authors*, pp. 15–34.

32 Blake, *Walt Whitman and the Culture of American Celebrity*, pp. 21ff., 197f.

33 Braudy, *The Frenzy of Renown*, pp. 491–505; Bluford Adams, *E pluribus Barnum: The Great Showman and the Making of U.S. Popular Culture*, Minneapolis: University of Minnesota Press, 1997.

34 This applies for instance to politics. A prominent example is Theodore Roosevelt. See Fisher, 'Appearing and disappearing in public'. The early public interest in stardom is the object of a severe backlash, in the USA and elsewhere. This critique draws heavily on the romantic semantics of an expressive subjectivity which should ideally be kept away from the light of public observation and on the Christian notion of the vanity of fame. See Braudy, *The Frenzy of Renown*, pp. 380f., 445–50 and 464–8.

35 On the aesthetic of presence, see Doris Kolesch, 'Ästhetik der Präsenz: Theater-Stimmen', in Josef Früchtl and Jörg Zimmermann (eds), *Ästhetik der Inszenierung*, Frankfurt am Main: Suhrkamp, 2001, pp. 260–75; on the culture of presence in contradistinction to the culture of sense, see Hans Ulrich Gumbrecht, *Production of Presence: What Meaning Cannot Convey*, Stanford, CA: Stanford University Press, 2004.

36 On the differences between movie and music stars, see Marshall, *Celebrity and Power*, pp. 79–118, 150–84.

37 On the uncertain status of stage actors in the nineteenth century, see Edward Berenson and Eva Giloi (eds), *Constructing Charisma: Celebrity, Fame, and Power in Nineteenth-Century Europe*, New York: Berghahn Books, 2010. In music, scattered interpreters occasionally attained recognition as virtuosos, usually on the basis of the classicist aesthetic of perfection. Heinz von Loesch (ed.), *Musikalische Virtuosität*, Mainz: Schott, 2004.

38 Richard deCordova, *Picture Personalities: The Emergence of the Star System in America*, Urbana: University of Illinois Press, 1990. On the film star in general, see Edgar Morin, *The Stars*, Minneapolis: University of Minnesota Press, 2005; Richard Dyer, *Heavenly Bodies: Film Stars and Society*, New York: St Martin's Press, 2003; Christine Gledhill (ed.), *Stardom: Industry of Desire*, London: Routledge, 1991.

39 Hollywood movie stars from the 1920s to the 1940s were the prototypes for Leo Löwenthal's study of stars in which he contrasts consumer idols with high media visibility with production idols. Löwenthal, *Literature, Popular Culture and Society*, Englewood Cliffs, NJ: Prentice Hall, 1961.

40 Dyer, *Stars*, pp. 38–65.

41 Edward Dwight Easty, *On Method Acting*, New York: Ivy Books, 1989. On the connection between performance stars and method acting, see also Christine Geraghty, 'Re-examining stardom: questions of texts, bodies and performance', in Christine Gledhill and Linda Williams (eds), *Reinventing Film Studies*, London: Arnold, 2000, pp. 183–201.

42 Marli Feldvoß and Marion Löhndorf (eds), *Marlon Brando*, Berlin: Bertz, 2004. Hamilton Carroll, *Affirmative Reaction: New Formations of White Masculinity*, Durham, NC: Duke University Press, 2011, pp. 79ff. (chapter '"A very patriotic theme": myths of mobility and blue-collar celebrity').

43 Admittedly, not every movie star conforms to the model of the performance star. The old Hollywood system frequently produced movie stars whose film performances lagged behind their personal fame, as well as type stars characterized not by individual performances but by the recognizability of their roles. On this distinction, see Geraghty, 'Re-examining stardom'.

44 Geoff King, *New Hollywood Cinema: An Introduction*, New York: Columbia University Press, 2002, pp. 85–115; Diedrich Diederichsen, 'Artists, auteurs, and stars: on the human factor in the culture industry',

Media Art Net (2004), www.medienkunstnetz.de/themes/art_and_cinematography/auteurs.

45　On the postmodern artist, see chapter 3.5.

46　On the pop star in general, see Marshall, *Celebrity and Power*, pp. 150–84; Edda Holl, *Die Konstellation Pop: Theorie eines kulturellen Phänomens der 60er Jahre*, Hildesheim: Univ, 1996. On the genre of the pop or rock concert, see Simon Frith, *Performing Rites: On the Value of Popular Music*, Cambridge, MA: Harvard University Press, 1996.

47　On the experience of the voice, see Doris Kolesch and Sybille Krämer (eds), *Stimme: Annäherung an ein Phänomen*, Frankfurt: Suhrkamp, 2006.

48　Marshall, *Celebrity and Power*, p. 162.

49　John Clarke, 'Style', in Stuart Hall and Tony Jefferson (eds), *Resistance through Rituals: Youth Subcultures in Post-War Britain*, London: Routledge, 1996, pp. 175–91.

50　Marshall, *Celebrity and Power*, pp. 152ff.

51　Keir Keightley, 'Reconsidering rock', in Simon Frith et al. (eds), *The Cambridge Companion to Pop and Rock*, Cambridge: Cambridge University Press, 2001, pp. 109–42; Lawrence Grossberg, 'Another boring day in paradise: rock and roll and the empowerment of everyday life', in Sarah Thornton and Ken Gelder (ed.), *The Subcultures Reader*, London: Routledge, 1997, pp. 477–93; Heike Klippel and Hartmut Winkler, 'Der Star – das Muster', in Kemper, *'But I like it': Jugendkultur und Popmusik*, Stuttgart: Reclam, 1998, pp. 333–43.

52　On the structure of the pop event, see Holl, *Die Konstellation Pop*. On the particular form of the pop and rock concert in contradistinction to the bourgeois concert, see Frith, *Performing Rites*.

53　Tom Holert and Mark Terkessidis (eds), *Mainstream der Minderheiten: Pop in der Kontrollgesellschaft*, Berlin: ID-Archiv, 1997, pp. 5–19. See also my examination of the countercultural hip/square distinction in chapter 4.4.

54　Ronald D. Cohen, *Rainbow Quest: The Folk Music Revival & American Society, 1940–1970*, Amherst: University of Massachusetts Press, 2002.

55　Richard Lester, *A Hard Day's Night*, 1964 [film].

56　Kenneth Womack and Todd Davis (eds), *Reading the Beatles: Cultural Studies, Literary Criticism, and the Fab Four*, Albany: State University of New York Press, 2006; Kenneth Womack (ed.), *The Cambridge Companion to the Beatles*, Cambridge: Cambridge University Press, 2009; P. David Marshall, 'The celebrity legacy of the Beatles', in Ian Inglis (ed.), *The Beatles, Popular Music and Society*, Basingstoke: Macmillan, 2000, pp. 163–75.

57　Hans Ulrich Gumbrecht, *In Praise of Athletic Beauty*, Cambridge, MA: Harvard University Press, 2006; Martin Seel, 'Die Zelebration des Unvermögens: Aspekte einer Ästhetik des Sports', in Seel, *Ethisch-ästhetische Studien*, Frankfurt am Main: Suhrkamp, 1996, pp. 188–200.

58 Richard Giulianotti, *Football: A Sociology of the Global Game*, Cambridge: Polity, 1999, pp. 122ff.; Barry Smart, *The Sport Star: Modern Sport and the Cultural Economy of Sporting Celebrity*, London: Sage, 2005.

59 John Albert Walker, *Art and Celebrity*, London: Pluto Press, 2003.

60 See chapter 3.5. The artist as a type of subject can now become particularly interesting for the audience on the level of personality creativity. This is demonstrated by the upsurge of artist's biopics since the 1990s. Manfred Mittermayer, 'Darstellungsformen des Schöpferischen in biographischen Filmen', in Bernhard Fetz (ed.), *Die Biographie: Zur Grundlegung ihrer Theorie*, Berlin: de Gruyter, 2009, pp. 501–33.

61 On these areas of the creative industries, see chapter 4.4. On star architects, see Donald McNeill, *The Global Architect: Firms, Fame and Urban Form*, New York: Routledge, 2009, pp. 59–81. The star chef, the most prominent international example being Jamie Oliver, is an interesting intermediate entity. On the one hand he is a work creator, inventing a style, a way of making a distinctive kind of culinary, aesthetic object. On the other hand, he is a television chef and therefore a performance star, exhibiting himself in the act of cooking.

62 Joe Littler, 'Celebrity CEOs and the cultural economy of tabloid intimacy', in Redmond and Holmes (eds), *Stardom and Celebrity*, pp. 230–43. A given social field can produce stars to the extent that it can become aesthetic. Professionals in administration, technology, social services and law are unlikely to become stars. Politics represents a special case. Political stars combine aspects of the expressive creative subject with the ancient tradition of the famous leader. Personality stars have been emerging in politics since the 1990s, Silvio Berlusconi being a prime example.

63 Charles Fairchild, 'Building the authentic celebrity: the "idol" phenomenon in the attention economy', *Popular Music and Society*, 3 (2007): 355–75; Albert Moran (ed.), *TV Formats Worldwide: Localizing Global Programs*, Chicago: Intellect, 2009. Practical strategies for becoming a star are contained in Irving J. Rein et al., *High Visibility: The Making and Marketing of Professionals into Celebrities*, Lincolnwood, IL: NTC, 1997.

64 Rojek, *Celebrity*, pp. 143–80; David Schmid, *Natural Born Celebrities: Serial Killers in American Culture*, Chicago: University of Chicago Press, 2005.

65 On the aesthetic of evil in cultural history, see Peter-André Alt, *Ästhetik des Bösen*, Munich: Beck, 2010.

66 Daniel Boorstin, *The Image: A Guide to Pseudo-Events in America*, New York: Vintage, 1992, p. 57.

67 Joshua Gamson, 'The assembly line of greatness: celebrity in twentieth-century America', *Critical Studies in Media Communication*, 1 (1992): 1–24; Graeme Turner, *Understanding Celebrity*, London: Sage, 2004. For a theoretical account of this process, see Franck, *Ökonomie der Aufmerksamkeit*, pp. 113ff.

68   On the problematic relation between achievement and success as an attribute of the creativity dispositif, see chapter 8.4.

Chapter 7   Creative Cities

1   John Dominis, 'Living big in a loft', *Life*, 68/11 (1970): 61–5.
2   The New York press had been reporting on this theme for several years. In the 1960s it was still an obscure subcultural phenomenon. Gilbert Millstein, 'Portrait of the loft generation', *New York Times Magazine*, 7 January 1962, pp. 24–36.
3   See chapter 3.1.
4   Michael Guggenheim, 'Mutable immobiles: change of use of buildings as a problem of quasi-technologies', in Thomas Bender and Ignacio Farias (eds), *Urban Assemblages: How Actor-Network Theory Changes Urban Studies*, London: Routledge, 2009, pp. 161–79.
5   Sharon Zukin, *Loft Living: Culture and Capital in Urban Change*, Baltimore: Johns Hopkins University Press, 1982, pp. 58ff.
6   Lewis Mumford, 'What is a city?', *Architectural Record*, 82 (1937): 58–62.
7   The tipping point into the mainstream was finally reached in New York in 1979, when the *New York Times* featured large-format real-estate advertisements under the title 'THE ULTIMATE in Loft Living'. See Zukin, *Loft Living*, p. 64.
8   Charles Landry, *The Creative City: A Toolkit for Urban Innovators*, London: Earthscan, 2009.
9   Sharon Zukin, *The Cultures of Cities*, Oxford: Blackwell, 1995.
10   This is suggested by Peter Hall's historiography of the city; see Hall, *Cities of Tomorrow: An Intellectual History of Urban Planning and Design in the Twentieth Century*, Oxford: Blackwell, 1989.
11   On the spread of the term 'urban experience', see Allan Jacobs and Donald Appleyard, *Toward an Urban Design Manifesto*, Berkeley: University of California, Institute of Urban & Regional Development, 1982.
12   Louis Wirth, 'Urbanism as a way of life', *American Journal of Sociology*, 44 (1938): 1–24.
13   On the theory of space, see Henri Lefebvre, *Production of Space* [1974], Oxford: Blackwell, 1991; Anthony Giddens, *The Constitution of Society: An Outline of the Theory of Structuration*, Berkeley: University of California Press, 1986, pp. 110–61 (chapter 3: 'Time, space and regionalization'); Martina Löw, *The Sociology of Space: Materiality, Social Structures, and Action*, Basingstoke: Palgrave Macmillan, 2016.
14   Bruno Latour, *We Have Never Been Modern*, Cambridge, MA: Harvard University Press, 1993.
15   David Harvey speaks in this context of the replacement of 'urban planning' by 'urban design'. See Harvey, *The Condition of Postmodernity:*

An Enquiry into the Origins of Cultural Change, Oxford: Blackwell, 1989, pp. 66ff.

16 On organized modernity, see chapter 8.1.

17 See Max Weber, 'The city (non-legitimate domination)', in *Economy and Society: An Outline of Interpretative Sociology*, Berkeley: University of California Press, pp. 1212–372, here pp. 1236–65 ('II: The occidental city').

18 Thilo Hilpert, *Die funktionelle Stadt: Le Corbusiers Stadtvision – Bedingungen, Motive, Hintergründe*, Braunschweig: Vieweg, 1978, pp. 14–20, 39–57.

19 Le Corbusier developed the plan for a 'contemporary city of three million inhabitants' divided into geometrical, high-density districts, while Frank Lloyd Wright proposed the suburban vision of a 'broadacre city' made up of single family houses. Le Corbusier, 'A contemporary city' [1922], in Le Corbusier, *The City of Tomorrow and its Planning*, London: Architectural Press, 1987, pp. 163–80; Frank Lloyd Wright, 'Broadacre city: a new community plan', *Architectural Record*, 4 (1935): 243–54.

20 Robert Imrie and Mike Raco, *Urban Renaissance? New Labour, Community and Urban Policy*, Bristol: Policy Press, 2003; Richard G. Rogers, *Towards an Urban Renaissance: Final Report of the Urban Task Force*, London: Department of the Environment, Transport and the Regions, 1999.

21 Critical urbanism was influenced by the metropolis discourse cultivated by members of the avant-garde, ranging from Baudelaire to Walter Benjamin and Virginia Woolf, which generated the figure of the *flâneur* as a mobile subject of experience receptive to urban attractions. Avant-garde discourse had been led within the context of a late bourgeois city on the verge of breaking its own outer limits. Meanwhile, critical urbanism acquired stringency by being juxtaposed to the functional city.

22 Lewis Mumford, *The City in History*, New York: Harcourt, Brace & World, 1961; for an earlier document along similar lines, see Mumford, *The Culture of Cities*, New York: Harcourt, Brace, 1938. See also Mumford, 'What is a city?' [1937], in Richard T. LeGates and Frederic Stout (eds), *The City Reader*, London: Routledge, 2003, pp. 91–5; for the terms cited above, see p. 93.

23 Kevin Lynch, *The Image of the City*, Cambridge, MA: MIT Press, 1960.

24 Ibid., p. 5.

25 Ibid., p. 91.

26 Tom McDonough, *The Situationists and the City*, London: Verso, 2009.

27 Guy Debord, 'Writings from the Situationist International 1957–61' [1981], in Charles Harrison and Paul Wood (eds), *Art in Theory 1900–1990: An Anthology of Changing Ideas*, Oxford: Wiley-Blackwell, 1993, pp. 693–700.

28 Lefebvre, *Production of Space*, pp. 362ff. In comparison to Lefebvre, the attempts of the Situationist International to provide alternative architecture in opposition to functionalism remained merely an episode,

an example of which was Mark Wigley Constant's supiciously futuristic *Orange Construction*, a prototype for a world free of the compulsion to work. The same applies to attempts at revolutionary radicalization opposing the spectacle with urban 'fêtes' in communard style.

29 Jane Jacobs, *The Death and Life of Great American Cities: The Failure of Current Planning*, New York: Vintage, 1961.

30 Ebenezer Howard, *Garden Cities of Tomorrow*, London: Swan Sonnenschein, 1902.

31 Jacobs, *The Death and Life of Great American Cities*, p. 20.

32 Ibid., p. 255.

33 Alvar Aalto, 'The humanizing of architecture', *Technology Review*, 43/1 (1940): 14–16, repr. in Göran Schildt, *Alvar Aalto in His Own Words*, New York: Rizzoli, 1998, pp. 102–7; Oscar Niemeyer, 'Form and function in architecture' [1960], in Joan Ockman and Edward Eigen (eds), *Architecture Culture 1943–1968: A Documentary Anthology*, New York: Rizzoli, 1996, pp. 308–14.

34 Robert Venturi, *Complexity and Contradiction in Architecture*, New York: Museum of Modern Art, 1966; Venturi et al., *Learning from Las Vegas: The Forgotten Symbolism of Architectural Form* [1977], Cambridge, MA: MIT Press, 2001; Aldo Rossi, *The Architecture of the City*, Cambridge, MA: MIT Press, 1982.

35 Hans Hollein, 'Everything is architecture' [1968], in Ockman and Eigen (eds), *Architecture Culture 1943–1968*, pp. 459–62, here p. 462.

36 Martin Gropius, 'Der stilbildende Wert industrieller Bauformen', in *Jahrbuch des Deutschen Werkbundes 1914*, pp. 29–32, here p. 30.

37 On the post-materialist values of the new middle class, see Paul Leinberger and Bruce Tucker, *The New Individualists: The Generation after The Organization Man*, New York: HarperCollins, 1991.

38 For some case studies, see Bastian Lange, *Die Räume der Kreativszenen: Culturepreneurs und ihre Orte in Berlin*, Bielefeld: Transcript, 2007; Richard Lloyd, *Neo-Bohemia: Art and Commerce in the Postindustrial City*, London: Routledge, 2010; Thomas Dörfler, *Gentrification in Prenzlauer Berg? Milieuwandel eines Berliner Sozialraums seit 1989*, Bielefeld: Transcript, 2010; Tim Butler and Garry Robson, *London Calling: The Middle Classes and the Re-Making of Inner London*, Oxford: Berg, 2003; Michael Jager, 'Class definition and the aesthetics of gentrification: Victoriana in Melbourne', in Neil Smith and Peter Williams (eds), *Gentrification of the City*, London: Allen & Unwin, 1986, pp. 78–91.

39 Ernest W. Burgess, 'The growth of the city: an introduction to a research project' [1925], in Robert E. Park et al. (eds), *The City: Suggestions for Investigation of Human Behavior in the Urban Environment*, Chicago: University of Chicago Press, 1967, pp. 47–62.

40 Jon Caulfield traces in detail this process of inner-city upgrading in Toronto since the 1970s, elaborating the way 'postmodernist urbanism' is at first brought about by various collective agents – bourgeois conservative heritage protectors, radical planners and architects, the alterna-

tive movement and the art scene – then later taken over above all by the younger educated middle classes. Caulfield, *City Form and Everyday Life: Toronto's Gentrification and Critical Social Practice*, Toronto: University of Toronto Press, 1994.

41 Ruth Glass, *London: Aspects of Change*, London: Centre for Urban Studies, 1964. On gentrification in general, see Loretta Lees and Tom Slater (eds), *The Gentrification Reader*, New York: Routledge, 2010.

42 For this reason, none of the stages of a gentrification process can be explained by cost–benefit calculation of factors such as the initially lower cost of rent, the ensuing benefits or prestige. This is shown in the way neighbourhoods incapable of aestheticization, such as areas with mass housing units, generally do not manage to attract new inhabitants from artistic and alternative scenes in the same way as the historical and industrial areas, even when they would seem to promise pecuniary advantages.

43 Lange, *Die Räume der Kreativszenen*.

44 Lloyd, *Neo-Bohemia*, pp. 38f.

45 The Berlin districts of Mitte and Prenzlauer Berg serve as such spaces of semiotic density for more recent inhabitants, with the associations of the former Jewish Scheunenviertel or the GDR alternative scene in Prenzlauer Berg.

46 Fredric Jameson, *Postmodernism, or, The Cultural Logic of Late Capitalism*, Durham, NC: Duke University Press, 1991, pp. 16ff.

47 Mónica Montserrat Degen, *Sensing Cities: Regenerating Public Life in Barcelona and Manchester*, London: Routledge, 2008.

48 Caulfield, *City Form and Everyday Life*, pp. 195f.

49 Martina Löw, *Soziologie der Städte*, Frankfurt am Main, Suhrkamp, 2008; part translated in Löw, 'The city as experiential space: the production of shared meaning', *International Journal of Urban and Regional Research*, 37/3 (2013): 894–908.

50 Diedrich Diedrichsen, 'Der grüne Frack: Wo und wie die Künstler leben und was in ihren Vierteln passiert', *Texte zur Kunst*, 16 (1994): 81–100.

51 Degen, *Sensing Cities*, p. 71.

52 Ibid.

53 Berlin again provides excellent examples of this cycle. Before the fall of the wall in 1990, the West Berlin districts of Charlottenburg, Schöneberg and Kreuzberg all underwent a different cultural upsurge. After 1990, the cycle shifted to Mitte-Nord and Prenzlauer Berg, then marched further eastward into Friedrichshain, before turning south to conquer Kreuzburg and Neukölln-Nord. See Andrej Holm, 'Die Karawane zieht weiter – Stationen der Aufwertung in der Berliner Innenstadt', in Mario Pschera et al. (eds), *Intercity Istanbul–Berlin*, Berlin: Dağyeli, 2010, pp. 89–101.

54 On the expansion of the *creative industries* as a whole, see John Howkins, *The Creative Economy: How People Make Money from Ideas*, London 2001; David Hesmondhalgh, *The Cultural Industries*, London: Sage, 2002.

55 Melvin M. Webber, 'The post-city age', *Daedalus*, 97 (1968): 1091–110.

56 The term is borrowed from Alfred Marshall's theory of the interconnection between innovation and place. See Marshall, *Principles of Economics*, London: Macmillan, 1920. On the difference between networks and clusters, see Bas van Heur, *Creative Networks and the City: Towards a Cultural Political Economy of Aesthetic Production*, Bielefeld: Transcript, 2010.

57 Sebastiano Brusco, 'The Emilian model: productive decentralization and social integration', *Cambridge Journal of Economics*, 6 (1982): 167–84.

58 Phil Hubbard, *City*, London: Routledge, 2006, pp. 206ff.

59 Elizabeth Currid, *The Warhol Economy: How Fashion, Art, and Music Drive New York City*, Princeton, NJ: Princeton University Press, 2007.

60 In the artistic field, this migration from the periphery to the centre has been a popular theme since the nineteenth century. For a good example, see Honoré de Balzac, *Lost Illusions* [1837], Harmondsworth: Penguin, 1976.

61 Charles R. Simpson, *SoHo: The Artist in the City*, Chicago: University of Chicago Press, 1981.

62 Mark Granovetter, 'The strength of weak ties: a network theory revisited', *American Journal of Sociology*, 78 (1973): 1360–80.

63 John Urry, *The Tourist Gaze*, London: Sage, 1990.

64 Mike Featherstone, *Consumer Culture and Postmodernism*, London: Sage, 1991; Joseph Pine and James Gilmore, *The Experience Economy: Work is Theatre & Every Business a Stage*, Cambridge, MA: Harvard Business School Press, 1999; Gerhard Schulze, *Die Erlebnisgesellschaft: Kultursoziologie der Gegenwart*, Frankfurt am Main: Campus, 1992. See also chapter 4 in this volume, in particular 4.4.

65 This development is exemplified by the rise of urban gastronomics, particularly in the form of 'eatertainment'. David Bell and Gill Valentine, *Consuming Geographies: We Are Where We Eat*, London: Routledge, 1997.

66 On the micro-level, the stores often display their wares as though presenting aesthetic objects in a museum. Gail Reekie, 'Changes in the Adamless Eden: the spatial transformation of a Brisbane department store 1930–90', in Rob Shields (ed.), *Lifestyle Shopping: The Subject of Consumption*, New York: Routledge, 2004, pp. 170–97.

67 Ilpo Koskinen, 'Semiotic neighborhoods', *Design Issues*, 21 (2005): 13–27.

68 George Ritzer, *Enchanting a Disenchanted World: Continuity and Change in the Cathedrals of Consumption*, Los Angeles: Sage, 2010.

69 Paul Knox, *Cities and Design*, London: Routledge, 2010, pp. 136ff.

70 Bernadette Quinn, 'Arts festivals and the city', *Urban Studies*, 42 (2005): 927–43.

71 Tony Bennett, *The Birth of the Museum: History, Theory, Politics*, New York: Routledge, 1995.

72 Kylie Message, *New Museums and the Making of Culture*, Oxford: Berg, 2006; Kevin Hetherington, 'The time of the entrepreneurial city:

museum, heritage and kairos', in Anne M. Cronin and Hetherington (eds), *Consuming the Entrepreneurial City: Image, Memory, Spectacle*, New York: Routledge, 2008, pp. 273–94; Urry, *The Tourist Gaze*, pp. 120ff.

73 In the case of historical inner-city or industrial neighbourhoods, the border between the museum and the surroundings can start to crumble until whole districts become museum-like.

74 Message, *New Museums and the Making of Culture*.

75 Examples include the National Museum of the American Indian in Washington, DC, the Museum of New Zealand Te Papa Tongarewa in Wellington, and the Schwules Museum (exhibiting LGBT life) in the Kreuzberg area of Berlin.

76 Viv Golding, 'Dreams and wishes: the multi-sensory museum space', in Sandra H. Dudley (ed.), *Museum Materialities*, London: Routledge, 2010, pp. 224–40; Kate Gregory and Andrea Witcomb, 'Beyond nostalgia: the role of affect in generating historical understanding', in Simon Knell et al. (eds), *Museum Revolutions*, London: Routledge, 2007, pp. 263–75.

77 On the 'Bilbao effect', see Knox, *Cities and Design*, pp. 184–7.

78 Richard Florida, *Cities and the Creative Class*, New York: Routledge, 2005. For a critique of Florida, see Allen Scott, 'Creative cities: conceptual issues and policy questions', *Journal of Urban Affairs*, 28 (2006): 1–17.

79 Florida, *Cities and the Creative Class*, p. 104.

80 Charles Landry and Franco Bianchini, *The Creative City*, London: Demos, 1995; Landry, *The Creative City: A Toolkit*.

81 Ibid., p. 4.

82 Ibid., p. 8. An illuminating example from Landry's own planning work is the transformation of Helsinki into a 'city of light'. Helsinki, like other Scandinavian cities, is plagued by its long, dark winter. This otherwise negative quality can be turned around to become a distinguishing cultural feature for inhabitants and visitors alike. The city needs constant lighting and cultivates traditions such as the Lucia Parade. Following Landry's suggestion, the planners strengthened this feature in an attempt to transform the city into a city of light, introducing a winter light festival, supporting lamp design, etc. See ibid., p. 88.

83 Hilmar Hoffmann, *Kultur für alle: Perspektiven und Modelle*, Frankfurt am Main: Fischer, 1984.

84 Paul Bray, 'The new urbanism: celebrating the city', *Places*, 8 (1993): 56–65, here p. 58; Jacobs and Appleyard, *Toward an Urban Design Manifesto*.

85 Stephanie Hemelryk Donald and Eleonore Kofman (eds), *Branding Cities: Cosmopolitanism, Parochialism, and Social Change*, New York: Routledge, 2009.

86 Guy Julier, *The Culture of Design*, London: Sage, 2008, pp. 123ff.

87 Julier, 'Urban designscapes and the production of aesthetic consent', *Urban Studies*, 42 (2005): 869–87.

88 On signature architecture, see Donald McNeill, *The Global Architect: Firms, Fame, and Urban Form*, New York: Routledge, 2009.

89 Diane Dodd, 'Barcelona – the making of a cultural city', in Dodd, *Planning Cultural Tourism in Europe*, Amsterdam: Boekman Foundation, 1999, pp. 53–64. For a detailed study of culturalization in British cities, see John Punter (ed.), *Urban Design and the British Urban Renaissance*, London: Routledge, 2010.

90 See chapters 3.5, 4.4.

91 Gernot Böhme, *Atmosphäre: Essays zur neuen Ästhetik*, Frankfurt am Main: Suhrkamp, 1995. For an example of a type of architecture that consciously strives to produce this type of atmosphere, see Anna Klingmann, *Brandscapes: Architecture in the Experience Economy*, Cambridge, MA: MIT Press, 2007.

92 Helmut Willke, *Systemtheorie II: Interventionstheorie: Grundzüge einer Theorie der Intervention in komplexe Systeme*, Stuttgart: Lucius & Lucius, 1999.

93 Michel Foucault, *Security, Territory, Population: Lectures at the Collège de France, 1977–78*, Basingstoke: Palgrave Macmillan, 2007; Foucault, 'The subject and power', p. 221.

94 See chapter 5.6.

95 Michel Foucault, *Security, Territory, Population*, pp. 19f.

96 The governmentality of culture contains elements of the other three forms: the advancement of life transforms into a vitalism of creativity, social planning turns into incentives for social processes of symbolic production, and marketization becomes the competition for attention between cities. The economization of the late modern city has been frequently demonstrated: see Tim Hall and Phil Hubbard (eds), *The Entrepreneurial City: Geographies of Politics, Regime and Representation*, Chichester: Wiley, 1998. Culturalization and aestheticization do not contradict this economization, although they cannot quickly be shown to have derived from it. On the structural homology between aestheticization and economization, see chapter 8.3 in this volume.

97 Marc Roseland, *Toward Sustainable Communities: Resources for Citizens and Their Governments*, Gabriola Island, BC: New Society, 2005.

98 Landry, *The Creative City: A Toolkit*, pp. 266ff.

99 These alternative approaches to aesthetics and creativity will be elaborated below in chapter 8.5.

Chapter 8   Society of Creativity

1 Max Weber, *The Protestant Ethic and the Spirit of Capitalism* [1930], New York: Oxford University Press, 2011, p. 177.

2 Michel Foucault, 'The confession of the flesh' [1977], in *Power/Knowledge: Selected Interviews and Other Writings 1972–1977*, ed. Colin Gordon, Brighton: Harvester Press, 1980, pp. 194–228, here p. 195.

3   On bourgeois and organized modernity, see Peter Wagner, *Sociology of Modernity*, London: Routledge, 1994; Andreas Reckwitz, *Das hybride Subjekt: Eine Theorie der Subjektkulturen von der bürgerlichen Moderne zur Postmoderne*, Weilerswist: Velbrück Wissenschaft, 2006.

4   David Riesman, *The Lonely Crowd: A Study of the Changing American Character* [1949], New Haven, CT: Yale University Press, 2001.

5   The claim being made here is not that there exists an intrinsic human need to live out affects. We want instead to assert the socio-historical fact that modernity's deficiency of affect was perceived and felt by the culture, which developed various counter-strategies.

6   On the causes of de-aestheticization, see chapter 1.2.

7   The theory that modernity involved affect deficiency or at least reduction has been reiterated in various forms by writers from Norbert Elias to Klaus Theweleit. For an empirical analysis of the affect culture in organized modernity, see Peter N. Stearns, *American Cool: Constructing a Twentieth-Century Emotional Style*, New York: New York University Press, 1994.

8   Max Weber, *The Protestant Ethic and the Spirit of Capitalism* [1930], London and New York: Routledge, 2005, p. 123.

9   A call for an affect cartography has been made by Gilles Deleuze and Félix Guattari, *A Thousand Plateaus: Capitalism and Schizophrenia*, Minneapolis: University of Minnesota Press, 2005, pp. 474–500. Recent investigations of the history of emotions and affects have provided additional impulses; see William M. Reddy, *The Navigation of Feeling: A Framework for the History of Emotions*, Cambridge: Cambridge University Press, 2001.

10 Émile Durkheim provided the seminal examination of the role of religion as a source of affect in society. Durkheim, *The Elementary Forms of the Religious Life: A Study in Religious Sociology*, New York: Macmillan, 1915. On the relevance of religion in late modernity, see Hans Joas and Klaus Wiegandt (eds), *Secularization and the World Religions*, Liverpool: Liverpool University Press, 2009. On the term *residual culture* as distinct from *dominant* and *emergent culture*, see Raymond Williams, *Marxism and Literature*, Oxford: Oxford University Press, 1977, pp. 121ff.

11 On the cultural relevance of the political, see Shmuel N. Eisenstadt, *Die Vielfalt der Moderne*, Weilerswist: Velbrück, 2000, chapter 1. There is reason to suppose that organized modernity, with its seemingly rationalist politics, was in fact contingent on patterns of intensive affect which erupted in the age of the 'European civil wars'.

12 The aesthetic and the political can both be interpreted as cultural, historical heirs to the sacredness of religion, as expressions such as *Zivilreligion* (civic religion) and *Kunstreligion* (cult of art) would suggest. However, from a contemporary perspective, the aesthetic can be interpreted in modernity as the form of culture providing the pre-eminent alternative to the political, an affect culture of purpose-free sensuousness in contrast to collective political mobilization. The religious field in

modernity thus appears either to tie itself to the aesthetic complex, informing the 'mystic' piousness of Western religious counter-cultures from romanticism to new age, or to the political complex, as manifest in the activism of religious fundamentalism.

13   Friedrich Nietzsche, 'The birth of tragedy' [1872], in *The Birth of Tragedy and Other Writings*, Cambridge: Cambridge University Press, 2007, pp. 1–116.

14   There is no doubt that certain aestheticization processes in modernity, such as the influential bourgeois ideal of romantic love or the emotional intensity of family life, cannot be understood entirely as forerunners to the creativity dispositif. These and other examples certainly cannot be subsumed under the regime of aesthetic novelty and the model of the audience. For an overview of the agencies of aestheticization in modernity, see chapter 1.2.

15   This list does not cover all the social fields in contemporary society in which processes of aestheticization are taking place. Other complexes include personal relations, sport and the use of digital media. There is a good deal of evidence that, since the 1970s, values such as morals, social status and the ability to provide have lost significance in partnership and friendship, which have come instead to be regarded as means of intensifying individual experience. See Anthony Giddens, *The Transformation of Intimacy: Sexuality, Love and Eroticism in Modern Societies*, Cambridge: Polity, 1992. We addressed above the aestheticization of sport in connection with the sport star. However, late modern individual sport also includes the promise of bodily experiences and an escape from the rational-purposive quotidian. These promises are broadly aesthetic. See Ronald Lutz, *Laufen und Läuferleben: Zum Verhältnis von Körper, Bewegung und Identität*, Frankfurt am Main: Campus, 1989. The open-ended practices of internet use in which consumption and production are linked together can count to a certain degree as a prominent training field for creative subjects and creative practices. Howard Gardner and Katie Davis: *The App Generation: How Today's Youth Navigate Identity, Intimacy, and Imagination in a Digital World*, New Haven, CT: Yale University Press, 2013.

16   On this notion of the social, see Bruno Latour, *Reassembling the Social: An Introduction to Actor-Network-Theory*, Oxford: Oxford University Press, 2005. Boltanski and Thévenot also take the social in the plural. However, they conceive of the social primarily as an order of normative legitimacy. Luc Boltanski and Laurent Thévenot, *On Justification: Economies of Worth*, Princeton, NJ: Princeton University Press, 2006.

17   Jürgen Habermas, 'Labour and interaction: remarks on Hegel's Jena "Philosophy of Mind"', in *Theory and Practice*, Boston: Beacon Press, 1973, pp. 142–69.

18   Each of these theoretical assertions takes its point of departure from a specific empirical background that is left out of the account. The first view is rooted in the normative rationality of the modern legal system

and the bourgeois family, while the second view is derived from productive labour and objectified trade in goods in the modern economy.

19   For a critique of the anti-aesthetic stance of traditional sociology, see Wolfgang Eßbach, 'Antitechnische und antiästhetische Haltungen in der soziologischen Theorie', in Andreas Lösch (ed.), *Technologien als Diskurse: Konstruktionen von Wissen, Medien und Körpern*, Heidelberg: Synchron, 2001, pp. 123–36.

20   Karin Knorr Cetina, 'Sociality with objects: social relations in postsocial knowledge societies', *Theory, Culture & Society*, 14 (1997): 1–30, and Bruno Latour, 'On interobjectivity', *Mind, Culture, and Activity*, 3 (1996): 228–44.

21   As we have shown, breaking the rules has now become the rule. As such, creative action in the context of the creativity dispositif can also be grasped within the paradigm of rule-guided action. However, the rule of breaking the rules leads to a transformation of social practices, confronting actors with constantly new events. This causes action to become more complex than anticipated by the paradigm of rule-guided behaviour.

22   On the concept of mobilization, see Peter Sloterdijk, *Eurotaoismus: Zur Kritik der politischen Kinetik*, Frankfurt am Main, Suhrkamp, 1989, pp. 30ff.

23   Guy Debord, *The Society of the Spectacle* [1967], New York: Zone Books, 1994.

24   On the concept of heightening (*Steigerung*), see Gerhard Schulze, *Die beste aller Welten: Wohin bewegt sich die Gesellschaft im 21. Jahrhundert?*, Munich: Hanser, 2003, pp. 81ff.; on acceleration as a specific form of heightening, see Hartmut Rosa, *Social Acceleration: A New Theory of Modernity*, New York: Columbia University Press, 2015.

25   See chapter 1.3 in this volume.

26   The creative activity can also be undertaken by groups, in a 'creative team' or a creative partnership sharing a common form of life. The collective aspect intensifies the sense of autonomy and authenticity.

27   On the theory of attention, see Bernhard Waldenfels, *Phänomenologie der Aufmerksamkeit*, Frankfurt am Main, Suhrkamp, 2004; Aleida Assmann and Jan Assmann (eds), *Aufmerksamkeiten*, Munich: Fink, 2001. On the historical dimension of the problem of attention, see Jonathan Crary, *Suspensions of Perception: Attention, Spectacle, and Modern Culture*, Cambridge, MA: MIT Press, 1999.

28   Waldenfels, *Phänomenologie der Aufmerksamkeit*, chapter 4.

29   This position differs from that of Boris Groys, who also addresses the constellation of cultural novelty but sees contemporary culture as determined essentially by processes of evaluation to decide which works are assigned to the cultural archive. See Groys, *On the New* [1992], London: Verso, 2014.

30   See chapter 2.2 in this volume.

31 There are two main ways to increase the potential for attention. The first is simultaneous focus (for example, by training in multi-tasking), which is necessarily limited in aesthetic perception. The second is to broaden and diversify audiences, so that a larger number of different cultural elements attract the attention of smaller groups.

32 On the genealogy of marketization, see Fernand Braudel, *Civilization and Capitalism: 15th–18th Century*, vol. 2: *The Wheels of Commerce*, Berkeley: University of California Press, 1992; for a sociological theory of the market, see Max Weber, *Economy and Society: An Outline of Interpretive Sociology* [1922], Berkeley: University of California Press, 1978, pp. 635ff. For a more recent discussion, see Klaus Krämer, *Der Markt der Gesellschaft: Zu einer soziologischen Theorie der Marktvergesellschaftung*, Wiesbaden: VS Verlag für Wissenschaften, 1997; Jens Beckert, 'The social order of markets', *Theory and Society*, 38 (2009): 245–69.

33 Ulrich Bröckling et al. (eds), *Gouvernementalität der Gegenwart: Studien zur Ökonomisierung des Sozialen*, Frankfurt am Main: Suhrkamp, 2000; Uwe Schimank, 'Modernity as a functionally differentiated capitalist society: a general theoretical model', *European Journal of Social Theory*, 18 (2015) 413–30. Governmentality studies have tended to neglect the interconnectedness of processes of economization and aestheticization.

34 The historical and structural distinction between marketization and capitalism (both trade and industrial) is made with reference to Braudel, *The Wheels of Commerce*, pp. 21ff.

35 There exist other strategies for capital accumulation, such as the reduction of labour costs or the discovery of new consumer groups for basic goods on the national or global level. Capitalism is therefore freed from the need to focus on new commodities and new needs. The radical capitalist regime of novelty with its special focus on aesthetic, cultural novelty turns out to have been constricted in bourgeois and organized modernity, not unfolding its wings to full span until late modernity (see chapter 4).

36 Affect deficiency does not entail the absence of affects altogether. Before the advent of the aestheticization of work and consumption, people were already experiencing affective motivation of a market-specific type, such as feelings of victory and defeat in competition.

37 Chapter 6 examines this aspect of mediatization's regime of novelty in connection with the star system. For an analysis of this media structure of time and attention in the case of television, see John Ellis, *Visible Fictions: Cinema, Television, Video*, London: Routledge, 1992, pp. 109–71.

38 The regime of novelty made possible by mediatization should not be seen as a mere product of marketization, even though they are frequently interconnected. The regime is also present in non-commercial media products such as public television, alternative radio stations and non-commercial blogs.

39 A strictly cognitive, informational process of mediatization would seem to be a marginal empirical case, at least for the mass media. This kind of mediatization would be most classically found in the scientific field and the scientific media of writing and publishing. However, it remains an open question as to what extent aestheticization processes in the guise of the creativity dispositif have perhaps seeped into science, increasing the relevance of the emotional value of surprise and the attraction to 'appealing' scientific work.

40 See chapter 1.3 in this volume.

41 David Harvey is inclined to reduce aestheticization to capitalization in this way. David Harvey, *The Condition of Postmodernity: An Enquiry into the Origins of Cultural Change*, Oxford: Blackwell, 1989.

42 Richard Florida has undertaken a study of the relation between class stratification and the creative form of life. See Florida, *The Rise of the Creative Class: And How It's Transforming Work, Leisure, Community and Everyday Life*, New York: Basic Books, 2002. On the creative scene, see Cornelia Koppetsch, *Das Ethos der Kreativen: Eine Studie zum Wandel von Arbeit und Identität am Beispiel der Werbeberufe*, Konstanz: Universitätsverlag Konstanz, 2006.

43 The seminal systematic critique of the aesthetic form of life remains Søren Kierkegaard's *Either/Or: A Fragment of Life* [1843], London: Penguin, 1992.

44 For a popular version of this convergence, see David Brooks, *Bobos in Paradise: The New Upper Class and How They Got There*, New York: Simon & Schuster, 2000.

45 Critique is understood here by Boltanski as social discourses of critique. See Luc Boltanski, *Soziologie und Sozialkritik*, Berlin: Suhrkamp, 2010. For the beginnings of a critical discussion of creativity in the humanities, see Christoph Menke and Juliane Rebentisch (eds), *Kreation und Depression: Freiheit im gegenwärtigen Kapitalismus*, Berlin: Kulturverlag Kadmus, 2011.

46 On the concept of achievement, see Talcott Parsons, *The Social System*, Glencoe, IL: Free Press, 1951, pp. 181ff.

47 This derivation from the performance to the subjective core is parallel to the case of gender analysed by Judith Butler in *Gender Trouble: Feminism and the Subversion of Identity*, London: Routledge, 1999, pp. 18–32.

48 A duty to be creative can also be imposed on larger social collectives such as organizations and cities.

49 Marion von Osten (ed.), *Norm der Abweichung*, Zurich: Voldemeer, 2003.

50 This marginalization of the non-creative can apply to individuals or to whole groups. The non-creative class is a class of routine workers who receive lower social recognition on the justification that they lack the relevant cognitive skills for a knowledge society. But it is also because they lack creative skills.

51 This potentially menacing lack of distance between professional achievement and personal identity haunts above all the creative professions. Diedrich Diederichsen, 'Kreative Arbeit und Selbstverwirklichung', in Menke and Rebentisch, *Kreation und Depression*, pp. 118–28.

52 Alain Ehrenberg, *The Weariness of the Self: Diagnosing the History of Depression in the Contemporary Age* [1998], Montreal: McGill–Queen's University Press, 2010; see also Elisabeth Summer, *Macht die Gesellschaft depressiv? Alain Ehrenbergs Theorie des 'erschöpften Selbst' im Licht sozialwissenschaftlicher und therapeutischer Befunde*, Bielefeld: Transcript, 2008.

53 On this distinction, see Sighard Neckel, '"Leistung" und "Erfolg": Die symbolische Ordnung der Marktgesellschaft', in Eva Barlösius et al. (eds), *Gesellschaftsbilder im Umbruch: Soziologische Perspektiven in Deutschland*, Opladen: Leske & Budrich, 2001, pp. 245–65.

54 In the creative professions, this experience of dissonance and injustice is displayed in the discourse of the 'precariat', which has led to the emergence of a precariat movement. Marion Hamm, *Performing Protest: Media Practices in the Trans-Urban Euromayday Parades of the Precarious*, PhD thesis, Department of Sociology, University of Lucerne, 2011, https://zenodo.org/record/44514/files/Hamm_PhD_FrontMatter.pdf.

55 Accumulations of attention can generally be cashed in as social and economic capital. Georg Franck, *Ökonomie der Aufmerksamkeit: Ein Entwurf*, Munich: Carl Hanser, 1998, pp. 113ff.; part translated in 'The economy of attention', *Telepolis* www.heise.de/tp/features/The-Economy-of-Attention-3444929.html (1999).

56 The discussion of stimulus overload and stimulus protection is as old as the audio-visual media and the city. Georg Simmel, 'The metropolis and mental life' [1903], in Gary Bridge and Sophie Watson (eds), *The Blackwell City Reader*, Oxford: Wiley-Blackwell, 2002, pp. 11–19. Jonathan Crary, *Suspensions of Perception: Attention, Spectacle, and Modern Culture*, Cambridge, MA: MIT Press.

57 Waldenfels, *Phänomenologie der Aufmerksamkeit*, pp. 65ff.

58 Christoph Türcke, *Erregte Gesellschaft: Philosophie der Sensation*, Munich: Beck, 2002, pp. 294ff. A pointed critique of distraction has been made more recently by Byung-Chul Han in *Duft der Zeit: Ein philosophischer Essay zur Kunst des Verweilens*, Bielefeld: Transcript, 2009.

59 On the historical conditions of attention deficit syndrome, see Peter Matussek, 'Aufmerksamkeitsstörungen: Selbstreflexion unter den Bedingungen digitaler Medien', in Assmann and Assmann, *Aufmerksamkeiten*, pp. 197–215.

60 Martin Seel, *Ethisch-ästhetische Studien*, Frankfurt am Main: Suhrkamp, 1996, Juliane Rebentisch, *The Art of Freedom: On the Dialectics of Democratic Existence*, Cambridge: Polity, 2016.

61 Elisabeth Klaus, 'Der Gegensatz von Information ist Desinformation, der Gegensatz von Unterhaltung ist Langeweile', *Rundfunk und Fern-*

sehen, 3 (1996): 403–17; Fritz Wolf, *Wa(h)re Information – Interessant geht vor relevant*, Frankfurt am Main: Netzwerk Recherche, 2011.

62 Eva Illouz, *Consuming the Romantic Utopia: Love and the Cultural Contradictions of Capitalism*, Berkeley: University of California Press, 1997; for a popular account, see Sven Hillenkamp, *Das Ende der Liebe: Gefühle im Zeitalter unendlicher Freiheit*, Stuttgart: Klett-Cotta, 2009.

63 Colin Crouch, *Post-Democracy*, Cambridge: Polity, 2004, pp. 19ff.

64 Luc Boltanski and Eve Chiapello, *The New Spirit of Capitalism*, London: Verso, 2005, pp. 343ff.

65 With the convergence of aestheticization and marketization in late modernity, this limitation or containment of the aesthetic is also a bulwark against marketization.

66 The concept of alienation gains new relevance in this context. Rahel Jaeggi, *Alienation*, New York: Columbia University Press, 2014.

67 Seel, *Ethisch-ästhetische Studien*.

68 Profane creativity is here consciously juxtaposed to sacred creativity. The latter remains within the horizon of the cult of genius. For a similar approach, see Tim Edensor (ed.), *Spaces of Vernacular Creativity: Rethinking the Cultural Economy*, London: Routledge, 2010; Elizabeth Hallam and Tim Ingold (eds), *Creativity and Cultural Improvisation*, Oxford: Berg, 2007; also Thomas Osborne, 'Against "creativity"', *Economy and Society*, 32 (2003): 507–52; Stefan Nowotny, 'Immanente Effekte', in Gerald Raunig and Ulf Wuggenig (eds), *Kritik der Kreativität*, Vienna: Turia & Kant, 2007, pp. 15–27 (translated as 'Immanent effects: notes on cre-activity', *Transversal* (February 2007), http://eipcp.net/transversal/0207/nowotny/en).

69 Similar concepts of creativity were formulated by Bergson and Whitehead. See Henri Bergson, *Creative Evolution* [1907], New York: Sheba Blake, 2015; Alfred N. Whitehead, *Process and Reality* [1929], New York: Free Press, 1990. See also Tim Ingold, *The Perception of the Environment: Essays on Livelihood, Dwelling and Skill*, London: Routledge, 2000.

70 Edensor, *Spaces of Vernacular Creativity*.

71 Ava Bromberg, 'Creativity unbound: cultivating the generative power of non-economic neighbourhood spaces', ibid., pp. 214–25.

72 This collapse of the distinction between creativity and routine is examined from the perspective of a theory of creativity by Amar Mall in the case of the kolam painting ritual performed by the Tamil Nadu women. The women produce interior and exterior wall paintings by means of routinized craftwork employing techniques and motifs from pattern books. At the same time natural improvisation occurs. The improvisations are a feature of the painting process, in which astonishing and successful new patterns are generated by the participants. Amar S. Mall, 'Structure, innovation and agency in pattern construction: the kolam of southern India', in Hallam and Ingold, *Creativity and Cultural Improvisation*, pp. 55–78.

73 Christoph Menke, 'A different taste: neither autonomy nor mass consumption', *Texte zur Kunst*, 75 (2009): 108–12; repr. in Bernd Fischer and May Mergenthaler (eds), *Cultural Transformations of the Public Sphere: Contemporary and Historical Perspectives*, Oxford: Peter Lang, 2015, pp. 183–202.

74 Marcel Proust is the paradigm of a weaver of new hermeneutic webs. The character Marcel in *Remembrance of Things Past* threads a wealth of resemblances, analogies and echoes into everyday observations. Fabian Heubel, *Das Dispositiv der Kreativität*, Darmstadt: Wissenschaftliche Buchgesellschaft, 2002, pp. 124ff.

75 In the 1960s and 1970s, Cultural Studies was foremost in elaborating profane creativity at work in the working class and in youth and subculture. Paul E. Willis, *Common Culture: Symbolic Work at Play in the Everyday Cultures of the Young*, Boulder, CO: Westview Press, 1990; Raymond Williams, 'Culture is ordinary' [1958], in Williams, *Resources of Hope: Culture, Democracy, Socialism*, London: Verso, 1989, pp. 3–14. This profane, subcultural creativity was able to provide impulses for the aesthetic economy, postmodern art and the culturalization of the city, thereby contributing unintentionally to the establishment of the creativity dispositif. The dispositif then immediately turned around and devalued profane creativity as banal, amateurish and derivative. As we have seen, both avant-garde art and postmodern art, with their practical and theoretical deconstruction of the myth of the artistic genius, frequently generate a consciousness for the profanity of creativity, while their artistic objects and events nevertheless assume the character of exhibition art soliciting audience attention.

76 Openness for profane creativity would then entail not placing it under observation but instead letting it happen and not making it an object of social classification. The borderline between openness for the profane and systematic creativity training is of course fragile, as newer creativity psychology has shown. See chapter 5.4 in this volume.

77 Max Bense, *Aesthetica: Einführung in die neue Ästhetik* [1965], Baden-Baden: Agis, 1982, pp. 208ff., 276ff.

78 Andreas Reckwitz, 'Toward a theory of social practices: a development in culturalist theorizing', *European Journal of Social Theory*, 5 (2002): 245–65.

79 François Jullien, *In Praise of Blandness: Proceeding from Chinese Thought and Aesthetics* [1991], New York: Zone Books, 2007.

80 Ibid., pp. 42–3.

81 Ibid., pp. 36ff.

82 On Zen meditation, see Shunryu Suzuki, *Zen Mind, Beginner's Mind*, New York: Walker/Weatherill, 1970. On the question of the original and the copy in East Asian culture, see Byung-Chul Han, *Shanzhai: Dekonstruktion auf Chinesisch*, Berlin: Merve, 2011.

83 Foucault employs texts from the Greek and Roman tradition to oppose an 'aesthetic of existence' to the later, restrictive morality of the Christian form of life. This aesthetic of existence also presents an alternative to

the regime of novelty. The technologies of the self elaborated by Foucault involve routine everyday self-care in which aesthetic perception and feeling are attached not to originality but, rather, to the long-term cultivation of a relation to the soul, the body, everyday objects and other people. Michel Foucault, *Ästhetik der Existenz: Schriften zur Lebenskunst*, Frankfurt am Main: Suhrkamp, 2007; see also Wilhelm Schmid, *Auf der Suche nach einer neuen Lebenskunst; Die Frage nach dem Grund und die Neubegründung der Ethik bei Foucault*, Frankfurt am Main: Suhrkamp, 1991.

84 Ruth Groh and Dieter Groh, 'Von den schrecklichen zu den erhabenen Bergen: Zur Entstehung ästhetischer Naturerfahrung', in Groh, *Weltbild und Naturaneignung: Zur Kulturgeschichte der Natur*, vol. 1, Frankfurt am Main: Suhrkamp, 1991, pp. 92–149.

85 See chapter 7.3 in this volume.

86 In the context of the conduct of life, this means that self-creation is not necessarily identical with constant self-transformation and the constant search for new aesthetic experiences. Self-creation can also consist of the constant repetition of the same set of practices and reiteration of the same meanings of the self. Richard Shusterman, *Pragmatist Aesthetics: Living Beauty, Rethinking Art*, Lanham, MD: Rowman & Littlefield, 2000, pp. 236ff.

87 Discussion has emerged recently around the concept of stillness. See David Bissell and Gillian Fuller (eds), *Stillness in a Mobile World*, London: Routledge, 2011. Many works of contemporary art open up awareness of deceleration by repetition or stillness. Prominent examples are works by John Cage and Christoph Marthaler.

88 The cultural imaginary of the creative form of life is currently being attacked across the globe, above all by a radical new moralism. Diverse religious fundamentalist movements can be interpreted as driven by opposition to the perceived decadence of the urban West and its creative 'lifestyle'.

89 On first signs of *creative economy*, *creative class* and *creative cities* in East and South Asia, see Lily Kong and Justin O'Connor (eds), *Creative Economies, Creative Cities: Asian-European Perspectives*, Dordrecht: Springer, 2009; Douglas Webster et al., 'The emerging cultural economy in Chinese cities: early dynamics', *International Development Planning Review*, 33 (2011): 343–69.

90 For an ecological approach to the aesthetic, see Gernot Böhme, *Atmosphäre: Essays zur neuen Ästhetik*, Frankfurt am Main: Suhrkamp, 1995, pp. 13ff. (Individual essays available in English: 'Atmosphere as the fundamental concept of a new aesthetics', *Thesis Eleven*, 36 (1993): 113–26; 'Contribution to the critique of the aesthetic economy', *Thesis Eleven*, 73 (2003): 71–82; 'Acoustic atmospheres: a contribution to the study of ecological aesthetics', *Soundscape: The Journal of Acoustic Ecology*, 1 (2000).)

Index